Teach Decoding

Why and How

SECOND EDITION

J. LLOYD ELDREDGE

Brigham Young University

PEARSON

Merrill
Prentice Hall

Upper Saddle River, New Jersey
Columbus, Ohio

Library of Congress Cataloging-in-Publication Data

Eldredge, J. Lloyd (Joseph Lloyd)-
  Teach decoding : why and how / J. Lloyd Eldredge—2nd ed.
    p. cm.
  Includes bibliographical references and index.
  ISBN 0-13-117685-4
    1. Language arts (Elementary) 2. Reading comprehension. 3. Reading—Phonetic method.
  I. Title.
LB1576.E37 2005
372.6—dc22

2004044936

Vice President and Executive Publisher: Jeffery W. Johnston
Senior Editor: Linda Ashe Montgomery
Assistant Editor: Dawne Brooks
Editorial Assistant: Laura Weaver
Production Editor: Mary M. Irvin
Production Coordination: Jolynn Feller, Carlisle Publishers Services
Design Coordinator: Diane C. Lorenzo
Cover Designer: Michelle Yandrich
Cover Image: Comstock
Production Manager: Pamela D. Bennett
Director of Marketing: Ann Castel Davis
Marketing Manager: Darcy Betts Prybella
Marketing Coordinator: Tyra Poole

This book was set in New Baskerville by Carlisle Communications, Ltd., and was printed and bound by Phoenix Book Tech. The cover was printed by Phoenix Color Corp.

Pearson Education Ltd.
Pearson Education Singapore Pte. Ltd.
Pearson Education Canada, Ltd.
Pearson Education—Japan

Pearson Education Australia Pty. Limited
Pearson Education North Asia Ltd.
Pearson Educación de Mexico, S.A. de C.V.
Pearson Education Malaysia Pte. Ltd.

10 9 8 7 6 5 4 3 2 1
ISBN: 0-13-117685-4

For my wife (Cherie), my seven children (Lloyd, Steve, Gaylene, Kristin, Brad, Michelle, Nicole), and my 27 grandchildren, who make my life worthwhile.

About the Author

J. Lloyd Eldredge is a professor in the College of Education at Brigham Young University. He teaches both graduate and undergraduate literacy courses. Dr. Eldredge is a former elementary school teacher, school principal, and school superintendent. He has also served as the Utah Director of Chapter I, the Utah Director of Early Childhood Education, and the Utah Director of Elementary Education.

His interests are in literacy education and motivation. He was one of the first educators to implement and research "whole language" practices in the public schools. The editors of *The Reading Teacher* acknowledge his article on "alternatives to traditional reading instruction" as the first "whole language" article published in that journal. However, his work has been focused on keeping literacy instruction balanced so children can both learn about the written language and use it in meaningful ways. During the past 21 years he has focused his research on phonemic awareness, a reconceptualization of decoding instruction in the early years of schooling, holistic teaching practices, oral reading, fluency, and the effects of various forms of "assisted reading" strategies (dyad reading, group assisted reading, and taped assisted reading) on young and "at-risk" readers. His work has been published in many journals, including *Journal of Educational Research, Reading Research and Instruction, Journal of Reading, The Reading Teacher,* and *Reading Research Quarterly.*

Preface

Teach Decoding: Why and How was written to help preservice and practicing teachers understand decoding and teach it in a balanced, comprehensive literacy program. Designed for those who want to help children develop the ability to decode while they also engage in reading and writing activities relevant to them, this book covers all aspects of decoding, and provides an in-depth view of each aspect. At present, there are no other books that do this.

Decoding is defined as the process of translating written text into language. There are various ways text can be decoded: word recognition, analogy, context, phonics, morphemic analysis, and syllabic analysis/phonics. This book will examine each of these ways, and discuss the strengths and weaknesses of each approach.

Decoding Strategies

Some decoding approaches are more efficient than others. Some are used more by proficient readers and some are used more by emerging readers. Proficient readers decode by automatic, fluent word recognition. The end goal of all decoding instruction is to help students decode like proficient readers.

There are also many strategies used to teach students how to decode. These strategies, informal and formal, are described. In addition to commonly known holistic strategies—the shared book experience, writing using invented spelling, and the Language Experience Approach—other less- well-known strategies such as dyad reading and group-assisted reading are presented. These strategies are unique because they allow students to read interesting but "frustration level" text while improving their decoding and comprehension abilities in the process.

Text Organization

Among other things, the first four chapters present research evidence to support the positions taken on "best literacy practices," decoding, phonemic awareness, phonics, word recognition, fluency, and reading comprehension. These chapters also provide a historical view of decoding, and an introduction to assessment and teaching. Many of the strategies introduced in the last seven chapters have been tried and tested in experimental classrooms. These strategies have had a positive effect on children's attitudes, and on their reading and writing achievement.

Teaching decoding is an essential part of a literacy program. A balanced and comprehensive approach to literacy instruction incorporates decoding and phonics as a part of the following literacy principles.

- Children learn much about reading and writing by attempting to read and write. Therefore, it is perfectly appropriate for teachers to involve children in reading and writing *before* they develop all the skills needed by independent readers and writers.
- If young children are unable to spell words correctly as they write, teachers either transcribe their work or encourage them to "spell" words by sounds.
- Children are intrinsically motivated to read and write, and enjoy reading and writing more when teachers immerse them in early literacy experiences.
- The use of shared book experiences, tape-assisted reading, and other "connected-text" strategies enhances literacy development.
- Phonemic awareness is necessary for the development of phonics knowledge, writing, and spelling. There are different levels of phonemic awareness. Certain levels are necessary for successful literacy development. Teachers can identify these levels and provide activities to improve phonemic awareness.
- Phonics knowledge is necessary for the development of word recognition and literacy growth. There are different ways to teach phonics, some more effective than others. There are also different ways for students to apply their phonics knowledge for the identification of unfamiliar words. Phonics knowledge provides students with a system for storing and retrieving words in lexical memory.

Traditional decoding approaches emphasize the *teaching* of skills, rather than the *application* of skills. These approaches also take considerable classroom time, leaving little time for children to read and write. *Teach Decoding: Why and How* describes how to teach encoding and decoding through writing and reading, and also by direct instruction. The mini-lessons for writing and the direct instruction for phonics described in this book take only 10 minutes a day. Because so little time is required for these brief lessons, teachers are able to allocate more classroom time for children to *use* language, thus achieving a better "balance" for children and teachers alike.

Perhaps the most important message of the book is "teach decoding!" Don't assume that the ability to decode will develop by chance.

Acknowledgments

My interests in literacy development heightened while I was serving as a young elementary school principal in the Granite School District, a suburban district near Salt Lake City, Utah. It was at that time that I became emotionally involved with certain children who were to soon move on to the junior high school, but were unprepared for the experience. These children had struggled in school for years because they had been incapable of dealing with the normal reading and writing tasks required of them.

I can still remember the conferences I had with their parents. A common thread ran through all of the stories they told. Their child's reading difficulties had surfaced early—by first grade. Efforts to correct the problem by the child's teacher, the child, and the parents were unsuccessful. The problem continued to worsen over the years. Year after year, the child and the parents sought remedies for the problem. Year after year, their attempts were unsuccessful. When the time arrived for the child to move on to the junior high school, the parents panicked and redoubled their efforts to help. They requested help from me that I could not deliver. I promised myself at that time that I would study the issues related to literacy development until I could respond appropriately to such pleas for help.

I owe much to the children and parents at the Hillsdale Elementary School who helped me focus on this important problem. I thank and acknowledge parents, children, and colleagues at the West Kearns, Taylorsville, and Robert Frost Elementary Schools for their contributions to this book as well.

I owe a debt of gratitude to my students and colleagues at Brigham Young University, and the teachers and administrators in Utah, who have helped me in my research efforts, and who have challenged many of the conclusions I have drawn from my studies.

I am grateful to the following reviewers whose input and valuable suggestions contributed greatly to this text: Pat Simpson, Abilene Christian University; Joseph A. Fusaro, University of Scranton; LaVerne Raine, Texas A & M University, Commerce.

To Linda Montgomery, I express appreciation for her willingness to support a project of this kind, and for her counsel and advice regarding the book. I thank Mary Irvin and her associates for their meticulous attention to detail in the preparation and production of the manuscript.

It is my hope that all who read the book will find the information interesting, useful, and challenging. Furthermore, I hope that readers can visualize the practical applications of the information presented herein. Most importantly, it is my hope that the book might contribute in some small way to the solution of literacy problems facing us all.

Contents

2

Decoding 14

The Coding System in Written English 14
Defining Decoding 16
Different Levels of Decoding 17

All Decoding Strategies Are Dependent on Phonics Knowledge 19
What Are the Strengths and Limitations of the Various Word Identification Strategies? 19

The Relationship of Decoding to Reading 22
Theoretical Underpinnings of Decoding 23

The Auditory Communication Channel 23
Language Meanings Are Initially Developed From Sound 23
Reading Theory 24

Enhancing Decoding 25

Quantitative and Qualitative Dimensions of Decoding 25

Application Activities 26

3

Phonemic Awareness and the Alphabetic Principle 27

The Alphabetic Principle 27
Phonemic Awareness 28

What Are Phonemes? 28
What Is Phonemic Awareness? 29
The Difference Between Phonemic and Phonological Awareness 30
What Are Some Phonemic Awareness Tasks? 31
Assessing Phonemic Awareness Levels 32
Why Phonemic Awareness Is Important 32
How Children Develop Phonemic Awareness 35

Application Activities 40

4

Phonics and the Alphabetic Principle 42

Defining Phonics 42
Differentiating Between Implicit and Explicit Phonics Approaches 44

Implicit Approaches 44
Explicit Approaches 45

5

Developing Phonemic Awareness Through Stories, Games, and Songs   60

8

Decoding Instruction: Phonics, Morphemic Analysis, and Syllabic Analysis

9

Improving Decoding, Fluency, Comprehension, Motivation, and Writing

10

Teaching Phonics in 10 Minutes a Day   180

11

Assessment   203

Chapter 1

Perspectives on Literacy Instruction

Introduction

Technically speaking, literacy is about reading and writing. A literate person is one who can read and write; however, since the development of these abilities is so highly related to the development of speaking and listening abilities, literacy instruction is also about oral language. Therefore, when effective literacy teachers teach children how to read, they also focus on writing and oral language.

Concerns

Efforts to teach our nation's children to read and write are under scrutiny. Perhaps at no other time in the United States' history has there been more national dialogue on how to improve reading instruction (National Assessment of Educational Progress [NAEP], 2000; Pearson, 2000a; Rayner, Foorman, Perfetti, Pesetsky, & Seidenberg, 2001, 2002). Today, the widening achievement gap among children, the increasing cost of reading failure to both society and individuals, and the increasing divisiveness among reading educators espousing different pedagogical points of view have resulted in an unprecedented national focus on literacy instruction.

Looking Back in Time

Phonics

There are few topics in literacy instruction that have been as controversial as phonics. This controversy began in the 1800s (Johnson & Baumann, 1984). Prior to 1800 reading instruction in America was focused on the alphabet and the sounds represented by letters. The approach was largely a synthetic phonics approach; (i.e., children were taught letter sounds first, and then taught how to synthesize sounds to form words).

It was Horace Mann in the early 1800s who introduced a whole-word method of teaching that competed with this phonics approach. Horace Mann's method prospered until 1880, when phonics again became popular. From 1880 to 1915 there was a heavy emphasis on word identification, and the schools utilized rigorous phonics programs. In the early 1900s a new look-and-say approach emerged. It grew in popularity and led to the development of the first basal reading programs published in the 1930s. These programs were popular until about 1940. Much of the research conducted during this period compared the effectiveness of look-and-say approaches with phonics approaches. The research results suggested phonics programs were more effective than look-and-say approaches.

The years from 1940 to 1965 were again plagued with a phonics controversy. This time, however, the debate shifted from a sight word versus a phonics debate to a debate regarding which phonics approach was better, analytical or synthetic phonics. The **analytical phonics** approach (sometimes called intrinsic phonics) helped children analyze the sight words they had learned by rote to learn phonics. Teachers selected sight words containing common letter-sound relationships, presented them to children, and helped them discover the relationships. Analytical phonics programs relied heavily on context as a word identification process while **synthetic phonics** approaches (sometimes called intensive phonics) taught children to "sound out" words.

Most of the basal readers during this period incorporated one approach or the other. However, analytical phonics basals were more popular. The studies conducted during this period suggested that synthetic phonics approaches were significantly more effective than analytical phonics (Johnson & Baumann, 1984).

Jeanne Chall's (1967) research on reading programs, sponsored by the Carnegie Corporation, had a significant impact on educators in the 1960s. Her analysis of existing programs revealed that there were some major differences. While reading programs addressed both decoding and comprehension, some basal authors placed more emphasis on "reading for meaning" in the early years of instruction while others focused more on "breaking the code" (decoding). Therefore, she used the labels "meaning-emphasis" and "code-emphasis" to differentiate reading programs. Programs using analytical phonics approaches were included in her meaning-emphasis programs, and programs using synthetic phonics approaches were included in her code-emphasis programs along with such programs as the Initial Teaching Alphabet (ITA), Words in Color, and Linguistic Readers.

Chall (1967) found that the synthetic phonics approaches, and other code-emphasis programs, were significantly superior to analytical phonics or meaning-emphasis programs for young children. Years later Chall again reviewed the phonics controversy (Chall, 1983, 1996) and concluded that systematic instruction in phonics resulted in better reading performance than instruction based on a whole-word approach using analytical phonics.

At the close of this era, the famous First Grade Studies (Bond & Dykstra, 1967) were conducted. This research, among other things, revealed that reading instruction with an intensive phonics component was significantly more effective than all other types of reading instruction without that component.

During the 1970s and early 1980s the controversy regarding the merits of analytical and synthetic phonics programs continued, but new names for these phonics approaches emerged. In the seminal publication, *Becoming a Nation of Readers,* the terms *implicit phonics* and *explicit phonics* appeared, replacing the terms *analytical phonics* and *synthetic phonics*. Once again, however, evidence supporting the superiority of explicit phonics programs ("sounding out" programs) over implicit phonics approaches ("context" programs) was provided (Anderson, Hiebert, Scott, & Wilkinson, 1985).

Whole Language

When the whole language movement started to grow in 1983, the phonics controversy intensified. Whole language purists were totally against the teaching of phonics, and anyone supporting phonics teaching became an enemy to the movement. Fortunately most whole language advocates in the United States were not as dogmatic as the purists. They believed that some phonics instruction was okay if it was taught in the context of "authentic" reading material. Almost everyone associated with the whole language movement, however, rejected the practice of teaching of phonics in isolation. Therefore, educators who taught isolated phonics "mini-lessons" were "out of sync" with the whole language movement. It was during the whole language movement that educators in the United States became polarized on the phonics issue more so than at any other time in the history of reading instruction.

The whole language movement was based on the assumption that children could learn to read and write in the same natural way they learned to listen and speak. Children did not need to be "taught" about the alphabetic system upon which the written language was based; knowledge of this system could be "caught" while immersed in a print-rich environment. This assumption proved to be false.

In 1990 Marilyn Adams published the data she had been commissioned, indirectly by the U.S. Office of Education, to collect and analyze (Adams, 1990). Her data influenced her to suggest that the holistic approaches supported by advocates of whole language ought to be accompanied by some sort of phonics instruction. Effective reading instruction, she suggested, could include both holistic activities and phonics.

By the early 1990s the whole language movement had begun to seriously falter. Declining test scores in reading, and the increased numbers of reading failures in those geographical areas of the United States where whole language had been so popular, were considered to be its downfall. Legislatures in California, Texas, Ohio, and other states passed laws requiring more emphasis on phonics instruction for children and better preparation for the teachers who would teach them.

Balanced Literacy

During the whole language movement a grassroots "balanced literacy" movement had begun in various schools across the nation. Educators who liked much of what whole language had to offer, but who also recognized the need for phonics and some direct instruction, were responsible for the movement. In 1990 a small group of educators wrote a manifesto supporting balanced reading instruction (Thompson, 1997). This manifesto was followed by the report of the 1994 National Assessment of Educational Progress (NAEP) emphasizing students' reading problems, and the Snow, Burns, and Griffin (1998) report emphasizing the importance of phonemic awareness and phonics knowledge in the prevention of children's reading difficulties. Furthermore, in the early 1990s, the Superintendent of Public Instruction in California, Bill Honig, called for a balanced reading approach, because whole language had not met the needs of California's diverse student body. These events, among others, legitimized balanced literacy as a national movement.

While most educational leaders seemed to embrace the concept of "balance," and seemed to recognize the importance of phonemic awareness and phonics knowledge in learning to read and write, confusion and controversy regarding literacy instruction still prevailed. Some felt that balanced literacy was just another name for whole language, and ought to be shunned. Others believed that it was an attempt to combine the views of phonics and whole language advocates. Some believed that balance meant equal time for phonics and whole language activities, while others believed that it meant holistic activities balanced by some phonics instruction. Others were not even sure what it was they were to balance.

Attempts to define balanced literacy (Fitzgerald, 1999; Spiegel, 1999; Pearson, 2000b) have still not resulted in a definition to which all educational leaders can resonate. Nonetheless, most classroom teachers seem to have some sense of what balance means. A national survey of elementary classroom teachers conducted near the end of the twentieth century revealed that the majority of teachers embraced "a balanced, eclectic approach to elementary reading instruction, blending phonics and holistic principles and practices" (Bauman, Hoffman, Moon, & Duffy-Hester, 1998, p. 641).

The National Reading Panel

In 1997 Congress asked the National Institute for Child Health and Human Development (NICHD) and the Department of Education to establish a National Reading Panel to assess the status of reading instruction. The National Reading Panel (NRP) issued its report in April 2000. They had studied, among other things, computer technology in reading, fluency, comprehension, phonemic awareness, and phonics.

The panel concluded that there was not enough quality research to make valid conclusions in some of the areas they studied. However, they did draw conclusions about the impact of phonemic awareness and phonics instruction on children's reading growth. First, they concluded that phonemic awareness instruction helps all children learn to read. Normally developing readers, children at risk, disabled readers, preschoolers, kindergartners, first graders, and children in the second through sixth grades, across various socio-economic levels, all seem to benefit from phonemic awareness instruction. Second, they concluded that systematic phonics instruction helps children, at all socio-economic levels, learn to read more effectively than nonsystematic phonics instruction or instruction teaching no phonics. They also noted that phonics instruction produces the largest impact on children's reading growth when it is introduced in kindergarten or first grade.

Looking at the Future

What Have We Learned From Phonics Research?

Each time the phonics debate has been revisited by researchers, the conclusion is always the same: phonics knowledge is essential for becoming a proficient reader, and instructional procedures teaching phonics explicitly seem to be more effective than those that do not (Rayner et al., 2001). Some educators (Rayner et al., 2002) ask, "If researchers are so convinced about the need for phonics instruction, why does the debate continue?" It continues for a myriad of reasons. Perhaps the most important one involves the ideological and philosophical differences among educators that seem to be difficult to bridge. Learning to bridge those differences is a challenge for us all.

What Have We Learned From the Whole Language Movement?

A first step in bridging differences is to look for the good in all things—even when we seem to be disposed to do otherwise. Many positive things happened to children and teachers during the whole language movement, and literacy instruction today should be more effective because of what was learned.

Whole language was not an educational program, but a philosophy about learning, language development, and children. The philosophy, unfortunately, was never clearly defined, making it difficult for educators to communicate meaningfully with one another (for different definitions see Farris & Kaczmarski, 1988; Goodman, 1986, p. 5; Newman, 1985; Rich, 1985, p. 719). Bergeron (1990, p. 312), after analyzing 64 whole language articles, found it to be defined differently in each article. Further confusion occurred when some whole language advocates stated that direct instruction and whole language were compatible (Fountas & Hannigan, 1989; Newman & Church, 1990; Slaughter, 1988; Spiegel, 1992), while others explicitly or implicitly stated otherwise (Altwerger, Edelsky, & Flores, 1987; Doake, 1987; Goodman, 1986, 1989, 1992b; Newman, 1985; Watson, 1989).

However, whole language was based upon some logical, refreshing points of view. A major whole language premise was that language acquisition (both oral and written) was natural, not in the sense of being innate or inevitably unfolding, but in the sense that when individuals unfamiliar with a language were placed in an environment where the language was an integral component, they would learn something about it (Altwerger et al., 1987, p. 145). This premise, if not taken too far, is logical, and is supported by research (Eldredge, 1990a, 1990b; Hoskisson, 1974; Eldredge & Butterfield, 1986; Eldredge & Quinn, 1988).

Whole language was also based on other logical beliefs. For example:

- Reading and writing abilities develop when there is a reason for them to develop.
- Individuals constantly exposed to written language, in authentic situations, will react to those experiences naturally, and learn more about the language in the process.

- Reading, writing, speaking, and listening are reciprocal processes.
- Literacy experiences for children should be meaningful; and children should be given opportunities to read and write as they learn about the world in which they live.

An analysis of whole language should include an examination of the context in which it evolved. The evolution was, in large measure, a reaction against the "skill and drill" teaching approaches introduced in the early part of the twentieth century. These programs were based on principles of learning advocated by behavioral psychologists, some good, some bad. The basal reader approach in those days was simple: identify the decoding, vocabulary, and comprehension skills necessary to be a good reader and then teach them to children.

Program designers provided teachers with lists of skills to be taught, and tests to assess whether children possessed the skills. The designers instructed teachers in how to teach children the skills, and also how to manage the assessment data obtained from the diagnostic tests so they could group children with common skill needs together for instruction.

In these skill and drill programs, so much classroom time was taken giving tests, recording test results, and teaching skills that children had little time left to read. Children didn't like reading, and teachers didn't enjoy teaching it. By the mid-1980s many teachers were ready for alternative teaching perspectives, and the ideas associated with whole language found a receptive audience.

What Have We Learned From Literacy Research?

The following practices are supported by research and/or classroom experience.

Reading Practices

1. *Use literature books for some reading instruction.* Children enjoy reading literature books, and their reading achievement can be enhanced through this medium (Cohen, 1968; Cullinan, Jaggar, & Strickland, 1974; Eldredge, 1991; Eldredge & Butterfield, 1986). When literature books are used for instructional purposes, select books that accommodate a wide range of student interests, and remember to give students some choice in the books they read. Researchers have found that reading comprehension is positively affected when children are interested in the reading material (Asher, 1980; Corno & Randi, 1997; Henk & Holmes, 1988; Reutzel & Hollingsworth, 1991a). Furthermore, interest can also compensate for a child's lack of reading ability (Spangler, 1983; Sweet, 1997).

2. *Encourage students to read extensively.* Involving children in actual reading is a major component affecting reading growth (Allington, 1977, 1980, 1984; Fielding, Wilson, & Anderson, 1986; Reitsma, 1988; Reutzel & Hollingsworth, 1991b). Not only do students who read extensively become better readers through the "practice," but increased reading improves writing abilities, as well (Devries, 1970; Mills, 1974). Furthermore, when teachers provide time for students to talk about the books they read, positive attitudes toward reading are enhanced (Guthrie & McCann, 1997).

3. *Encourage students to read favorite books over and over again.* Encourage them to practice their oral reading skills so they can read favorite books to younger children, peers, and parents. Repeated readings of moderately difficult text tend to produce student growth in word recognition, reading fluency, and reading comprehension (Dowhower, 1987; Herman, 1985; Samuels, 1979; Taylor, Wade, & Yekovich, 1985).

4. *Read stories, nonfiction literature, or articles aloud with children using "big books" or other enlarged text.* This strategy is called **shared reading** or the shared book experience. During the shared book experience, teachers model how readers process print (Barrett, 1982). They model directionality of print, written word–pronunciation connections, and they model expressive, fluent reading. Several research studies have found shared reading to be particularly helpful for young children (Eldredge, Reutzel, & Hollingsworth, 1996; Reutzel & Hollingsworth, 1993; Reutzel, Hollingsworth, & Eldredge, 1994).

5. *Involve struggling readers of all ages in assisted reading practices such as taped assisted reading, shared reading, dyad reading, and group assisted reading.* Children learn to read by practicing reading, and a teacher's prime concern must be to do as much reading as is necessary with children until they can make progress on their own (Smith, 1976, p. 297).

Assisted reading strategies help students read interesting, relevant material that is too difficult for them to read independently. Furthermore, consistent use of these connected-text reading experiences enables students to repeatedly see written words as they are read for them, which eventually has a positive impact on their sight vocabulary skills (Bridge & Burton, 1982; Bridge, Winograd, & Haley, 1983; Eldredge, 1990a; Eldredge & Quinn, 1988), their reading fluency (Dowhower, 1987; National Reading Panel, 2000; Samuels, 1979; O' Shea, Sindelar, & O' Shea, 1985), and their reading comprehension (Eldredge, 1988–1989; Eldredge, 1990a; Eldredge, 1991; Eldredge & Butterfield, 1986; Eldredge & Quinn, 1988).

6. *When reading good literature (both fiction and nonfiction) to and with young students, stop and discuss the information, the story line, the picture, word characteristics, or sentence features.* Reading trade books aloud, and interacting with children in the process, helps young children become successful readers (Bennett, 2001; Campbell, 1992; Dickinson & Tabors, 2001; Labbo, 2001; Neuman, 1999).

7. *Use guided reading strategies with students to help them become independent readers.* Effective teachers provide young children with three types of reading experiences: assisted reading, guided reading, and independent reading. "Book leveling" is used to help teachers identify reading materials appropriate for each type of experience.

Assisted reading experiences help students read text material too difficult for them to read by themselves. **Independent reading** gives students reading practice with materials they are capable of reading by themselves. Books chosen for independent reading are not only easy for students to read, but interesting as well. Teachers use **guided reading** with text materials that are not too easy, and not too difficult. While students read, teachers provide the guidance they need for word identification and reading comprehension; that is, they provide prompts and feedback to help students become strategic, independent readers. There are a number of ways guided reading can be implemented (Fountas & Pinnell, 1996, 2001; Mooney, 1990; Opitz & Ford, 2001).

8. *Use direct instruction, when appropriate, to help children develop phonics knowledge.* While the whole language purists rejected direct instruction (Newman, 1985) and phonics (Watson, 1989), most teachers now recognize that some direct instruction in phonics is not incompatible with the concepts of student empowerment and meaningful learning. The assumption of primacy of either "skills over meaning" or "meaning over skills," fostered during the whole language movement, simply does not make sense (Goldenberg, 1991).

All **decoding strategies** (word recognition, analogy, context, "sounding out words," morphemic analysis, and syllabic analysis/phonics) are dependent upon phonics knowledge; students, without the ability to decode words accurately and automatically, will not progress toward the strategic, fluent reading needed for comprehension (Adams 1990, 2001; Blevins, 1998; Breznitz, 1997a, 1997b; Gough & Tunmer, 1986; Pressley, 2000; Tan & Nicholson, 1997).

9. *Improve children's comprehension of stories by focusing their attention on the basic elements of story grammar.* Ask them to make predictions about the setting, characters, and story line from book titles, book covers, and story previews before reading a story, and/or to identify basic story grammar elements after reading. Story schema seems to influence both what individuals recall from a story and what they anticipate while reading a story (Fitzgerald, 1984; Mandler & Johnson, 1977). An understanding of how authors organize and structure their ideas in texts is important for good reading comprehension (Pearson & Duke, 2002; Pressley, 2000; Simmons & Kameenui, 1998; Vallecorsa & deBettencourt, 1997).

When needed, provide less proficient students with instruction on story grammar. Fitzgerald and her colleagues found that instruction on story structure positively influenced poorer students' reading and writing of narrative text (Fitzgerald & Spiegel, 1983; Fitzgerald & Teasley, 1986).

Story grammar activities are appropriate when stories are read *to* children, *with* them, or *by* them. When stories are independently read by children, a simple story frame, such as the following, can be given to them to fill in the blank spaces, focusing their attention on major story grammar elements:

This story took place _____ .

The main characters were _____ .

The problem in this story was _____ .

The problem was solved by _____ .

Prior to reading stories to or with young children, time spent on appropriate vocabulary/schemata issues affecting the comprehension of the story is well spent (see Tierney & Cunningham, 1984).

10. *Use teaching strategies known to improve children's vocabulary knowledge, and teach individual words and word-learning strategies directly, when appropriate.* Obviously, read-

ing and writing are dependent on words, and the meanings students develop for words. When elementary students improve their vocabulary, reading comprehension improves (Beck, Perfetti, & McKeown, 1982; McKeown et al., 1983; McKeown, Beck, Omanson, & Pople, 1985). Students who are "language deprived" in any way must be helped to improve their vocabulary knowledge if they are to become successful readers (Johnson, 2001; National Research Council, 1998).

While most of an individual's vocabulary knowledge is developed indirectly through his or her experiences, either firsthand experiences or vicarious experiences through books, children can be directly taught words (Johnson, 2001) through a variety of strategies. For a scientific review of vocabulary instruction, review the work of Nagy and his associates (Nagy, Herman, & Anderson, 1985), Stahl (1986, 1998), and his associates (Stahl & Fairbanks, 1986; Stahl & Jacobson, 1986; Stahl, Hare, Sinatra & Gregory, Krashen, 1993), Allington & Cunningham, 1996), and Burns, Griffin, & Snow, 1999).

11. *Help students develop their own comprehension processing strategies.* Durkin (1978) helped educators realize that asking students questions about their reading, even high-level questions, does not teach them how to comprehend. The ability to comprehend, among other factors, includes the use of strategic thinking abilities, and research supports the effectiveness of teaching these abilities to students (Dole, Brown, & Trathen, 1996; Gordon, 1985; Pressley, 2004; Reutzel & Hollingsworth, 1988). Explicit comprehension strategy instruction for imagery, inferencing, critical thinking, and metacognition can improve students' comprehension. Teachers providing demonstrations, and explanations utilizing "think alouds," in a "gradual release of responsibility" teaching format (Pearson & Gallagher, 1983) seem to experience the most success.

12. *Provide students with expository (nonfiction) reading material, and teach them how authors organize the information in this material.* Sometimes we call **expository materials** "information books" because they are the books we read to get information about the world in which we live. Authors of expository texts use predictable text patterns, or structures, appropriate for the information they are trying to convey. These patterns have been researched (Armbruster & Anderson, 1981; Meyer, 1979), and readers who understand them recall more from reading expository texts than readers who do not (Meyer, Brandt, & Bluth, 1980).

The predictable text patterns most used by authors of expository text are: **sequencing pattern** (organizing information into a chronological sequence); **causation pattern** (showing cause and effect relationships); **comparison pattern** (examining similarities and differences among concepts or events); **response pattern** (asking questions and providing answers to the questions *or* presenting problems along with solutions); **description pattern** (describing concepts, events, or processes); **collection pattern** (presenting generalizations in either a deductive or inductive format).

Literacy experts are concerned about the lack of expository reading material in primary grade classrooms (Duke, 2000a, 2000b). Teachers may need to provide more expository books for young children. Learning to read and comprehend expository material gets at the very heart of "reading to learn."

Grouping Practices

Replace Traditional Reading Groups with Student Dyads, Total Class Activities, Ad Hoc Groups, and Small Heterogeneous Groups. Not only do children enjoy their experiences in these grouping patterns, but they feel better about themselves and learn more than when placed in traditional reading groups (Eldredge & Butterfield, 1986).

Writing Practices

1. *Use students' speech, during the early years of schooling, to help them make the transition from the oral to the written language.* Students' own vocabulary and sentence patterns are easier for them to read and write than adult vocabulary and syntax patterns. This transition from oral to written language is relatively easy for young children when they are engaged in individual writing activities, or when teachers use the Language Experience Approach (LEA) to teach them to read. When using the Language Experience Approach, children see their own speech written before they attempt to read it, and when young children write, they attempt to encode their own speech.

The Language Experience Approach has been shown to be as effective as basal programs in teaching young children how to read (Hall, 1981). The approach is especially effective with beginning readers, and with older children not too familiar with English vocabulary or syntax patterns.

2. *Encourage children to spell words by sounds (invented spelling) when they want to use words they cannot spell.* Writing activities where children are encouraged to use invented spelling are known to have a positive impact on reading development (Clarke, 1988; Robinson, 1991; Tierney & Shanahan, 1991), spelling growth, and quality of writing (Eldredge & Baird, 1996).

Clarke (1988) found that first-grade students not only wrote better when they had the freedom to spell without emphasis on standard forms, but their word recognition abilities and reading achievement improved significantly as well. Spelling words according to their sounds focuses children's attention on the individual phonemes in words and requires them to apply their knowledge of letter–sound relationships. Both phonemic awareness and phonics knowledge are related to word recognition abilities. Therefore, it is not surprising that researchers have found that writing has a positive impact on the young children's word recognition abilities when they are encouraged to use invented spelling as they write (Tierney & Shanahan, 1991).

3. *Involve young children in interactive writing sessions where teachers write with students.* Sometimes these sessions are called "sharing the pen" (McCarrier, Pinnell, & Fountas, 1999). In these interactive writing sessions teachers do most of the writing for the children, following the format of the Language Experience Approach. However, with time and student development, the teacher invites children to write the beginning letter of a word, several letters of a word, an entire word, a series of words, or an entire sentence.

4. *Encourage students to write daily for "intrinsic" purposes, on topics relevant to them.* Not only do children learn to write well when given meaningful opportunities to

write, but their reading abilities are also enhanced when writing is a part of a literature-rich environment (Calkins, 1982; Graves, 1983).

   5.   *Stress the content of written work over its form during the drafting and revising stages of the writing process.* Encourage children to write anything they can say, even when they do not know how to spell the words they want to use. Children write better when they are free to focus on what they want to say (Clarke, 1988; Eldredge & Baird, 1996).

Practice Integrating the Language Arts

Integrate the Teaching of Reading, Writing, Speaking, and Listening. Studies indicate that reading and writing are interrelated processes (Doctorow, Wittrock, & Marks, 1978; Taylor & Berkowitz, 1980), and growth in one process tends to facilitate growth in the other. Success in writing can be predicted by reading scores (Evanechko, Ollila, & Armstrong, 1974), and increased reading results in improved writing (Stotsky, 1983). It has also been demonstrated that a) writing activities in a literature-rich environment (Graves, 1983), b) writing activities using invented spelling (Clarke, 1988), and c) writing activities designed to improve reading comprehension (Holbrook, 1987; Stotsky, 1983) enhance reading abilities. Many language arts researchers have concluded from their research that writing and reading should be taught together (Graves, 1983; Shanahan, 1988).

Reading and writing are interrelated in a complex relationship. Sometimes we observe good readers who are poor writers, and good writers who are poor readers. Further studies are needed to understand the exact nature of the reading–writing connection (see Tierney & Shanahan, 1991). However, reading and writing, when used together, involve students in a greater variety of reasoning operations than when either is used alone (Tierney & Shanahan, p. 272), enhancing literacy development in the process. In addition, teaching writing and reading together has been shown to motivate poor readers who have been "turned off to reading" (Dionisio, 1983).

How Does Decoding Fit in with What We Have Learned?

In all alphabet languages, a word's **phonemes** (its individual sound sequences) are represented by an alphabet code when the word is written. Therefore, when we write words we say that they have been *encoded* ("put into a code"). When readers *decode* words, they reverse the process; that is, they translate the encoded words back into speech, or, if reading silently, they translate them into "inner speech." The term **decoding,** as it is used in this book, therefore, refers to any process used to translate written text into language; (i.e., speech or inner speech).

You will learn about different decoding processes in this book; (i.e., different ways people translate written text into language). You will learn about the strengths and weaknesses of these processes, and you will also learn about the relationships existing among them. As you learn about decoding, try to visualize its unique role in the development of literacy, and remember the literacy instruction research presented in this chapter.

Effective teachers organize instructional programs in literacy to help students a) learn how to read and write, b) enjoy reading and writing, and c) use reading and writing to learn and enrich their lives. Teaching students to decode (or encode) is only one piece of the literacy puzzle teachers are trying to put together while helping students learn how to read and write. The decoding (encoding) piece is necessary to complete the puzzle, however, because the ability to translate written text into language is necessary for the reading act, and encoding words is necessary for the act of writing. Therefore, while the decoding/encoding piece of the puzzle is not sufficient to complete the puzzle because other pieces must be used for that purpose, the puzzle can never be completed without it.

Reading Theories

There are many different theories regarding what readers do when they read. All theories, however, acknowledge that a) decoding/encoding, b) language, and c) thinking play some role in the process of reading. If children are having difficulty in reading, generally speaking, it will be in one or more of these three areas. These elements in each area are displayed in Figure 1.1. They are all interrelated.

Decoding

The focus of this book is on decoding. The purpose of all decoding instruction is fluent reading, a necessary condition for reading comprehension. Therefore, decoding is not an end in itself. It is a means to an end, and reading comprehension is the end goal for developing readers; (i.e., readers "learning to read"). Everything about decoding discussed in this book is ultimately connected to improved reading comprehension.

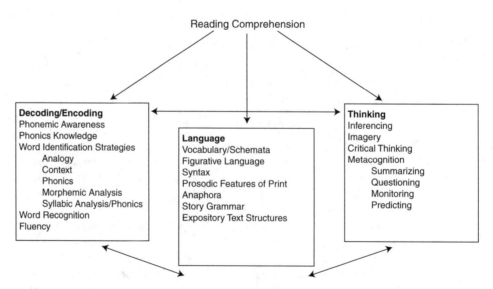

FIGURE 1.1   Reading Comprehension

The other reading goals are sometimes affectionately referred to as "reading for enjoyment" and "reading to learn." Decoding also plays an important role in achieving these goals since comprehension is necessary for both reading enjoyment and functional reading.

Application Activities

1. Organize small discussion groups, and do the following:
   (a) Define literacy.
   (b) Discuss the question, "Why is there such an unprecedented focus on literacy instruction today?"
   (c) Report some of the important findings of the National Reading Panel.
   (d) Share your personal feelings about the role of phonics in reading and writing.
2. Summarize, in writing, some of the effective teaching practices introduced during the whole language movement.
3. Describe your personal position regarding whole language. Is it consistent with existing research?
4. Summarize, in writing, some of the most important things we have learned from literacy research.
5. Visit one or two classrooms. Observe children and teachers in action. How are reading, writing, speaking, and listening taught in these classrooms?

Chapter 2

Decoding

The Coding System in Written English

The English alphabet is used to represent speech in print. Each word in the spoken language is comprised of individual sounds called **phonemes**, and the 26 letters of the alphabet are used by themselves, or in combination with other letters, to represent the 45 phonemes used in spoken words. The letter/s representing phonemes are called **graphemes**.

In Figure 2.1, the phonemes and graphemes in the word *cat* are identified. The spoken word contains three phonemes represented by three single-letter graphemes.

In Figure 2.2, the phonemes and graphemes in the word *box* are identified. The spoken word contains four phonemes represented by only three graphemes. *Most of the time* the number of graphemes in a word equals the number of phonemes. That is, each phoneme in a spoken word is represented by a separate grapheme in the written word. The letter *x*, however, is an unusual letter. It doesn't represent its own phoneme; (i.e., it has no sound of its own). In the word *box*, the letter *x* represents two phonemes: /k/ and /s/ blended together, or /ks/. Therefore, in the word *fox*, and in other words or syllables ending in *x*, we have an unusual situation where the number of graphemes in the word does not equal the number of phonemes.

Written word: **cat**

3 Phonemes in the spoken word: /k/ + /a/ + /t/
3 Graphemes in the written word: c + a + t
3 Letters to comprise 3 graphemes, which represent the 3 phonemes

---

FIGURE 2.1

Written word: **box**

4 Phonemes in the spoken word: /b/ + /o/ + /k/ + /s/
3 Graphemes in the written word: b + o + x
3 Letters to comprise 3 graphemes, which represent the 4 phonemes

FIGURE 2.2

 Written word: **mouse**

3 Phonemes in the spoken word: /m/ + /ou/ + /s/
3 Graphemes in the written word: m + ou + se
5 Letters to comprise 3 graphemes, which represent the 3 phonemes

FIGURE 2.3

In Figure 2.3 the phonemes and graphemes in the word *mouse* are identified. The word contains three graphemes representing three phonemes, which is the normal phoneme/grapheme relationship found in words. However, notice that five letters are used to represent only three phonemes. The first phoneme in the word is represented by a single-letter grapheme (*m*). The second phoneme is represented by a two-letter grapheme (*ou*), and the third phoneme is represented by a two-letter grapheme (*se*). From this example, it should become clear that letters and graphemes are not synonymous terms. Sometimes one letter is used to form a grapheme, and sometimes multiple letters are used.

In Figure 2.4 the phonemes and graphemes in the word *badge* are identified. The word contains three graphemes representing three phonemes. This time, however, the first phoneme in the word is represented by a single-letter grapheme (*b*). The second phoneme is represented by a single-letter grapheme (*a*), and the third phoneme is represented by a three-letter grapheme (*dge*). You may have noticed that letters within slash marks / / represent sounds (phonemes), while letters without slash marks represent graphemes.

However imperfect the alphabetic system may appear, a word's grapheme sequences in the English language represent its phoneme sequences. Said another way, speech is "mapped onto print" by representing the phonemes in spoken words, in the sequences in which they occur, with written symbols called graphemes.

Written word: **badge**

3 Phonemes in the spoken word: /b/ + /a/ + /j/
3 Graphemes in the written word: b + a + dge
5 Letters to comprise 3 graphemes, which represent the 3 phonemes

FIGURE 2.4

When individuals communicate through writing, such as I am now doing, they *encode* words into sentences, paragraphs, and larger units of discourse; that is, they represent speech with a written code comprised of alphabetic symbols. When spoken words are written with this code, the process is called encoding. When individuals read, they *decode* words; that is, they translate the written code back into language. If the decoding task is not difficult for readers, then they may be able to use their language and thinking abilities to construct meaning from the print. If the decoding task is difficult for readers then comprehension suffers.

Defining Decoding

Decoding is a term meaning different things to different people. Some definitions of decoding are extremely narrow, while others are quite broad. For example, some individuals use the term *word recognition* to describe the process students use when they recognize words instantaneously, and *decoding* to describe the process they use when they "sound out" words, thus excluding word recognition from their definition. Others use *decoding* to refer to word recognition, and the term *recoding* to refer to the process used to sound out words. Still others use the term to refer to both word recognition and sounding out words.

Ehri (1991, 1994) defines decoding as the process readers use when they convert letters into sounds, and blend those sounds to form recognizable words. The letters students use for this conversion might be individual letters, digraphs, or rimes. She explains that decoding is only one of four different ways students read words (National Reading Panel, 2000, pp. 2–107). The other three ways are by **sight**, **analogy**, and **prediction**. When students read by sight they are retrieving words they have already learned to read from memory. When they read by analogy they access in memory words they have already learned and use parts of the spellings to read new words having the same spellings (e.g., using -*atch* in *catch* to read *hatch*). When students use prediction they use their linguistic (syntax, phonics, semantics) and background knowledge to guess the identities of unknown words.

Decoding is defined fairly broadly in this book. In Chapter 1, we learned that decoding is defined as the process readers use to translate written language into speech or inner speech, regardless of the strategy used for the translation.

Different Levels of Decoding

Ehri's (1991, 1994) explanation regarding the different ways students read words is closely associated with my explanation of decoding levels. I developed my decoding model sometime before 1981; otherwise, I might have used hers. Nonetheless, our perceptions regarding "reading words" are similar. For example, the following terms describe essentially the same concepts:

Her Terms	*My Terms*
Sight	*Word Recognition*
Analogy	*Analogy*
Prediction	*Context*
Decoding	*Phonics, Syllabic Analysis/Phonics*
–	*Morphemic Analysis*

The term *decoding*, as used in this book, includes both a fast translation process, called *word recognition*, and slower processes, called *word identification*. Word recognition is the primary decoding process used by proficient readers, and implies an accurate, rapid, and automatic recognition of written words. The utilization of various word identification strategies, along with some word recognition, is associated with less proficient readers. Once readers have developed reading fluency their decoding efforts do not interfere with comprehension processing (Barr, 1972; Cohen, 1974–1975; Johnson & Baumann, 1984) as some researchers have suggested, but rather enhance it. Less fluent readers find comprehension difficult, then, not because of an overreliance on decoding, as some educators suggest, but because of insufficiently developed decoding skills.

Decoding strategies are shown in Figure 2.5. These strategies can all be used to translate written text into language. However, better readers use word recognition most of the time, relying on word identification strategies only when words are not recognized.

All of the strategies listed underneath word recognition are word identification strategies. All word identification strategies take more reader time to use than word recognition. However, some word identification strategies take less reader time than others. The word identification strategies in Figure 2.5 are arranged according to the amount of time readers take when using them. For example, identifying words by analogy takes less reader time than identifying words through context, and identifying words by context takes less reader time than identifying words by phonics ("sounding them out"). The amount of time taken for decoding is important, because comprehension suffers when decoding takes a lot of time and effort (LaBerge & Samuels, 1974; Perfetti, 1985).

All of the word identification strategies (analogy, context, phonics, morphemic analysis, and syllabic analysis/phonics) are interim decoding strategies students use until they develop large word recognition vocabularies some educators call "sight words." Notice in Figure 2.5 that there are two arrows going from the context strategy. One arrow goes to phonics and the other one goes to morphemic analysis. These arrows indicate that the analogy and context strategies can be used to identify both

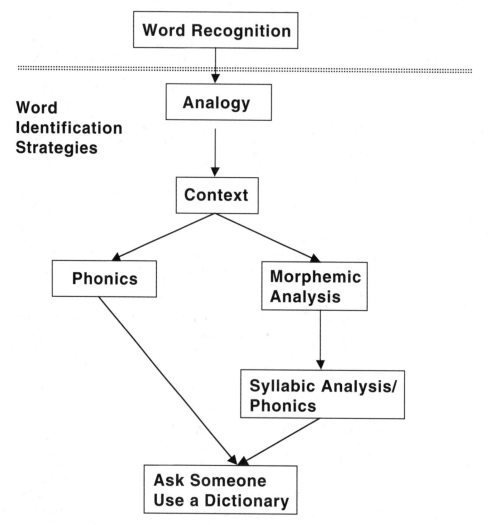

FIGURE 2.5 Decoding Strategies

single-syllable and multisyllabic words. However, after these strategies have failed to produce the desired outcome, the strategy to use next will depend upon whether the unrecognized word contains one vowel sound or more than one vowel sound. Phonics is the strategy to use if the word contains only one syllable. Morphemic analysis is the strategy to use if the word contains more than one syllable.

The average word recognition rate for adult readers is about 250 milliseconds per word. Furthermore, adult readers recognize words by their spellings since it is each word's spelling that sets it apart from all other words. Effective decoding instruction should help students remember word spellings and improve their reading rates so they can become proficient readers.

All Decoding Strategies Are Dependent on Phonics Knowledge

Ehri's research (1992) suggests that word recognition is a process where learners use phonics knowledge to help them remember the systematic connections between word spellings and word pronunciations. According to Ehri and Wilce (1983, 1985), the differences between skilled and unskilled readers is that skilled readers possess the phonics knowledge needed to form complete connections between word spellings and pronunciations, while unskilled readers lack that knowledge. Unskilled readers, therefore, form incomplete word-spelling–word-pronunciation connections, and have poorer word recognition abilities, because of their insufficient phonics knowledge.

Not only is word recognition dependent on phonics knowledge, but analogy and context strategies are also dependent on it (National Reading Panel, 2000, pp. 2-107). In a study conducted by Ehri and Robbins (1992) it was found that word identification by analogy was dependent upon phonics knowledge. Since one of the three language cueing systems children use to identify words by context is the phonics cue, the ability to use context as a word identification strategy is also dependent on phonics. Furthermore, if word recognition is dependent on phonics knowledge, then morphemic analysis would also be dependent on it since recognition of root words is a part of that strategy. The other two word identification strategies are phonics-based so, obviously, phonics is an integral part of those strategies. In sum, all decoding strategies are dependent upon phonics knowledge.

What Are the Strengths and Limitations of the Various Word Identification Strategies?

When readers use word identification strategies, they use them because word recognition fails. As a rule of thumb, if children do not read a word in a second or less, they are probably using some word identification strategy. Some of the word identification strategies may be learned by the children themselves (analogy, for example) while other strategies are usually taught.

The word identification strategies are a) identifying words by analogy, b) identifying words through contextual information, c) identifying words by "sounding them out" (phonics), d) identifying words through recognition of morphemic units (roots, prefixes, suffixes, or inflectional endings), and e) identifying words by locating syllable boundaries and sounding out the syllables (syllabic analysis and phonics). Readers are decoding when they use any of these word identification processes, even though they are using what are considered to be interim strategies, employed only because word recognition abilities have not developed sufficiently for accurate, automatic, rapid, fluent decoding.

Analogy. When children search their lexical memories for a word not immediately recognized, they may recall words that look something like the unrecognizable word. For example, a child might be trying to identify the word *bound,* in the sentence, "He was *bound* to do great things." While trying to identify the word, the child might realize that it looks like the words *ground, found, around,* and *sound,* which are already sight words stored in lexical memory. He notices the similarity between these words and the unrecognizable word, and since he knows the sound represented by the letter *b,* he quickly identifies the new word as *bound.* This process of word identification is called **analogy.**

The main advantage of using analogy as a word identification strategy is the speed at which the strategy produces results. It takes less time to use analogy than all of the other identification strategies. Its major weakness is that children need a large sight vocabulary before they can use it. Therefore, analogy is not a very useful strategy for children who do not read well.

Context. When words are identified by **context,** children use the three cueing systems written language provides for all readers: the syntax cue, the semantic cue, and the phonics (graphophonic) cue. Syntax, or grammar, is a study of sentence organization and word function. The syntax cue has to do with word function. Words serve different functions in sentences. Sometimes the same word will serve different functions in different sentences. For example, in the following sentences the word *baby* plays a different function in each sentence: "The *baby* cried." "The *baby* pictures are becoming worn." In the first sentence the word *baby* is a noun (it serves as a naming word). In the second sentence the word is an adjective (it serves as a desribing word). To use the syntax cue, therefore, the reader must determine the function of the unrecognizable word, and identify a word that would serve that same function.

The semantic cue is about meaning. When children focus on semantics, they want to know whether the word they identify for the unrecognizable word "makes sense" when used with the other words in the sentence.

The phonics cue is about letter–sound relationships. When children focus on the phonics cue, they want to know whether the word they identify begins with the sound represented by the beginning letter of the unrecognizable word.

When teachers ask children to identify a word through context, they are asking them to make an intelligent "guess" based on syntax, semantic, and graphophonic information. Try using the guessing game yourself. Read the following sentence: "The beautiful black cat p _____ gently as her master petted her." Ask yourself, "What action word (syntax focus) beginning with the letter *p* (graphophonic focus) would make sense (semantic focus) in this sentence?" Did you respond with the word *purred*? If you did, you made a good guess.

There are definite advantages to the context strategy because it focuses on "reading for meaning." There are some limitations in its use, however, and some problems with using it exclusively. The limitations of use are the same as those found with the analogy strategy. Readers must possess a sight vocabulary large enough to enable an intelligent word guess. They must be able to recognize *all* of the other words in the sentence surrounding the unrecognizable word. If there are two unrecognizable words in a sentence, the process breaks down. Therefore, the strategy cannot be used successfully with students who are struggling readers without teacher support.

Adams (1990) also found a problem associated with the teaching of contextual analysis exclusively. When children use that strategy they tend to look at only the first letter of the unrecognizable word, since that is all the phonics data they need to make an intelligent guess. The research she reviewed suggested that the strategy did not require young children to look closely enough at the letters of unknown words to enable them to remember their spellings. Hence, the strategy is probably not very powerful for building children's word recognition abilities.

Phonics. When students use phonics as a word identification strategy, they use a) their letter–sound knowledge, b) their ability to isolate, or segment, phonemes, and c) their ability to blend phonemes to "sound out" words. In other words, they use their phonics knowledge to identify words by sounds.

The greatest strength for the phonics identification strategy is that the phonics knowledge students learn while using it leads to greater word recognition abilities (Ehri & Wilce, 1983, 1985). Its greatest weakness is that it is not as efficient as context or analogy as a word identification strategy. Therefore, in guided reading lessons teachers should encourage students to try analogy or context strategies before asking them to sound out unrecognizable words. Since analogy and context are more efficient decoding strategies, they should be tried first. Then, if students are unsuccessful using them, phonics can be used.

Morphemic Analysis. Morphemes are the smallest units of meaning in words. Morphemes can be root words, prefixes, or suffixes in word derivatives; or morphemes can be root words, or inflectional endings in word variants (see Figure 2.6).

When students encounter word derivatives or word variants and do not initially recognize them, they may be able to identify these words by analyzing the morphemic units within them. If they are able to identify a word by its morphemes, they are using morphemic analysis for word identification.

Morphemic analysis can be a fairly rapid word identification process for students who have large word recognition vocabularies. These children look within words for roots, prefixes, suffixes, and inflectional endings (Durkin, 1989; Lass & Davis, 1985).

Word Derivative: ***disagreeable***

Morphemes: 1) ***dis*** (not)   2) ***agree*** (concur)   3) ***able*** (able to)
                        prefix   root   suffix

Meaning: "not able to concur"

Word Variant: ***smartest***

Morphemes: 1) **smart** (intelligent)   2) **est** (the most)
                          root   inflectional ending

Meaning: "the most intelligent"

FIGURE 2.6 Morphemes

However, for struggling readers morphemic analysis is not very effective—especially without teacher support.

Syllabic Analysis/Phonics. Phonics is a study of letter–sound relationships *within* syllables. Children with phonics knowledge have learned that the vowels in "open syllables" (*go, me*) predictably represent long vowel sounds, and the vowels in "closed syllables" (*can, must*) predictably represent short vowel sounds. *Note:* Open syllables end in vowels, and closed syllables end in consonants.

When children encounter multisyllabic words that cannot be recognized through any other identification strategy, phonics can be used if the syllable boundaries in multisyllabic words can be identified, revealing their closed and open syllables. For example, phonics could be used to sound out words like *fever* and *cabin* if children could visualize the open and closed syllables in each word: *fe.ver* and *cab.in.*

If children cannot identify the syllable boundaries in multisyllabic words, phonics strategies cannot be used to sound them out. It is just too confusing. Children often attempt to use their phonics knowledge by looking for familiar word parts in multisyllabic words. For example, they may look at the word *paper* and associate *ap* with sight words such as *nap, map,* and *lap,* and sound out the word as *pap.er.* Phonics as a word identification strategy, therefore, can only be used with multisyllabic words when students are taught how to visualize the syllable boundaries in the words.

Syllabic analysis/phonics is the most cumbersome and time-consuming of all word identification strategies. Therefore, it is not a strategy for students to use while reading unless everything else fails. In spite of the weakness of the strategy, however, when students are taught how phonics works in multisyllabic words they develop a greater ability to see multisyllabic word "chunks." This ability, in turn, facilitates growth in the recognition of multisyllabic words.

The Relationship of Decoding to Reading

Decoding is not equivalent to reading, since readers can sometime decode words without understanding them. At other times readers can decode, but may not be able to meaningfully organize the ideas presented among or between sentences. At still other times readers can decode, but cannot create mental images from the message, make inferences from text clues, or critically evaluate the message. Decoding is clearly not reading, but it is necessary for reading (Adams, 1990), for if print cannot be translated into language, then it cannot be understood (Gough & Tunmer, 1986, p. 7).

Reading fluency is dependent upon decoding and directly related to reading comprehension (Eldredge, Quinn, & Butterfield, 1990; Nathan & Stanovich, 1991). **Reading fluency** has been defined by cognitive psychologists as the ability to read with expression, which entails, among other things, the ability to recognize words accurately, rapidly, and automatically (see LaBerge & Samuels, 1974; Perfetti, 1985; Stanovich, 1980, 1986). Individuals who are fluent decoders (who recognize words automatically without giving conscious attention to them) generally comprehend written text better than those who are poor at decoding. In fact, inadequate decoding seems to be a hallmark of poor readers (Carnine, Carnine, & Gertsen, 1984;

Jorm & Share, 1983; Lesgold & Curtis, 1981). Good decoders find it easier to comprehend written text than poor decoders simply because they have less difficulty in translating print into language.

Cognitive psychologists reason that people have finite cognitive capacity to devote to any given task (Kahneman, 1973), and that since comprehension processing utilizes so much of this capacity (Freedman & Calfee, 1984), ways must be found to decrease the capacity needed for decoding and increase that available for comprehension. Readers who are poor decoders will use too much of the cognitive capacity needed for reading in attempts to translate the written symbols into words. Fluent readers will use less of their cognitive capacity for decoding, leaving more for comprehension.

Theoretical Underpinnings of Decoding

The definition of decoding embraced in this book is based on the premise that readers generally translate written words into internal speech as they read (Cunningham & Cunningham, 1978; McCutcheon, Bell, France, & Perfetti, 1991; Tannenhaus, Flanigan, & Seidenberg, 1980; Taylor & Taylor, 1983). This premise is derived from research on the effects of speech upon the development of word meanings (see Taylor & Taylor). Young children initially attach meanings to words from speech (i.e., each word's pronunciation). Readers translate written words into inner speech, while reading silently, because inner speech calls to mind the attached meanings and aids comprehension while reading.

Let us recapitulate the language development of children, and the effects of the auditory channel on the development of word meanings. Children first learn to understand speech, and then learn to speak. After speech is reasonably well developed, they learn to read. Reading is initially taught orally to children. It is only after children learn to read orally that they are capable of silent reading.

The Auditory Communication Channel

Even after children learn to read silently, they spend most of their time using oral language. Therefore, listening and speaking are practiced much more than reading and writting. People are more accustomed to, and have more practice with, the auditory channel for communication, and it is through the auditory channel that people (apart from those with hearing impairments and the deaf) learn to attach meanings to most words.

Language Meanings Are Initially Developed From Sound

Children attach meanings to spoken words early in life through trial and error. As they listen to their parents and others trying to communicate with them, they perceive sounds, or sometimes think they do, and attach meanings to them based upon how the adults in their environment use them. Children attempt to replicate the sounds of words so they can communicate with others through speech, sometimes making mistakes that adults find amusing; but through trial and error, children learn to listen and speak. Through early, meaningful, receptive, and expressive language experiences children begin to refine their listening and speaking abilities, and can eventually use the spoken language effectively to communicate with others.

Children learn to differentiate words from one another by their unique sound sequences (phonemes). It is the individual phonemes in a word, occurring in a specific sequence, that set it apart from all other words (homophones excepted). Therefore, children learn to identify individual words by processing specific sound sequences through the auditory channel. Children attach meanings to the words, based upon their sounds, and both the sounds and the meanings attached to them are stored in *lexical memory*. Huey (1908), speaking of inner speech, said, "Although it is a foreshortened and incomplete speech in most of us, yet it is perfectly certain that the inner hearing or pronouncing, or both, of what is read, is a constituent part of the reading of by far the most people" (p. 117).

When children begin to read they must use all of their language abilities and knowledge to make sense of the messages contained in written text. However, before they can employ this knowledge, they must be able to decode, or translate the text's written symbols into words. It is the words in the spoken language to which children have attached meanings, and it is the words in written text that bring those meanings to mind when reading. Therefore, when individuals read they do *not* go directly from the print to meaning, as some believe. They go from the graphic representation of the word to the word itself to the meanings attached to the word. For good readers, these connections occur nearly simultaneously.

Many studies demonstrate clearly that readers, when reading silently, are sensitive to the auditory components of words (see Taylor & Taylor, 1983). Readers take more time to read words containing many syllables than words of equal graphemic length containing fewer syllables. Readers also detect more misspellings in words when the spellings are not phonetically compatible with the spoken word, and they detect fewer misspellings when the misspellings are phonetically compatible with the spoken word.

Readers store inner speech in short-term memory until they can integrate it and comprehend it as a clause or sentence. Poor readers cannot use inner speech or auditory images to hold linguistic material in short-term memory as well as good readers do because of inadequate decoding (translating) abilities. Apparently, this ability to hold inner speech in short-term memory does not develop quickly (see Taylor & Taylor, 1983).

Reading Theory

The theory of reading embraced in this book suggests that proficient readers simultaneously process orthographic (spelling), phonological (speech), and meaning (syntax and semantic) information while they read, making predictions about immediate and subsequent text, and checking those predictions against the actual text. Because readers encounter written words first, it is their orthographic and phonological processors (see Adams, 1990) that initiate this parallel distributed processing, which in turn leads to reading comprehension. Decoding therefore plays an important role in reading.

Enhancing Decoding

Teachers can enhance children's word recognition development by providing them with meaningful experiences with written language that focus their attention on the letter sequences of specific words. When children perceive the relationships existing between the sounds of spoken words and the letters in written words, word recognition occurs more rapidly than when they do not perceive such relationships.

Quantitative and Qualitative Dimensions of Decoding

Children develop word recognition skills only through practice, and the more meaningful the practice is to children, the more likely they will continue to practice. Word recognition practice has both a quantitative and a qualitative dimension. The quantitative dimension is based on the belief that the more experiences children have associating spoken words with the letter sequences representing them, the greater their word recognition development will be. The qualitative dimension is based on the belief that when teachers provide children with experiences that focus their attention on words' letter–sound relationships, their word recognition development will be greater.

Students develop word recognition through the use of informal strategies such as shared book reading, dyad reading, group assisted reading, tape assisted reading, repeated reading, writing with invented spellings, and the Language Experience Approach to reading. These strategies are effective if students pay attention to the words' letter sequences as they read or are read to, and, in case of writing, if they try to recall the letter sequences of words as they write them. Informal decoding strategies (with the exception of writing with invented spellings) provide children with *quantitative* word recognition practice. Writing with invented spellings is probably more qualitative than quantitative.

Children may also develop their word recognition abilities through meaningful phonics instruction. Such instruction can enhance phonemic awareness and can help children learn how the sounds in spoken words are related to the letters in written words. In fact, carefully organized phonics instruction focuses children's attention on words' letter sequences more than any other type of activity (Adams, 1990). Planned phonics activities, therefore, provide *qualitative* word recognition practice.

In summary, then, decoding involves either: word recognition; identifying words by analogy; identifying words through the use of contextual clues; sounding out words using phonics; identifying words through the recognition of familiar root words, prefixes, suffixes, or inflectional endings; or identifying syllabic boundaries within multisyllabic words and sounding out the separate syllables. The goal of all decoding instruction should be to help readers develop word recognition abilities because accurate, rapid, automatic recognition of printed words is directly related to reading comprehension, and is a hallmark of all good readers. Word identification strategies are a means to the end, not ends themselves.

Application Activities

1. Describe, in writing, the role of "inner speech" in the reading process.
2. Summarize, in writing, the relationship of decoding to reading.
3. Summarize, in writing, the quantitative and qualitative dimensions of word recognition practice. Describe how teachers can provide both types of practice for students.
4. Interview two or three teachers. Ask them to define *decoding*. Compare their responses. How do they compare with each other? How do they compare with the definition of decoding in this text? How do they teach decoding in their classrooms?
5. Visit a second- or third-grade classroom. Ask the teacher to identify the two best and the two poorest readers in the classroom. Listen to these students read. Observe the decoding strategies they use. Ask them some questions about what they have read. How do their decoding abilities relate to their reading comprehension?

Chapter 3

Phonemic Awareness and the Alphabetic Principle

The Alphabetic Principle

The English language uses an alphabetic writing system to represent speech in print. If it was a perfect system each *phoneme,* or speech sound, would have its own distinctive graphic representation. But it doesn't, and it isn't a perfect system. There is not a one-to-one relationship between the 45 speech sounds comprising spoken English and the letters of the alphabet. In the first place, there aren't enough letters in the alphabet to match sounds and letters this way. Plus, when you consider that some of the 26 letters (*x, c, q,* and *y* as a vowel) could be eliminated from the system entirely, because other letters do what they do, the letters available for representing the 45 phonemes are even fewer than many teachers realize.

To make the system work; that is, to provide enough graphemes to represent the 45 phonemes, adjustments had to be made. First, certain letter combinations were used to represent phonemes. An example of one of these letter combinations would be the *sh* used to represent the first phoneme in the word *shop.* Second, writing patterns were used so that one letter could represent more than one phoneme. For example, all of the vowel letters are used to represent at least two sounds by using different ways to write syllables: m**ad**, m**ade**; n**ot**, n**ote**, etc.).

Imperfect as the alphabetic writing system is, it is predictable, and phonemes in spoken words are "mapped onto print" by graphemes, in a sequential order. The system is predictable enough for children to understand, and those who eventually understand it learn to read and write.

The system is called the **alphabetic principle**. The alphabetic principle could be explained as follows: "Spoken language is represented in writing by an alphabet. The sequence of sounds in each spoken word are represented by certain letters or letter combinations. The word sounds are called phonemes, and the letters representing them are called graphemes." The principle reveals how the sounds in spoken words are represented by the letters in written words. Therefore, the alphabetic principle provides students with the key to understanding how the oral and written forms of the language relate to each other.

Students need two sources of knowledge for them to understand the alphabetic principle. First, they need to be aware that spoken words are comprised of phonemes (the smallest units of sound within words), and second, they need to understand the relationship existing between these sound units and the alphabetic letters *(graphemes)* representing them.

When children become aware that spoken words are comprised of phonemes we say that they have **phonemic awareness**. When they are able to associate graphemes with these phonemes we say that they have letter–sound knowledge or **phonics knowledge**. Students who understand the alphabetic principle have developed some level of phonemic awareness and phonics knowledge. Educators and researchers are currently debating the exact nature of this knowledge and how much is needed to be a successful reader. However, there should be no debate about the importance of both phonemic awareness and phonics knowledge in writing and reading (National Reading Panel, 2000). Reading acquisition research suggests that knowledge in both areas is causally related to literacy development.

Phonemic Awareness

What Are Phonemes?

A *phoneme* is the smallest unit of sound in a word. The word *man* has three phonemes: /m/ /a/ /n/. The word *sleep* has four: /s/ /l/ /ē/ /p/, even though there are five letters in the word.

A single phoneme change in a word results in a meaning difference because word meanings are determined by phonemes. For example, consider how the phoneme differences in the following word pairs affect word meanings: **p**en, **p**in; so**d**, so**b**; **b**at, **f**at; and **c**attle, **r**attle. When individuals hear these words they automatically attach different meanings to them, even though they may not realize that a subtle difference of just one phoneme sets each of them apart from all other words. As stated earlier, except in the case of homophones, the unique sequence of phonemes in a word distinguishes it from all other words used in the spoken language.

Words are not our only means of communication. Meanings are also conveyed to us through the use of signals or signs, such as pictures, symbols ($), doorbells, or dog barks. In general, however, nonlinguistic systems are not as efficient as our spoken language. Because the signals used in nonlinguistic systems differ holistically from one another, recipients must perceive each signal or sign individually. In addition, the number of different signals in a nonlinguistic system is small, limiting the system's potential as a communication source. Words, however, are created by phoneme sequences, and individuals can produce an extremely large number of words by creating new sequences. The English language contains hundreds of thousands of words; almost all of them are perceived by their unique sequence of phonemes, yet each is not holistically different from other words. Liberman, Shankweiler, and Liberman (1989) described this phenomenon in the following words:

Language is different in a most important way. Meanings are not conveyed directly by signals that differ holistically, but rather by words that are distinct from each other in their internal structure. This structure is formed of a small number of meaningless phonological segments we know as consonants and vowels, and governed according to a highly systematic combinatorial scheme called phonology. The consequence is that words can (and do) number in the tens of thousands. Moreover, there is a perfectly natural basis for accommodating new words, since the phonological system, which all speakers of the language have in common, automatically recognizes a new, but legal, structure as a word that stands to have meaning attached to it. (pp. 7–8)

Liberman et al. (1989) explained that words, whether spoken or printed, are always phonological structures. Listeners or readers "may very well be unsure of [a word's] meaning—indeed, may even have got the meaning wrong—but if they have the phonological structure, they have [an] adequate basis for ultimately getting its meaning properly sorted out. As for going directly to meaning . . . independently of phonology—surely that is done when a person sees a picture, for example, or hears the roar of a lion, but not when one perceives a word as it is spoken or read" (p. 8).

Phonemes, therefore, are the smallest units of sound in a word that determine the meaning we attach to it. As children learn to speak a language, they are not consciously aware of its phonological structure because the biological specialization for speech manages the production and perception of phonemic structures below the level of consciousness; awareness of phonemes in words is not an automatic consequence of speaking a language. It is only when children attempt to make the transition from oral to written language that a conscious awareness of phonemes becomes necessary—children cannot understand the alphabetic transcription used in the written language if they are unaware of the phonological structure that transcription represents.

What Is Phonemic Awareness?

Phonemic awareness, sometimes incorrectly referred to as phonological awareness, has been defined in a variety of ways. Cunningham, for example, defined phonemic awareness as the ability to examine language independently of meaning, and manipulate its component sounds (Griffith & Olson, 1992). Isabelle Liberman defined it as the ability to analyze the internal structure of the word into its phonemic constituents (Shankweiler, 1991). Blachman (1991) defined it as an awareness of and the ability to manipulate the phonological segments in words. Yopp (1992) defined phonemic awareness as having control over the smallest units in speech, the phonemes. Griffith and Olson (1992) said that phonemic awareness is the realization of sound segments in words; a realization that speech can be segmented into phonemes. "It is an understanding of the structure of spoken language" (p. 518).

The Directors of the International Reading Association (Cunningham, Cunningham, Hoffman, & Yopp, 1998) claim that there is no single definition of phonemic awareness, but they explain that "phonemic awareness refers to an understanding about the smallest units of sound that make up the speech stream: phonemes" (p.1). Most educators believe that phonemic awareness refers to an understanding that spoken words are made up of individual sound sequences (Burns, Griffin, & Snow, 1999; Pikulski & Templeton, 1997).

All definitions of phonemic awareness focus on children's understanding of the nature of spoken words. Do children understand that words are comprised of individual sound sequences called phonemes? Can they segment or isolate the separate phonemes in words? If so, they are phonemically aware at a level we generally associate with successful reading and writing.

Technically, individuals could be phonemically aware and not even know the letters of the alphabet, because phonemic awareness involves speech sounds, not the letters representing them. In fact, the earliest phonemic awareness training programs we know of focused on phonemes without reference to letters (Elkonin, 1963, 1973; Zhurova, 1963). These early experiments established a strong connection between children's levels of phonemic awareness after training and later successful reading. Subsequent studies, patterned after these earlier ones (Olofsson & Lundberg, 1985; Torneus, 1984), not only found a strong connection between children's levels of phonemic awareness and later reading achievement, but also a strong connection to spelling. However, as successful as these experiments were, subsequent studies have revealed that children best develop phonemic awareness when they are taught to associate the letters in written words with the phonemes they represent (Ball & Blachman, 1991; Bradley & Bryant, 1985; Hohn & Ehri, 1983).

The Difference Between Phonemic and Phonological Awareness

Phonemic awareness and phonological awareness both play an important role in the development of literacy (Stahl, Duffy-Hester, & Stahl, 1998), but are not synonymous terms. Confusion arises when these terms are misunderstood. Speaking of this issue, Morais (1991) said: "The study of the relations between acquisition of literacy in an alphabetic writing system and phonemic awareness has been hampered to some extent by ambiguity [in defining terms]. Phonological awareness subsumes at least the following: awareness of phonological strings (a global, nonanalytical level of awareness); awareness of syllables; awareness of phonemes (also called segmental awareness); and awareness of phonetic features" (p. 6).

Phonological awareness, then, is a broader term referring to an awareness of all of the sound structures of speech (Armbruster, Lehr & Osborn, 2001; National Reading Panel, 2000; Yopp & Yopp, 2000):

- word awareness
- syllable awareness
- rhyming awareness
- awareness of alliteration
- phonemic awareness
- awareness of phoneme features (how the mouth, tongue, vocal cords, and teeth are used to produce each phoneme)

Some forms of phonological awareness seem to be acquired with ease at an early age, while other forms do not seem to emerge unless circumstances require them (Peterson & Haines, 1992). Bradley and Bryant (1985) claim that awareness of rhyme seems to occur almost spontaneously in even very young children, whereas awareness of phonemes is very difficult for them to acquire. Most researchers believe that children's awareness of the phonological structure of speech is developmental in nature. Children first become aware of words, then syllables, and finally phonemes (Leong & Haines, 1978; Liberman et al., 1974; Rozin & Gleitman, 1977).

It has been found that literacy instruction is not necessary for the development of all forms of phonological awareness. Studies convincingly demonstrate that awareness of syllables and awareness of phonological strings can be developed in many children before instruction (Bradley & Bryant, 1983; Liberman, ShankWeiler, Fischer, & Carter, 1974; Maclean, Bryant, & Bradley, 1987). However, Morais (1991) claims that phonemic awareness does not generally develop in the absence of explicit instruction on a graphic code that represents the phonemic information. His claim is supported by other researchers (Morais, Cart, Alegria, & Bertelson, 1979; Read, Zhang, Nie, & Ding, 1986).

What Are Some Phonemic Awareness Tasks?

The following phonemic awareness tasks have been used for both phonemic awareness assessment and training:

- *Phoneme Blending*
  Teacher: I will say a word using a magic code. The word is /m/ /a/ /n/. What is the word?
  Student: Man.
- *Phoneme Association*
  Teacher: Can you tell me a word that begins with /p/?
  Student: Pan.
- *Phoneme Segmentation*
  Teacher: Can you tell me the beginning sound in the word *box?*
  Student: /b/.
- *Segmenting Words*
  Teacher: Can you tell me all of the sounds in the word *fish?*
  Student: /f/ /i/ /sh/.
- *Phoneme Counting*
  Teacher: Can you tell me how many sounds are in the word *jump?*
  Student: Four.
- *Phoneme Manipulation (deletion)*
  Teacher: Say the word *mask*, without the /m/.
  Student: Ask.

- *Phoneme Manipulation (addition)*
  Teacher: Add /p/ to the beginning of the word *lace*, and what word do you get?
  Student: Place.
- *Phoneme Manipulation (substitution)*
  Teacher: Say the word *quack*, but substitute /a/ with /i/.
  Student: Quick.

Researchers disagree regarding the difficulty children have in completing various phonemic awareness tasks. However, most would agree with Griffith and Olson (1992) that recognizing rhymes occurs before phonemic awareness; phoneme blending occurs before phoneme segmentation; and that the most difficult phonemic awareness tasks involve word segmentation and manipulation of phonemes (p. 517).

Assessing Phonemic Awareness Levels

The Directors of the International Reading Association (Cunningham et al., 1998) have stated that there is no research evidence to suggest that there are phonemic levels students acquire in some sequence; only that they acquire increasing control over sounds in general. While there is still much more for us to learn about the development of children's phonemic awareness, we do have writing and spelling research suggesting that children become aware of beginning phonemes in words first, ending phonemes next, and middle phonemes last. Since children cannot make letter–sound connections for sounds they can't hear, the appearance of appropriate letters for phonemes suggests that they are hearing those phonemes. It is widely known that children begin writing graphophonically logical letters at the beginning of words first (*m* for *man*), logical letters for the endings of words next (*mn* for *man*), and vowel letters appear last of all (*man*).

Obviously, the determination of the phonemic awareness abilities of a group of children in a classroom will occur through teacher assessment. Teacher "action research" will provide the phonemic awareness insight teachers need regarding their own students' phonemic awareness development.

Eight phonemic awareness tasks have been described. Initially, the first four tasks are the ones recommended for assessment. Once children are able to segment all of the sounds in words (the fourth task), they should have the phonemic awareness necessary for successful reading and writing. Figure 3.1 outlines a recommended assessment sequence for normal and advanced phonemic awareness assessments. Individuals who can perform such tasks demonstrate that they are able to a) focus on words independently of their meanings, and b) have control over the smallest units of their speech. Such individuals are considered phonemically aware.

Why Phonemic Awareness Is Important

Phonemic awareness, understanding the internal structure of spoken language, would be irrelevant were it not for the fact that phonemes are the units encoded by the letters of the alphabetic languages used throughout the modern world. For chil-

For initial phonemic awareness assessment use single syllable words, containing a maximum of three phonemes. Suggested words: *so, me, on, it, at, up, wet, bed, sun, fat, dog, mud, jam, red, hot, nap, lake, yes, kite, game, tape, page, cup, zoo, tub, ox, safe, rock, room, doll, has, five*

1. Assess Phoneme Blending
2. Assess Phoneme Association (Beginning Phonemes in Words)
3. Assess Phoneme Segmentation (Beginning Phonemes in Words)
4. Assess Phoneme Association (Ending Phonemes in Words)
5. Assess Phoneme Segmentation (Ending Phonemes in Words)
6. Assess Phoneme Association (Vowel Phonemes in Words)
7. Assess Phoneme Segmentation (Vowel Phonemes in Words)
8. Assess Segmenting Words

For advanced phonemic awareness assessment use single syllable words, containing a maximum of four phonemes. Suggested words: *chin, peach, sharp, whale, sing, thin, bath, stop, skip, sleep, blouse, brush, plum, clock, crash, glass, grass, prize, truck, frog, dress, flag, smell, snow, spot, scab, throw, shrub, twin, jump, tent, sand, belt, wept*

FIGURE 3.1   Recommended Phonemic Awareness Assessment Procedures

dren to learn to write and read they must learn how spoken language maps onto written language, and phonemic awareness helps them grasp this understanding (Ball & Blachman, 1991). Phonemic awareness is a prerequisite for phonics knowledge, spelling development, and word recognition, and is a predictor of later reading, writing, and spelling achievement.

Prerequisite for Phonics Knowledge, Spelling Development, and Word Recognition. Phonemic awareness is not a synonym for phonics, but without it there would be no phonics knowledge, and phonics instruction would not make much sense. Children cannot connect letters to sounds if they cannot hear the phonemes in speech.

Studies of invented spellers suggest that an understanding of the alphabetic principle is necessary for spelling development since children must assign letters to represent sounds in the words they spell (Beers & Henderson, 1977; Morris, 1983; Read, 1971). The link between phonemic awareness and spelling development is supported by, among others, Juel, Griffith, and Gough (1986) and Lundberg, Frost, and Petersen (1988), who found a causal relationship between phonemic awareness and growth in spelling ability of first- and second-grade children.

Preschool, kindergarten, and first-grade children with the poorest phonemic segmentation skills are likely to be the poorest readers and spellers (Ball & Blachman, 1991; Tangel & Blachman, 1992). Juel (1988) found that phonemically unaware poor readers entering first grade remained poor readers at the end of fourth grade. She concluded that their lack of phonemic awareness contributed to their slow development of word recognition. Researchers generally agree that early problems in phonemic awareness reflect children's inability to break the alphabet code, resulting in poor word recognition and spelling strategies (Blachman, 1991). Children must be phonemically aware when trying to learn those essential literacy skills requiring them to manipulate phonemes—specifically phonics, spelling, and word recognition skills.

Predictor of Later Reading, Writing, and Spelling Achievement. Zhurova (1963) and Elkonin (1963, 1973) provided the first published evidence regarding the relationship between phonemic awareness and reading. Since that time, studies conducted in both the United States and abroad have shown that children's phonemic awareness abilities are significantly related to their success in reading, writing, and spelling.

Phonemic awareness and phonics knowledge provide a foundation for reading and writing. Reading and writing obviously involve more than constructing and recognizing written words; however, individuals could not read or write at all without being able to encode (represent phonemes by letters) and decode (translate letters into spoken words). These abilities require phonemic awareness and phonics knowledge; phonemic awareness and phonics knowledge are thus the raw materials of both reading and writing.

Many educators believe that young children should overlearn lower-order processes involving the manipulation of phonemes (the sound–spelling skills involved in writing, and the spelling–sound skills involved in reading) (LaBerge & Samuels, 1974; Scardamalia, 1981). These educators claim that it is only when these lower-order processes become automatic that children's conscious attention can be concentrated on the higher-order processes of comprehension when reading, and composing when writing.

In summary, over two decades of research suggest that some skill in phonemic analysis is a) directly related to the issue of understanding the pronunciation clues of written language; b) necessary for phonics knowledge; c) necessary for spelling development (Griffith & Olson, 1992; Lyon, 1997; National Reading Panel, 2000; Snow, Burns, & Griffin, 1998); d) related to efficient reading (Lyon, 1997; National Reading Panel, 2000; Snow et al., 1998; Stanovich, 1994); e) related to efficient writing (Eldredge & Baird, 1996); and f) a key feature of becoming conventionally literate (Sulzby & Teale, 1991, p. 746). Researchers also have indirectly linked phonemic awareness to reading comprehension, finding a causal link between phonics knowledge and reading comprehension (Eldredge, Quinn, & Butterfield, 1990; Tunmer & Nesdale, 1985).

Phonemic awareness is one of the hallmarks of a good reader. Good readers outperform poor readers in a variety of tasks measuring phonemic awareness, even when differences in intelligence and socio-economic background are controlled (Rosner & Simon, 1971; Torneus, 1984; Zifcak, 1981). The ability to segment individual phonemes in words correlates highly with reading achievement, and training programs that foster this ability appear to speed up overall writing (Eldredge & Baird, 1996) and reading development (Evans & Carr, 1985).

How Children Develop Phonemic Awareness

Phonological Awareness Can Develop Naturally in a Print-Rich Environment. The written language, predominant in the environment (signs, labels on food, letters, notes, books, magazines, and even print on TV), influences young children's language development, including their phonological awareness. As they interact with this language, they discover important concepts that contribute to their emerging literacy. The development of the following concepts indicates that children are becoming literate:

1. Words are represented by print.
2. Written word boundaries are established by spaces.
3. Print goes from left to right.
4. There are legitimate reasons why we read and write.
5. We create written words by using letters of the alphabet.
6. Written words are related to spoken words.

Parents help children develop an awareness that words are made up of sound elements by reading nursery rhymes and books emphasizing alliteration to them (Griffith, 1991). For a list of children's books that "play" with language sounds see Opitz (1998). The ability to recite nursery rhymes is strongly related to beginning levels of phonological awareness in 3- and 4-year-old children (Maclean et al., 1987). Children do not develop an awareness of phonemes in rhymes or syllables, however, until they have a genuine need to use them.

Phonemic Awareness Is Enhanced Through Writing. Encouraging children to write creates a natural need for phonemic awareness, although this need does not surface in young children's initial writing efforts. Young children don't use phonemes or letters in their beginning writing; they use scribbles and pictures to represent speech instead. When they learn that alphabet letters are used in writing, they begin to use them, although they use them initially without an understanding that letters and sounds are related to each other. It is only after a period of time that young children's writing reveals some understanding of the alphabetic principle. We are not exactly sure how this occurs, but we know that children's involvement with books and their attempts to write influence this development.

Studies of invented spellers (Beers & Henderson, 1977; Morris, 1983; Read, 1971, 1986) indicate that children go through predictable stages in their writing development. When they begin to write words according to sounds (invented spellings), they have to segment words into phonemes and assign letters to represent them. Therefore, when young children begin to use invented spellings it is a sign that they are becoming aware of the internal structure of both spoken and written words (Tangel & Blachman, 1992). As children's phonemic awareness and phonics knowledge increase, their invented spellings become more sophisticated.

Some educators suggest that phonemic awareness and phonics knowledge emerge when children attempt to write with invented spellings. Others suggest that the ability to write with invented spellings grows as a result of phonemic awareness and phonics training. All of them are probably right. Children cannot use invented spellings, at any level, without some phonemic awareness and some phonic knowledge. Writing with invented spellings requires a student to a) be aware of phonemes in words (phonemic awareness), b) identify appropriate symbols to represent the phonemes (phonics), and c) write the symbols identified. Consider for a moment the invented spelling scenarios in Figure 3.2. In all of the scenarios presented, some phonemic awareness and phonics knowledge is needed for the spellings observed. In scenario one, phonemic awareness and phonics knowledge is limited, but nonetheless some attempt was made to spell the word. In scenarios five and six, all of the phoneme sequences in the word were perceived, and all of the phonemes were represented by logical spelling symbols. Scenario six reveals a spelling for the word closer to correct orthography than found in scenario five, but both scenarios reveal complete phonemic awareness, and logical, though not complete, phonics knowledge. The important points to be made by these scenarios are that children cannot engage in invented spellings without some phonemic awareness and phonics knowledge, and the greater the phonemic awareness and phonics knowledge, the more sophisticated the invented spelling.

The assumption that phonemic awareness training improves children's growth in invented spelling is supported by a study conducted by Tangel and Blachman (1992). It also seems logical that, as children write with invented spellings, their skills

Scenario	Spelling	Phonemic Awareness	Phonics Knowledge	
One	k (for camped)	/k/ at beginning of word	/k/ = k	
Two	kt (for camped)	/k/ at beginning /t/ at the end	/k/ = k	/t/ = t
Three	km (for camped)	/k/ at beginning /m/ at the end	/k/ = k	/m/ = m
Four	kam (for camped)	/k/ at beginning /a/ in the middle /m/ at the end	/k/ = k /m/ = n	/a/ = a
Five	kampt (for camped)	/k/ at beginning /a/ in the middle /m/ at the end /t/ at the end	/k/ = k /m/ = m	/a/ = a /t/ = t
Six	campt (for camped)	/k/ at beginning /a/ in the middle /m/ at the end /t/ at the end	/k/ = c /m/ = m	/a/ = a /t/ = t

FIGURE 3.2 Invented Spellings Scenarios

in phonemic awareness, phonics knowledge, and word recognition would increase through the experience (Stahl et al., 1998).

In any event, the following studies suggest there is value in both encouraging children to write with invented spellings *and* in providing training in phonemic awareness and phonics. Ehri and Wilce (1987) found that teaching children to generate phonetic spellings of words resulted in improved phonemic segmentation skills. Clarke (1988) found that first-grade students encouraged to use invented spelling not only wrote better, but their word recognition ability and reading achievement improved significantly as well. Tierney and Shanahan (1991) found a positive influence on the word recognition ability of young children encouraged to use their phonemic awareness and phonics knowledge to spell words by their sounds. Eldredge and Baird (1996) found that first-grade children taught to write with invented spellings wrote longer and more sophisticated essays than children not trained to use invented spellings. They also found that the writing samples of children trained to use invented spellings contained a significantly greater number of correctly spelled words than the comparison group.

Research suggests that precocious children can spontaneously invent spellings without any formal instruction (Bissex, 1980; Burns & Richgels, 1989; Read, 1971, 1986). These children seem to deduce the alphabetic principle on their own, and as a result, generally become successful readers (Ferroli & Shanahan, 1987; Mann, Tobin, & Wilson, 1987). Several studies have also shown that some normally achieving students have used invented spellings without formal instruction (Bissex, 1980; Paul, 1976). We don't know all of the circumstances surrounding these accomplishments. However, we do know that children do not generally develop the phonemic awareness and phonics knowledge necessary for invented spellings such as those depicted in scenarios five and six (Figure 3.2) without some interaction with print and some adult intervention. There is no reason to suppose that children who have used invented spellings without formal instruction accomplished this feat without considerable exposure to print and adult input.

Children Do Not Develop Phonemic Awareness Through Normal Speech. Phonemic awareness does not develop naturally while using oral language. If we could explicitly hear phonemes when speaking and listening, then we would probably develop phonemic awareness naturally while using language. However, we neither represent spoken words, nor perceive them, as a sequence of individual phonemes. Words are stored in lexical memory and retrieved from memory as holistic patterns—holistic patterns of interacting phonemic elements described as gestures, features, or articulatory routines (Ferguson, 1986; Jusczyk, 1986; Menyuk & Menn, 1979; Studdert-Kennedy, 1986, 1987). In short, we don't isolate phonemes in the words we speak; we don't say, "/k/ /a/ /t/" and "/d/ /o/ /g/." We say, "cat" and "dog." Since phonemes in spoken words are coarticulated with other phonemes to produce the holistic sound units we call words, it is difficult to detect them.

Using words as holistic sound units, rather then words as isolated sequences of phonemes, makes speaking and listening a very efficient process. Learning phonemes for speech would be a waste of time. In fact, if we didn't need to read and write there would never be a need to become consciously aware of the individual phonemes in words.

Phonemic Awareness Can Be Developed Through Formal Instruction. Since individuals do not become aware of phonemes either by speaking or by listening to others speak, phonemic awareness must be explicitly taught, and/or children need to be given opportunities to write where the use of phonemic awareness is essential. Young children lack a conscious awareness of phonemes—preschoolers, for example, cannot tell you that the word *milk* has four separate sounds (Liberman et al., 1974; Yopp, 1992).

The realization that speech can be segmented into phonemes and that these units can be represented in print is believed to be a fundamental task facing the beginning writer (Read, 1986) and reader (Liberman, 1971, 1983). However, children do not ordinarily develop phonemic awareness without specific instruction, and even then rarely before age 5 (Liberman, 1989).

Explicit awareness of phonemes requires children to focus their attention on the formal attributes of words rather than on their meanings—a metalinguistic task difficult for young children. Jean Piaget has called this ability to shift attention from one aspect of a stimulus to another aspect as *decentering* and considers it to be a hallmark of the concrete operational stage of cognitive development beginning between the ages of 5 and 7. While intensive training efforts prior to age 5 have successfully taught children to segment or categorize on the basis of words or syllables (Content, Kolinsky, Morais, & Bertelson, 1986; Fox & Routh, 1976; Treiman & Breaux, 1982), these efforts have not produced awareness at the phoneme level (Fowler, 1991).

Many children need formal phonemic awareness training to make the transition from oral to written language. Liberman and Liberman (1992), referring to phonemic awareness and phonics knowledge, said, "It is now quite firmly established that neither experience with speech nor cognitive maturation is sufficient to acquaint a person with the principle that underlies all alphabets" (p. 354). Clay, discussing invented spelling, said, "Undoubtedly children can invent for themselves something like written English, but not all children will invent it" (1983, p. 122). Chomsky (1971), speaking of invented spelling over 30 years ago, said, "For those children whose phonetic awareness doesn't yet permit this kind of composition, the thing to do is to work on developing the awareness" (p. 299). Fortunately, more and more educators are realizing that many children need training in phonemic awareness for them to be successful writers and readers. It is only when children receive specific training, or become involved with the written language in a way that requires the use of phonemes, that phonemic awareness begins to develop.

Understanding Coarticulation and Learning to Isolate Phonemes. Developing phonemic awareness is not an easy task because phonemes are not discrete language units children can easily hear. Phonemes are **coarticulated** (overlapped or merged) with other phonemes as words are spoken, so even a spectrographic analysis of human speech cannot detect them (Liberman et al., 1967). Consider, for example, the four phonemes in the word *jump*. They are so thoroughly coarticulated that they produce a single unified segment of sound, rather than the four separate sounds /j/, /u/, /m/, and /p/. Spectrographs can pick up syllables, but cannot pick up the coarticulated phonemes within syllables.

Some teachers teach students how to "sound out" words. Identifying words by sounds requires phoneme segmentation (isolation) and blending. However, neither children nor adults can isolate coarticulated phonemes without some articulatory distortion. The distortion occurs largely because many consonant sounds cannot be isolated without an accompanying schwa sound. (The schwa sound is the /u/ sound you hear at the beginning of the word *up*.)

The following consonant phonemes cannot be articulated without some distortion: /b/, /d/, /g/, /j/, /l/, /r/, /v/, /w/, and /y/. All of these phonemes are coarticulated with the vowels that follow them. For example, when you try to isolate the phoneme represented by *b* in the word *box*, /bu/ is the result. When you attempt to isolate all of the phonemes in the word *box* you get the sounds /bu/ /o/ /ks/, and if you blend the isolated sounds you get a distorted version of the word /bu-oks/ rather than /boks/. If, however, you coarticulate the phonemes represented by b and o in the word *box*, /bo/ is the result, and no distortion of the consonant phoneme occurs.

The word distortion that occurs when isolating phonemes implies that our alphabetic representation of spoken words does *not* specify, on a segment by segment basis, how the speech organs are to be articulated and coarticulated so as to produce the sounds of speech—even though some individuals assume otherwise. The letters in written words are, in fact, an abstraction from speech, and do represent phonemes, but because of coarticulation this representation is hard for children to apprehend. Therefore, the difficult task facing emerging readers is to match the alphabetic transcription to the *abstract* phonological structure of the word it represents.

The pioneering work of Isabelle Liberman (1983) has helped us recognize the importance of phonological processes in reading. For nearly 20 years she and her colleagues studied the problems beginning readers encountered in learning to read. They concluded that children must develop phonemic awareness, and they must perceive how those phonemes map onto print (Liberman et al., 1989) in order to become successful readers and writers. Liberman and Liberman (1992) stated, "We take it as given . . . that in teaching children to read and write, our aim must be to transfer the wonders of phonology from speech to script. In our view, this can be done only if the child comes to understand the alphabetic principle. . . . [To teach this principle successfully,] we must first . . . understand how the phonemes are produced and perceived in speech, for only then can we see precisely how far these processes must be different in writing and reading" (p. 349).

Liberman and Liberman (1992) concluded that in all languages, utterances are formed by stringing together two or three dozen consonants and vowels in various ways. These strings inevitably run to considerable lengths, so, as a practical matter, there had to be a way of producing them at some reasonable rate. For example, speech would be impossibly tedious if, instead of saying *strict*, we could only say /s/ /t/ /ru/ /i/ /k/ /t/. Not only would communication be slow, but our sentence comprehension would be extremely difficult, if not impossible, due to the strain on our working memory limits. The Libermans concluded that speech and language became possible only because coarticulation of phonemes evolved—a specialization for the rapid and effortless production and perception of phonological structures.

> We and some of our colleagues believe that the strategy underlying this specialization was to define the phonemes not as sounds but as motor control structures we choose to call gestures. Thus, the phoneme we write as *b* is a closing and opening at the lips; the phoneme we write as *m* is that same closing and opening at the lips, combined with an opening of the velum, and so forth. In fact, the gestures are far more complex and abstract than this. . . but for our purposes the important consideration is only that the gestural strategy permits coarticulation. That is, it permits the speaker to overlap gestures that are realized by different organs of articulation (as in the case of lips and tongue in /ba/) and to merge gestures that are produced by different parts of the same organ (as in the case of the tip and blade of the tongue in /da/). The consequence is that people can and do regularly speak at rates of 10 to 20 phonemes per second. (Liberman & Liberman, 1992, p. 350)

The Libermans explained that language would pay a terrible price if it were not based upon phoneme articulation and coarticulation. If each phonological segment were distinctive then communicating phonological structures at rates of 20 phonemes per second would merge the sounds of language together into an unanalyzable buzz. Therefore, coarticulating several segments of the phonology into one segment of sound is extremely efficient for speech, even though beginning writers and readers may have difficulty apprehending such segments. Understanding this specialization helps us understand why many children do not develop phonemic awareness without some adult intervention.

Application Activities

1. Summarize, in writing, the alphabetic principle.
2. Describe how phonemes affect word meanings.
3. Describe phonemic awareness and summarize its importance in reading and writing.
4. Visit a first-grade classroom. Obtain permission to assess three or four children's phoneme counting ability. Assess each student individually, using the following steps:
   (a) Tell each student that there are two sounds in the word *on*.
   (b) Say each phoneme in the word *on*, slowly. As you say /o/ hold up one finger, and as you say /n/ hold up a second finger.
   (c) Ask the student to tell you how many sounds are in the following words (don't isolate the phonemes for the student): *at* (2), *man* (3), *last* (4), and *shop* (3).
   (d) Record your results. Ask the teacher to rank the children you tested according to their reading ability. Compare your phoneme counting results with her rankings.
5. Obtain a stopwatch. Time yourself as you read the following sentence: "I think it is difficult to isolate sounds in words." Ask another person to listen to you and

time yourself again as you read the sentence by phonemes: "I th-i-nk i-t i-s d-i-ff-i-c-u-l-t t-o i-s-o-l-a-te s-ou-n-d-s i-n w-or-d-s." Ask the person listening if he or she understood what you said. Compare the time required to read the sentence by words and by phonemes. What does this experience tell you about the importance of phoneme coarticulation?

6. The evidence supporting the relationship of phonemic awareness to reading and spelling is overwhelming. If you desire to review some of this evidence read the following documents: Blachman, 1983, 1984, 1989; Blachman and James, 1985; Bradley and Bryant, 1983, 1985; Calfee, Lindamood, and Lindamood, 1973; Fox and Routh, 1975, 1980; Helfgott, 1976; Juel, 1988; Juel, Griffith, and Gough, 1986; Liberman, 1973; Liberman, Shankweiler, Fischer, and Carter, 1974; Lomax and McGee, 1987; Lundberg, Olofsson, and Wall, 1980; Mann and Liberman, 1984; Rohl and Tunmer, 1988; Share, Jorm, Maclean, and Mathews, 1984; Stanovich, Cunningham, and Cramer, 1984; Tunmer and Nesdale, 1985; Wagner, 1986; Wagner and Torgesen, 1987; Williams, 1986.

You may also want to review the following documents indicating that phonemic awareness is considered to be the best predictor of reading achievement presently existing: Adams, 1990; Blachman, 1989; Fox and Routh, 1984; Golinkoff, 1978; Lundberg, Olofsson, and Wall, 1980; Mann, 1984; Stanovich, 1985; Vellutino and Scanlon, 1987.

Chapter 4

Phonics and the
Alphabetic Principle

Defining Phonics

Word meanings are not found in words, but in the people. It has been said that words do not "mean," only people "mean." Some people say, "Words do not mean the same to all people"; however, it is more accurate to say, "People do not mean the same by all words." In Chapter 2 decoding was defined as the process used by readers to translate written language into oral or inner speech. Phonics is one of the strategies used in this translation process. Furthermore, all of the other decoding strategies, including word recognition, are dependent upon phonics knowledge.

The word *phonics* means different things to different people. Even with the National Reading Panel report (2000) emphasizing the importance of phonics instruction on children's reading growth, different perceptions of, and different dispositions toward, phonics persist. These perceptions and dispositions seem to be deeply rooted, and resistant to change. Unfortunately therefore, many reading researchers and practitioners will probably continue to seek evidence to support a phonics point of view they already hold, regardless of the popular research at the time. The history of phonics in education suggests that this has happened in the past (Balmuth, 1992), and will undoubtedly continue to occur. Phonics instruction has become too entangled with politics, ideology, and disagreements about how children learn to read (Goodman, 1993; McKenna, Stahl, & Reinking, 1994; National Reading Panel, 2000; Stahl, 1999).

Over the years various educators have coined such terms as *intensive phonics, phony phonics, analytic phonics, synthetic phonics, implicit phonics,* and *explicit phonics* to communicate their specific notions about phonics, and to express their preferences regarding how it should be taught. In fact, the many different approaches to the teaching of phonics adds to the difficulty of defining it, and the confusion regarding its role and value in the instructional program.

In this book the term *phonics* is used in two different contexts. First, it refers to a knowledge students acquire regarding how the spoken and written language are related to each other. This knowledge is called "phonics knowledge." Second, it refers to instructional approaches used by teachers or parents to help students a) acquire phonics knowledge and/or b) use it to decode.

The two usages of the word are different, and if individuals do not differentiate between them, confusion results. For example, when discussing the impact of students' phonics knowledge on word recognition, some individuals might confuse students' phonics knowledge with specific approaches used to teach the knowledge. So instead of associating the effects of the knowledge with the outcomes observed, they associate the effects of a teaching approach with the outcomes. Researchers and educators who want to study the influences of each on reading must differentiate between phonics knowledge and the various strategies employed to acquire that knowledge.

Phonics knowledge refers to an individual's knowledge of letter–sound relationships within different written syllable patterns. This knowledge helps students see how the spoken and the written forms of the language relate to each other. The acquisition of this knowledge is dependent upon phonemic awareness.

Phonics knowledge is directly related to the acquisition of word recognition, which is directly related fluency, which is directly related to reading comprehension. Phonics knowledge can be assessed by asking students to read different pseudowords containing the basic phonics elements, organized in patterns identical to those used in real words.

Phonics instruction refers to the various ways teachers teach phonics. Some phonics instruction may be more effective than other approaches, at a given time, simply because of the developmental level of the students involved. For example, phonics instruction using onsets and rimes seems to be effective with children who are not fully phonemically aware; (i.e., they cannot hear all of the phonemes in single syllable words). Therefore, phonics instruction with onsets and rimes helps children focus on, and segment, initial phonemes in words, and then associate those phonemes with the letters representing them. This phonics approach is successful with children having limited phonological awareness, simply because it does not require them to isolate all of the phonemes in the word, and ask them to associate letters with phonemes they can't hear. However, teaching phonics with onsets and rimes, while effective at a particular stage of student development, has serious limitations at higher levels of development. These limitations will be discussed later.

It appears that the most effective phonics approaches for children, ultimately, are explicit approaches, which focus on all of a word's phoneme sequences, and all of a word's grapheme sequences. Explicit approaches teach children to segment phonemes in words (phonemic awareness), and to identify the graphemes representing them (phonics). Explicit phonics approaches also help students apply their knowledge of phonemes and phonics by teaching them to sound-out words by: a) associating the graphemes within the word with sounds (phonemes) they represent, b) isolating (segmenting) the individual phonemes in the word, and c) finally, blending the phonemes together.

There are also variations of explicit phonics approaches. The approach favored in this book differs from typical explicit phonics approaches in the following ways:

1. The instruction is process or strategy oriented rather than skills oriented.
2. Instruction takes little classroom time, about 10 minutes per day.
3. Instruction need not involve the use of workbooks or ditto masters.
4. It is inexpensive.

5. It teaches children how to determine vowel sounds in words based upon each word's written syllable pattern.
6. It avoids distortion of phonemes.
7. Instructional methods are designed to support any approach to literacy development.

Differentiating Between Implicit and Explicit Phonics Approaches

Studies and debates about how phonics should be taught, or if it should be taught, occupy considerable space in the literature. One position is based on the premise that children need to be explicitly taught how sounds in speech are represented by letters in written language, while the other position is based on the belief that explicit phonics instruction is probably not necessary. At one time the debate centered on the question, "Should early instruction in reading be based upon a 'look and say' approach or should it be based upon phonics?" Later on the question was, "Should we use analytic or synthetic phonics programs to teach young children how to read?" Chall's (1967) "great debate" was, "Should we teach 'code emphasis programs' or 'meaning emphasis programs' in the early years of schooling?" And again, in *Becoming a Nation of Readers* (Anderson, Hiebert, Scott, & Wilkinson, 1985), a major issue was, "Are implicit phonics programs better, no different, or less effective than explicit phonics programs in the primary grades?"

The labels "implicit phonics," "analytic phonics," and "meaning emphasis programs" reflect essentially one position regarding phonics instruction, while "explicit phonics," "synthetic phonics," and "code emphasis programs" reflect an alternative position. The names have changed over the years, but the basic issues have not.

Implicit Approaches

Advocates of implicit phonics approaches believe that meaning is deemphasized when children are taught to focus their attention on the written coding system. While these programs do not ignore decoding instruction, their major focus is on "meaning." Implicit phonics approaches stress the acquisition of a sight vocabulary and the use of context clues, teaching only enough phonics information to enable children to identify unfamiliar words through contextual analysis.

In early versions of implicit phonics programs, children were taught to read stories where the vocabulary was carefully selected and controlled. The stories were not very interesting because the words children needed to learn intentionally occurred over and over again in the story to facilitate word recognition. Newer versions of implicit phonics programs are characterized by less vocabulary control. Usually students are involved in "shared reading experiences" where teachers read stories to them from "big books," tracing the lines, and touching words while reading the books. Later they are involved in independent reading. After children have learned to recognize a number of commonly used words, those words are "analyzed" and the sounds common to them are identified along with the letters that represent them. Phonics is taught by "analysis" (analyzing known words to learn about their parts). In short, words are taught first, and then certain phonics elements are taught within those words.

Implicit phonics approaches emphasize letter–sound relationships, but purposely avoid isolating or blending sounds represented by letters. Children using these programs are never asked to sound out unfamiliar words. Instead, they are asked to "guess" unknown words using contextual information. Because the major decoding strategy employed in these approaches is contextual analysis, consonant letters are considered more important than vowels, and are therefore taught first. Since most of the words in the language begin with consonants, and since the sound associated with the initial letter is the most important word sound to know when using context clues for word identification, this practice is consistent with the desired outcome.

Many primary grade teachers use leveled books for reading *to, with,* and *by* students. Teachers use these leveled books for different purposes. They read difficult books *to* them. They read less difficult books *with* them. When books are read *by* students, they are read for enjoyment or for teacher guidance and support. Books read independently by students are the least difficult, generally speaking, of all the books available to them. When students read books, under the guidance of teachers, the books are a little more difficult so teachers can "guide" them in the development of comprehension and word identification strategies. When using "guided reading" most teachers use implicit phonics strategies. They emphasize the use of the three cueing systems of language for word identification, phonics being one of those systems. Thus, the phonics approach is implicit.

Explicit Approaches

Many explicit phonics programs emphasize meaning, and some of them have a strong children's literature component so these are not the factors differentiating implicit programs from explicit ones. Explicit phonics programs are based on the premise that children must master the code early. Because first-grade children have already learned to use the oral language fairly well, educators believe that most of them possess sufficient background, vocabulary, and syntax knowledge needed for early reading experiences. However, they possess little decoding knowledge, so their early reading experiences should help them learn to decode. Hence phonics becomes important.

In explicit programs children are taught the sounds represented by letters, but they are also taught how to isolate those sounds, and how to blend them for word identification. Phonics is taught through a "synthesizing" process (parts to whole) rather than by analysis. That is, letter–sound relationships are taught first, and then letter sounds are combined in various ways to form words.

Explicit approaches are based upon overwhelming evidence that children must master segmentation and blending before they can transfer the results of phonics instruction to the reading of unfamiliar words (Bausell & Jenkins, 1972; Fox & Routh, 1976; Jeffrey & Samuels, 1967; Jenkins & Muller, 1973).

Assessing Phonics Knowledge

Using real words to test phonics knowledge is not, generally speaking, an effective procedure to assess phonics knowledge since the test would probably be testing word recognition, rather than phonics. Therefore, an acceptable way to test phonics knowledge is to ask readers to read a list of pseudo-words created according to the graphophonic structure of real words (Doehring, Trites, Patel, & Fiedororwicz, 1981; Jorm & Share, 1983). Pseudo-words are not nonsense words! Pseudo-words are created according to the graphophonic structure of real words. The spelling-sound relationship of each pseudo-word used should be checked against the common spelling-sound relationships found in the written language. This is done by first comparing the spelling of the pseudo-word up to and including the vowel with spelling relationships found in commonly used words. For example, in the pseudo-word *nad* the *na* spelling for the /na/ sound is consistent with the *na* spelling in words like *nap, nag, nab,* and so forth. Second, the spelling of the pseudo-word from the vowel to the end of the word should be checked. In the pseudo-word *nad* the *ad* spelling for the /ad/ sound is consistent with the *ab* spelling in words like *mad, had, sad, bad,* and so forth. A pseudo-word like *mik* would not be used since there are no single syllable words where the /ik/ sound is spelled *ik*. In real words the /ik/ sound is spelled *ick* such as in *pick, stick, quick, trick,* and so forth.

Comprehensive individual and group phonics tests developed with pseudo-words are included in Appendix G and Appendix H. Assessment strategies and uses of assessment data are discussed in Chapter 11.

A simple phonics assessment is presented in Figure 4.1. This test measures only simple grapheme-phonics relationships and would be suitable for an early phon-

---

Instructions: Show the list of 16 pseudo-words to the student. Do not show the rest of the information in the figure. Explain that the words on the list are not real words, but are organized like real words. Ask the student to read the words. How many were read correctly?

Pseudo-words:	Rhymes with:	Phonics Elements Tested:
1. *nad*	*had*	initial consonant *n*, final consonant *d*, short vowel *a*
2. *bap*	*tap*	initial consonant *b*, final consonant *p*, short vowel *a*
3. *fid*	*hid*	initial consonant *f*, final consonant *d*, short vowel *i*
4. *dop*	*drop*	initial consonant *d*, final consonant *p*, short vowel *o*
5. *mem*	*them*	initial consonant *m*, final consonant *m*, short vowel *e*
6. *hun*	*run*	initial consonant *h*, final consonant *n*, short vowel *u*
7. *rit*	*sit*	initial consonant *r*, final consonant *t*, short vowel *i*
8. *wib*	*crib*	initial consonant *w*, final consonant *t* short vowel *i*
9. *jut*	*hut*	initial consonant *j*, final consonant *b*, short vowel *u*
10. *vad*	*mad*	initial consonant *v*, final consonant *d*, short vowel *a*
11. *lill*	*hill*	initial consonant *l*, final consonant *l*, short vowel *i*
12. *yab*	*cab*	initial consonant *y*, final consonant *b*, short vowel *a*
13. *kig*	*pig*	initial consonant *k*, final consonant *g*, short vowel *i*
14. *gan*	*ran*	initial consonant *g*, final consonant *n*, short vowel *a*
15. *tafe*	*safe*	initial consonant *t*, final consonant *f*, long vowel *a*
16. *pake*	*rake*	initial consonant *p*, final consonant *k*, long vowel *a*

FIGURE 4.1 Simple Phonics Assessment

ics assessment. The phonics elements tested in the test are analyzed next to each test item.

A phonics assessment for more advanced phonics knowledge is presented in Figure 4.2. An analysis of the phonics elements tested and the phonics principles involved are listed for each pseudo-word used in the test.

Under certain circumstances real words can be used to assess phonics knowledge. The procedures for testing phonics knowledge with real words are presented in Figures 4.3 and 4.4.

Why Phonics Knowledge Is Important

A research review provides convincing evidence that phonics knowledge is related to the acquisition of basic reading skills. Phonics knowledge positively affects decoding abilities (Stanovich & West, 1989), and inadequate decoding is a hallmark of a poor reader (Carnine, Carnine, & Gersten, 1984; Rack, Snowling, & Olson, 1992). Poor readers a) read slowly (Calfee & Drum, 1986); b) cannot decode pseudo-words

---

Instructions: Show the list of 14 pseudo-words to the student. Do not show the rest of the information in this figure. Explain that the words on the list are not real words, but are organized like real words. Ask the student to read the words. How many were read correctly?

Pseudo-words:	Rhymes with:	Phonics Elements:	Principles:
1. *eff*	*f*	*e, ff*	closed syllable
2. *dazz*	*jazz*	*d, a, zz*	closed syllable
3. *cen*	*ten*	*c, e, n*	*c*, followed by *e* = /s/
4. *milt*	*quilt*	*m, i, lt* blend	closed syllable
5. *scradge*	*badge*	*scr* blend, *a, dge*	closed syllable
6. *sheb*	*web*	*sh* digraph, *e, b*	closed syllable
7. *swush*	*brush*	*sw* blend, *u, sh* digraph	closed syllable
8. *plench*	*bench*	*pl* blend, *e, nch*	closed syllable
9. *naid*	*paid*	*n, ai* digraph, *d*	vowel team syllable
10. *girt*	*shirt*	*g, ir, t*	murmur diphthong
11. *mafe*	*safe*	*m, a, fe*	vowel-consonant-e
12. *yo*	*so*	*s, o*	open syllable
13. *phode*	*rode*	*ph* digraph, *o, de*	vowel-consonant-e
14. *choin*	*coin*	*ch* digraph, *oi* diphthong, *n*	vowel team syllable

Note: closed syllable = short vowel sound
open syllable = long vowel sound
vowel-consonant-e syllable = long vowel sound

FIGURE 4.2 Advanced Phonics Assessment

Teacher Action:	Teacher Instruction:	Student Response:
1. Write: *or*	"Say the phoneme represented by these letters."	/or/
2. Write: *por*	"Say what I have written."	/por/
3. Write: *ch*	"Say the phoneme represented by these letters."	/ch/
3. Write: *porch*	"Read the word."	/porch/

FIGURE 4.3 Procedure #1 for Assessing Phonics Knowledge Using Real Words

Sample Grapheme Tiles:

| s | oa | p | oo | ir | au | ch | ur | ch |

Teacher: "Pick up the tile that represents the sound of /ō/." Student: | oa |

Teacher: "Pick up the tile that represents the sound of /s/ and make /sō/."

Student: | s | oa |

Teacher: "Pick up the tile that represents the sound of /p/ and make the word /sōp/."

Student: | s | oa | p |

Note: An alternative way to use this test is to have the student say the phonemes represented by *all* of the tiles, before asking him/her to make various words using the tiles.

FIGURE 4.4 Procedure #2 for Assessing Phonics Knowledge Using Real Words

created according to the graphic structure of real words (Doehring et al., 1981); and c) do not use spelling–sound patterns when attempting to identify unfamiliar real words (Biemiller, 1970). All of these indicators are directly linked to poor or inadequate phonics knowledge.

The use of contextual information while reading does not differentiate good readers from poor ones since research indicates considerable use of context by all early readers. In fact, between 70 and 95% of the oral reading errors of first graders are contextually appropriate (Biemiller, 1970, 1979; Weber, 1970). Two tasks that clearly differentiate good from poor comprehenders, however, are accuracy (see Tunmer & Nesdale, 1985) and speed (see Perfetti & Hogaboam, 1975) of naming pseudo-words, such as *naid* and *moach*. These differences are observed even when younger fluent readers are matched with older, poor readers (Manis & Morrison, 1985; Snowling, 1985). Pseudo-word reading reflects readers' phonics knowledge (since they could not have been seen before and could not have been learned by sight). Phonics knowledge, therefore, clearly differentiates readers with good comprehension abilities from those with poor abilities.

Good readers store written representations of words in lexical memory. They have associated meaning(s) with each word, and they recognize each word by a specific letter sequence. When good readers see the spelling of a word, the word associated with that spelling is immediately called to mind as inner speech, along with the meaning(s) associated with it. Good readers translate written words into audio images very rapidly, and hold this inner speech in short-term memory until after they apprehend complete sentences. Phonics is a critical component in this process; specific letter sequences represent specific audio images. Therefore, readers who have difficulty with phonics will also have difficulty with word recognition.

Visual–Phonological Connections

Ehri (1992) developed a theory of sight word reading that explains how phonics knowledge affects word recognition. Her theory proposed that readers do not use a "visual route" to go from print to meaning when recognizing words by sight, but use a "visual–phonological route" instead, going from print to pronunciation to meaning.

> The critical connections that enable readers to find specific words in lexical memory by means of this visual–phonological route are connections linking spellings to pronunciations rather than to meanings. However, connections between spellings and meanings are easily formed in the process of establishing visual–phonological routes. . . . The visual–phonological connections that readers have formed for a word make that spelling a visual symbol for its pronunciation. This means in effect that readers "see" the pronunciation when they look at the spelling, and this event creates direct links between the spelling and its meaning. Thus, readers access not only pronunciations but also meanings directly when they learn to read words by means of a visual–phonological route. (pp. 115–116)

Ehri said, "My view of sight word reading makes letter–sound knowledge a necessity. This knowledge is needed to form a complete network of visual–phonological connections in lexical memory" (p. 138). Ehri (1998) also said, "Sight word learning is at root an alphabetic process in which spellings of specific words are secured to their pronunciations in memory" (p. 105).

Ehri and McCormick (1998) reinforced this concept 6 years later when they said, "Knowledge of letter-sound relations provides a powerful mnemonic system that bonds the written forms of specific words to their pronunciations in memory" (p. 140).

Reading Model

Ehri's "visual–phonological" route theory for word recognition is supported by the theory of reading embraced in this book. Proficient readers simultaneously process information from a) word spellings in text, b) word pronunciations in lexical memory, and c) meanings from schemata. They make predictions about immediate and subsequent text while processing this information, and they check those predictions against the actual text. They construct meanings, therefore, from the print *while* they read. Consider the following two sentences:

The beautiful satin dress was torn.

A tear in your _____ doesn't help the situation.

The word missing in the second sentence was *eye*. You might have supplied other words such as *dress* or *garment* since the schema activated from the first sentence was probably "a torn dress." Reading about something torn would influence you to predict the pronunciation for *tear* in the following sentence as a word rhyming with the word *bear*. As you read both sentences you simultaneously processed word spellings, word pronunciations, and meanings from schemata. You also made some predictions in the process.

Now ask someone else to read the following sentences for you. Ask them to read the sentences to you out loud, word by word. Use a piece of paper to cover up the sentences, and uncover the words one by one as the individual reads:

The beautiful satin dress was torn.

A tear in your eye doesn't help the situation.

The person who read the sentences for you probably pronounced the word *tear* the way you did. However, as the word *eye* was presented for her to read, she probably changed the pronunciation for the word *tear* as a word rhyming with the word *deer*. This reveals how readers check their predictions against the actual text, and make corrections when their predictions are wrong. The important issues revealed in this activity are that mature readers a) construct meaning from text while reading; b) make predictions regarding the text, and the content of the text, while reading; c) process word spelling–word pronunciation connections and meanings simultaneously; and d) make corrections when the text–pronunciation– meaning connections don't work.

Stages of Reading Acquisition

Frith's (1980, 1985) theory of reading by full or partial letter cues supports the beliefs about reading advocated in this book, supports Ehri's sight word reading theory, and explains why some children rely on contextual information for word identification.

According to Frith, there are three stages of reading acquisition: logographic, alphabetic, and orthographic. At the beginning, or **logographic**, stage readers look at words like they look at pictures, selectively focusing on some feature or aspect of a printed word to help them remember what it looks like. Lacking a knowledge of letter–sound relationships, the associations they make with the written word are largely visual. According to Ehri (1994) they associate "nonphonemic visual characteristics" with words. Remembering words this way is extremely difficult, and word recognition is slow and ineffective. The number of words children are able to learn is extremely small (Gough & Hillinger, 1980).

As children become phonemically aware and begin to develop some phonics knowledge, they move into the **alphabetic** stage (Byrne, 1992). Children at the beginning of the alphabetic stage begin to perceive letter–sound relationships, but tend to focus on only a few letters in a word for purposes of identification. While children may learn words in this manner, the method has at least two serious problems: a) readers will eventually confuse words containing common letters; (e.g., *cane, came),* and b) readers will not develop the knowledge needed to identify unfamiliar words.

As children become more phonemically aware and develop more phonics knowledge, during the alphabetic stage, they begin to process more letters in words as they read. When they write they spell many words incorrectly (*gat* for *gate, wisht* for *wished,* etc.) but, at the end of the alphabetic stage, they are able to hear all of a word's phonemes and represent each phoneme with some grapheme.

When children reach the **orthographic** stage, they realize that, because a word's full spelling is the only thing distinguishing it from all other words, they must use all of its letters for word recognition. At this stage children become aware that some words are spelled in predictable ways, and that some words are not. They begin to focus more intently on the complete letter sequences in words as they read.

The phonics knowledge acquired during the alphabetic stage provides students with a system for remembering word spellings (Ehri, 1992). Students who lack phonics knowledge form incomplete word spelling—word pronunciation connections in lexical memory, and read by partial letter cues. According to Frith, children who read by partial letter cues are not able to adequately discriminate words that contain similar letters, such as *horse–house, pin–pen,* and *peach–poach.* Therefore, since they can't adequately recognize words by their unique letter sequences they must rely on contextual information in the sentence to help them read.

Some investigators subscribe to the view that children can, and do, learn to read a certain number of words by partial letter cues, before developing the phonics knowledge sufficient for complete word spelling–word pronunciation connections (Gough & Hillinger, 1980; Gough & Walsh, 1991; Gough, Juel, & Griffith, 1992). However, some of them warn that children's progress will be hindered without adequate phonics knowledge:

> Children could continue to learn in this way, but they face two serious problems. Although it is easy to find partial cues that distinguish a handful of words, this task becomes increasingly difficult as additional words must be added. In the end, many words can be identified on the basis of no partial cue, for every one of their proper subsets of ordered letters is shared with some other word; the only thing that distinguishes such a word is its full spelling. The result then is that learning by selective association begins easily but gets progressively harder.

The second problem is that selective association provides no way of recognizing a novel word. . . . To read ordinary text, children must be able to identify unfamiliar words. (Gough, Juel, & Griffith, 1992, pp. 37–38)

The Whole Word Hypothesis

It is no secret that beginning readers read in a different manner than skilled readers. Explanations of the nature of these differences vary among educators. Some subscribe to the theory that both skilled and unskilled readers perceive words as "wholes," and that the only difference between them is the speed and ease of word perception. They believe that skilled readers perceive words faster than unskilled readers because of their background knowledge, their attempts to make reading meaningful, and the quantity and quality of their previous experiences with written text.

Other educators reject the whole word theory. These individuals believe that skilled readers recognize words by the letters that distinguish them while unskilled readers do not. They believe that unskilled readers select some cue, attribute, or feature of a word to distinguish it from other words simply because they have not learned how to associate the phonemes in spoken words with letters in written words.

The holistic word perception theory (whole word hypothesis) goes back to Cattell's (1886) studies of word perception. According to the hypothesis, words are perceived by their shapes and word length, along with some letter cues. The whole word hypothesis is very popular with some educators, but is not founded on solid research. Perfetti (1992) wrote, "It is now fairly clear that, whatever the appeal of the whole word hypothesis at the phenomenal level, word identification is mediated by letter perception. The individual constituent letters of the word are the units of its identification. Cues of word shape and word length appear to be of some significance, but they carry a very small share of the identification burden compared with letters" (pp. 146–147).

Advocates of the whole word hypothesis believe that beginning readers view words globally, registering each word as a gestalt. They agree that readers must know the alphabetic principle, but believe they do not need to look at all of the letters in words to recognize them. Opponents of the whole word hypothesis suggest that early readers perceive words by partial letter cues, not by wholes, using a process of "selective association" (Gough et al., 1992) to help them remember written words. This view is consistent with Frith's theory of reading with full and partial letter cues, and with the research suggesting that skilled readers do not view words globally, but by letters. When skilled readers read, they quickly survey each word's component letters to ensure accurate recognition (Balota, Pollatsek, & Rayner, 1985; Pollatsek, Rayner, & Balota, 1986; Rayner & Bertera, 1979). This process occurs so rapidly that some mistakenly conclude that the words must have been perceived "globally."

Several researchers (Adams, 1990; Barron, 1981, 1986) state that phonics instruction facilitates the development of accurate orthographic representations of words simply because it forces children's attention to words' interior details. Studies show that poor readers do not fully analyze the interior components of words

(Stanovich, 1992; Vellutino & Scanlon, 1984); therefore, instruction focusing children's attention on a word's letters, and the sounds representing them should help them read by full cues, and move to the orthographic reading stage. Frith also claims that students using full cues to read also become better spellers because they have stored more complete orthographic representations for words in lexical memory.

Beginning readers must eventually learn that there is systematic correspondence between elements of spoken and written language to advance beyond the stage of reading where words are recognized by selective association. Children who continue to read words as though they were pictures will be limited to reading the specific words they have learned as arbitrary patterns.

Developing Word Recognition

The evidence is strong that phonics knowledge provides the foundation for the development of word recognition abilities. Ehri and Wilce (1985) compared kindergartners' ability to learn to read nonsense words with both systematic (*msk* for *mask*) and arbitrary (*uhe* for *mask*) spellings. They found that nonreaders learned to read arbitrary spellings more readily than systematic phonetic spellings. However, beginning readers learned systematic spellings more readily than arbitrary spellings. They hypothesized that nonreaders lacked letter–sound knowledge needed to form visual–phonological connections in memory, which was verified on tests showing that the nonreaders knew only a few letter–sound relations. Ehri and Wilce speculated that beginning readers learned systematic spellings better than arbitrary spellings because they used letter–sound knowledge to form systematic connections in memory. Beginning readers' phonics knowledge was verified by tests revealing that these students knew all of the letter names and most letter sounds.

Ehri and Wilce (1983) also compared the speed with which skilled and unskilled readers in the first, second, and fourth grades read familiar real words (*cat, red*) and pseudo-words (*mig, fup*), and named single digits. All subjects read real words and pseudo-words over several practice trials. This practice enabled the skilled readers to read the pseudo-words as fast as the real words and digits. However, even 18 practice trials did not allow poor readers to read pseudo-words as fast as real words and real words as fast as digits. They hypothesized that only the skilled readers possessed adequate phonics knowledge to form complete connections between spellings and pronunciations in memory.

Effective phonics instruction affects word recognition in two separate, but related, ways. (Note that we are now talking about phonics as a *method* rather than phonics as *knowledge*.) First, children who are taught how to segment and blend word sounds learn how to sound out unfamiliar written words. Words accessed in this manner are remembered better than when using contextual analysis since students pay attention to all of the letters in a word rather than just the beginning letter (Adams, 1990).

Second, phonics instruction helps students learn the regular graphophonic patterns found in the written language, facilitating the recognition of other words not yet encountered in print; students who are taught to focus on all of the letter sequences within words become consciously aware of basic letter and sound patterns needed to identify words by analogy. Dank (1976) found that students learned graphophonic patterns quickly in the early grades when they were taught how to segment and blend sound in words, and Fox and Routh (1984) found that the learning of such strategies strongly affected students' later ability to acquire new words. As young children become acquainted with the principles involved in stringing letters together to form words they use this knowledge both to learn new words and to rapidly access familiar words.

Ehri (1991) suggested that it may be necessary for beginning readers to learn to say the sounds represented by letters in words for them to learn to decipher words. The National Reading Panel (2000) stated that the primary way to build students' word recognition vocabularies is to involve them in phonics or analogizing strategies for word identification (p. 2–107). These strategies enable students to form alphabetic connections needed to establish words in memory as sight words (Ehri, 1992; Share, 1995).

Children with large sight vocabularies can identify unfamiliar words by analogy, searching through their store of words in memory to find a word containing a pattern similar to the unfamiliar one, and using the analog to identify the word. Analogy, as a word identification strategy, was discussed in Chapter 2. If a child's word recognition vocabulary included the word *match*, the unfamiliar word *patch* might be identified by associating it with that word already existing in memory. Ehri and Robbins (1992) found that children could not identify words by analogy until they possessed sufficient phonics knowledge. Therefore, phonics knowledge seems to be the primary factor affecting growth in word recognition. Educators might argue on how beginning readers may best acquire phonics knowledge, but there should be little argument about its importance in word recognition. Children *must* acquire phonics knowledge if they are to progress successfully in reading.

Reading Irregular Words. Phonics knowledge also helps children learn to read irregular words. For years educators believed (and some still do) that children learned to read irregular, or exceptional, words differently than they learned to read graphophonically regular words. However, there is now strong evidence that children learn how to read both regular and irregular words similarly, and that phonics knowledge is needed for learning both.

Orthographic irregular words contain letters that are pronounced differently than expected (e.g., come, any, Wednesday). In a sense, however, all English words are regular, and all nonwords are irregular, since the written system is alphabetic and letters are used to represent word sounds. Even words considered to be irregular have some predictability. For example, there are three phonemes in the word *come* and there are also three graphemes representing those three phonemes. The word is considered to be irregular because the spelling of the word would predict the vowel letter *o* to represent its long sound. The first and last phonemes in the word are predictably represented by the letters *c* and *m*, respectively. The middle phoneme is represented by the letter *o* which unpredictably represents the short sound of *u*.

The fact is that most English words are spelled in predictable ways. Those that are spelled unpredictably, however, are often referred to as *irregular* or *exceptional*.

One frequently heard criticism is that English is not a regular language (Harris & Sipay, 1990). One could argue with that position. It is true that written words in English are not always spelled in consistent ways. However, English spellings are much more consistent than inconsistent. Many "inconsistently" spelled words are actually borrowings from other languages that have not been conformed to English orthography. Ehri (1992) wrote of English word spellings:

> . . . few English word spellings are totally arbitrary in the sense that they contain no letters that conform to English letter–sound spelling conventions. Most spellings that are considered irregular are only partially so. For example, *island* and *sword* each contain only one irregular letter. All the other letters correspond to sounds in the words' pronunciations. In using memory processes to read these words, readers are more apt to take advantage of any available systematic relations than to ignore them and rote memorize the entire form. (pp. 111–112)

All English words are comprised of specific letter sequences that represent specific phoneme sequences whether or not the spellings are consistent. Therefore, it would seem reasonable to assume that readers store exceptional words in lexical memory in the same fashion as they store regular words. This assumption is supported by Ehri (1992), who claims that learning to recognize regular and exceptional words by sight is not a rote memory process, but a process involving the establishment of systematic connections between spellings and pronunciations of words in lexical memory (p. 137). The assumption is also supported by research indicating that children process regularly spelled words, irregularly spelled words, and pseudo-words similarly (Gough & Walsh, 1991; Lovett, 1987; Treiman & Baron, 1983).

Phonics Knowledge Affects Reading Comprehension

In a study conducted by Eldredge, Quinn, and Butterfield (1990), a direct causal connection from phonics to reading comprehension was established. The study is supported by other research suggesting the following causal connections:

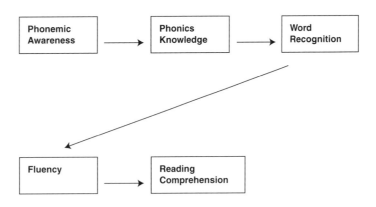

It is important to note that the causal connections outlined in this illustration do not, in any way, minimize the importance of other factors impacting reading comprehension. The variables in the causal path leading to reading comprehension (phonemic awareness, phonics, word recognition, reading fluency), therefore, are not to be considered inclusive. While each of the variables would appear to be "necessary" for reading comprehension, they are not "sufficient." Other variables are also involved.

It has been shown in this chapter that phonics knowledge affects growth in word recognition. Word recognition, in turn, affects reading comprehension. If children cannot recognize written words, they will not comprehend the meaning intended by those words (Adams, 1990; Metsala & Ehri, 1998). In addition to accurate word recognition, however, good readers read fluently; (i.e., they read words quickly, automatically, and with expression). If children read too slowly, comprehension suffers (Breznitz, 1997a, 1997b; Samuels, Schermer, & Reinking, 1992; Snow et al., 1998; Tan & Nicholson, 1997). Studies supporting this important role of fluency report strong correlations between speed and accuracy of context-free word recognition and reading comprehension, especially among children in the lower grades (see Lesgold, Resnick, & Hammond, 1985; Perfetti, 1985).

Strategies to improve children's reading fluency are presented in Chapter 9. The research studies supporting the use of these strategies to improve fluency are reported in the National Reading Report (National Reading Panel, 2000).

Reading fluency facilitates reading comprehension since students who are not struggling with decoding are able to give their full attention to the content of the text. The role of phonics in the development of fluency was discussed in 1985 by the National Commission on Reading. The commission stated that phonics knowledge contributed to the development of word recognition, and that rapid, accurate, automatic word recognition, in turn, was needed for effective reading comprehension (Anderson, Hiebert, Scott, & Wilkinson, 1985).

Before children can read fluently, word spelling–word pronunciation connections must be firmly rooted in lexical memory. Children develop the ability to read fluently from reading practice, or they develop it through strategies specifically designed to make them become fluent readers. Sometimes these strategies are designed to improve both word recognition and fluency.

The commission acknowledged that word recognition was not a "sufficient condition" for reading comprehension, but insisted that it was a "necessary" one. That is, while word recognition is only one of the many factors influencing an individual's reading comprehension, without it there *is* no reading comprehension. Adams (1990), who also extensively studied decoding research, came to the same conclusion. She compared decoding and reading with gasoline and a car: Without gas the car does not run; without decoding there is no reading.

Explicit Phonics Instruction Is Powerful

It has long been known that children taught to read with explicit phonics programs emphasizing segmentation and blending have an advantage over children taught to read with implicit programs (Anderson et al., 1985; Bond & Dykstra, 1967; Pflaum,

Walberg, Karegianes, & Rasher, 1980). Students' knowledge of the graphophonic patterns in the written language is an outcome associated with explicit phonics instruction (Dank, 1976; Norton & Hubert, 1977). Implicit phonics strategies do little to enhance this knowledge, other than teach beginning grapheme–phoneme patterns.

In the past, some educators were concerned that explicit phonics instruction might have negative effects on young children's reading comprehension. As Johnson and Baumann (1984) cautioned, "It may be that the excessive reliance upon code–emphasis instruction obscures the more important goal of obtaining meaning from print" (p. 595). Their concerns were supported by studies revealing that first-grade children taught by explicit phonics programs made more nonsense errors while reading than children taught by implicit programs (Barr, 1972; Cohen, 1974–1975; DeLawter, 1975; Norton, 1976). For example, children taught by explicit phonics programs might misread the word *horse* as *house* because *horse* and *house* are graphophonically similar, while children taught by implicit phonics programs might misread the word *horse* as *pony* because it made sense in the sentence. From these studies researchers found a) that young children taught by explicit phonics programs focused more on graphophonic clues than on the semantic clues when attempting to identify words; and b) that young children taught by implicit phonics programs focused more on meaning than on print clues. From this data it was concluded that implicit phonics programs were better than explicit programs because the former programs were more focused on meaning, and the latter programs had negative effects on meaning.

This line of reasoning contains several fallacies. First, the bulk of the research evidence regarding explicit versus implicit phonics programs indicates that children get a better start in reading when taught with explicit phonics than when taught with implicit phonics (Anderson et al., 1985).

Second, researchers have discovered that children taught by explicit programs pass the stage of making nonsense errors as reading abilities improve (Biemiller, 1970), usually around the second or third grade (Carnine et al., 1984). Furthermore, at this point they surpass their peers who were taught by implicit approaches (i.e., they make fewer reading errors).

Third, although the errors made by first-grade children using implicit programs were semantically correct, making sense in the sentence, they *were* errors. Those errors demonstrated obvious defects in decoding, and poor understanding of the alphabetic principle.

Fourth, research findings indicate that good readers use both graphophonic and contextual cues when reading, but it is the graphophonics knowledge, not the ability to use context, that is important for fluent reading (Stanovich, 1980; Tulving & Gold, 1963). It appears that good readers resort to contextual cues for word identification only when graphophonic knowledge breaks down.

Fifth, explicit phonics approaches need not take much classroom time to be effective. Phonics is only one component of a comprehensive literacy program. Children will make few nonsense errors in their reading when teachers follow the "best literacy practices" outlined in Chapter 1.

In sum, *phonics instruction should be well planned, systematic, and explicit* (Fielding-Barnsley, 1997; Foorman, Fletcher, Francis, Schatschneider, & Mehta, 1998; National Reading Panel, 2000).

Conclusions From the National Reading Panel

Based upon their metaanalysis of phonics research, the National Reading Panel (2000, pp. 2–132 through 2–135) concluded the following:

1. Systematic phonics instruction makes a more significant contribution to children's growth in reading than do alternative programs providing unsystematic or no phonics instruction.

2. Various types of systematic phonics approaches are more effective than non-phonics approaches in promoting substantial growth in reading.

3. Systematic phonics instruction is effective when delivered through tutoring, through small groups, and through teaching classes of students.

4. Systematic phonics instruction produces the biggest impact on growth in reading when it begins in kindergarten or first grade before children have learned to read independently.

5. Systematic phonics instruction is significantly more effective than nonphonics instruction in helping to prevent reading difficulties among at-risk students and in helping to remediate reading difficulties in disabled readers.

6. Growth in word-reading skills is strongly enhanced by systematic phonics instruction when compared to non-phonics instruction for kindergartners and first graders as well as for older struggling readers. Growth in reading comprehension is also boosted by systematic phonics instruction for younger students and reading disabled students.

7. Systematic phonics instruction contributed more than nonphonics instruction in helping kindergartners and first graders apply their knowledge of the alphabetic system to spell words. However, it did not improve spelling in students above first grade.

8. Systematic phonics instruction is beneficial to students regardless of their socio-economic status.

9. Students taught systematic phonics outperformed students who were taught a variety of nonsystematic or nonphonics programs, including basal programs, whole language approaches, and whole word programs.

10. Systematic phonics instruction on children's growth in reading were evident in the most rigorously designed experiments. Significant effects did not arise primarily from the weakest studies.

After sharing their conclusions, the National Reading Panel (2000) made this statement:

> Finally, it is important to emphasize that systematic phonics instruction should be integrated with other reading instruction to create a balanced reading program. Phonics instruction is never a total reading program. (p. 2–136)

Effective Phonics Instruction

Effective phonics instruction should be integrated with instructional practices described in Chapter 1. The ideal program :

1. Will not absorb much classroom time.
2. Will not communicate to children that phonics is reading.

3. Will teach children how to determine vowel sounds in words according to syllable patterns.
4. Will avoid the distortion of phonemes.
5. Will teach phonics as a decoding strategy to be used rather than a set of skills to be learned.
6. Need not involve the use of workbooks or photocopied masters.
7. Will be based upon sound linguistic principles.
8. Will support any literacy program.
9. Will help students identify written words by sounds.

Application Activities

1. Obtain a copy of any basal first-grade teacher's manual. Browse through the manual. Determine whether it is an implicit or explicit phonics basal. Justify your determination.
2. Listen to two or three first graders read. Identify whether each child is at the logographic stage, alphabetic stage, or orthographic stage of reading. Justify your conclusions.
3. Describe to another person how you believe phonics knowledge affects reading ability.
4. Describe and justify the type of phonics instruction you believe teachers should provide for children.
5. The evidence supporting the relationship of phonics knowledge to the acquisition of basic reading skills is overwhelming. If you desire to review some of this evidence read the citations listed in the chapter, and the following documents: Backman, Bruck, Herbert, and Seidenberg 1984; Hoover and Gough, 1990; Jorm et al., 1984; Juel et al., 1986; Juel, 1988; Snowling, 1980, 1981; Stanovich, Cunningham, and Freeman, 1984a, 1984b; Thompson, 1986; Tunmer et al., 1988; Tunmer, 1989.

Chapter 5

Developing Phonemic Awareness Through Stories, Games, and Songs

Phonology is the study of language sounds. *Phonological awareness* is a general term used to indicate that children are aware of the basic units of sound in the language: words, syllables, and phonemes. *Phonemic awareness* is a specialized term used to indicate that children are aware of the smallest units of sound in the language: phonemes.

Most linguists believe that children's awareness of phonology develops in a natural sequence from words to syllables to phonemes. Phonemes are the last sound units children learn to perceive, and the most difficult. Phonemic awareness does not develop as naturally as other forms of phonological awareness, but teachers can provide experiences for children that will help them become phonemically aware. The research reviewed in the previous chapters indicates that children will not become successful readers and writers without this knowledge. Phonics instruction is meaningless without phonemic awareness since children must understand what letters and spellings are supposed to represent. Phonemic awareness training must precede or accompany phonics instruction. Children must be aware of the units of sound within words (phonemes) and the letters that represent them (phonics) so they can spell (write the letters that stand for word sounds) and read (retrieve words from memory by their spellings). In this chapter we discuss different levels of phonological and phonemic awareness, and explore a few of the many different ways children's phonemic awareness can be enhanced through songs, games, and stories.

Phonological Awareness Stages

Phonological awareness develops in stages. Children first become aware of the larger units of sound, the words. Next, children become aware of syllables and rhymes within words, and last of all, phonemes.

Some teachers are unaware that young children must develop word awareness. "After all, my students understand me when I speak to them. They must be aware of words," these teachers say. Yet many young children write without leaving spaces between words, reflecting the difficulty they are having with word awareness.

The difficulty young children have with word awareness might be better understood after you do a little experiment: Say the word *excitement*. Then say the sentence,

"You can't come." Say the word *disenchantment.* Then say the sentence, "Don't bother me." *Excitement* is a three-syllable word. The sentence, "You can't come" is also three syllables long. *Disenchantment* and "Don't bother me" are both four syllables long. To a non-English-speaking person, words and sentences with the same number of syllables are nearly indistinguishable.

People attach meanings to speech sounds. Sometimes these speech sounds represent one word and other times they represent more than one word. When we speak, we speak in a fairly steady flow, pausing only to cluster words into phrases. The spaces we place between written words are not to separate each word's sounds, as some might believe; they are artificial breaks, used only to separate words, and came into common use in alphabetic written languages less than 2,000 years ago (relatively recently, historically speaking). Young children frequently confuse words, syllables, and phrases in adult speech. Even when young children speak they are not always aware of word breaks. Children's word awareness problems are often difficult for teachers to understand; adults have learned to "hear" word breaks simply because they already know the words. If you have ever listened to someone speak a language that you don't understand, you might have experienced the word awareness problem that many young children experience when they hear adults speak.

As a teacher, you can help young children develop word awareness, informally, during normal discussion periods throughout the school day. For example, you might occasionally ask, "How many words did you hear in my last sentence?" Children's responses to the question may vary because of their individual word awareness development. However, if you repeat the sentence, and ask the students to say it in unison, many of them will be able to count the words. If children have difficulty with word awareness, you may repeat the sentence and make a mark on the chalkboard after each word is said. Writing words underneath those marks will also help children visualize the connections between the spoken and written language. You also can help them discover relationships between the length of written and spoken words with such questions as, "Which words are short words?" and "Which word is the longest?"

The first level of phonological awareness, then, is word awareness. Children must come to understand what a word is. They must be able to differentiate words from syllables, and eventually they must be able to hear phonemes in both words and syllables.

Syllabic awareness is the second level of phonological awareness. A **syllable** is a part of a word containing one vowel sound. When we speak multisyllabic words, we *say* the individual syllables because of the natural speech breaks separating them. Syllables can be isolated without distorting speech, while phonemes cannot. For this reason, syllabic awareness is easier for children to develop than phonemic awareness. How many syllables (vowel sounds) do you hear in the following words: *apple, engage, disagree, justification?*

You may use an *auditory blending* game called the "secret code" game to help children develop syllabic awareness. Begin the game by saying, "I am going to say some words in a secret code. Tell me the word, if you can discover how to break my code. The word is /pen/ /sul/." (Wait for a response.) As children become more acquainted with written words, you might write the word *pencil* on the chalkboard and underline its syllables, as the word is repeated, so students can make the connection between the spoken and written forms of the word. In the meantime, you will probably want to divide the class into two groups and have one half of the class compete with the other half to add some motivation to the secret code game.

The following words, familiar to young children, are appropriate for use in the secret code game: *bun-ny, can-dy, car-pet, fun-ny, emp-ty, but-ter, bas-ket, foun-tain, chil-dren, dol-lar.* You will easily think of other words to with your students.

If children have difficulty hearing syllables in these words, you may want to begin the secret code game with compound words such as the following: *bed-room, air-plane, cook-book, birth-day, gold-fish, flash-light, grand-ma, play-house, snow-ball, rail-road.*

When children are able to manipulate sounds in words, we have evidence that they are more phonologically aware than when they demonstrate the ability to complete auditory blending with syllables. For example, if children can respond to such directions as, "Say *cupcake* without *cake*," "Say *football* without *foot*," "Say *carpet* without *car*," or "Say *candy* without *can*," they are more phonologically advanced than children who cannot respond to those directions. You may want to play classroom games with children using these manipulation tasks.

Phonemic Awareness Levels

Demonstrating phonemic awareness involves performing the following tasks:

1. Phoneme blending (identifying words when pronounced in isolated phonemes)
2. Phoneme association (matching phonemes with words beginning with those phonemes)
3. Phoneme segmentation (isolating phonemes)
4. Segmenting words (isolating all of the phonemes in words)
5. Phoneme counting (counting the phonemes in words)
6. Phoneme manipulation (deletion)
7. Phoneme manipulation (addition)
8. Phoneme manipulation (substitution)

Some researchers claim that these tasks, in the order presented, represent phonemic awareness levels. However, there is some disagreement regarding levels of phonemic awareness. Furthermore, children respond differently to various phonemic awareness tasks.

Phonemic Awareness Tasks

Current research suggests that most children hear rhyming words, and words that begin alike, before they develop the ability to hear, isolate, and blend individual phonemes in words. After developing the ability to hear rhymes and beginning sounds, many children seem to be able to perform the phonemic awareness tasks, roughly speaking, in the order listed. The following examples specify the tasks involved.

Phoneme Blending

1. The teacher says, "I will say a word in a secret code. If you can break my code, tell me the word. The word is /ba/ /k/. What is the word?"

2. The teacher says, "I will say a word in a secret code. If you can break my code, tell me the word. The word is /b/ /ak/. What is the word?"
3. The teacher says, "I will say a word in a secret code. If you can break my code, tell me the word. The word is /b/ /a/ /k/. What is the word?"

Phoneme Association

1. The teacher places three pictures in front of the child and says, "Point to the picture that begins with /f/."
2. The teacher says, "Tell me a word that begins with /s/."
3. The teacher places three pictures in front of the child and says, "Point to the picture that ends with /p/."
4. The teacher says, "Tell me a word that ends with /t/."
5. The teacher places three pictures in front of the child and says, "Point to the picture that has a /u/ sound in the middle of the word."
6. The teacher says, "Tell me a word that has an /i/ sound in the middle."

Phoneme Segmentation

1. The teacher says, "I can 'machine gun' the first sound of *top*. T-t-t-top. Can you 'machine gun' the first sound of *cat?*"
2. The teacher says, "The beginning sound of *man* is /m/. Tell me the beginning sound of *no*."
3. The teacher says, "The beginning sound of *man* is /ma/. Tell me the beginning sound of *lock*."
4. The teacher says, "The ending sound of *lip* is /p/. Tell me the ending sound of *kiss*."
5. The teacher says, "The word *catch* can be said in two parts: /ka/ /ch/. Say the word *pan* in two parts."
6. The teacher says, "The middle sound in the word *top* is /o/. Say the middle sound in the word *man*."

Segmenting Words

1. The teacher says, "Listen to the sounds in the word *so*. /s/ /ō/. Say the sounds in the word *up*."
2. The teacher says, "Listen to the sounds in the word *dog*. /d/ /o/ /g/. Say the sounds in the word *cat*."
3. The teacher says, "Listen to the sounds in the word *church*. /ch/ /ir / /ch/. Say the sounds in the word *up*."
4. The teacher says, "The sounds in the word *jump* are /j/ /u/ /m/ /p/. Tell me the sounds in the word *last*."
5. The teacher says, "Listen to the sounds in the word *stop*. /s/ /t / /o/ /p/. Say the sounds in the word *sleep*."

Phoneme Counting

1. The teacher says, "Listen to the sounds in the word *go*. /g/ /ō/. Count the sounds in the word. /g/ /ō/."
2. The teacher says, "Count the sounds in the word *me*."
3. The teacher says, "Count the sounds in the word *scratch*."

Phoneme Manipulation

1. The teacher says, "Say *tan* without /t/."
2. The teacher says, "Say *tan* without /n/."
3. The teacher says, "Add /p/ to the beginning of the word *an*, and what word do you get?"
4. The teacher says, "Say *tan* with /m/ at the beginning instead of /t/."
5. The teacher places various lettered squares in front of the child and, while moving the appropriate squares to make words, says, "This word says *man*. Make it say *pan*." After waiting for the child to move the appropriate lettered squares, the teacher says, "Make *pan* say *pat*." After the appropriate student response, the teacher says, "Make *pat* say *pit*."

Phoneme to Symbol

1. The teacher places lettered squares in front of the child. One square has the letter *i* on it, and the other one has the letter *t*. The teacher places them in front of the child and, while pointing to the appropriate letters, says, "This letter says /i/ and this letter says /t/." The teacher points to the letter /i/ and says, "Tell me the sound of this letter." While pointing to the letter *t*, the teacher says, "Tell me the sound of this letter."
2. The teacher places various lettered squares in front of the child and, while moving the appropriate squares to make words, says, "I am going to make the word *up*. This letter says /u/ and this letter says /p/. When /u/ and /p/ are put together they make the word *up*. Make the word *an*. Move and sound each letter as you make the word."
3. The teacher says, "Write the sound of /i/." After the student responds, the teacher says, "Write the sound of /t/." After the student responds, the teacher says, "Touch and sound each letter you have written and tell me the word."

Activities to Enhance Rhyme and Alliteration

Teachers are generally concerned about whether learning experiences are relevant to children. They know that lessons requiring children to use language which involve them in activities they can relate to enhance their language development. When children discover that reading is enjoyable, they will want to read and they will learn something from the experience. When they have someone to write to, they will try to write and they will learn from the process. When teachers and children are discussing an interesting subject, children may want to read books about the subject, and write about it. Relevance is important to all of us, children included. Phonemic awareness activities can and should be relevant to children.

Listening to teachers read nursery rhymes and books that play with language is a natural way for children to learn about words and the sounds of words. Children enjoy reading books that emphasize rhyme and alliteration. Some favorites follow:

Across the Stream, by Mirra Ginsburg (illustrated by Nancy Tafuri), Puffin, 1985

Alphabears: An ABC Book, by Kathleen Hague (illustrated by Michael Hague), Scholastic, 1984

Aster Aardvark's Alphabet Adventures, by Steven Kellogg, William Morrow: Mulberry, 1987

Bears on the Stairs: A Beginner's Book of Rhymes, by Muriel and Lionel Kalish, Scholastic, 1993

Beast Feast, by Douglas Florian, Harcourt Brace, 1994

Busy Buzzing Bumblebees and Other Tongue Twisters, by Alvin Schwartz (illustrated by Kathie Abrams), Harper & Row, 1982

Chicken Soup with Rice, by Maurice Sendak, Scholastic, 1962

Don't Forget the Bacon, by Pat Hutchins, Puffin, 1976

Down by the Bay, by Raffi, Crown, 1987

Each Peach Pear Plum, by Janet and Allan Ahlberg, Puffin, 1978

Eek! There's a Mouse in the House, by E. Y. Wong, Houghton Mifflin, 1992

Fire! Fire! Said Mrs. McGuire, an old jingle adapted by Bill Martin, Jr. (illustrated by Ted Schroeder), Holt, Rinehart and Winston, 1970

Goodnight Moon, by Margaret Wise Brown (illustrated by Clement Hurd), Harper & Row, 1975

"I Can't," Said the Ant, by P. Cameron, Coward, 1961

I Met a Man, by John Ciardi (illustrated by Robert Osborn), Houghton Mifflin, 1961

It Does Not Say Meow and Other Animal Riddle Rhymes, by Beatrice Shenk De Regniers (illustrated by Paul Galdone), Houghton Mifflin, 1972

It's Raining Said John Twaining (translated and illustrated by N. M. Bodecker), Atheneum, 1973

Jesse Bear, What Will You Wear? by Nancy White Carlstrom (illustrated by Bruce Degen), Scholastic, 1986

Little Chicks' Mothers and All the Others, by Mildred Luton (illustrated by Mary Maki Rae), Puffin, 1983

Over in the Meadow by Ezra Jack Keats, illustrator Scholastic, 1971

Peek-A-Boo! by Janet and Allan Ahlberg, Puffin, 1981

Pretend You're a Cat, by J. Marzollo, Dial, 1990

Roar and More, by Karla Kuskin, Harper & Row, 1956

Silly Times With Two Silly Trolls, by N. Jewell, Harper Collins, 1996

Teddy Bear Teddy Bear, by M. Hague, Morrow, 1993

Time for Bed, by M. Fox, Harcourt Brace, 1993

Tomie dePaola's Mother Goose, by Tomie dePaola, Putnam, 1985

After reading a book emphasizing alliteration or rhyming to children, call the children's attention to that characteristic of the book that makes it so much fun to read (rhyme or alliteration). During subsequent readings of the book, you might ask the children to clap their hands when they hear rhymes or words beginning with certain sounds. You may also want to ask the children if they can think of other words that rhyme with those used in the story. For example, in the book *Goodnight Moon,* a little rabbit is saying goodnight to everything around him. He says, "Goodnight bears, Goodnight chairs." Ask the children if they can think of other words that rhyme with *bears* or *chairs.* The children might come up with, "Goodnight stairs, Goodnight pears."

Children also enjoy rhyming games. For example, you could develop rhyming questions for them where the last word in the question either rhymes or doesn't rhyme with other words in the sentence. If the last word in the question rhymes with other words, the children would respond with a "yes" to the question. (You: "Will a bear share a pear?" Children: "Yes.") If the last word in the question does not rhyme with other words in the sentence, the response would be "no." (You: "Will a bear share a peach?" Children: "No.")

Sample questions:

Will a dog chase a frog?	Will a pig wear a big hat?
Will a clown frown?	Will Kate clean her plate?
Will Jake bake a cake?	Will Alice find the treasure?
Is the queen fifteen?	Will Dot pet the cat?
Will a bee land in a bush?	Will Sam feed the hamster?

Another rhyming game children enjoy playing requires them to supply the rhyming word:

A little white mouse

Was playing in the _____ (house).

A large black cat

Chased a fat brown _____ (rat).

Eventually, you will want children to see the text of the books, poems, and songs they read and sing (we discuss shared book, music, and rhythm experiences in Chapter 9). When doing this, emphasize the written representations of rhyme and alliteration to help them perceive sound–letter relationships.

Children enjoy participating in joint writing activities with teachers. In these activities, both develop the ideas for the written product together, but the teacher does the actual writing. (When children are able, "share the pen" with them as described in the interactive writing sessions in Chapter 1.) Teacher and children read the finished piece aloud together. The teacher might also make copies for the children to read to their parents. Your first joint writing activity might be *couplets,* two successive lines of poetry that rhyme. Each line is approximately equal in length. For example:

> In my favorite dream
> I eat chocolate ice cream.

The first step in creating a couplet is to identify a topic, for example, *food.* The second is to make a list of all of the words related to the topic: *ice cream, pizza, hamburger, corn, peas, carrots, peaches, apples,* and so on. In step three, identify rhyming words for the words related to the topic, such as *peach—reach, teach, beach, preach, bleach.* Finally, use one of the rhyming sets to create a couplet:

> On the beaches,
> I eat peaches.

More mature children will enjoy creating limericks with the teacher. A *limerick* has five anapestic lines, of eight, eight, five, five, and eight syllables, respectively. Lines one, two, and five each contain three stresses; lines three and four each contain two. The lines rhyme a-a-b-b-a. For example:

> I know an old fellow named Ray,
> Who goes to the beach every day.
> "I swim in the sea—
> Because it is free.
> The surfers stay out of my way."

Children also enjoy creating tongue twisters. Tongue twisters use alliteration and help children become consciously aware of common phonological elements. After children create tongue twisters they enjoy seeing how fast they can say or read them without stumbling. For example:

Robert's **r**abbit **r**an a **r**ace with a **r**accoon.

Hank **h**eld a **h**ealthy **h**amster in **h**is **h**and.

Big **b**ad **b**ashful **B**en **b**uilt a **b**anjo from a **b**undle of **b**ranches **B**en's **b**rother **b**rought **b**ack from **b**eautiful **B**ritain.

Seven **s**ad **s**elfish **s**isters **s**uddenly **s**tarted **s**inging the **s**ame **s**imple **s**ong they **s**ang to **s**ix **s**ea **s**erpents **s**o **s**lowly **s**everal **s**easons ago.

One-two-three-four poetry also uses alliteration. This type of poetry is relatively easy for a teacher and students to create. For example, after a field trip to the zoo, ask the students to list all of the animals they saw: *horses, monkeys, elephants, lions, snakes.* Then ask the students to think of something each animal does that begins with the same sound heard at the beginning of the animal's name: *horses heave; monkeys munch; elephants eat; lions lick; snakes sit.* Ask students to think of a word to describe each animal that begins with the same sound as the animal's name: *healthy horses; moody monkeys; elegant elephants; large lions; slithery snakes.* Finally, ask the students to think of words with the same beginning sound that describe how the animals do what they do: *heave heavily; munch merrily; eat endlessly; lick lazily; sit slyly.* Students put these elements together and have a one-two-three-four poem:

Healthy **h**orses **h**eave **h**eavily.

Moody **m**onkeys **m**unch **m**errily.

Elegant **e**lephants **e**at **e**ndlessly.

Large **l**ions **l**ick **l**azily.

Slithery **s**nakes **s**it **s**lyly.

We saw interesting animals at the zoo.

Rhyme Association Game

Children love riddles and guessing games. The rhyme association game is a guessing game requiring children to solve riddles using rhyming words.

Present a riddle by saying, "I am thinking of something that we eat. It is baked in an oven. It rhymes with *red*." Answer: *bread.* Sample riddles follow:

I am thinking of an animal that some children have as a pet. Its name rhymes with *log.* (Answer: *dog*)

I am thinking of something dogs do. It rhymes with *shark.* (Answer: *bark*)

I am thinking of an animal that dogs sometimes chase. Its name rhymes with *fat.* (Answer: *cat*)

I am thinking of something cats eat. It rhymes with *silk.* (Answer: *milk*)

I am thinking of something that you can climb. It rhymes with *bee.* (Answer: *tree*)

I am thinking of something we put on a floor. It rhymes with *bug.* (Answer: *rug*)

I am thinking of something we use to put food on before we eat. It rhymes with *gate.* (Answer: *plate*)

I am thinking of something we use when we eat. It rhymes with *pork.* (Answer: *fork*)

I am thinking of something we throw. Its name rhymes with *tall.* (Answer: *ball*)

I am thinking of something we use to move us from one place to another when we don't want to walk. Its name rhymes with *jar.* (Answer: *car*)

I am thinking of a place where we go to learn. Its name rhymes with *pool.* (Answer: *school*)

I am thinking of an animal we sometimes find on a farm. Its name rhymes with *dig.* (Answer: *pig*)

I am thinking of an animal that gives milk. Its name rhymes with *how.* (Answer: *cow*)

I am thinking of a color. It rhymes with *bed.* (Answer: *red*)

I am thinking of another color. It rhymes with *shoe.* (Answer: *blue*)

I am thinking of a number. It rhymes with *see.* (Answer: *three*)

I am thinking of a fruit that we eat. It rhymes with *bear.* (Answer: *pear*)

Using Songs to Enhance Phonemic Awareness

Young children enjoy singing. By creating new words for old familiar songs, children's phonemic awareness can be enhanced through music.

Phoneme Blending

[Song: The Mulberry Bush]

Now we will say the word out loud,

The word out loud,

The word out loud,

Now we will say the word out loud,

So put the sounds to-geth-er.

(Say, "/ka/ /t/"—simple level. Children respond, "*cat.*" Say, "/k/ /a/ /t/"—advanced level. Children respond, "*cat.*")

Sample words for sound blending activities: *wax, bed, sun, fog, dig, men, jam, red, hug, nap, van, lid, yes, kiss, gas, ten, pot, cut, zip, quick, gym, queen, zoom, coat, page, teeth, kite, yard, lawn, nose, horse, rope, jail, mice, dime, food, soap, beach, week.*

Note: Whenever, letters are placed between slashes/ /, *sounds* are said, not letters!

Phoneme Association

Beginning Sounds—Option 1 [Song: Skip to My Lou (Modified)]

Who has a word that starts with /k/?

Starts, starts, starts with /k/?

Who has a word that starts with /k/?

Skip to my Lou, my darling!

(Call on a student who knows a word that starts with /k/. The word is repeated, and used in the song.)

Cat is a word that starts with /k/.

Starts, starts, starts with /k/.

Cat is a word that starts with /k/.

Skip to my Lou, my darling!

Sample words for other beginning consonant sounds: **b**ox, **s**ack, **w**ig, **d**og, **m**an, **j**et, **r**ock, **h**en, **n**est, **l**og, **y**es, **k**iss, **g**um, **t**ub, **p**ig, **z**oo.

Beginning Sounds—Option 2 [Song: Skip to My Lou (Modified)]

Who has a word that starts with /fi/?

Starts, starts, starts with /fi/?

Who has a word that starts with /fi/?

Skip to my Lou, my darling!

(Call on a student who knows a word that starts with /fi/. The word is repeated, and used in the song.)

Fish is a word that starts with /fi/.

Starts, starts, starts with /fi/.

Fish is a word that starts with /fi/.

Skip to my Lou, my darling!

Sample words for other beginning consonant sounds: **w**itch, **b**adge, **s**ack, **f**ox, **d**esk, **m**ap, **j**am, **r**at, **h**and, **n**ut, **l**ock, **k**ick, **t**en, **p**an, **c**up, **c**oat, **p**aint, **t**eeth, **g**oat, **k**ite, **y**ard, **l**ake, **n**ose, **h**ome, **r**ope, **r**oad, **j**ail, **m**oon, **d**ime, **f**ace, **s**oap.

Ending Sounds

Who has a word that ends with /t/?

Ends, ends, ends with /t/?

Who has a word that ends with /t/?

Skip to my Lou, my darling!

Cat is a word that ends with /t/.

Ends, ends, ends with /t/.

Cat is a word that ends with /t/.

Skip to my Lou, my darling!

Sample words for other ending consonant sounds: cu**p** (rope), fo**x**, bi**b** (robe), kni**fe**, su**n** (bone), du**ck** (cake), gu**m** (dime), be**ll** (smile), be**d** (food), bu**g**, pa**ge**, hor**se** (ice), fi**ve**, no**se**.

Vowel Sounds

Who has a word with an /a/?

With, with, with an /a/?

Who has a word with an /a/?

Skip to my Lou, my darling!

Apple is a word with an /a/.

With, with, with an /a/.

Apple is a word with an /a/.

Skip to my Lou, my darling!

Sample words for other vowel sounds:

itch, **o**x, **u**p, **e**dge

ice, **a**te, **o**pen, **u**se, **e**at

hat, bed, big, dog, bus

face, bone, music, bike, seed.

Phoneme Segmentation

Beginning Sounds [Song: The Farmer in the Dell (Modified)]

What sound starts the words?

What sound starts the words?

Hi-ho, the der-ri-o,

What sound starts the words?

(Say, *"man, moon, mouse."* Everyone repeats, *"man, moon, mouse."*)

/m/ starts the words.

/m/ starts the words.

Hi-ho, the der-ri-o,

/m/ starts the words.

(Everyone repeats, *"man, moon, mouse."*)

Sample words for isolating beginning consonant sounds: **c**oat, **c**ook, **c**ap; **p**ain, **p**oint, **p**up; **t**oy, **t**est, **t**ape; **g**oat, **g**ood, **g**um; **k**iss, **k**ing, **k**eep; **y**es, **y**ell, **y**ard; **l**og, **l**eg, **l**ake; **v**est, **v**an, **v**oice; **n**ail, **n**ice, **n**oise; **h**ill, **h**ome, **h**at; **r**ope, **r**oom, **r**ain; **j**ump, **j**ob, **j**unk; **d**ay, **d**ance, **d**ish; **f**ood, **f**oot, **f**ish; **s**oap, **s**un, **s**and; **b**ox, **b**us, **b**adge; **w**et, **w**ood, **w**ig; **ch**eese, **ch**ain, **ch**urch; **sh**op, **sh**ed, **sh**irt; **th**in, **th**ick, **th**orn; **th**at, **th**em, **th**is; **wh**ip, **wh**eat, **wh**eel.

Ending Sounds

What sound ends the words?

What sound ends the words?

Hi-ho, the der-ri-o,

What sound ends the words?

(Say, *"fish, wash, wish."* Everyone repeats, *"fish, wash, wish."*)

/sh/ ends the words.

/sh/ ends the words.

Hi-ho, the der-ri-o,

/sh/ ends the words . . . *fish, wash, wish.*

Sample words for isolating ending consonant sounds: to**p**, cu**p**, a**p**e; we**b**, jo**b**, ro**b**e; si**x**, mi**x**, o**x**; kni**f**e, o**ff**, sa**f**e; rai**n**, bo**n**e, te**n**; sna**ke**, du**ck**, boo**k**; ki**t**e, boa**t**, ra**t**; gu**m**, na**m**e, ho**m**e; dol**l**, nai**l**, smi**l**e; toa**d**, foo**d**, mu**d**; wi**g**, le**g**, ba**g**; ca**ge**, a**ge**, pa**ge**; hou**se**, mou**se**, bo**ss**; ro**se**, no**se**, noi**se**; fi**ve**, sto**ve**, ca**ve**; tea**ch**, cou**ch**, di**tch**; mo**th**, too**th**, mou**th**; sin**g**, lon**g**, rin**g**.

Vowel Sounds

> What sound is in the mid-dle?
>
> What sound is in the mid-dle?
>
> Hi-ho, the der-ri-o,
>
> What sound is in the mid-dle?
>
> (Say, *"man, cap, jam."* Everyone repeats, *"man, cap, jam."*)
>
> /a/ is in the mid-dle.
>
> /a/ is in the mid-dle.
>
> Hi-ho, the der-ri-o,
>
> /a/ is in the mid-dle . . . *man, cap, jam.*

Sample words for isolating vowel sounds: **mail**, **rain**, **name**; **heat**, **teeth**, **geese**; **five**, **dime**, **ride**; **bone**, **road**, **home**; **cute**, **fuse**, **mule**; **bed**, **men**, **red**; **fish**, **dish**, **lid**; **bus**, **pup**, **nut**; **box**, **rock**, **top**.

Segmenting Words

[Song: London Bridge]

> Lis-ten to the words I say,
>
> Words I say,
>
> Words I say,
>
> Tell me all the sounds you hear,
>
> Lis-ten to this word.

(Say, *"Cat."* Children respond, "/ka/ /t/"—simple level. Children respond, "/k/ /a/ /t/"—advanced level.)

Sample words for sound isolating activities: witch, badge, sand, farm, dance, moon, joke, reach, house, nurse, voice, lawn, yes, kiss, gum, tooth, paint, count, quake, geese, chop, shake, peach, wish, whale, bang, thick, bath.

Phoneme Manipulation

[Song: Little White Duck]

> There's a lit-tle white duck
>
> Sit-ting in the wa-ter,
>
> A lit-tle white duck
>
> Do-ing what he ough-ter.
>
> He took a bite of a lil-y pad,
>
> Flapped his wings and he said, I'm glad,

I'm a lit-tle white duck

Sit-ting in the wa-ter.

Quack! Quack! Quack!

(Say, "Sing the song again and say *quack* without /kw/"—simple level. Say, "Sing the song again and put the /z/ sound in place of the beginning sound of *quack*"— more difficult level. Say, "Sing the song again and put the /k/ sound in place of the ending sound of *quack*"—more advanced level. Say, "Sing the song again and put the /i/ sound in place of the /a/ sound in *quack*"—most advanced level.)

Using Games to Develop Phonological and Phonemic Awareness

Word Awareness Games

Many times during the school day teachers and children discuss the experiences they share. These experiences are varied and might include stories read, art projects completed, songs sung, filmstrips viewed, or field trips taken. During these discussions, teachers often ask students to talk about their experiences while they write what the children say on the chalkboard. Students then usually read these sentences with assistance from the teacher. It is on occasions such as these that the first word awareness game is appropriate.

The steps to the game follow:

1. Write each word of a dictated sentence on a separate word card.
2. Select a child to stand in front of the classroom and give him the first word in the sentence to hold. Select another child to stand next to the first child and hold the second word. Repeat this process until you have the words in the sentence held by students in the correct order.

3. Reread the sentence and touch the head of each child holding the appropriate word as it is read.
4. Tell the students that you will read the sentence again, but this time the child holding the appropriate word should raise it above her head as it is read.
5. Ask the children at their seats to close their eyes. Have one student in the sentence line turn her card over so a blank space appears.

6. Ask the children to open their eyes and guess which word is missing.
7. Repeat this process with other words in the sentence.

A second word awareness game follows:

1. Divide the class into two groups. Give each group the assignment to sort the words used in the sentence according to their length, shortest to longest. Give the students time to consult with each other in their groups.
2. Ask group one to send one of their members to the sentence line to take the shortest word from the student holding it. If the student selects the correct word, group one gets a point and the word is taped to the chalkboard. If he selects the wrong word, no points are given and the word is returned to the student holding it.
3. Ask group two to send one of their members to the sentence line to take the shortest word remaining. If the student selects the correct word, group two gets a point and the word is taped beneath the first word on the chalkboard. If he selects the wrong word, no points are given and the word is returned to the student holding it.
4. The game continues until all of the words in the sentence line have been taped to the chalkboard according to length. When the game is over, students, with your assistance, read the words taped on the chalkboard. You then help students perceive length relationships between spoken and written words.

Phoneme Counting Game

The phoneme counting game is designed to help children become aware of phonemes by listening to words spoken by the teacher and counting the phonemes heard. Each child participating in the game should have at least three 2-inch squares made of tag board, or cut from magnetic sheets. These squares may be blank or each may have an alphabet letter written on it. Educators originally believed that letters confused children when teaching them to count phonemes in words; however, that assumption has been proven to be false if the letter–sound relationships are kept simple. So you may choose to use either blank or lettered squares when playing the phoneme counting game. *Note: If you use letters on the squares, however, do not use words containing vowel digraphs (ai), diphthongs (oy), murmur diphthongs (er), or vowel-consonant-e words (cake). Young children with limited phonemic awareness would find the graphemes representing these phonemes to be confusing.*

You should have the same number of squares that the students have, but your squares should be larger so all children in the classroom can see them. If you decide to use lettered squares then you and the students should have the appropriate lettered squares for the words selected for the game.

Your squares should have cloth glued on the back so you can put them on a flannel board and move them as the occasion requires. If a flannel board is not available, put masking tape on the back of each so they can be used on the chalkboard. If magnetic squares are used they will stick to a magnetic board.

Introduce the game by placing the three squares so that each square is in a line:

Say, "Listen to the sounds in the word *at*." As you say each phoneme in the word, move one square down about four inches. "/a/ /t/. How many sounds are in the word *at*?" Wait for a response. Say, "You say the word *at* and move down one of your squares for each sound you hear in the word. /a/ /t/." Wait for a response, then say, "How many squares did you move down?" Wait for a response. Say, "How many sounds are in the word *at*?" Wait for a response.

Continue the game using two-phoneme and three-phoneme words, such as the following:

Two-phoneme, two-grapheme words: *at, an, as, am, Ed, it, in, if, is, on.*

Use only blank squares for the following words: *toy, for, fur, jar, jaw, joy, say, saw, row, hay, her.*

Three-phoneme, three-grapheme words: *web, wig, win, wet, wag, bus, bib, bed, bad, big, beg, bat, bag, bug, bun, but, bit, bet, sit, sob, sin, sad, set, sun, sat, fib, fan.* Use only blank squares for the following words: *wait, wave, week, weed, wife, wood, beach, bead, bean, boil, book, boot, born, safe, sail, same, seat, soap, soon, south, face, fake, farm.*

Phoneme Association Game

The phoneme association game is a guessing game that requires children to match isolated phonemes with familiar words containing those phonemes. The game can be played with half of the class competing with the other half, or it can be played in one group without the "friendly competition." If the game is played with all members of the class, children raise their hands when they think they have the answer to a riddle. You would then call upon various students to respond.

If class members enjoy competition, the classroom should be divided into two groups. Each group takes a turn trying to guess a riddle. The group gets only one guess. Each member of the group takes a turn responding for the group, but other members of the group may prompt the person responding if they believe they know the answer. If the team member responsible for responding for the group gives the correct answer, the team gets a point. If the answer is incorrect, no points are given.

Present a riddle by saying, "I am thinking of something that children ride. It has two wheels. It begins with the /bi / sound (simple level)." Answer: *bike.* If the students are able to respond to a more difficult matching level task, then the teacher replaces the last sentence with, "It begins with the /b/ sound." Sample riddles follow.

Beginning Sounds

I am thinking of a furry animal that dogs chase. Its name begins with the /ka/ sound (optional: the /k/ sound). Answer: *cat*

I am thinking of an animal that can fly and likes to swim. Its name begins with the /du/ sound (optional: the /d/ sound). Answer: *duck*

I am thinking of something that goes high up in the sky. It has a string attached to it that I hold while it flies. It begins with the /kī/ sound (optional: the /k/ sound). Answer: *kite*

I am thinking of something that shines in the sky. It begins with the /su/ sound (optional: the /s/ sound). Answer: *sun*

I am thinking of an animal that likes to eat cheese. Its name begins with the /mou/ sound (optional: the /m/ sound). Answer: *mouse*

I am thinking of something that we hit with a hammer. It begins with the /nā/ sound (optional: the /n/ sound). Answer: *nail*

I am thinking of an animal that has a curly tail. Its name begins with the /pi/ sound (optional: the /p/ sound). Answer: *pig*

I am thinking of something that I use when I take a bath. It begins with the /tu/ sound (optional: the /t/ sound). Answer: *tub*

I am thinking of something that policemen have. It begins with the /gu/ sound (optional: the /g/ sound). Answer: *gun*

I am thinking of something that lives in the water. Its name begins with the /fi/ sound (optional: the /f/ sound). Answer: *fish*

I am thinking of something that we see pictures of during Halloween. Its name begins with the /wi/ sound (optional: the /w/ sound). Answer: *witch*

I am thinking of something that needs a key. It begins with the /lo/ sound (optional: the /l/ sound). Answer: *lock*

I am thinking of something that grapes grow on. It begins with the /vī/ sound (optional: the /v/ sound). Answer: *vine*

I am thinking of something that we use to get the leaves off the ground. It begins with the /rā/ sound (optional: the /r/ sound). Answer: *rake*

I am thinking of something that we put on our heads. It begins with the /ha/ sound (optional: the /h/ sound). Answer: *hat*

I am thinking of something that we sometimes find on coats. It begins with the /zi/ sound (optional: the /z/ sound). Answer: *zipper*

I am thinking of another name for a penny. It begins with the /se/ sound (optional: the /s/ sound). Answer: *cent*

I am thinking of something good to eat. It begins with the /ja/ sound (optional: the /j/ sound). Answer: *jam*

I am thinking of something children do when they try to call to a friend down the street. It begins with the /ye/ sound (optional: the /y/ sound). Answer: *yell*

I am thinking of something that we put on a horse to ride. It begins with the /sa/ sound (optional: the /s/ sound). Answer: *saddle*

I am thinking of a piece of furniture. It begins with the /ch/ sound. Answer: *chair*

I am thinking of an animal. This animal was lost by Little Bo Peep. Its name begins with the /sh/ sound. Answer: *sheep*

I am thinking of something that is round. It is found on a bike. It begins with the /wh/ sound. Answer: *wheel*

I am thinking of something on a vine that hurts if you touch it. Its name begins with the /th/ sound. Answer: *thorn*

Ending Sounds

After children get the right answers to these riddles, ask them to repeat the word, then the ending sound. For example, "*Dad, /d/.*"

I am thinking of something people usually eat with butter. It ends with the /d/ sound. Answer: *bread, /d/*

I am thinking of something that we use to throw on a fire to keep it burning. It ends with the /g/ sound. Answer: *log, /g/*

I am thinking of a very small animal with a tail. Its name ends with the /s/ sound. Answer: *mouse, /s/*

I am thinking of something a bear lives in sometimes. It ends with the /v/ sound. Answer: *cave, /v/*

I am thinking of an animal that has horns, and some people say eats cans. Its name ends with the /t/ sound. Answer: *goat, /t/*

I am thinking of something a spider walks on. It ends with the /b/ sound. Answer: *web, /b/*

I am thinking of a color. Its name ends with the /k/ sound. Answer: *black, /k/*

I am thinking of an animal that lives in the ground. Some people use it for fishing. Its name ends with the /m/ sound. Answer: *worm, /m/*

I am thinking of something that you throw. Its name ends with the /l/ sound. Answer: *ball, /l/*

I am thinking of something we generally use when we drink something warm. It ends with the /p/ sound. Answer: *cup, /p/*

I am thinking of something you see at night. Its name ends with the /n/ sound. Answer: *moon, /n/*

I am thinking of a number. Its name ends with the /ks/ sound. Answer: *six,* /ks/

I am thinking of something that falls off trees in the fall. Its name ends with the /f/ sound. Answer: *leaf,* /f/

I am thinking of something you get when you win a contest. It ends with the /z/ sound. Answer: *prize,* /z/

I am thinking of something a policeman wears. Its name ends with the /j/ sound. Answer: *badge,* /j/

I am thinking of something you put on your finger. Its name ends with the /ng/ sound. Answer: *ring,* /ng/

I am thinking of something that you put food on. Its name ends with the /sh/ sound. Answer: *dish,* /sh/

I am thinking of a fruit. Its name ends with the /ch/ sound. Answer: *peach,* /ch/

I am thinking of something you take when you get dirty. Its name ends with the /th/ sound. Answer: *bath,* /th/

Vowel Sounds

After children get the right answers to these riddles, ask them to repeat the word, then the vowel sound. For example, "*Top,* /o/."

I am thinking of something that we wear on Halloween. Its name has an /a/ sound in the middle. Answer: *mask,* /a/

I am thinking of something that uses ink for writing. Its name has an /e/ sound in the middle. Answer: *pen,* /e/

I am thinking of a dessert that we eat on birthdays. Its name has an /ā/ sound in the middle. Answer: *cake,* /ā/

I am thinking of something people wear on their heads when they don't have any hair. Its name has an /i/ sound in the middle. Answer: *wig,* /i/

I am thinking of a number. Its name has an /ī/ sound in the middle. Answer: *five,* /ī/

I am thinking of a color. Its name has an /ē/ sound in the middle. Answer: *green,* /ē/

I am thinking of something we put on the floor. We walk on it. Its name has an /u/ sound in the middle. Answer: *rug,* /u/

I am thinking of an animal that is something like a horse. Its name has a /ū/ sound in the middle. Answer: *mule,* /ū/

I am thinking of something that we use to scrub floors. Its name has an /o/ sound in the middle. Answer: *mop,* /o/

I am thinking of a part of the face. Its name has an /ō/ sound in the middle. Answer: *nose,* /ō/

I am thinking of something we use to carry money. Its name has an /ir/ sound in the middle. Answer: *purse,* /ir/

I am thinking of something a dog does. It has an /ar/ sound in the middle of the word. Answer: *bark,* /ar/

I am thinking of something we use when we eat. It has points on it. Its name has an /or/ sound in the middle. Answer: *fork,* /or/

I am thinking of something that is used to buy things. It is flat and round. Its name has an /oi/ sound in the middle. Answer: *coin,* /oi/

I am thinking of something that we find in the sky. Its name has an /ou/ sound in the middle. Answer: *cloud,* /ou/

I am thinking of something that growls and lives in caves. Its name ends with the /âr/ sound. Answer: *bear,* /âr/

Phoneme Blending Game

The phoneme blending game is another guessing game. In this game you isolate phonemes, and the children mentally blend the phonemes to form words. The phoneme blending game can be played with or without student competition. Group students for the game in the same manner as for the phoneme association game. Tell the students that you are thinking of something that you will reveal through a secret code. Then tell them the word in your secret code. If the students understand the code they identify your word. For example, say, "I am thinking of a /k/ /a/ /t/. Can you tell me my word?" Wait for a correct response, which in this case is *cat.*

A variation of the game requires the use of a large bag of objects, much like the bag Santa Claus is supposed to carry. Reach into the bag, touch an object, and say, "I am touching a /k/ /a/ /n/. What am I touching?" The students then respond to your question, in this case saying *can.*

You can adjust the complexity of the game to meet the phonemic awareness levels of your students. At the simplest level, your secret code involves segmenting the word in two parts. The first part ends with the vowel, and the second part includes everything after the vowel: /ma/ /d/. At a more advanced level, the secret code also segments the word in two parts, but this time the first part is everything before the vowel, and the second part begins with the vowel and includes everything after it: /m/ /ad/. At the most advanced level, the secret code involves the segmentation of every phoneme in the word: /m/ /a/ /d/.

The following words, familiar to young children, are appropriate for use in the phoneme blending game. These words include most of the basic phonemes of speech: *bike, book, ball, dog, duck, dish, kite, key, king, six, sun, mouse, moon, match, nose, nine, nail, purse, pen, pig, tent, tail, tub, goat, gun, gate, five, fox, fish, wing, wall, witch, log, lock, lamp, vine, vest, van, rose, rake, ring, hook, hat, house, zest, jam, jet, queen, yarn, yell, sing, bed, head, can, nut, rain, jeep, soap, girl, coin, shout, fork, tooth, wig, chain.*

Phoneme Segmentation Game

In the phoneme isolation game, the children play the teacher's role, isolating phonemes in words (saying words in a secret code) for other children to identify. The secret code they use depends upon their phonemic awareness level. Some children may isolate words in two parts, breaking the word after the vowel, such as /ju/ /j/ for the word *judge*. Others may be able to isolate the word in two parts, breaking the word before the vowel: /j/ /uj/. More advanced children might be able to isolate every phoneme in the word: /j/ /u/ /j/.

Students select words for this game that they are able to say in a "secret code." The game is enjoyed both by the students who can say the words in a secret code, and by those who try to identify them.

Using Literature Books to Enhance Phonemic Awareness

Teachers help children develop phonological awareness by reading books to them that stress rhyming and alliteration. Other literature books can also be used to enhance children's phonological and phonemic awareness.

Literature books are meant to be enjoyed by children; the primary purposes for using them in classrooms are for enjoyment, learning, and enrichment. However, after children are well acquainted with specific books, teaching activities using words or ideas from those books are appropriate, and often extremely effective.

Creative teachers can find a variety of ways to use children's books to teach the phonemic awareness tasks described in this chapter. Activities involving phoneme blending, phoneme association, phoneme segmentation, phoneme counting, phoneme manipulation, and segmenting words can all be developed from themes, concepts, and/or words used in children's literature books. We close this chapter by illustrating three of the many ways in which children's books can be used to enhance phonemic awareness.

Example One: Phoneme Association

In Steven Kellogg's book, *Can I Keep Him?* (Dial, 1971), a small boy wants to take all kinds of animals home and keep them. His mother explains why he can't. Dogs bark; cats have fur that affect people's allergies; deer have hooves and antlers that tear up furniture; bears smell; tigers eat too much; and pythons are messy because they shed their skins all over the house.

You could follow this story with a phoneme matching activity centered around other animals that do each of these things. You could, for example, use the following riddles:

I am thinking of another animal that barks. Its name begins with the /sē/ sound (optional: the /s/ sound). Answer: *seal*

I am thinking of another animal that causes allergies for some people. Its name begins with the /hor/ sound (optional: the /h/ sound). Answer: *horse*

I am thinking of another animal that has horns and feet that can destroy furniture. Its name begins with the /gō/ sound (optional: the /g/ sound). Answer: *goat*

I am thinking of another animal that smells. Its name begins with the /sku/ sound (optional: the /sk/ sound). Answer: *skunk*

I am thinking of another animal that eats a lot. Its name begins with the /pi/ sound (optional: the /p/ sound). Answer: *pig*

I am thinking of an animal that sometimes sheds fur all over the house. Its name begins with the /do/ sound (optional: the /d/ sound). Answer: *dog*

Example Two: Phoneme Association

In Patricia Reilly Giff's book, *Today Was a Terrible Day*, illustrated by Susanna Natti (Puffin, 1984), a second-grade boy named Ronald Morgan couldn't do anything right until the end of the school day. By extracting sentences from that book and substituting a syntactically correct word for one of the words, you can provide phoneme matching activities for children (use a substitute word so that children cannot guess the word from memory). Read the sentence and say the first sound of the missing (substitute) word, and have the children guess the missing word. For example:

"Today was a terrible day.

It started when I dropped my [/boo/ or /b/]."

Answer: *book*

"I tiptoed to the closet and ate a [/pē/ or /p/]."

Answer: *peach*

"When lunchtime came, I had no money for [/ka/ or /k/]."

Answer: *candy*

Example Three: Phoneme Manipulation and Blending

In H. A. Rey's *Curious George* (Houghton Mifflin, 1969), a monkey named George gets into all sorts of trouble because of his curiosity. After reading the story, you might pick a few words from the story to do sound substitution and sound blending activities. For example, you might select the words: *had, man, hat, take, him, came, bag*.

When doing sound substitution and blending activities write the word on the chalkboard and say, "This word is *had*. Say the word *had* without the /h/ sound." The correct response would be *ad*. After the students respond appropriately, write *ad* underneath the word *had* so the children can visualize the sound–symbol connections, then say, "Say the /m/ sound and the /ad/ sound together and tell me what word you get." The students should respond with the word *mad*. When they respond correctly, write the word *mad* underneath the word *ad*, then say, "Replace the /m/

sound in *mad* with the /s/ sound and tell me the word you get." When the children respond with *sad,* write that word underneath the word *mad.* If this activity were to continue, you would create the following words by substituting and blending phonemes:

had	man	hat	take	came
ad	an	at	cake	name
mad	ran	rat	rake	tame
sad	tan	sat	sake	same
bad	can	cat	bake	fame
pad	pan	pat	make	game

Application Activities

1. Summarize, in writing, the stages of phonological awareness.
2. Use the "secret code" game with some preschool child. Use both compound and multisyllabic words in the game. Afterwards, see how well the child can respond to sound manipulation activities with these words. Write a paragraph describing your experience.
3. Use the phonemic awareness tasks outlined in this chapter and assess a child's level of phonemic awareness.
4. Create a game or song to enhance children's phonemic awareness.

Chapter 6

Using Writing to Teach Phonemic Awareness and Phonics

Writing is essential in classrooms. Reading and writing are reciprocal language processes, and many children learn to read through their early writing experiences. Writing is also an effective vehicle to help young children develop an understanding of the alphabetic principle. For those phonemically unaware, writing creates a natural need for phonemic awareness and phonics knowledge. As they try to write words, they attempt to isolate the word's phonemes (phonemic awareness) and write something for each phoneme identified (phonics). There are many ways to teach young children to isolate phonemes and associate those phonemes with letters, but perhaps none more effective than writing, especially if it is accompanied by brief periods of systematic phonemic awareness and phonics training.

Children cannot write effectively without some level of phonemic awareness and phonics knowledge. Therefore, activities to teach children to be phonemically aware and develop letter–sound knowledge are essential. At the same time, phonemic awareness and phonics knowledge can be enhanced through writing, especially when children are encouraged to spell words by sounds. Because of the reciprocal relationship between writing and phonemic awareness/phonics knowledge, young children should be encouraged to write, and teachers should concurrently provide them with relevant mini-lessons to enhance their understanding of the alphabetic principle.

The phonemic awareness and phonics training described in this chapter is designed to complement any writing program. The program helps children spell words by sounds, and takes no more than 10 minutes of daily classroom time to implement. Classroom studies indicate that children receiving this training write better, spell better, read better, and move through the stages of invented spelling earlier than children who do not receive it (Eldredge & Baird, 1996; Funke, 1997).

The Writing Process

Most writers, when producing publishable documents, generally follow a series of predictable steps: prewriting, drafting, revising, editing, and publishing. Educators now generally believe that children should learn these steps; that is, they should learn the process writers go through when they write. It is assumed that if children learn this process, they will become better writers.

In the first step, *prewriting*, authors get ideas, develop needed writing skills, obtain information about various subjects, and choose writing topics. This step takes considerable time for most authors.

After writers have selected their topics and prepared themselves to write about them, they begin *drafting* their document, putting their topic-related ideas on paper. Their primary attention is on the content of the message they are trying to convey, not on the form or mechanics of writing.

After completing a draft, writers usually have other individuals read and critique it. They then use this critical feedback to *revise* and improve the written product.

During the fourth step, *editing*, writers closely examine the form and mechanics of their document. They ask themselves such questions as, "Are there any misspellings? Do I have any punctuation errors? Is my grammar usage proper? Is the written product attractive to the reader?"

After editing the written product, it is *published* so it can be shared with the intended audience. The five writing steps (prewriting, drafting, revising, editing, and publishing) are known as "the writing process."

Introducing the Writing Process to Children

Many teachers introduce children to the writing process by *writing with them;* that is, teacher and children go through the steps together, jointly producing written documents. First, they spend time, often several days, pursuing an area of interest to the group. The teacher reads books about the subject aloud; they see films, filmstrips, and videos on the subject; they go on field trips related to it; they listen to guests speak about it, and so on. At the conclusion of this step, the teacher and children jointly decide to write something about the subject studied.

After identifying a specific writing topic, the teacher and children select a title for their proposed document. Then, individual children dictate sentences about the topic. The teacher writes them on the chalkboard, and the teacher and children read them together. After the chalkboard has been filled with children's sentences, the children read them all again with teacher assistance (see Chapter 9 on assisted reading strategies). They talk about the sentences and decide how to organize them. The teacher numbers the sentences to identify the students' chosen sequence. Before erasing the chalkboard, the teacher makes a copy of the written draft.

The next day, the teacher projects a copy of the draft on a screen, using an overhead projector, so the children can watch as revisions are made to the original document. Every line of print is double spaced on the draft copy so there is room to make revisions. With the teacher's assistance the children read the draft copy. The teacher and students then talk about how to improve each sentence; (i.e., how to better say what is intended). Suggestions for improvement are elicited from the group, and revisions agreed upon by the majority of students are made to the document.

The following day, the teacher projects a copy of the revised draft on the screen so the children can participate in the editing phase of the process. The teacher had purposely misspelled some simple words, and made a few simple punctuation errors on the revised draft. The teacher and students focus on the mechanics and form of the written product. The teacher asks the students to look for any misspelled words or punctuation errors so they can be corrected.

The next day, the teacher distributes copies of the final version of the document to the children. A copy of the document is also projected on the screen. The children and the teacher read it several times. Children who desire to do so illustrate their individual copies of the document. The teacher encourages the children to take the document home and read it to their parents.

Writing on Their Own

After teachers have introduced children to the writing process by sufficiently involving them in "supported writing experiences," students are encouraged to go through the process by themselves. They choose their own writing topics after spending the necessary prewriting time. They do their own written drafts, supported by teacher guidance. During the drafting phase, teachers encourage students to focus on what they want to say, and not to worry about spelling. Teachers also encourage students to use "invented spellings" when they are unsure of word spellings. Teachers often provide "spelling helps" through picture–sound reference charts, and high-frequency word lists, which are given to each student or posted on word walls in the classroom.

It is appropriate at this point to comment about spelling and grammar in children's writing. Most educators believe that the substance of children's writing is more important than its form during the initial stages of the writing process. Therefore, they tend to deemphasize spelling and punctuation when children write drafts so they can better focus on what they want to say. That is not to imply that spelling and grammar are unimportant. Spelling and syntax knowledge greatly influence the quality of anyone's writing. Individuals who understand how sentences are legitimately structured, and written sentences punctuated, are better writers than those who lack that knowledge, and people not worried about word spellings are better able to focus on what they want to say than those concerned about spelling. However, when children are trying to put their ideas onto paper, they need to be free of spelling and punctuation concerns. There is a time and a place to worry about spelling, punctuation, and grammar in children's written documents; however, that time is not when children are trying to focus on what they want to say. Improving children's syntax and spelling knowledge, during the writing process, is important, but it should be done in ways unobtrusive to the constructive thinking processes children are required to use during the initial phases of writing.

After the children complete their written drafts, they share them with classmates. Students form small groups for this purpose, and take turns reading their drafts to one another. After each reading, members of the group react to the draft, making positive comments about the author's work before they offer any suggestions for improvement. It is during the revision stage that children focus on those grammar issues that will improve communication. Therefore, ideas about sentence improvement are shared during this stage. After children receive feedback from their peers, they are free to make whatever revisions they want to make in their work.

After children revise their documents, they are encouraged to proofread and edit them for spelling, punctuation, and grammar. Other students then have the opportunity to proofread them. These students become "editors," and identify spelling, punctuation, and grammar problems. The authors of the documents make the needed corrections after the editors complete their work.

The final editor of children's work is the teacher. The teacher may want to edit students' documents after the author and two or three other students proofread them. The teacher may want to write the correct spelling above all misspellings the children did not find. These corrections should be written above misspelled words in small, neat, legible, manuscript writing. The student then makes a final copy of the document, illustrates it if desired, and makes it available for others to read. The final draft copy, containing the teacher's spelling corrections, may be placed in the student's assessment portfolio.

The quantity and quality of children's writing are influenced by teachers. Teachers create a writing climate in the classroom; they provide relevant reasons for children to write; they motivate children to write; and they help children improve their writing abilities. One of the best ways to help *young* writers improve their writing is to provide them with systematic phonemic awareness and phonics training.

Other Writing Activities

Young children's early writing experiences often include, among other things, writing captions underneath their artwork. (The artwork might in fact be produced after the written document.) During the writing "sharing time," opportunities for students to display their artwork and read their captions are provided. Afterwards, each student's written work is made available for others to read and enjoy. Sharing time is important for students because they tend to be more motivated to write when there is an audience ready to hear what they have to say.

Children unable to write captions might dictate their thoughts to someone else to write until they develop the rudimentary skills needed for such writing activities. These children should also be able to participate in the writing "sharing time." They should be able to read the captions underneath their pictures, even though they were written by someone else, since the written text will represent their own language and sentence structures.

Teachers sometimes ask children to bring magazine or newspaper pictures to school for writing captions. Many teachers collect newspapers and magazines so students not having access to them can participate in activities such as this one. Caption writing for single pictures eventually leads to caption writing for three or four related pictures. The short, captioned stories produced by children in this manner are usually interesting and creative, and the writing experience helps children view themselves as authors. Before long, they are writing and illustrating their own stories.

Teachers often use wordless picture books as tools for young children's writing. Children write simple stories for these books by creating captions for each picture in the book. These captions are loosely taped underneath each picture in the book while the children read their stories during the sharing time.

Some teachers have children keep simple journals. Children write in their journals at the end of the school day, recording anything they want about the day.

It is recommended that writing activities be an important part of the curriculum for all children, even kindergarten children. The simple writing products these young children are able to create in the early part of the year should become more sophisticated as the year progresses if writing activities are maintained as an integral part of the kindergarten curriculum.

Phonemic Awareness and Phonics Mini-Lessons

Even though phonemic awareness is about sounds rather than print, there are many advantages in teaching phonemic awareness *and* phonics together. In fact, many research studies, and educators, suggest that children develop phonemic awareness best when they are taught to associate letters with the phonemes they represent (Ball & Blachman, 1991; Bradley & Bryant, 1985; Ehri et al., 2001; Hatcher, Hulme, & Ellis, 1994; Hohn & Ehri, 1983; Iversen & Tunmer, 1993; National Reading Panel, 2000; Stuart, 1999; Torgesen, Wagner, & Rashotte, 1997).

The amount of phonics knowledge one can teach while teaching phonemic awareness, however, is limited since phonics knowledge growth is dependent on phonemic awareness growth. Therefore, phonics instruction usually differs when teaching children with limited phonemic awareness, and when teaching children with higher levels of phonemic awareness. For this reason, the phonics instruction presented in this chapter is designed for young children with limited phonemic awareness. As these children develop greater capacities to isolate and manipulate phonemes, the phonics instruction becomes more sophisticated. The training is designed to improve phonemic awareness, and phonics knowledge through writing, accompanied by brief mini-lessons focusing on phonemic awareness tasks involving letters. The phonics knowledge learned will help children read and write better.

The phonics strategy presented later in this book is designed for first-grade children with slightly higher levels of phonemic awareness. The major focus is on reading rather than writing. Phonics is then taught as a decoding process for children to use when other decoding strategies fail. The skills children learn, while learning how to use the strategy, include phoneme blending for word identification, a skill needed for successful decoding (Kroese et al., 2000; Pullen, 2000; Wesseling & Reitsma, 2000).

Background

Phonemic awareness/phonics activities presented in this chapter are an appropriate supplement to children's writing activities. These "sound to symbol" activities explicitly reveal to children the relationships existing between phonemes and the letters representing them. Once children perceive these relationships, they approach invented spelling with more confidence and their written products reflect a more sophisticated vocabulary.

The sound to symbol phonemic awareness activities described herein systematically teach children how to spell most of the 45 basic speech sounds in the English language.

The activities should not take much classroom time; 10 minutes a day is usually sufficient. If you choose to use the activities, you should use them daily. Short periods of instruction provided regularly will have a greater impact on children's learning than longer periods provided only once or twice a week. Therefore, it is recommended that the activities be provided for young children throughout the year until they are able to use invented spellings to spell any word they can pronounce.

Matching Phonics Instruction with Phonemic Awareness Abilities

By ages 4 and 5 most children are able to identify rhyming words and beginning sounds (Juel & Minden-Cupp, 2000). Some consider that the ability to identify rhyming words and beginning sounds as one single level of language awareness (Armbruster et al., 2001). However, children seem to be able to manipulate rimes before they are able to manipulate the beginning sounds appearing before the rimes (Cardoso-Martins, Michalick, & Pollo, 2002; Norris & Hoffman, 2002).

Most of the research on phonemic awareness suggests that children first develop the ability to manipulate rimes, then initial phonemes, then ending phonemes, and lastly middle phonemes. Goswami (2001) suggests that the awareness of rimes in words may influence children to look for the letters in written words representing the rime, and Norris and Hoffman (2002) suggest that children probably learn how to manipulate the initial phonemes *after* they develop an awareness of rhyming words. Therefore, it has been suggested that phonemic awareness instruction should begin with beginning sounds, followed by ending sounds, followed by middle sounds (Foorman, Jenkins, & Francis, 1993). The phonemic awareness and phonics training outlined in this chapter begins with a) onsets and rimes, followed by b) beginning phonemes, followed by c) ending phonemes, followed by d) middle phonemes.

Writing and Mini-Lessons

All of the mini-lessons outlined in this chapter are designed to be used with an ongoing writing program. A writing program includes a) writing *to* children, b) writing *with* children, and c) writing *by* children. Teachers who write messages to children each day help to create an interest in writing and a sense of importance for writing. The messages teachers write can be short, but should be purposeful. Some children will be able to read the messages without assistance, but some will not be able to read them without help. An effective practice is to give children the opportunity to work in triads (groups of three) where all members of the group help each other read the message. Afterwards, the entire class reads the message as a group, with assistance, if needed, from the teacher. Regardless of who leads the group in reading the message (teacher or student) the words should be touched with a pointer as each is read. Teachers may also write individual notes to students occasionally.

Teachers also write with children. According to the developmental level of the children, teachers "share the pen" with various students, asking them to write letters, words, phrases, or even sentences in the jointly produced documents. Writing with children is an important writing component, and should be continued throughout the school year.

Children also do their own writing, encouraged by the teacher to spell words by sounds; (i.e., use invented spellings). They are given opportunities to write to class-mates, the teacher, significant other people, the principal, and other authority fig-ures. They are given opportunities to keep journals, to write short reports, to write about their personal experiences, or to write for any relevant purpose. They are also given opportunities to share their writing with others in the classroom.

Beginning Writing Supports

The knowledge students derive from mini-lessons should be utilized in teacher sup-ported "sharing the pen" activities, and in the students' individual writing. It is sug-gested that several writing supports be provided for students struggling with their independent writing. First, provide a word wall where the most frequently used words are displayed. The word wall shown in Figure 6.1 contains the 36 most frequently

a	b	c	d	e	f
a	but	can	do		for
at					
and					
all					
are					
g	**h**	**i**	**j**	**k**	**l**
	he	I			little
	her	it			
	his	in			
	have	is			
m	**n**	**o**	**p**	**q**	**r**
my	not	on			
		of			
		out			
s	**t**	**u**	**v**	**w**	**x**
said	the	up		was	
she	to			we	
	that			what	
	they			will	
				with	
y	**z**				
you					

FIGURE 6.1   Word Wall for Frequently Used Words

used words in first-grade basal readers, and 231 literature books used in first grade. Each of these words were used more than 1,000 times in the first-grade materials. Other words considered to be important for writing may be added to the word wall, as appropriate. The words should be reviewed (read) with the students from time to time, until they can be read without help.

Another writing support helpful to young students is a consonant reference chart (see Figure 6.2). The consonant reference chart should be reviewed with the stu-

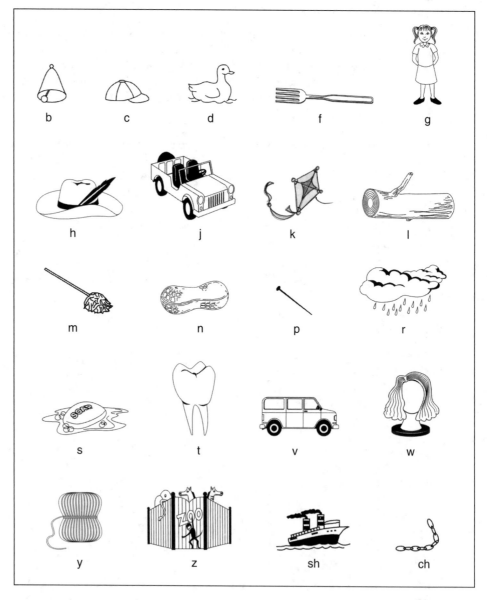

FIGURE 6.2 Consonant Reference Chart

dents from time to time so they can become familiar with the picture names, and the phonemes represented by the letters.

Onsets and Rimes

Phonics is a study of phoneme–grapheme relationships within syllables. There are different ways to analyze syllables. One popular way is to analyze them according to their onsets and rimes. The syllable's rime is the rhyming component in the syllable (*jump, dump, stump*). All rimes begin with a vowel, and include everything after the vowel. The syllable's onset is everything before the vowel (*jump, dump, stump*).

Onsets can be single consonants *(rub)*, consonant blends *(stub)*, consonant digraphs *(chub),* or consonant digraphs blended with another consonant *(shrub).* The vowels in rimes can be open *(no)*, closed *(not)*, or vowels followed by a consonant, followed by an *e (note).*

After developing an awareness of rhyming words, it is a relatively easy task for children to learn how to perceive the phonemes preceding the rhyming part of the word, and to associate the phonemes with the onsets representing them. Initially it is best to use rhyming words with single consonants. Rhyming words containing consonant blends, or consonant digraphs blended with another consonant, should not be used until children have learned to manipulate the simpler onsets.

Figure 6.3 presents the visuals needed for an onsets and rimes activity. These visuals can be made for the overhead projector, or they can be made of tagboard, with tape pasted on the back, so both the pictures and the onsets and rimes can be moved

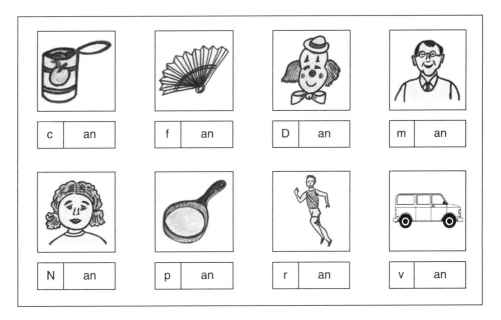

FIGURE 6.3 Onsets, Rimes, and Pictures

around. Organize the students in dyads (groups of 2). Each dyad group should have a copy of Figure 6.3, a set of onset tiles: *c, f, D, m, N, p, r,* and *v,* and one rime tile: (*an*).

Onset and Rimes Lesson (Sample). The main purpose of this onset and rime lesson is to help students isolate beginning phonemes in words and write correct graphemes for each phoneme isolated. This is a crucial skill for learning to write with invented spellings.

The tasks involved in the lesson are: a) blending (identifying words when the first phoneme is isolated from the rest of the word), b) phoneme association (matching phonemes with words beginning with those phonemes), c) phoneme segmentation (isolating the first phoneme in the word), d) phoneme manipulation (deletion, addition, substitution), and e) phoneme to symbol (writing graphemes for phonemes). In addition to these five tasks, students will be asked to apply their knowledge to complete sentences or rhymes written by the teacher.

All of the tasks presented below are not complete, just samples. Teachers using the onset and rimes lesson should incorporate all eight onsets and/or pictures in each task.

(Remember: Whenever, letters are placed between slashes / /, sounds are said, not letters!)

Blending (Sample)

Teacher: "Point to the picture of /m/. . . /an/, and say the word."

The students in each dyad point to the picture of the man and say "*man.*"

Phoneme Association (Sample)

Teacher: "Point to the picture that begins with /f/, and say the name of the picture."

The students in each dyad point to the picture of the fan and say "*fan.*"

Teacher: "Tell me another word that begins with /f/." The students may say words like *fish, feet, food, farm, find, four.*

Phoneme Segmentation (Sample)

Teacher: "I can 'machine gun' the first sound of *pan*. P-p-p-p-p-*pan*.

Can you 'machine gun' the first sound of *can?*"
Students: "K-k-k-k-k-*can.*"

Teacher: "The beginning sound of *pan* is /p/. Tell me the beginning sound of *can*."
Students: "/k/."

Phoneme Manipulation (Sample)

1. The teacher places all of the onset tiles on the overhead projector (or chalkboard if tagboard squares are used). The rime is also displayed.

    The students in the dyads place their onset and rime tiles in front of them.

c	f	D	m	N	p	r	v

an

Teacher: "Make the word *fan.*"

f	- - - - - - ▸	an

The students move an onset to the rime:

The teacher reinforces the correct response by moving the onset *f* to the rime *an* to make the word *fan* on the overhead projector top, or chalkboard.

2. *Teacher:* "Say *Dan* without /d/."

Students: "*an.*"   **D**an

3. *Teacher:* "Add /v/ to *an,* and what word do you get?"

Students: "*van.*"   **V**an

Phoneme to Symbol (Sample)

1. *Teacher:* "Write the letter we use for the /m/ sound to make the word *man.*"

	a	n

Students write the letter *m*. This writing activity may be continued with *c, f, m,* and *r*.

2. *Teacher:* "Write the letter that we use for the /f/ sound."

   Each student writes the letter *f*.

Application Activity (Sample)

All of the students should have a copy of the culminating lesson activity which requires them to apply their phonics knowledge to complete sentences or rhymes. All of the words in the sentences should be read by the teacher, except the words the students are expected to complete. Read two sentences at a time. When you come to any incomplete word, say *"an."* For example, the first two sentences would be read, "Come along with me, if you *'an'*. To visit a clown named *'an'*." Give the students time to complete the incomplete words, and then read the next two sentences, and so on.

Come along with me, if you _____ *an.*

To visit a clown named _____ *an.*

He was such a funny young _____ *an,*

and drove such a funny old _____ *an.*

His wife was a young girl named _____ *an,*

who never cooked dinner in a _____ *an.*

Her dinner was cooked in a _____ *an,*

given with love, by a friend named Jan.
I met this clown, one hot day in July.
The weather was miserable, I can't deny.
When the weather is hot, we can all use a _____ *an.*

Especially, when to the neighborhood store, you _____ *an.*

Other Onset and Rimes Lessons. The rimes contained in the following 35 words can be used for other onset and rimes lessons: *tack, bag, nail, chain, cake, whale, game, lamp, hat, gate, hay, ring, sink, ship, sit, lock, woke, mop, pot, duck, bug, jump, bunk, bank, cap, cash, meat, bell, hen, vest, chick, hide, hill, pin,* and *nine.* Literally, hundreds of words can be produced by students using these rimes and the 21 consonants listed in the Consonant Reference Chart, Figure 6.2.

Vowel Phonemes

Once children are able to segment initial consonant phonemes in words, they are ready to learn how to segment vowel phonemes at the beginning of words. The first vowel reference chart (see Figure 6.4) is provided to help children associate vowel letters with short vowel phonemes. The chart also provides students with a sound–spelling reference as they attempt to write words by sounds (invented spellings).

Vowel Phoneme Lesson (Sample). The main purposes of the vowel phoneme lesson are to help students isolate vowel phonemes in the initial position of words, write

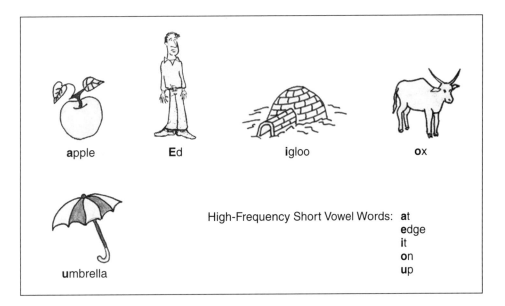

apple   **E**d   **i**gloo   **o**x

umbrella

High-Frequency Short Vowel Words: **at**
edge
it
on
up

FIGURE 6.4   Short Vowel Reference Chart

correct graphemes for each phoneme isolated, and to write words containing short vowel phonemes.

The tasks involved in the lesson are: a) blending phonemes (identifying words when pronounced by phonemes), b) phoneme association (matching phonemes with words beginning with those phonemes), c) phoneme segmentation (isolating the first phoneme in the word), d) phoneme manipulation (deleting, adding, or substituting phonemes), and e) phoneme to symbol (writing graphemes for phonemes).

Organize the students in dyad groups. Each dyad group should have a copy of Figures 6.2 and 6.4, and a set of grapheme tiles: *a, e, i, o, u, dge, f, p,* and *t.*

Blending Phonemes (Sample)

Teacher: "Point to the picture of /e/. . . /d/, and say the word."

The students in each dyad point to the picture of Ed   and say *"Ed. "*

Phoneme Association (Sample)

Teacher: "Point to the picture whose name begins with /a/, and say the name of the picture."

The students in each dyad point to the picture of the apple   and say *"apple. "*

Teacher: "Tell me another word that begins with /a/."

The students may respond with words like *ask, after, ant, and, at.*

Phoneme Segmentation (Sample)

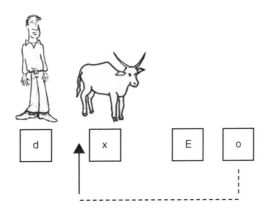

Umbrella

Teacher: "I can 'machine gun' the first sound of *umbrella.* U-u-u-u-u-umbrella.

Ox

Can you 'machine gun' the first sound of *ox?*"
Students: "O-o-o-o-ox."
Teacher: "The beginning sound of umbrella is /u/. Tell me the beginning sound
   of ox, /o/. . . /ks/."
Students: "/o/."

Phoneme Manipulation (Sample)

1. The teacher places the following pictures and tiles on the overhead projector
   top, and says, "Move one of the letters in front of the *x* (point to the letter) to
   make the word *ox,* /o/. . . /ks/.":

The students move the *o* in front of the *x:*

The teacher reinforces the correct response by moving the *o* to the *x* on the overhead projector top, and asks the students to say the sounds represented by both
letters in the word as each letter is touched.

The students respond, receiving assistance from the teacher, if needed.

The teacher moves the letter *o* away from the picture of the ox, and repeats the
process with the word *Ed.*

2. The teacher places grapheme tiles on the overhead projector top as follows:

The teacher moves the tiles in the word *at* away from the others so children can focus on the word's graphemes, while listening to the phonemes that represent them:

Teacher: "There are two sounds in the word *at.* Watch while I touch the letters used for each sound." The teacher touches each letter and isolates the sound of each as they are touched, " /a/ . . . /t/ ."

"Tell me the sound of each letter as I touch it." The teacher touches each letter and helps the children respond with the appropriate sounds, "/a/ . . . /t/ ."

The teacher repeats this process with the word *if:*

The teacher then arranges the tiles in the words *at* and *if* in random order:

Teacher: "Say the sound of each letter as I touch it." The teacher touches each letter and the children respond.

"Make the word it, /i/ . . . /t/. To make this word, find the /i/ letter, and move it away from the other letters." (Students respond.) "Now find the /t/ letter and place it after the /i/ letter." As the students respond, the teacher moves the appropriate letters on the overhead projector top to form the word *it:*

"Say the sounds of the new word as I touch each letter in the word." (Students respond.) "Spoken words are made up of sounds, and letters represent those sounds. So when we make written words we choose letters to represent their sounds."

Put the letter tiles in random order again:

"Make the word at, /a/ . . . /t/. First, find the /a/ letter, and move it away from the other letters." (Students respond.) "Now find the /t/ letter and place it after the /a/ letter." As the students respond, the teacher moves the letters on the projector top to form the word *at*:

"Say the sounds of the new word as I touch each letter in the word." (Students respond.)

Continue this activity with the words *on, up,* and *edge*. Students should be able to make the following words by manipulating phoneme tiles: *at, an, it, in, if, on, up,* and *edge*.

Phoneme to Symbol (Sample)

1. *Teacher:* "Write the letter we use for the /o/ sound to make the word *ox*."

Continue this writing activity with the words *an, if, at, it, in, on, up,* and *edge*.

2. *Teacher:* "Write the letter we use for the /a/ sound."
Each student writes the letter *a*.

   Teacher: "Write the letter we use for the /n/ sound after the letter *a*."
Each student writes the letter *n*.

   Teacher: "Read the word we wrote."

   Students: "*an.*"

With the assistance of the short vowel reference chart (Figure 6.4), students should be able to write the following words by sounds: *at, ox, it, in, if, on, up,* and *edge*. With the introduction of the word *edge,* children are shown for the first time that graphemes may be comprised of more than one letter.

> *Note:* The grapheme for the /j/ phoneme at the end of words is never the letter j. The grapheme is usually dge for words with short vowels (dodge), and ge for words with long vowels (huge).

Extending Word Writing Skills by Letter Addition

After children are able to write the following words by sounds: *at, an, it, in, if, on, ox, up, Ed,* and *edge,* they should also be able to use the consonant reference chart (Figure 6.2) to write additional words by letter addition. They should be able to write the following words: *at, an, it, in, if, on, up, edge, sat, mat, fat, rat, hat, cat, bat, vat, pat, chat, man, fan, tan, Dan, ran, Nan, can, ban, van, Jan, pan, sit, fit, lit, hit, bit, pit, wit, zit, mit, sin, fin, tin, chin, pin, win, Don, Ron, pup, cup, ledge, hedge, Ed, fed, Ted, red, led, Ned, bed, wed, shed, ox, fox, box, pox.*

Letter Addition (Sample)

Materials needed: Consonant reference chart.

Teacher: "Write the letter for /a/" (Children respond.) "Write the letter for /t/ after the letter *a.*" (Children respond.) "What word did we write?"

Children: "*at.*"

Teacher: "Let's say all of the names of the pictures on the consonant chart, and say the sound of the letter underneath each picture. The letter underneath each picture is how we write the first sound of the word."

Teacher and students: "*bell,* /b/, *cap,* /k/, *duck,* /d/, *fork,* /f/," and so on.

Teacher: "If I blend /b/ and /at/ together I would get the word *bat.* What letter would I need to write in front of *at* to write the word *bat*?" (Children respond.) "See how many words you can write using the consonant letters on the chart with the word *at.*"

The children should be able to write the words: *sat, fat, mat, rat, hat, cat, bat, vat,* and *pat* by adding different consonant onsets to the rime.

Long Vowel Phonemes

The long vowel phonemes and the names of the vowel letters are one and the same. Vowel letters predictably represent their long sounds (the sound of their names) when they are in vowel-consonant-*e* words *(bone),* and when the word ends in a vowel sound *(me).* To help children learn to write long vowel sounds another vowel reference chart is needed (see Figure 6.5).

Segmenting Short and Long Vowel Phonemes. After the students have learned to write graphemes for short vowel phonemes, and after they have learned how to write graphemes for two phoneme words, the children are ready to learn about long vowel phonemes, and to distinguish between the long and short vowel sounds.

The teacher places grapheme tiles on the overhead projector top as follows:

a	t		i	f		o	n		u	p		e	dge

Teacher: "Say each of these five words, and then say the two sounds in each word."

Under the direction of the teacher, the students read each word and segment the two sounds in each word. The teacher separates the grapheme tiles for the word *at*

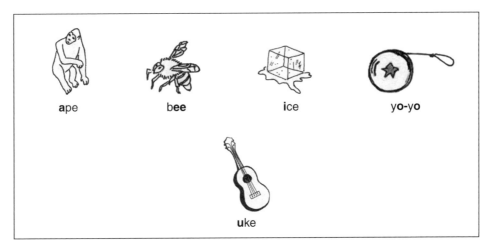

FIGURE 6.5 Long Vowel Reference Chart

from the rest of the tiles, and places the picture of the *ape,* and two grapheme tiles for the word *ape,* underneath those tiles:

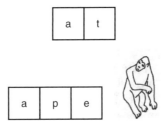

The teacher helps the students segment the two sounds in each word, and helps them distinguish the short vowel phoneme from the long vowel phoneme that are both represented by the vowel letter *a.*

The teacher repeats the process with the words *if* and *ice,* and the words *up* and *uke.*

When the teacher gets to the word *bee,* the students are helped to segment the two phonemes in the word. When the long vowel sound in *bee* is contrasted with the short vowel sound in *edge,* the teacher might say, "The long vowel sound in the word *bee* is /ē/, and that sound is the same as the name of the letter *e*. The short sound of *e* is the /e/ sound heard at the beginning of the word *edge.*"

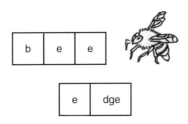

When the teacher gets to the word *yo-yo,* the students are helped to segment the two sounds in each syllable of the word. When the long and short vowel sounds in the words *yo-yo* and *on* are compared, the teacher might say, "The long vowel sound in the word *yo-yo* is /ō/. There are two long vowel sounds in *yo-yo,* and those sounds are the same as the name of the letter *o.* The short sound of *o* is the /o/ sound heard at the beginning of the word *on.*"

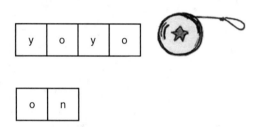

The teacher helps the students recognize that the long vowel sounds for all vowel letters are the same as the vowel letter names.

Long Vowel Phoneme Lesson (Sample). The main purposes of the long vowel phoneme lesson are to help students isolate vowel phonemes in the initial position of words, write correct graphemes for each phoneme isolated, and to write words containing long vowel phonemes.

The tasks involved in the lesson are: a) blending phonemes (identifying words when pronounced by phonemes), b) phoneme association (matching phonemes with words beginning with those phonemes), c) phoneme segmentation (isolating the first phoneme in the word), d) phoneme manipulation (deleting, adding, or substituting phonemes), and e) phoneme to symbol (writing graphemes for phonemes).

Organize the students in dyad groups. Each dyad group should have a copy of Figures 6.2 and 6.5, and a set of grapheme tiles: *a, e, i, o, u, b, c, f, h, k, p, t,* and *w.*

Blending Phonemes (Sample)

Teacher: "Point to the picture of /ā/. . . /p/, and say the word."

The students in each dyad point to the picture of the ape and say "*ape.*"

Phoneme Association (Sample)

Teacher: "Point to the picture that begins with /ī/, and say the name of the picture."

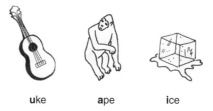

The students in each dyad point to the picture of ice and say "*ice.*"

Phoneme Segmentation (Sample)

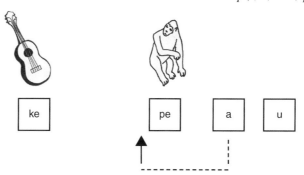

Teacher: "The beginning sound of *uke* is /ū/. Tell me the beginning sound of *ape*, /ā/ . . . /p/."

Students: "/ā/."

Teacher: "Tell me the beginning sound of *ice*, /ī/ . . . /s/."

Students: "/ī/."

Phoneme Manipulation (Sample)

The teacher places the following pictures and tiles on the overhead projector top, and says, "Move one of the tiles to make the word *ape,* /ā/ . . . /p/:"

The students move the *a* in front of the *pe:*

The teacher reinforces the correct response by moving the *a* to the *pe* on the overhead projector top, and asks the students to say the sounds represented by both graphemes in the word as each grapheme is touched.

The students respond, receiving assistance from the teacher, if needed.

The teacher moves the letter *a* away from the picture of the ape, back to its position next to the letter *u,* and follows the same procedure with the word *uke.*

Writing Long Vowel Phonemes

Teacher: "Look at the letter *e* at the end of the words *uke, ape,* and *ice.* One of the ways we write long vowel phonemes is to write an *e* after the consonant before the vowel. The *e* doesn't make any sound when we do this, but it tells the reader that the vowel letter in the word is used for the long vowel sound.

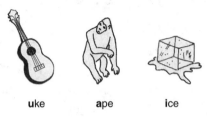

uke　　　　ape　　　　ice

1. *Teacher:* "Write the letter we use for /a/."

   The students write the letter *a.*

   Teacher: "After the letter *a,* write the letter we use for /t/."

   The students write *at.*

   Teacher: "What word did we write?"

   Students: "*at.*"

   Teacher: "Write a letter *e,* after the *t.*"

   The students write *ate.*

   Teacher: "Now the letter *a* in this word is used for a different sound. It is used for the /ā/ sound because there is an *e* after the *t.* Say all the sounds in the word we wrote, as I touch each letter."

   The teacher touches the letters, except *e,* and the teacher and students say, /ā/ . . . /t/.

   Teacher: "What word did we write?"

   Students: "*ate.*"

2. *Teacher:* "Write the word *at,* /a/ . . . /t/."

   The students write *at.*

   Teacher: "Write a consonant letter in front of *at* to make the word *hat.*"

   The students write *hat.*

   Teacher: "Write a letter *e* after the *t.*"

   The students write *hate.*

   Teacher: "What word did we write?"

   Students: "*hate.*"

This writing activity could be continued with the words *can* and *cane, bit* and *bite, fin* and *fine, win* and *wine.*

3. *Teacher:* "Write the letter we use for the /i/ sound to make the word *in.*"

"Write the letter we use for the /f/ sound to make the word *fin.*"

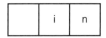

"Write the letter we use to make the word *fine.*"

This writing activity could be continued with the words *can* and *cane, bit* and *bite, hat* and *hate, win* and *wine.*

Writing More Long Vowel Phonemes

Teacher: "There are some other ways we can write long vowel sounds. Look at the letter *o* at the end of the two parts of the word *yo-yo.* Another way we write long vowel phonemes is to write a single vowel letter at the end of a word, or a word part.

If we write a consonant letter after a vowel letter, and don't write an *e* after the consonant letter, we are usually writing short vowel phonemes."

The teacher helps students understand the concept of open and closed syllables with words like *me* and *men.* As children are helped to segment the individual phonemes in the words *me* and *men,* they begin to understand how the same vowel letter represents different phonemes just by the way the syllables are written.

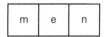

1. *Teacher:* "Write the letter we use for /s/."
   The children write *s.*
   Teacher: "Write the letter we use for /ō/"
   The students write *so.*
   Teacher: "What word did we write?"

Students: "so."

Teacher: "Write the letter we use for /b/, after the vowel *o*."
The students write *sob.*

Teacher: "Now the letter *o* is used for a different sound. It is used for the /o/ sound because there is a consonant after it. Say all of the sounds in the word we wrote, as I touch each letter."
The teacher touches the letters, and the teacher and students say, "/s/... /o/.../b/."

Teacher: "What word did we write?"

Students: "sob."

This writing activity may be continued with the words *go* and *got, no* and *not, be* and *bet, he* and *hen, we* and *web.*

Teacher: "Write the letter we use for the /ō/ sound to make the word *go*."

"Say all of the sounds in the word go, as I touch each letter."
The teacher and students say, "/g/.../ō/."
"Write the letter we use for the /t/ sound, after the letter *o*.

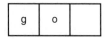

"Say all of the sounds in the word, as I touch each letter. Remember that the letter *o* will represent a different sound than the sound we hear in the word *go* because there is a consonant letter after the *o*."
The teacher and students say, "/g/.../o/.../t/."
What word did we write?"
Students: *"got."*
"Write the letter we use for the /ē/ sound to make the word *me*."

"Write the letter we use for the /t/ sound, after the letter *e*."

"What word did we write?"
Students: "met."

Ending Consonant Phonemes

Once children are capable of segmenting and writing two phoneme words, and able to write three phoneme words by letter addition, they are ready to segment and write three phoneme words. An ending consonant reference chart is provided to help accomplish this task (see Figure 6.6).

FIGURE 6.6 Consonant Reference Chart for Ending Consonant Phonemes

Ending Consonant Phoneme Lesson (Sample). The main purposes of the ending consonant lesson are to help students segment phonemes in the final position of words, write correct graphemes for the phonemes isolated, and to write words.

The tasks involved in the lesson are: a) blending, b) phoneme association, c) phoneme segmentation, d) phoneme manipulation, and e) phoneme to symbol. All of the tasks presented in this lesson are just samples. Teachers using the lesson should incorporate all ending consonant phonemes and/or pictures at - some time.

Blending (Sample)

Teacher: "Point to the picture of the /ka/. . . /t/, and say the word."

The students in each dyad point to the picture of the cat, and say *"cat."*

Phoneme Association (Sample)

Teacher: "Point to the picture that ends with the /p/ sound, and say the name of the picture."

The students in each dyad point to the picture of the top, and say *"top."*
Teacher: "Tell me another word that ends with /p/."
The students may say words like *cup, pup, mop, hop, nap, map, lap, lip, up.*

Phoneme Segmentation (Sample)

Teacher: "Tell me the ending sound of bed, /be/. . . /d/."
Students: "/d/."

Phoneme Manipulation (Sample)

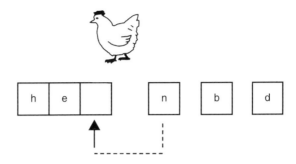

1. *Teacher:* "Move the letter used for the /n/ sound to the blank space, so you can make the word, /he/ . . . /n/."
   The students move the *n* to the blank space.

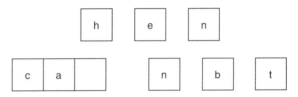

2. *Teacher:* "Move the letter used for the /b/ sound to the blank space, so you can make the word, /ka/ . . . /b/."

Students: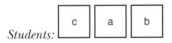

Continue this activity using the words *can* and *cat.*

Phoneme to Symbol (Sample)

   Teacher: "Write the letter we use for the /a/ sound."
   The students write *a.*
   Teacher: "Write the letter we use for the /d/ sound after the letter *a.*"
   The students write *ad.*
   Teacher: "What word did you write?"
   Students: "ad."
   Teacher: "Write the letter we use for the /s/ sound before the letter *a.*"
   The students write *sad.*
   Teacher: "What word did you write? If you have any trouble, say all of the sounds in the word, and blend the sounds together."
   Students: "sad."
   This activity may be continued using such words as: *mad, had, dad, bad, pad, fad,* and *lad.*

Middle Phonemes

Lesson (Sample). The middle phonemes are the most difficult for children to hear in words. This lesson is designed to help students hear phonemes in the middle of words so they can write words by sounds.

The tasks involved in the lesson are: a) blending, b) phoneme association, c) phoneme segmentation, d) phoneme manipulation, and e) phoneme to symbol. Writing words by sounds, even if the words are not always spelled correctly, is the main purpose of these phonemic awareness/phonics mini-lessons. After children can hear all of the phonemes in words and are able to write something for everything they hear, they should be able to write any word they can say.

Blending (Sample)

Teacher: "Point to the picture of the /w/ . . . /i/ . . . /g/, and say the word."

The students in each dyad point to the picture of the wig, and say *"wig."*

Phoneme Association (Sample)

Teacher: "Point to the picture with the /a/ sound in the middle, and say the name of the picture."

The students in each dyad point to the picture of the ham, and say *"ham."*

Teacher: "Tell me another word with the /a/ sound in the middle of the word."
The students may say words like *pan, gas, cap, lamp, sack, bad.*

Phoneme Segmentation (Sample)

Teacher: "Tell me the middle sound of bed, /b/ . . . /e/ . . . /d/."
Students: "/e/."

Phoneme Manipulation (Sample)

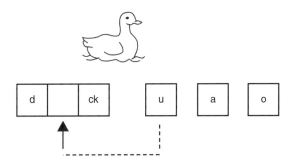

1. *Teacher:* "Move the letter used for the /u/ sound to the blank space, so you can make the word, /d/. . . /u/. . . /k/."

The students move the *u* to the blank space:

2. *Teacher:* "Move the letter used for the /e/ sound to the blank space, so you can make the word, /p/. . . /e/. . . /n/."

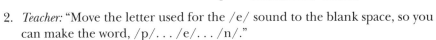

Students:

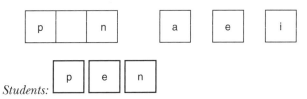

Continue this activity using the words *pan,* and *pin.*

Phoneme to Symbol (Sample)

1	2	3	4

1. *Teacher:* "Write the letter we use for the /l/ sound in box 1."

1	2	3	4
l			

"Write the letter we use for the /u/ sound in box 2."

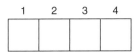

"Write the letter we use for the /n/ sound in box 3."

1	2	3	4
l	u	n	

"Write the letters we use for the /ch/ sound in box 4."

1	2	3	4
l	u	n	ch

"What word did we write?"

2. *Teacher:* "Write the letter we use for the /s/ sound."
   The students write *s.*

   Teacher: "Next, write the letter we use for the /t/ sound."
   The students write *st.*

   Teacher: "Next, write the letter we use for the /o/ sound."
   The students write *sto.*

   Teacher: "Lastly, write the letter we use for the /p/ sound."
   The students write *stop.*

   Teacher: What word did you write? If you have any trouble, say all of the sounds in the word, and blend the sounds together."

   Students: "stop."

3. *Teacher:* "Write the word *wish.* Listen to the sounds in the word, and then write letters for the sounds. You may need to use some of your consonant and vowel charts if you have forgotten the letters to write."

You may have noticed that the three "phoneme to symbol" samples above included the writing of words with consonant blends *(st)* and consonant digraphs *(ch, sh)*. At this point in the children's instruction, they should be ready to write words containing these phonics elements.

Other Phonemes and Graphemes

Figure 6.7 contains other phonemes and graphemes for children to learn. It includes consonant and vowel digraphs (two letters representing one sound), vowel diphthongs (gliding vowel sounds), and murmur diphthongs (*r*-controlled vowels).

The words in Figure 6.7 introduce children to consonant digraph graphemes and the phonemes they represent (*dish, chain, them, tooth, ring*); vowel digraph graphemes and the sounds associated with them (*book, zoo, rain, jeep, soap, tie*); vowel diphthong digraphs (*boy, trout*); and murmur diphthongs (*fork, girl, yarn, bear*).

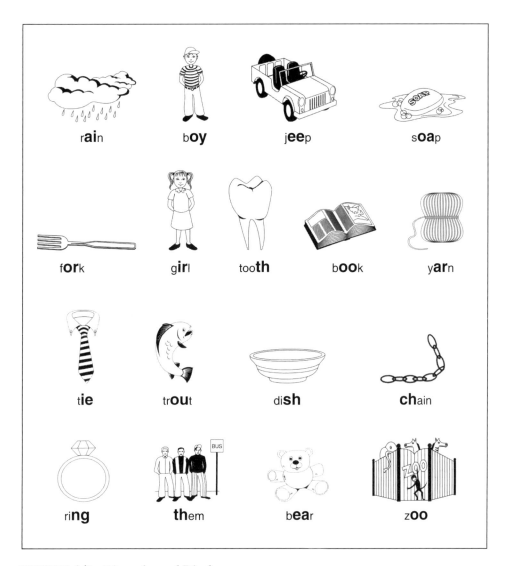

FIGURE 6.7 Digraphs and Dipthongs

The reference words listed in Figures 6.2, 6.4, 6.5, 6.6, and 6.7 provide children with the graphemes they need to write 44 of the 45 phonemes used to make English words. The only phoneme that cannot be written from the graphemes provided is /zh/, which is represented by the letter *s* in the word *treasure*. Therefore, the children who go through this training should be able to write any word they can segment into phonemes. This enables them to engage in writing activities with confidence, and to be able to concentrate on what they want to say without worrying about spelling. They know that they are not always spelling the words the way adults do, or that they, themselves, will be able to do when their literacy abilities improve. However, they learn to love writing and their writing, spelling, and reading abilities improve in the process.

Two research studies support these observations. The first study (Eldredge & Baird, 1996) compared the writing of 23 first-grade children, who were given this training in kindergarten, with the writing of 26 first-grade children who were taught to write through the Language Experience Approach during the same period of time.

Samples of children's writing taken in February of their first-grade year indicated that the training provided for the experimental group was extremely effective. The children in this group were significantly better writers than those in the control group. Their compositions revealed that they were at developmentally higher writing stages; they spelled more total words correctly in their compositions (51 versus 36), and they spelled more unique or different words correctly (23 versus 17). Both of these differences were statistically significant (.03 level).

The experimental students' compositions contained more words (72 versus 48); more unique or different words (40 versus 28); more difficult words (6 versus 3); and more sentences (11 versus 6) than the compositions of children in the control group. All of these differences were statistically significant (.03 to .002 level). The experimental children's holistic "quality of writing" scores were also significantly larger (36 versus 21). The effect sizes on all of these measures were large. The results of this experiment suggest that teaching young children to spell words by sounds can be very effective.

The second study (Funke, 1997) examined the effects of this training on 32 first-grade students at risk for reading failure, during a six-week period. The experimental students were compared with a matched control group who received special training in "assisted reading." Significant differences were found in both phonemic awareness growth and basic reading skills, in favor of the experimental group.

Application Activities

1. Visit a kindergarten classroom and select a child, or locate a kindergarten-age child in your own circle of acquaintances. Obtain permission to try phonemic awareness training lessons with this child. Use one of the early phonemic awareness training lessons. Share the results of this experience with the parent or teacher involved, and with your colleagues.
2. Without the help of the text, see if you can identify the 45 sounds used in speech. Try to identify the various ways we "spell" each sound in the English language.
3. Develop a plan for implementing a writing program in either kindergarten, first, or second grade.

Chapter 7

Decoding Instruction:
Word Recognition,
Analogy, and Context

Social Mediation and Scaffolding

Sociolinguists believe that language learning is a social process (Vygotsky, 1978, 1986). We live with and around people, and we use language to communicate with each other in a variety of different social settings. Even young children use the language to communicate and share experiences with others. All of us learn early in life that there is power in being able to use language. We use language so we can meet our needs, control other people's actions, acquire information, share information, and so on (Halliday, 1973). According to sociolinguists, we learn how to effectively use language as we attempt to use it with other people.

Sociolinguists also believe that as adults interact with children, they systematically help them become increasingly more sophisticated language users. For example, Bruner (1978) claimed that parents contributed to children's language development by expanding and extending their talk. If a child said, "Leg hurt?" a parent might respond with, "Yes, Mother's leg hurts because she fell down." Bruner used the term **scaffold** to describe these parent interactions because they helped to move children to higher levels of language understanding, eventually raising their level of language development. Scaffolds are supports that mature language users provide for children to stimulate their language development to more complex levels. Any mature language user (parent, teacher, or older student) can provide scaffolds for children as they learn. Rosenshine and Meister (1992) offered the following definition: "Scaffolds are forms of support provided by the teacher (or another student) to help students bridge the gap between their current abilities and the intended goal. . . . Instead of providing explicit steps, one supports, or scaffolds, the students as they learn the skill" (p. 26).

Vygotsky (1978) used the term **zone of proximal development** to describe how children learn through their social interactions with adults. According to Vygotsky, the zone of proximal development is that level just beyond children's actual development. When mature language users, such as teachers, consistently help children perform language tasks at their zone of proximal development, where they cannot function independently, they eventually become able to perform at that level without support. Then, as teachers move children to a new zone of proximal development and work with them at that level, they "scaffold" them, leading them to a still higher level.

Social mediation is the term used to describe the scaffolding process mature language users use with children as they perform language tasks with them at their zone of proximal development. Teachers *mediate* students' learning in a *social* setting by helping them perform language tasks at their *zone of proximal development*, and then they *scaffold* them to higher language tasks when their language development level rises.

Social mediation involving the concept of scaffolding has been used effectively in both vocabulary (May, 1994) and comprehension (Pearson & Fielding, 1991) instruction. There is also a role for social mediation in informal and formal decoding instruction. The assisted reading strategies, the shared book experience, shared music and rhythm experiences, literature book activities, the Language Experience Approach, and writing activities described in Chapter 9 are all informal decoding strategies utilizing some form of social mediation. The formal phonics lessons presented in Chapter 10 also utilize social mediation. In both situations, children, in a "psychologically safe" environment, are assisted to perform tasks they cannot perform independently until they are able to perform those tasks without adult support.

Decoding Strategies

Decoding, the processes readers use to translate written text into either speech or inner speech, involves both a fast translation process called word *recognition,* and slower processes called word *identification.* Word recognition is the decoding process used by proficient readers. Word recognition implies an accurate, rapid, and automatic recognition of printed words. Utilization of various word identification strategies, along with some word recognition, is associated with less proficient readers. (See Chapter 2 for a fuller discussion of decoding.)

Words not recognized may be identified by readers through the use of strategies readers develop themselves, or through strategies teachers teach them to employ: a) analogy, b) context, c) phonics, d) morphemic analysis, and e) syllabic analysis/phonics. Word identification strategies are considered interim strategies, employed only because word recognition abilities have not developed sufficiently for accurate, automatic, rapid decoding.

In this chapter, we will discuss three decoding strategies: a) sight word recognition, b) identifying words by analogy, and c) using contextual information to identify words. In Chapter 8, we will discuss using phonics to identify single-syllable words, using morphemic analysis to identify words, and using phonics to identify polysyllabic words.

Sight Word Recognition

Sight word recognition is a near-instantaneous recognition of written words. It does not refer to a global, whole-word recognition process, based upon word "shape," as some reading educators propose. It is the recognition of words based upon each word's unique sequence of letters.

Skilled readers have stored the written representations of many words in their lexical memories. When they see a particular letter sequence, the word associated with that letter sequence is immediately called to mind as inner speech, along with the meaning(s) previously attached to it. This is called sight word recognition, or simply word recognition. It occurs very rapidly, enabling skilled readers to hold the inner speech obtained from word recognition in short-term memory until they have apprehended complete sentences.

There are many different instructional approaches available to help readers develop the ability to recognize words by sight, both informal and formal. All approaches are built on the same basic principle: teachers must provide children with opportunities to see the written representation of words frequently enough for the letter sequences of those words to become firmly established in lexical memory.

Issues of Word Frequency

Estimates of the number of words existing in the English language vary from 500,000 to 750,000, depending on whether one includes inflected word forms and word variants. Some English words are considered *high-frequency words,* meaning that they are used frequently in both spoken and written discourse. The identification of high-frequency words was considered important in the past because both writers of basal readers and teachers had to determine which words should be taught as sight words. Identifying these words is considered important today because of their impact on children's reading fluency, and on word identification utilizing contextual information.

Over the past 60 years or so, many studies have been conducted to identify the most frequently used words in print (Carroll, Richman, & Davies, 1971; Dolch, 1936, 1948; Horn, 1926; Kucera & Francis, 1967; Rinsland, 1945; Thorndike & Lorge, 1944;) and to assess the speaking and listening vocabularies of children (Dale & O'Rourke, 1976; Hopkins, 1979; Moe, Hopkins, & Rush, 1982; Wepman & Hass, 1969). Studies have also been conducted to identify those words "easy" for elementary school children so readability formulas could be developed (Dale & Chall, 1948; Harris & Sipay, 1980).

Word frequency research reveals that a relatively small number of English words account for most of the words children encounter in spoken and written discourse. Fry (1980) claimed that one-half of the written material available for children to read is composed of 100 words and their common variants. Walker (1979) claimed that his list of 1,000 high-frequency words, plus their variants and derivatives, accounted for about 85 percent of the more than 5 million words of running text analyzed in the Carroll, Davies, and Richman (1971) study.

The Carroll et al. study was one of the most extensive word frequency studies ever conducted. Words from 1,657 publications used in grades three through nine, covering a broad range of content areas, were counted, sorted, and listed in rank order by computer, and the results were published in the *American Heritage Word Frequency Book.* Walker's (1979) 1,000 high-frequency words were taken from this book. Walker combined the frequencies of a base word (e.g., *jump*) and all of its variants (e.g., *jumps, jumping, jumped*), whereas the book listed each word variant frequency separately. Walker (1979, p. 804) believed that the base word was the vital element in word recognition. This belief is interesting, and sounds reasonable, but needs to be substantiated by research. There is little doubt that the recognition of base words aids in the identification of words containing those elements. However, the vital element in word recognition, according to the most recent literature on the subject, is each word's unique letter sequence.

The rapid recognition of frequently used words is not the only factor related to fluent reading, but is essential. The instantaneous recognition of frequently used words is also essential for the identification of words through context. Readers must be able to recognize the words around the unfamiliar one in order to use the contextual information available for its identification. As Walker reasoned, " . . . if a student had instant recognition control of each of these thousand words, he or she would seldom meet a reading passage in which more than one word per sentence would need to be decoded by use of context and letter–sound association" (p. 804).

The Carroll et al. study analyzed word usage in a range of reading materials read by students in grades three through nine. Are the high-frequency words identified from these materials similar or different from those identified from young children's literature? In an attempt to answer the question here, I analyzed the words used in 235 primary-grade children's literature books. The books contained a total of 156,859 running words. Over 6,000 of the 156,859 words were names of people or characters, repeated many times. The 919 most frequently used words in these books comprised 85% of the running words analyzed. An examination of both studies suggests that while there are definite differences between the lists, there are also many similarities, particularly within the first 100 words on each list.

The first 100 words on the literature list comprised 55% of all the words used in the literature books analyzed. The first 300 words comprised 70.5% of all the words used. The literature book frequency list is presented in Appendix A for teachers interested in high-frequency words used in young children's books.

Editions of three first-grade basal programs (Ginn, McGraw-Hill, and Silver, Burdett, & Ginn) were analyzed along with 231 literature books used in first-grade literature-based classrooms. These reading materials contained a total of 235,930 running words. From these words over 1,400 high-frequency words were identified. The 300 most frequently used words were each used over 100 times in these materials. They comprised 72% of all the words used in the books analyzed, and the instant recognition of these words by first-grade students should enable them to read and comprehend first-grade reading material. Thirty-six words comprised 39% of all the words analyzed in the study. Each of these 36 words was used over 1,000 times in the materials analyzed: *the, and, to, a, I, said, you, in, it, of, he, was, is, on, that, she, for, can, they, his, all, what, we, will, not, little, with, my, do, but, are, at, up, her, have,* and *out.* See Figure 7.1.

A knowledge of high- and low-frequency words is important to teachers. Teachers generally want to know if their students can rapidly recognize high-frequency words since reading fluency and comprehension are directly related to this ability. Some teachers may want to implement strategies that will help students instantaneously recognize high-frequency words. Others may want to evaluate their decoding instruction in terms of its effect upon students' ability to recognize high-frequency words.

The ability to comprehend text material is also directly related to students' ability to recognize and understand low-frequency words, so teachers may want to

a	called	fun	jumped	off
about	came	garden	just	oh
after	can	gave	keep	old
again	can't	get	king	on
all	cat	girl	know	once
along	children	give	last	one
always	city	go	left	only
am	come	going	let	or
an	could	good	let's	other
and	couldn't	got	like	our
animals	cried	great	little	out
another	dad	green	live	over
any	dark	grow	long	people
are	day	had	look	picture
around	did	hand	looked	pig
as	didn't	happy	looking	place
asked	do	has	made	play
at	does	hat	make	pulled
ate	dog	have	man	put
away	don't	he	many	rabbit
baby	door	head	may	ran
back	down	hear	maybe	read
bad	each	heard	me	red
ball	eat	help	mom	ride
be	end	hen	more	right
bear	even	her	morning	road
because	ever	here	mother	room
bed	every	hill	mouse	run
been	everyone	him	Mr.	said
before	eyes	his	Mrs.	sat
began	far	home	much	saw
behind	fast	house	must	say
best	father	how	my	school
better	find	I	name	sea
big	fine	I'll	need	see
bird	first	I'm	never	she
birds	fish	if	new	show
blue	fly	in	next	sister
book	for	inside	nice	sky
books	found	into	night	sleep
box	fox	is	no	small
boy	friend	it	not	so
brown	friends	it's	nothing	some
but	frog	its	now	something
by	from	jump	of	soon

continued

FIGURE 7.1   The Eldredge Instant Word List: The 300 Most Frequently Used Words in Children's Literature Books and First-Grade Basal Readers

119

started	then	told	walked	why
stay	there	too	want	will
still	these	took	wanted	wind
stop	they	top	was	witch
stories	thing	tree	water	with
story	things	truck	way	wizard
sun	think	try	we	woman
take	this	two	well	words
tell	thought	under	went	work
than	three	until	were	would
that	through	up	what	write
that's	time	us	when	yes
the	to	very	where	you
their	toad	wait	while	you're
them	together	walk	who	your

FIGURE 7.1 *Continued*

identify difficult low-frequency words in children's text materials for prereading activities. Knowledge about word frequencies is also important for informal and formal reading assessment since teachers generally want to know if students can fluently read and comprehend text material involving both high- and low-frequency words.

Regular and Irregular Graphophonic Word Patterns

Written languages based on alphabetic systems use letters to represent word sounds, even if the letters don't consistently predict the same sounds. Teachers use the term *regular* to help them differentiate those English words spelled in predictable ways from those that are spelled in less predictable ways. Those words that are spelled in unpredictable ways are often referred to as *irregular* words.

Some teaching strategies are more appropriate for teaching regular words while others are more appropriate for irregular ones. For example, phonics instruction is generally appropriate if a word's letter–sound relationships are predictable, while sight word instruction is more appropriate if those relationships are not so predictable. In both situations, however, children should be taught to associate a word's phonemes with its graphemes since words stored in lexical memory are best established in this fashion.

The term *graphophonics* is often used in place of the word *phonics*. The morpheme "graph" (a *morpheme* is a meaning unit in a word) refers to letters and the morpheme "phonics" refers to sounds. *Graphophonics* is often used specifically to refer to letter–sound relationships within words, rather than using the broader term *phonics*.

The letter–sound relationships in most words are predictable. For example, the words *up, can, step, branch, stretch,* and *trip* all contain predictable letter–sound sequences. They are all closed-syllable words (a closed syllable is one that ends in a consonant sound) and the vowel sound in each word is short. More will be said about predictable letter–sound sequences in Chapter 8.

A smaller percentage of English words contain letter–sound relationships that are not so predictable. For example, in the words *mind, most,* and *wild* the sound represented by the vowel letter in each word is unexpected, or occurs rarely. These three words are closed syllables; therefore, short vowel sounds are generally expected rather than long sounds.

Although the vowel sounds represented by *mind, most,* and *wild* are unexpected, all of the other letter–sound relationships in the words are predictable. This is an important concept, and should not be passed by lightly. Research evidence suggests that readers store irregular words in lexical memory in the same manner as they store the regular ones (Gough & Walsh, 1991; Lovett, 1987; Treiman & Baron, 1983). That is, readers relate a word's letters with the sounds those letters represent as they store both regular and irregular words (Ehri, 1992) in lexical memory. The predictable letter–sound relationships in regular words make this storage process easy, but the rare relationships slow it down. This reasoning is supported by research indicating that irregular words are not learned as quickly as regular ones.

Sometimes the letter–sound relationships in words are difficult to predict. In these cases, the sound usually associated with a particular letter or cluster of letters is just different or unusual. For example, in the word *of* the letter *f* represents the /v/ sound rather than the /f/ sound usually associated with it. Other examples of words containing letters that are pronounced differently than expected are: *m<u>a</u>ny, fr<u>o</u>nt, w<u>or</u>k.*

Children learn to recognize many high-frequency words, both regular and irregular, through the use of the informal decoding strategies discussed in Chapter 9. Repeated exposures to high-frequency words in meaningful reading may eventually lead students to recognize them by sight. If students do not learn them through these means, however, explicit phonics instruction and/or sight word instruction can help solve the problem.

Brief but meaningful phonics instruction will help children learn how speech sounds normally map onto print. Brief but meaningful sight word instruction will help children learn to recognize graphophonically irregular words not learned through assisted reading strategies. Such instruction will therefore complement the decoding knowledge students acquire through informal decoding strategies, and may give students insights into the alphabetic principle and unusual letter–sound relationships not always perceived by students using informal, holistic reading strategies.

Some teachers may want help determining whether students are learning irregular words through the use of informal decoding strategies. Appendix B contains 275 high-frequency irregular words drawn from the 919 high-frequency words derived from children's literature books. This list can be used by teachers to determine if students are able to instantaneously recognize graphophonically irregular high-frequency words after extensive involvement in the informal decoding activities described in Chapter 9, and also to determine which words need to be explicitly taught when the time for such instruction seems appropriate.

The list in Appendix 2 comprises about 30% (29.9) of the high-frequency words from which it was drawn, which does not reflect the true proportion of irregular to regular words in the language. The percentage is inflated for two reasons. First, the number of irregular words occurs proportionately more in the first 300 high-frequency words than anywhere else. Second, there are many words with recognizable letter–sound patterns on the lists that some researchers would consider consistent enough to be considered regular. For example, the letter *a* generally represents the vowel sound heard at the beginning of the word *all* when it is followed by an *l* or *r*, and when preceded by a *w*. Words on irregular word lists consistent with this pattern include *water, called, also, small, warm, tall, talking, walrus, wants,* and *watching.*

Other graphophonics patterns on the lists that some researchers consider regular are: the phonogram *ome* frequently says /um/—*some, come, something, sometimes, comes, coming, someone, becomes, become, somebody;* when *or* is preceded by a *w, or* represents the /ir/ sound—*words, work, word, world, working, works;* the *o* in the phonogram *old* represents the long *o* sound—*old, told, cold, hold, gold, sold, holding;* and the letters *oul* represent the same sound as the letters *oo* in the word *wood*—*would, could, should, couldn't, wouldn't.*

Teaching Sight Words

When you determine that explicit sight word instruction is needed for any student or group of students, you may want to teach brief sight word lessons according to the following model. Such lessons should take no more than 10 minutes of classroom time, and are based upon the following principles:

1. Children will more likely remember the words taught to them if those words are meaningful to them.
2. Children will more likely retain words if they focus on the words' letter sequences along with the sounds represented by those letter sequences.
3. The likelihood that children will remember words will be enhanced if they see each word taught at least six times during the lesson.
4. Children will more likely remember words if teachers explicitly emphasize any unusual letter–sound relationships.
5. Children will more likely retain words if they see them in context.
6. The likelihood that children will remember specific words will be enhanced if teachers involve their senses of touch, sight, and sound while learning each word's letter–sound sequences.

Model Lesson

Step 1: Select three or four words students need to learn from the irregular word list or from some other source (example: *any, come, move*). Write each word in manuscript form on the chalkboard. Read each word as you write it. Distribute three blank tagboard cards for each student or student team to use to make word cards. Ask the students to write each word on one of the cards provided for that purpose. Supervise this process carefully, making sure that students spell each word correctly.

Step 2: Point to the first word on the chalkboard (example: *any*). Read the word. Ask the students to read the word. Ask them to find the card on their desks that has the same word written on it and hold it up so you can see it. Repeat this process with the other two words.

Step 3: Ask the students to create several sentences using the three target words. As the students dictate the sentences, write each in manuscript form on the chalkboard. Help students who have difficulty thinking of sentences. After dictating each sentence, ask the students to read it while you point to each word. When you come to the new words, underline them (example: I don't have <u>any</u> crayons in my desk).

Step 4: Ask the students to trace each letter on the *any* card with their fingers, naming each letter as they trace it. When they finish tracing the last letter, ask them to say the word once more. Repeat this process with the other two words.

Step 5: Ask the students to write the target words in manuscript form on a piece of paper. (Remind them not to look at the words on the chalkboard or on their desks.) After writing, have them check the words against their word cards for accuracy.

Step 6: Ask the students to read the sentences on the chalkboard again. Help them with any words they may have forgotten. However, they should be able to read the underlined words without any help.

Step 7: Ask the students to copy each sentence in manuscript form in a special notebook or on a sheet of paper for reading to their parents or some other person that day. Have them save the sentences so they can read them periodically.

Step 8: Refer to the words on the chalkboard again. Point out the distinguishing characteristics of each word. (For example, the word *come* is a word that looks like it should be pronounced /kōm/. However, the letter *o* in the word represents the /u/ sound rather than the /ō/ sound.) Say the sounds of each word as you point to the letters representing those sounds. (For example, for the word *come*, say /k/../u/../m as you point to the letters *c o me*.) Ask the students to say the sounds of each word as you point to the letters representing those sounds.

Step 9: Ask the students to place their word cards in front of them. Do not let them see the written word. As you say each word, the students should pick up the appropriate card and hold it up for you to see. Go through the word cards several times.

When you finish this step, ask the students to file their word cards in a special container (a recipe box works well) to be used later to construct sentences, to use in word games, or to review.

Identifying Words by Analogy

When children encounter unknown words they often identify them by analogy, associating word parts in the unfamiliar words with word parts in familiar words. For example, the unfamiliar word *tame* might be identified by associating it with the familiar word *name*. Then by substituting the *n* in *name* with *t,* the new word can be identified. After associating the ending analogs in *tame* and *name,* some children might even associate the sound represented by the letters *ta* in the word *tame* with those found in the word *tape.* Ending analogies (rimes) seem to be easiest for children to access. However, it appears that readers of all ages associate patterns whether at the beginning (**back**, **bat**), middle (*peach*, *team*), or end (**poach**, *coach*) when identifying unknown words by analogy.

Interesting reciprocal relationships seem to exist among various decoding abilities. Children are able to identify words by analogy only when they have fairly large sight vocabularies since they must be able to find patterns in known words to associate with those found in unknown words. However, subsequent sight word recognition is enhanced when readers begin to recognize familiar analogs in unknown words; these words need fewer exposures for storages in lexical memory. Finally, phonics knowledge seems to be necessary for both word recognition (Ehri & Wilce, 1983, 1985) and word identification by analogy (Ehri & Robbins, 1992). Activities emphasizing onsets (*tap*) and rimes (*tap*) seem to help word identification by analogy (National Reading Panel, 2000), and phonics instruction helps the learning of the regular graphophonic language patterns because its instructional focus is on letter–sound sequences. As students become more consciously aware of basic letter–sound sequences, their ability to recognize analogs increases.

Several researchers have suggested that reading by analogy does not develop until after first or second grade (Manis, Szeszulski, Howell, Horn, Marsh, Friedman, Desberg, & Saterdahl, 1981; Marsh, Friedman, Welch, & Desberg, 1981, 1986; Zinna, Liberman, & Shankweiler, 1986). However, it appears that even young children can identify words by analogy if they have a sufficient store of familiar words in memory (Ehri & Robbins, 1992; Goswami, 1986, 1988).

Analogy Identification Activities

The letter substitution activities, frequently found in teaching materials written by implicit phonics advocates, help students identify common rimes students frequently access for the identification of unknown words by analogy. Furthermore, these activities also help teach and reinforce letter–sound relationships found in the initial position of words.

Begin letter substitution activities by writing a word containing a common word ending (rime) on the chalkboard: *cake*. Then write ___*ake* under the word *cake*. For example,

cake

_*ake*

Pointing to the word *cake*, say, "This word is *cake*. Tell me what letter I need to write in the blank space below the word *cake* to make the word *rake*." This activity could be continued by using the following words: *bake, fake, lake, make, sake, take, wake,* and *quake.*

Using Contextual Information to Identify Words

If students' word recognition abilities are fairly substantial, and if they have been taught that reading should be meaningful, they may not need to recognize every word in a sentence in order to understand the message the author intends to convey. Furthermore, those few words children do not recognize may be identified by deriving contextual information from the sentences containing them.

When using contextual information for word identification, students are not technically unlocking the alphabetic code. Instead, they are identifying words by making "intelligent guesses." Those guesses are based upon readers' knowledge of syntax, graphophonics, and semantics. Syntax refers to the structure of the sentence, and each word's function in the sentence. Graphophonics refers to words' letter–sound relationships. Semantics refers to word meanings. The process children employ to identify unfamiliar words by using these three language cueing systems is called **contextual analysis.**

Effective readers use contextual information to determine the unfamiliar word's function. Is the unfamiliar word a naming word, a describing word, or an action word? Sentence cues suggest the word's function. For example, "The young man took off his shoes and socks, rolled up his pant legs, and went wading in the _____." The missing word names some place where the young man went wading, and is therefore a naming word.

Readers also use graphophonics information; they look at the initial letter in an unfamiliar word, think of the sound associated with that letter, and think of words beginning with that sound. Readers also use semantic information along with the graphophonic information obtained. If students know the meanings of all the other words used in the sentence, they can use that information to eliminate word options that begin with the "right sound," but just don't make sense in a particular sentence.

Readers use whatever information they can acquire to make intelligent guesses at unknown words in specific sentences. They do not retrieve information in any particular sequence, nor are they always able to retrieve information from all three cueing systems. However, the thinking processes involved when using contextual analysis communicate to students that reading involves meaning, plus these thinking processes help students identify unfamiliar words quickly, much quicker than when using phonics.

Read the following sentence: "The young man took off his shoes and socks, rolled up his pant legs, and went wading in the l _____." Effective readers could use their syntax knowledge to conclude that the unknown word is a noun or naming word. They could use their graphophonics knowledge to conclude that the unknown word begins with the /l/ sound, and they could use their semantics or vocabulary knowledge to make sure that the word selected makes sense in the sentence. They might ask themselves, "What 'naming' word, beginning with the letter *l*, would make sense in this sentence?"

Contextual analysis has been called the "supervisor" of all of the other word identification strategies because its major focus is on meaning. Readers should verify all words identified using other strategies (analogy, phonics, morphemic analysis, or syllabic analysis with phonics) by asking the question, "Does the word make sense in this sentence?"

Teaching Children to Use Contextual Information

If children have difficulty identifying words in context, consider teaching them how to make logical word guesses from the contextual information available in sentences. The most important of the three text cues is the *semantic,* or vocabulary, cue since contextual analysis is based on logic and meaning. Therefore, the first question you want to teach students to ask is, "What word would make sense in this sentence and the rest of the text?"

Another language cue is *syntax.* The syntax cue helps students identify the function of a word in a sentence. Is the word functioning as a name, an action, or is it serving a describing function in the sentence? For example, nouns are naming words, verbs are action words, and adjectives and adverbs are describing words. Therefore, the question students should be taught to ask should include the syntax dimension, "What naming (or describing or action) word would make sense in this sentence and the rest of the text?"

There might be many words that would be semantically and syntactically appropriate in a particular sentence. Therefore, students should also be taught to use *graphophonic* cues as well. For example, consider the logical word options for the following sentence: "Maria went boating in the _____." The words *ocean, lake, water, river,* and *pond* are all naming words, and all of them make sense in the sentence. However, if students learn to consider the sound of the first letter of the unknown word, then they reduce the number of acceptable options. Therefore, students should be taught to ask themselves questions focusing on all three language cueing systems. In the sentence above, if the unknown word began with the letter *o,* students might ask themselves, "What naming word beginning with the letter *o* would make sense in this sentence and the rest of the text?"

Context clues, of course, have limitations. First, students must be able to recognize all of the words around the unknown word they are trying to identify. If students' sight vocabulary skills are limited, contextual analysis becomes an ineffective strategy, as they will be unable to derive the information needed to use it. Second, sometimes more than one word fits the syntactic, semantic, and graphophonic clues in the text. For example, consider the options for the following sentence: "The young man took off his shoes and socks, rolled up his pant legs, and went wading in the p_____." The words *pond, pool,* and *puddle* are all nouns, they all make sense, and they all begin with the letter *p.*

Because of the limitations of contextual analysis, you should also teach students phonics strategies to supplement it. Effective phonics teaching will help students both sound out words and speed up their word recognition development.

In spite of its limitations, contextual analysis is effective, and it is efficient. A *modified cloze* activity is an excellent way to help children learn to use the three language cueing systems necessary for the identification of unfamiliar words. The following modified cloze activity was adapted from the children's book, *I Will Not Go to Market Today,* by Harry Allard, illustrated by James Marshall (Dial, 1981). In the activity, key words found in the original story (*looked* and *blizzard*) have been substituted with synonyms (*gazed* and *storm*) for two reasons. First, the activity should *not* replace children's experiences with the story. The story should be read and enjoyed by children before introducing the modified cloze activity. By using synonyms, the children will not be able to identify the omitted words from memory. Second, since children may remember the original words used in the story, the activity will also enhance children's vocabulary abilities by helping them associate words with similar meanings.

You might want to introduce the modified cloze activity to students as a total-class activity. If you do, enlarge and display the portion of the story you are using so everyone can read it together. When you come to a blank space students should be taught to say "blank" and then read the rest of the sentence. After reading the sentence, model the questioning strategy you hope students will eventually adopt when reading by themselves. For example, read the first three sentences as they are written. Read the fourth sentence as, "Fenimore B. Buttercrunch 'blanked' out the window." Then say, "What action word beginning with the letter *g* would make sense in this sentence?" Help students use the semantic information, "out the window," to help them identify the word *gazed*. (Students might select the word *glanced*, instead of *gazed*. If they do, compliment them for their reasoning, but tell them to identify a word that begins with the single consonant *g*.)

After students have learned how to ask the right questions, provide them with modified cloze activities they can complete in small cooperative learning groups (two or three students).

I Will Not Go to Market Today

Fenimore B. Buttercrunch awoke one morning to find there was no jam for his morning toast and tea. "No jam!" he said. "I must go to market today."

Fenimore B. Buttercrunch g_____ out the window. There was a
          (verb)

st_____ raging. "I cannot go to market today," he said.
  (noun)

Context and the Alphabetic Principle

Goodman (1967) developed his "psycholinguistic guessing game" concept by watching children read. From his observations he concluded that children selectively used three cueing systems—graphophonic, syntactic, and semantic—as they sought meaning from written text. He embraced a theory of reading that placed more importance on readers' use of prediction, print sampling, and context than upon word recognition abilities. He reasoned that meaning-oriented readers do not need to process every letter of every word or even to recognize all words in a text to get meaning from print. Readers who seek meaning as they read, he believed, will focus more on syntax and semantic cues than on the graphophonic cues.

Goodman therefore based his model on the premise that readers predict words by means of cues provided by context and then confirm or refute their predictions by the print samples that follow. He encouraged teachers to help students develop and use prediction skills, deriving the meanings of words from context cues and confirming or refuting their predictions with further reading. His message to teachers was simple: Meaning is the major reading focus, so teachers should not be too concerned about decoding errors as long as those errors are syntactically and semantically appropriate to the text being read.

Most of what Goodman taught is sound. However, the decoding errors children make, even though those errors are syntactically and semantically appropriate, must not be ignored. Errors that are graphophonically inappropriate must be addressed. Research suggests that phonemic awareness and phonics knowledge are much more important in the reading process than Goodman realized.

The written language system is based upon the alphabetic principle, involving phonemes and graphemes. Even the use of context is dependent upon graphophonic knowledge.

Regardless of the importance of context, the importance of graphophonic knowledge should not be minimized. Good readers use both. Consider the following information about the use of each. First, the use of context for the identification of words is not a variable separating good readers from poor readers, nor is it a cause of reading failure (Stanovich, 1992). Even less skilled readers make substantial use of contextual information to help them identify written words (Nicholson, Lillas, & Rzaska, 1988; Simpson & Foster, 1986; Stanovich, West, & Freeman, 1981; West & Stanovich, 1978).

Second, studies have shown that the effect of context on word recognition speed decreases with age, grade level, word recognition ability, and stimulus quality (see Stanovich, 1984, 1986 for reviews).

Third, *poor* readers tend not to fully analyze the interior components of words (i.e., they seem to lack concern for word details beyond the beginning of the word) (Venezky, 1976).

Fourth, eye movement studies have revealed that the time required for *fluent* readers to recognize words in and out of context is nearly the same, and that word length and word familiarity, not context, account for much of the variation of eye fixations (see Adams, 1990; Just & Carpenter, 1987; Rayner & Pollatsek, 1989; Stanovich, 1991).

Fifth, research indicates that *fluent* readers sample the letter sequences in words rather completely, even when reading fairly predictable words (Just & Carpenter, 1980, 1987; Rayner & Pollatsek, 1989). Good readers do not reduce their sampling of letter sequences in words when context is present, nor are they in the habit of skipping difficult words (Stanovich, 1992).

Sixth, even though fluent readers are better than poor readers in language prediction abilities, they rely less on context to identify words as they read (Perfetti, Goldman, & Hogaboam, 1979).

Seventh, research suggests that while good readers use both graphic and contextual cues when reading, words' *spelling patterns* are most important to fluent reading (Tulving & Gold, 1963). Better readers are so fast and accurate at word recognition that they do not need to rely on contextual information. It is only when graphophonic knowledge breaks down that good readers resort to contextual information for word identification (Stanovich, 1980; Tulving & Gold).

This research also helps us understand why Goodman observed young children using all three cueing systems (graphophonic, syntax, and semantic) to identify unfamiliar words. Readers with undeveloped word recognition skills would need to compensate for that deficit by using contextual information. As readers' word recognition skills improve, context would have less effect on recognition speed as context would only be referred to when word recognition fails. Biemiller (1970) supports this reasoning, finding in a longitudinal study of first graders' oral reading errors that progress in reading was determined in part by how early children began to shift their attention to the letters within words. In addition, Perfetti's (1985, 1986) verbal efficiency theory maintains that children will have difficulty reading if they cannot recognize individual words quickly and accurately. Research supports his position (see Adams, 1990; Gough, Ehri, & Treiman, 1992).

Researchers now generally believe that a) written words are identified by their spellings (orthography); b) meanings of words (semantics) are associated with their pronunciations (phonology); and c) meaning ambiguities (problems distinguishing meanings of multiple-meaning words) are resolved by the context in which the words occur. The brain processes all of these sources of information in parallel, or simultaneously, but it is the "orthographic processor," using Adams' (1990) words, "that kicks the system in." This parallel distributed processing good readers employ while reading occurs very quickly. The brain is capable of recognizing written words and associating meaning with them in a fraction of a second.

Application Activities

1. The 36 alphabetized words that follow are considered to be the most frequently used words in young children's books: *a, all, and, are, at, but, can, do, for, have, he, her, his, I, in, is, it, little, my, not, of, on, out, said, she, that, the, they, to, up, was, we, will, what, with,* and *you.* Analyze one or two pages in any children's book to determine how often these words occur.

2. Use the word list in Appendix B and assess a first- or second-grade child's irregular word sight vocabulary. Ask the child to read the words on the list as quickly as he or she can. If any word is not instantly recognized (within a second or less), count the word wrong. When the child misses a total of five words, stop. How far into the list did the child go before making five errors?

3. Identify a first- or second-grade child who needs sight word instruction. Following the nine steps outlined in this chapter, teach four high-frequency irregular sight words to this child.

4. The ability to use analogy as a decoding strategy is dependent upon a child's word recognition vocabulary. Visit an elementary classroom. Ask the teacher to identify an "excellent" reader and a "poor" reader. Use the following analogy activity with each child:
   (a) Write the word *deep* on the chalkboard. Say, "This word is *deep.*"
   (b) Write the word *keep* underneath the word deep. Say, "What is this word?"
   (c) Repeat step b using the following words: *peep, weep, creep, sheep, sleep, sweep,* and *steep.*

   Write a paragraph describing what you have concluded from this experience about word identification by analogy.

Chapter 8

Decoding Instruction: Phonics, Morphemic Analysis, and Syllabic Analysis

Phonics

Traditional Phonics

Phonics has traditionally been perceived as a set of "skills" that should be taught to children. These skills are usually organized in a certain order, and then integrated into an instructional program for children from kindergarten through grade three or beyond. Explicit phonics programs are generally completed before grade three, while many implicit programs extend into grade six. "Scope and sequence charts" outline the skills to be taught, and the grades in which they are to be introduced, reinforced, and mastered. Traditional phonics instruction consists of teachers teaching children some phonics skill followed up by activities designed to help them practice, or reinforce, the skill. Worksheets or ditto sheets are the most popular vehicles used to practice skills.

Phonics rules are often taught to children so they can determine when to associate specific sounds with letters or letter clusters, even though there is little evidence that children apply those rules to improve their reading performance. In explicit phonics basals, children are taught how to "say" the sounds of letters, and how to blend those sounds together so unfamiliar written words can be identified by "sounding them out." In implicit phonics basals, children are taught how to associate sounds with letters so they can use that knowledge to identify unfamiliar words through context.

In many traditional phonics programs, only the children who can read are able to do the phonics lessons. In these situations, it is difficult to justify taking valuable classroom time for phonics lessons. For example, a teacher, using one implicit phonics program, taught children the two sounds represented by the letters *ea*. The children were told that the *ea* vowel team represented either the vowel sound heard in the word *teach* or the vowel sound heard in the word *bread*. Children were then given examples of words, each containing one sound or the other. After the examples, various words were written on the chalkboard and read for the children. The children were asked to identify whether the vowel sound in each word was like the sound heard in *teach* or *bread*. They were shown how to place marks over the vowels to differentiate between the two vowel sounds (a breve to designate the short sound of *e*, and a macron to designate its long sound).

When the teaching part of the lesson was finished, the children were given a worksheet to complete. The worksheet contained about 15 words. Each word contained an *ea* vowel team. The students were instructed to read the words, listen to the vowel sound in each word, and identify whether it was the sound heard in *teach* or *bread*. They were asked to write a breve over the *e* if the vowel sound in the word was like the one heard in the word *bread* and a macron over the *e* if the vowel sound was like the one heard in the word *teach*.

The phonics lesson just described is representative of traditional phonics programs; it is not atypical. It was designed to help children associate specific sounds with the *ea* vowel team. While one may not want to argue about the lesson's intent, it is certainly justifiable to argue about the effectiveness of the lesson design. The lesson, in fact, proved to be ineffective for both good and poor readers.

Only the good readers were able to successfully complete the worksheet. The other children could not read the words, so they could not identify the vowel sounds in each word, which made it impossible for them to complete the culminating assignment. Remember that phonics knowledge is supposed to help children "sound out" words when words are not recognized, and it is also supposed to help them improve their word recognition abilities. For the children who could already read the words on the worksheet, the lesson was a waste of time. There was no need to help them "sound out" or recognize words they could already read. For the children who could not do the culminating activity, the lesson did not help them "sound out" unfamiliar words containing the *ea* vowel team, nor did it teach them to recognize the words containing those elements.

At no time in the *ea* vowel team lesson just described, did the teacher either isolate (segment) the vowel sounds for children or teach children to isolate them. Furthermore, children were never taught to blend sounds so they could use phonics to identify unfamiliar words. Yet, there is overwhelming evidence indicating that children must master segmentation and blending before the results of phonics instruction are transferable to the reading of unfamiliar words (Fox & Routh, 1976; Jeffrey & Samuels, 1967; Jenkins, Bausell, & Jenkins, 1972; Muller, 1973), and there is strong evidence indicating that explicit phonics instruction, incorporating segmentation and blending, enhances word recognition (Adams, 1990).

Problems with Phoneme Distortion

Although research evidence tends to favor explicit phonics approaches over implicit ones, these approaches are not without problems (Anderson et al., 1985; National Reading Panel, 2000). As Anderson et al., writing for the Reading Commission, indicated, one of the problems with explicit phonics programs is the distortion of phonemes that occurs when children attempt to isolate and blend them for word identification: " . . . a problem with explicit phonics is that both teachers and children have a difficult time saying pure speech sounds in isolation. The *b* sound becomes /buh/, for instance. When figuring out a new word, the child who has been taught the sounds of letters in isolation may produce /buh-ah-tuh/ and never recognize that the word is *bat*" (1985, p. 41). It should be pointed out that the Reading Commission followed this quoted comment with a statement indicating that they were uncertain about whether the distortion problem was hypothetical or real (Anderson et al., 1985, p. 41). The National Reading Panel (2000), however, reported the same concerns:

> . . . the synthetic strategy presents two difficulties for children. One is that blending words containing stop consonants requires deleting "extra" (schwa vowel) sounds produced when letters are pronounced separately, for example, blending "tuh-a-puh" requires deleting the "uh" sounds to produce the blend "tap." The second problem is that when the sounds to be blended exceed two or three, it becomes harder to remember and manage the ordering of all those sounds, for example, blending "stuh-r-ea-m" to say "stream" (p. 2–104).

The evidence reviewed in previous chapters suggests that phoneme distortion is a problem for children. It makes the development of phonemic awareness difficult, and the application of phonics knowledge for word identification awkward.

As discussed previously, words are comprised of *coarticulated* (overlapped or merged) phonemes. (A few words, however, are single phoneme words, such as *I* and *a*.) Coarticulated phonemes are not discrete language units that children can easily hear or reproduce. Coarticulation is an advantage for speech because it enables people to create thousands of words, each distinguished from all other words by its unique sequence of phonemes, and it enables individuals to speak words rapidly. Coarticulation is a disadvantage for reading, however, because phonemes and words become distorted when readers try to isolate and blend coarticulated phonemes. This problem is particularly acute when isolating certain voiced consonant sounds. For example, when sounding out the word *dog*, the reader gets /du/ /o/ /g/, which is a distorted version of /dog/.

It is possible, however, to eliminate the phoneme distortion problem in phonics instruction and application. Furthermore, the connection between the oral and written language is more visible to young children when those distortions are eliminated. The key to the solution of the distortion problem lies in a rethinking of the syllable structure. The popular way to view syllables is to view them as comprising both an onset and a rime. In the word *dime*, the onset is the *d* and the rime is *ime*. When pronouncing onsets and rimes there is no sound distortion in the rime, but there is frequently a distortion in the onset. For example, /bu/ oks/ for *box*, and /du/ /īm/ for *dime*.

There is another way to view the structure of the syllable. Every syllable, and hence every single-syllable word, contains one vowel sound. Vowels are voiced sounds and can be articulated without any distortion. Every consonant element preceding that vowel is coarticulated with it, and can be said as a unit without any sound distortion. Furthermore, the consonant sound(s) following the vowel can be isolated without distortion. Ending consonant sounds are said no differently when isolated from, or coarticulated with, the vowel preceding it. (This is not true with beginning consonant sounds.) Therefore, all single-syllable words can be said in two parts without distorting either part, if the first isolated part ends with the vowel sound. For example, the word *box* could be said in two parts (/bo/ /ks/) without sound distortions in either part. Consider all of the following examples: *beach* = /bē/ /ch/; *church* = /chir/ /ch/; *dog* = /do/ /g/; *stand* = /sta/ /nd/; *strap* = /stra/ /p/; *rain* = /rā/ /n/; *shrub* = /shru/ /b/; and *bird* = /bir/ /d/.

The vowel is the key element in a syllable. In fact, a *syllable* is defined as a word, or part of a word, containing one vowel sound. The first part of a syllable can be viewed as the *vowel and everything in front of it,* and the second part as *everything after the vowel.*

Viewing syllables as being comprised of onsets and rimes may be useful for rhyming and other related activities. However, viewing syllables as onsets and rimes distorts the relationship between the spoken and written forms of the language when those parts are pronounced. The relationship between the spoken word *brick* and its written representation is more visible when pronouncing the syllable parts as /bri/ /k/ than when pronouncing them /bu/ /ru/ /ik/ or /bru/ /ik/. Furthermore, the former pronunciations of the syllable parts do not distort any of the phonemes in the syllable, while the latter ones do. Finally, when viewing syllable parts in the manner described herein, the letters in written words more nearly represent actual speech, rather than an abstraction of speech.

Using Phonics to Identify Single-Syllable Words

Teaching a Phonics Strategy Students Can Use

Unless students can use their phonics knowledge to improve their reading performance, there is little reason to teach it. Fortunately, readers can use phonics knowledge in two distinctively different ways. First, they may use it to help identify words through context, and second, they may use it to sound out words.

When phonics knowledge is combined with syntax and semantic knowledge, children can use contextual information to identify unfamiliar words if they also know enough sight words. A knowledge of letter–sound relationships is sufficient for students when using phonics in this manner since the sound represented by the initial letter in the word is the best graphophonic clue to use when identifying words in context. However, when using phonics knowledge to sound out words, this level of phonics knowledge is insufficient. To identify words by sounds, children must also learn how to segment the sounds represented by the letters, and they must learn how to blend those sounds.

There are limitations to the use of context as a word identification strategy. Using phonics knowledge to identify unfamiliar words in context is ineffective when children possess weak word recognition abilities; they just cannot recognize enough words to obtain the information needed for the analysis. Furthermore, when identifying words through context, students do not focus attention on the letter sequences of words sufficiently to store them in lexical memory. Hence, future word recognition is delayed unless teachers supplement contextual analysis instruction with phonics instruction requiring students to focus all of the letters within words.

Children need a word identification strategy to help them when their word recognition skills are limited and when other identification strategies fail. Phonics meets that need. The phonics strategy described herein was developed in the early 1980s and has been field tested in many classrooms since then. Research suggests that it helps students sound out unfamiliar words, and increases their ability to store written words in lexical memory (Eldredge, 1991; Eldredge & Butterfield, 1986).

Children learn to use the following steps when using phonics as a process to identify unfamiliar words:

1. Determine the vowel sound in the word, and isolate that sound.
2. Blend all of the consonant sounds in front of the vowel sound with the vowel sound.
3. Isolate the consonant sound(s) after the vowel sound.
4. Blend the two parts of the word together so the word can be identified.

The following examples demonstrate the application of this process to various types of written words:

Example 1: *dog.* First step: /o/. Second step: /do/. Third step: /g/. Fourth step: /dog/.

Example 2: *stop.* First step: /o/. Second step: /sto/. Third step: /p/. Fourth step: /stop/.

Example 3: *bend.* First step: /e/. Second step: /be/. Third step: /nd/. Fourth step: /bend/.

Example 4: *soap.* First step: /ō/. Second step: /sō/. Third step: /p/. Fourth step: /sōp/.

Example 5: *bark.* First step: /ar/. Second step: /bar/. Third step: /k/. Fourth step: /bark/.

Example 6: *shrub.* First step: /u/. Second step: /shru/. Third step: /b/. Fourth step: /shrub/.

This phonics strategy determines which phonics elements are to be taught. For example, the first step in the process requires students to determine the vowel sound in words. Therefore, children need to be taught how to identify vowel sounds in words according to the pattern or structure of the syllable. The second step requires students to blend all of the consonants occurring before the vowel sound with the vowel. There are four different consonant-vowel patterns children could encounter in this step: a) a single consonant preceding a vowel (*time*); b) a consonant blend preceding a vowel (*strap*); c) a consonant digraph preceding a vowel (*shine*); and d) a consonant digraph/consonant combination preceding a vowel (*throat*). Therefore, children need to be taught these consonant elements, and taught how to blend them with the vowel sounds following them. The third step requires students to isolate the consonant sound(s) after the vowel. The same four consonant patterns occur in step three: a) a single consonant (*job*); b) a consonant blend (*send*); c) a consonant digraph (*wish*); and d) a consonant/consonant digraph combination (*lunch*). Therefore, children need to be taught to isolate these sounds at the end of words.

Phonics Elements

The phonics elements used in teaching phonics are single vowels, vowel teams (including regular and irregular vowel digraphs, vowel diphthongs, and murmur diphthongs), single consonants, consonant digraphs, consonant blends, and *y* as a vowel and consonant. These phonics elements are used to represent, in writing, all of the phonemes utilized in the spoken language.

Much could be said about the relationships existing between phonics elements and phonemes, particularly those found in graphophonically irregular words. However, the position taken in this book is that graphophonically irregular words, if not learned through informal decoding strategies, are best taught by explicit sight word instruction which, incidentally, includes a phonics component. The unusual, rare, unpredictable, or low-frequency letter–sound relationships found in graphophonically irregular words are addressed when students have a need, so there is little reason to devote space to discuss them here. However, if the reader is interested in low-frequency letter–sound relationships, see Appendix C.

Graphophonically regular words, however, are best learned through phonics. Predictable letter–sound relationships are emphasized in phonics instruction so children can quickly apprehend these predictable patterns. The speed at which children learn to recognize new words is directly related to their familiarity with predictable letter–sound relationships. However, whether children learn words through phonics, sight word instruction, or any other strategy, they will store and retrieve them from lexical memory more accurately and efficiently if they learn to associate each word's graphemes with its phonemes. Poor readers read by partial letter cues, focusing on only a few of the letters in a word to help them remember it, and therefore, do not decode accurately and efficiently.

Vowel Phonemes and Graphemes. Vowel phonemes are voiced sounds that vibrate the human larynx when produced. Single vowel graphemes and various vowel team graphemes represent these phonemes in written words. The pattern of the written syllable or word, in which a single vowel occurs (*a, e, i, o, u,* and *y*), predicts the sound the letter represents, while the sounds represented by vowel team graphemes (*ai, ay, ea, ee, aw, au, oa, igh, ow, ew, ue, oo, oi, oy, ou, or, ar, ir, er, ur, ire, air, are, ear, ere, eer*) remain fairly constant. There are 20 English vowel phonemes represented by vowel graphemes:

/a/ *at*	/ē/ *eve, feet, eat, me*
/ā/ *ate, raid, say, ba.con*	/o/ *off, saw, fraud, ball*
/i/ *it*	/ō/ *so, oak, ode, show*
/ī/ *ice, ci.der, high*	/oo/ *book, put*
/u/ *up*	/ōo/ *moon, rude, blue, grew*
/ū/ *use, few, cue, u.nite*	/ar/ *car*
/ir/ *bird, fur, fern*	/oi/ *boy, oil*
/or/ *for*	/âr/ *hair, care, there, bear*
/ou/ *cow, found*	/īr/ *fire*
/e/ *edge, bread*	/ir/ *deer, year*

Single vowels are said to represent either long (<u>bo</u>n<u>e</u>, s<u>o</u>) or short (t<u>o</u>p) vowel phonemes. Vowel teams also represent vowel phonemes. Vowel teams can be a regular vowel digraph (s<u>oa</u>p), an irregular vowel digraph (d<u>ea</u>d), a vowel diphthong (<u>ou</u>t), or a murmur diphthong (d<u>ir</u>t).

A *vowel digraph* is a vowel team, comprised of two letters, representing one vowel sound. A vowel digraph is regular when the first vowel in the vowel team represents its long sound or letter name (*pain*). A vowel digraph is irregular when the first vowel in the vowel team represents a sound other than its long sound (*moon, book, saw, fraud, bread, blue, grew*). An inconsistent vowel team rule often taught is, "When there are two vowels in the word, the first vowel does the talking (says its own name), and the second one does the walking (is silent)." This rule describes regular vowel digraphs, but doesn't work with any of the other vowel teams.

A *vowel diphthong* is a gliding vowel sound. There are two vowel diphthong sounds, both of which are heard in the word *cowboy*. Two graphemes represent the first diphthong sound (*plow* and *out*), and two represent the second (*toy* and *coin*).

A *murmur diphthong* is a vowel followed by the letter *r*. The vowel and the *r* should be viewed as a single unit. Some phonics teachers try to separate the sounds in a murmur diphthong. However, murmur diphthongs each represent one gliding, "murmuring" vowel phoneme, and teachers and children should never attempt to separate them into two sounds. Three murmur diphthongs represent the same sound (*fir, fur, fern*). These three vowel teams are often called the /ir/ triplets. The murmur diphthong *ar* represents the sound heard in the word *car*, and the murmur diphthong *or* represents the sound heard in the word *fork*.

There are 20 vowel teams that consistently represent certain sounds and occur frequently in written words:

ir as in *sir*	*ue* as in *glue and cue*
er as in *herd*	*igh* as in *fight*
ur as in *burn*	*oy* as in *joy*
ar as in *cart*	*ea* as in *seat and bread*
or as in *sort*	*ou* as in *trout*
oi as in *join*	*ow* as in *now and crow*
oo as in *spoon and look*	*au* as in *cause*
ew as in *blew and few*	*aw* as in *lawn*
ee as in *feet*	*ai* as in *aim*
oa as in *coat*	*ay* as in *stay*

Other vowel teams are less consistent in predicting the phonemes, or occur less frequently in written words: *ie, ui, ey, ei*. I analyzed the 5,000 most frequently used words in the language and found that the vowel team *ie* represented the long sound of *e* (*piece*) about 65% of the time, and the long sound of *i* (*pie*) about 26% of the time and the short sound of *e* (*friend*) 9% of the time. The vowel team *ui* represented the long *oo* sound (*fruit*) about 67% of the time, and the short sound of *i* (*build*) about 33% of the time. The *ey* represented the long *e* sound (*key*) about 70% of the time, and the long *a* sound (*they*) about 30% of the time. The *ei* represented the long *a* sound (*vein*) about 52% of the time, the long sound of *e* (*seize*) 39% of the time, and other phonemes (*heifer*) about 9% of the time. These consistency percentages are a little higher than those found by Johnston (2001), who analyzed the 3,000 most frequently used words.

Consonant Phonemes.   Consonant phonemes can be either voiced or voiceless. Voiced sounds vibrate the larynx while voiceless sounds are produced by forcing air through the mouth in various ways. When words beginning with consonant phonemes are pronounced, those phonemes, both voiced and voiceless, are coarticulated with the vowel sounds that follow them. If teachers and children try to isolate these phonemes, particularly the voiced consonants, phoneme distortion often results. The consonant phonemes that end syllables and words, however, can be isolated without distortion.

There are 25 consonant phonemes, represented by the following graphemes:

/b/	*bat*	/zh/	*measure*
/f/	*fish*	/d/	*dog*
/h/	*had*	/g/	*go*
/k/	*kiss, cat, kick*	/j/	*jump, gem, rage, fudge*
/m/	*man*	/l/	*lamp*
/p/	*pan*	/n/	*no*
/s/	*sun, cent, geese*	/r/	*run*
/v/	*voice*	/t/	*teeth*
/y/	*yes*	/w/	*watch*
/sh/	*shoe*	/hw/	*white*
/th/	*the*	/z/	*zoo, dogs, rose*
/ng/	*sing*	/ch/	*church*
/th/	*thing*		

Consonant elements are single consonants, consonant digraphs, or consonant blends. The following *single* consonant letters are used to represent consonant phonemes: *b, c, d, f, g, h, j, k, l, m, n, p, q, r, s, t, v, w, x, y,* and *z.* The letters *c* and *x* have no sounds of their own. The letter *c* represents the /s/ sound when it is followed by an *e, i,* or *y* (*cent, fence, cycle, city*). At all other times the letter *c* represents the /k/ sound (*crack, cap, cup, cod, car, coat*). The letter *x* represents the /ks/ sound at the end of words (*six, fox*). At the end of syllables, the letter *x* sometimes represents the /gz/ sound (*exam, exit*), and sometimes the /ks/ sound (*express, explode, export*).

The letter *g* has its own sound (*go*), but when it is followed by an *e, i,* or *y* it may represent either the /j/ sound (*gem, ginger, gym*), or its own sound (*get, gift, gynecology*). However, when the letter *g* is followed by an *e* at the end of words, it always represents the /j/ sound (*huge, badge*). Also notice that the letter combinations *ge* and *dge* represent the same sound. When the vowel letter in the word represents the long sound, the /j/ sound is spelled *ge*, and when the vowel letter represents the short sound, the /j/ sound is spelled *dge*.

The letter *q* is always followed by a *u* in English words, and the *qu* represents the /kw/ sound (*quiet, quit, question*). The /k/ phoneme is represented by the letters *ck* when it follows short vowel sounds (*back, pick, sock, deck, duck*). However, when the /k/ sound is preceded by long or other vowel sounds, it is represented by the letter *k* (*take, took, bike, oak*). English words do not end with the letter *v*. Therefore, an *e* is always placed after a word ending with the /v/ phoneme (*live, have*).

The letter *y* represents a consonant sound when it is used to begin a word (*yes*) or a syllable (*canyon*). At all other times it is used to represent vowel sounds (*myth, cry, rhyme*).

Based on physiological data regarding children's speech development and the frequency at which various consonant letters are found in words, you may want to teach consonant letter–sound relationships in the following order: *m, p, s, b, t, d, f, l, r, n, w, h, c/k/, k, j, g, g/j/, c/s/, y, v, z, qu.*

Consonant digraphs are two or more consonant letters representing one consonant sound (*peach, shop, thing*). The following consonant digraphs are used to begin words or syllables: *shine, chirp, when, then, thing, phone.* With the exception of the *ph* digraph, all of the other digraphs represent unique sounds. The letters *gh* are a digraph in words such as *laugh* and *cough.* However, the few words containing this digraph are best taught as sight words. Most of the time when *gh* is used in words, it is a part of a vowel (*sigh, right*). The *wh* digraph represents the /hw/ sound heard at the beginning of the words *white, while,* and *which;* however, because of lazy speech habits over the years many individuals are now pronouncing these words the same way they pronounce words beginning with *w* (*wine, wine, was*).

The following consonant digraphs are used to end words or syllables: *teach, catch, wish, sing, with, bathe.* The *ch* and *tch* digraphs represent the same sound, but the spelling of the sound is usually *ch* when it follows long, or other vowel sounds (*reach, couch, roach*), and *tch* when it follows short vowel sounds (*stitch, batch, stretch*). There are five words that are exceptions to this spelling pattern: *much, such, rich, which, touch.* The letters *nk* found at the end of syllables or words represent a combination of the /ng/ and /k/ sounds (*bank, sink, honk*). The only difference between the pronunciations of the words *sing* /sing/ and *sink* /singk/ is the /k/ phoneme at the end of the word *sink.*

Instead of representing one sound, *consonant blends* are clusters of consonant letters representing blended consonant phonemes (*stop, bend, strap, first*). While each consonant in a consonant blend represents its own sound, it is blended with the other consonants in the cluster. Because consonant blends are blended consonant sounds, teachers and children can take them apart and put them back together when sounding out words. Consider, for example, an analysis of the phonics process described earlier in this chapter. The first step in sounding out the word *stop* would be to determine the vowel sound in the word. The sound of the letter *o* in the word *stop* is /o/ (a more detailed explanation on how to determine vowel sounds is found in the next section). The next step would be to blend all of the consonants in front of the vowel with the vowel. The sounds represented by the letters *st* when blended with the /o/ sound result in /sto/. However, children could blend the sound represented by the letter *t* with /o/ first, and get /to/, and then blend the sound represented by the letter *s* with /to/ to get /sto/. The third step in the process would be to isolate the sound represented by the letter *p*, which is /p/; and the final step would be to blend /sto/ with /p/ to get /stop/.

Consonant blends can be separated and blended back together, if children cannot initially recall the sound represented by the entire consonant cluster; however, consonant digraphs cannot be separated in this fashion. For example, if children tried to sound out the word *shop* by /o/ /ho/ /s/ /ho/ /p/, the end result would be /s/ /hop/ rather than /shop/.

Phonics Patterns

Written words are structured by patterns, and syllables within words are structured by patterns. Furthermore, many word parts (letter combinations within words) are organized in patterns. Letter, syllable, and word patterns occur repeatedly in the written language, and successful readers, consciously or subconsciously, recognize them and associate them with predictable sounds.

A knowledge of phonics patterns is important in decoding. The pattern of the written syllable, or word, informs readers whether the vowel letter in the syllable, or word, is long or short. Furthermore, readers see certain letter combination patterns within words and associate specific sounds with them. Vowel digraphs, vowel diphthongs, murmur diphthongs, and consonant digraphs are examples of letter patterns. Other letter patterns, such as *wa* (**water, want, wall**), *wor* (**work, world, worm**), and *al* (**call, already, also**), are also associated with predictable sounds.

There are about 3,000 single-syllable words in an unabridged dictionary. They are familiar to most adults. An analysis of these words reveals that there are 74 distinct syllable patterns among them. The most common pattern is the consonant-vowel-consonant-consonant pattern (CVCC) represented by such words as *just, send,* and *tell.* A little over 17% of all single-syllable words fall into this pattern.

Forty-three of the 74 patterns each represent less than 10 words; 37 represent less than 5 words; and 19 are represented by only one word—therefore, there are only 31 predominant single-syllable word patterns. A close analysis of these 31 distinct patterns reveals that many of them are variations of the same basic group. For example, all of the patterns containing only one vowel and ending in one or more consonants belong to the same group. After analyzing the 31 patterns in this manner, it was concluded that there are only four basic single-syllable word patterns in the English language.

The most frequently occurring word pattern is what is commonly referred to as the *closed* syllable: there is one vowel in the syllable and the syllable ends with a consonant sound. There are 13 variations of this pattern, and 45 percent of the words analyzed belonged to this group. The variations of the pattern are listed, according to frequency of occurrence, in descending order:

Pattern	Example
CVCC	*sand*
CVC	*cup*
CCVCC	*trash*
CCVC	*slip*
CVCCC	*witch*
CVCCe	*badge*

CCVCCC	*crutch*
CCVCCe	*grudge*
CCCVCC	*script*
VCC	*add*
VC	*up*
CCCVC	*scrap*
VCCC	*inch*

The vowel letters in closed syllable patterns generally represent short sounds. Good readers either consciously or subconsciously make this association. They may also begin to realize that short vowel sounds occur more frequently in words than long vowel sounds.

The second most frequently occurring word pattern is the *vowel team* pattern. About 37.5% of the words analyzed fell into this group. Words containing the 20 vowel teams (vowel digraphs, vowel diphthongs, and murmur diphthongs) discussed earlier in the chapter belong to this group. There are 12 variations of the pattern, given here according to frequency of occurrence, in descending order:

Pattern	Example(s)
CVVC	*seat, bird*
CCVVC	*train, stork*
CVVCC	*peach, march*
CVV	*day, car*
CCVV	*clay, scar*
CVVCe	*leave, force*
CCVVCC	*bleach, thirst*
CCVVCe	*freeze, charge*
CCCVVC	*sprain*
VVC	*air, ark*
VVCC	*each, arch*
CCCVV	*three*

About 15.8% of the words analyzed fell into the vowel-consonant-silent *e* pattern. There were only four variations of this pattern. They are, according to frequency of occurrence, in descending order:

Pattern	Example
CVCe	*nice*
CCVCe	*slave*
CCCVCe	*stride*
VCe	*ace*

The letter *e* in these word patterns does not represent any sound. It does, however, signal to the reader that the first vowel letter in the word represents its long sound.

The last syllable pattern group is commonly referred to as the *open* syllable. There is only one vowel letter in the syllable, and the syllable ends with the vowel's sound. Words in this pattern represent only about 1.5% of the single-syllable words in the language. Since the pattern occurs so infrequently one might wonder why it should be mentioned at all. If the pattern occurred only in single-syllable words, this concern would be valid. However, the pattern occurs frequently in polysyllabic words, and children need to become familiar with it so they can associate the appropriate vowel sound with the letters found in the pattern. There are two variations of the pattern:

Pattern	Example
CCV	*she*
CV	*he*

The four syllable patterns just discussed occur in both single-syllable and polysyllabic words. Since the syllable pattern helps readers predict the vowel sound represented by the vowel letters in the pattern, this knowledge is important for readers when attempting to identify both types of words. The knowledge also facilitates readers' sight word recognition and their ability to identify words by analogy.

Phonics Scope and Sequence

The phonics process can be introduced to children beginning with the first phonics lesson. Since the principle of social mediation is applied in the phonics lessons, teachers will help students perform any task they are unable to perform by themselves until they develop independence.

The phonics elements and phonics patterns to be taught are organized in a systematic fashion according to what is known about children's developmental stages of decoding (Eldredge, 2004, pp. 127–9), and the utility of the elements and patterns. Since short vowel sounds are the most frequently occurring vowel sounds in English words, and since children are able to sound out simple CVC words before they are able to sound out other patterns, it is recommended that the phonics elements and patterns be taught as follows:

1. Teach children the five short vowel sounds.
2. Teach children the sounds represented by the beginning consonant letters *m, p, s, b, t, d, f, l, r, n, w, h, c/k/, k, j, g, g/j/, c/s/, y, v, z, qu,* and teach them how to blend these consonants with any vowel sound following them.
3. Teach children to isolate the consonant sounds ending words, represented by the following consonant letters: *p, b, x, f, n, ck, k, t, m, l, d, g, ge, dge, s, z, ve,* and *ce.*
4. Teach children that syllable patterns help readers predict whether the vowel in the syllable is long or short. Teach them how to identify vowel sounds in closed, open, and vowel-consonant-*e* syllable patterns.
5. Teach children the sounds associated with the 20 vowel teams most frequently used in English words: *ir, er, ur, ar, or, au, aw, ai, ay, ee, oa, oi, oy, ea, ou, ow, oo, ew, ue,* and *igh.*
6. Teach children the sounds associated with consonant digraphs (*sh, ch, th, tch, wh, ng,* and *nk*), and help them blend the sounds represented by beginning consonant digraphs with the vowel sounds following them, and isolate those that occur at the ending of words.

7. Teach children the sounds associated with consonant blends, and teach them to blend those that begin words with the vowel sounds following them, and isolate those that occur at the ending of words. The beginning consonant blends, according to frequency of use, in American English words are *st, pr, tr, gr, pl, cl, cr, str, br, dr, sp, fl, fr, bl, sl, sw, sm, sc, thr, sk, gl, tw, scr, spr, sn, spl,* and *shr.* The ending consonant blends, according to frequency of use, are *st, nt, nd, ct, nce, nk, mp, lt, ft, nge, sk, pt, nch, nse,* and *sp.*

8. Teach children the vowel sounds represented by the letter *y,* and teach them how to determine those sounds by syllable pattern.

Morphemic Analysis

Using Morphemic Analysis for Building Vocabulary

Morphemes are meaning units. For example, in the word *unwise,* "un" is a morpheme meaning "not," and "wise" is a morpheme meaning "having or using good judgment." Morphemes may either be a root word (dis**agree**able), a prefix (**dis**agreeable), a suffix (disagree**able**), or an inflectional ending (toy**s**, church**es**, woman**'s**, boys**'**, walk**ed**, walk**ing**, walk**s**, smart**er**, smart**est**). An inflectional ending is a morpheme at the end of a root word. Inflectional endings (**s**, **es**, **s'**, **'s**, **ed**, **ing**, **er**, **est**) are used to communicate a) possession; b) plurality; c) comparison; d) tense (present, past, future); and e) person (first person, "I"; second person, "you"; and third person "he, she, they"). For example:

The boy**s** went to the store. (Plurality)

The boy**'s** shirt was torn. (Possession)

I walk**ed** to school yesterday. (Past tense)

I walk to school every day. She walk**s** to school on Fridays. (Second person)

He runs fast**er** than Brad. (Comparison)

Students are generally taught how to use morphemic analysis as a tool for improving vocabulary knowledge. It is assumed that if students know the meanings of frequently used prefixes and suffixes they will be better able to independently determine the meanings of words containing those morphemes when they are encountered in print.

The most frequently taught prefixes are:

Prefix	Meaning/s	Example
un	*not, opposite of*	*unhappy, unlock*
dis	*not, reversing of an action*	*disloyal, disappear*
re	*do again*	*retell*
en	*to make (into), to put into*	*enslave, entrap*
co	*together with*	*coexist*
mis	*wrong*	*misinterpret*
in, im, il, ir	*not*	*incorrect, impolite, illegal, irregular*
anti	*against*	*antiwar*

extra	*beyond*	*extraordinary*
fore	*in front*	*foreground*
inter	*between*	*interstate*
intra	*within*	*intrastate*
non	*not*	*nonsense*
post	*after*	*postseason*
pre	*before*	*predate*
pro	*in favor of*	*prowar*
semi	*half*	*semicircle*
sub	*under*	*submarine*
super	*above*	*supernatural*

The most frequently taught suffixes are:

Noun Suffixes	Meaning	Examples
al, ance, ment, ation, *ion, sion*	*act of*	*dismissal, continuance,* *payment, presentation, connection,* *division*
ation, ment, ness, hood, *dom, ship, ion, ice*	*state of*	*desperation, bewilderment, dimness,* *manhood, freedom, friendship,* *corruption, cowardice*
ist, er, or, eer	*one who*	*pianist, worker, creditor, auctioneer*

Adjective Suffixes	Meaning	Examples
ful, ish, y, ive, *able*	*full of, having* *capable of*	*hateful, selfish, guilty, inventive* *peaceable*

Using Morphemic Analysis to Identify Words

Root words with prefixes and/or suffixes are called word *derivatives*. Root words with inflectional endings are called word *variants*. Sometimes children do not immediately recognize word derivatives or word variants, but are able to identify a familiar morpheme within the word that facilitates full identification. When children recognize familiar roots, prefixes, suffixes, or inflectional endings, and identify words from those elements, they are using morphemic analysis. Because children have been known to use their knowledge of morphemic elements to identify written words, teachers occasionally engage them in activities where they are required to identify those elements in written text.

Syllabic Analysis

Using Phonics to Identify Multisyllabic Words

When children use phonics to sound out single-syllable words, they isolate and blend letter sounds. This task is not too difficult for children who have been taught to do it. However, the key to successful phonetic decoding (often called *recoding*) is knowing how to identify the vowel sound in the word before trying to sound it out. The sounds represented by consonants are fairly predictable, so identifying these sounds before-hand is not necessary, but the sounds represented by vowels vary from word to word. The right vowel sound must be determined before blending a word's sounds. For example, imagine a child trying to sound out the word *scrap* by isolating the letter sounds in the word. The child begins by saying, "/s/ /k/ /ru/ . . . " and then pauses to determine the vowel sound. The vowel letter *a* represents three sounds, so the child might try out the three possibilities, "/ā/ /ä/ /a/." When the child interrupts the blending process to determine which vowel sound is appropriate, the entire process breaks down. It's like standing in line to buy a ticket to a cultural or sporting event and not checking to see if you have enough money before you get to the cashier's window. Some things have to be determined beforehand or you will never reach your goal. Therefore, readers must be helped to determine vowel sounds in words by the structure of the syllable, before they attempt to sound out words.

In a very real sense, phonics is a study of letter–sound relationships within written syllable patterns. A knowledge of the four basic patterns described in this chapter helps readers identify *appropriate* sounds to associate with vowel letters that represent more than one phoneme. So when children see an unfamiliar word like *map*, they identify the appropriate vowel sound with the letter *a* (/a/ in this case) because they know that vowel letters represent short sounds in closed syllables.

Phonics knowledge, however, is not so valuable to children when they encounter unfamiliar polysyllabic words. If they can't identify the syllable boundaries in poly-syllabic words, they won't know the syllable's pattern and the appropriate vowel sound to associate with the vowel letter in the syllable. For example, children might encounter an unfamiliar word such as *maple*, and associate the first part of it with the word *map*. If they view the first syllable in *maple* as *map* and the second one as *le* they will sound the word out as /map/ /ul/ rather than /mā/ /pul/. Children often associate inappropriate sounds with vowel letters in words such as this, simply because they don't know where the first syllable in the word ends and the second one begins. The problem is compounded in words of three or more syllables. In short, phonics as a word identification strategy breaks down for many children when they encounter unfamiliar polysyllabic words, simply because they can't perceive the syllable patterns within each word.

In order to use phonics to identify such unfamiliar words, children must be able to identify the syllable boundaries within words so they can determine the correct vowel sound in each syllable. After vowel sounds in syllables have been determined, the rest of the blending process is fairly simple.

In the past, the teaching of syllabication has been a "can of worms." Children were taught rules for breaking words into syllables and rules for accenting them. Many children and teachers found the experience difficult and confusing. Furthermore, there is little or no evidence that the information taught was ever used by children, or ever improved their reading performance. Teachers need a simple syllabication strategy to help young children identify syllable boundaries in unfamiliar multisyl-labic words so their phonics knowledge can be used to identify them. Before introducing a simple, logical approach for determining syllable boundaries, a brief review of syllables is appropriate.

The Syllable

Ten Basic Principles:

1. *The smallest pronunciation unit in a word is the syllable.*

Syllables are pronounced without any sound distortions; therefore, it can be said that they are pronunciation units. For example, in the word *yesterday,* the three pronunciation units are *yes ter day.* Each syllable in the word can be clearly spoken without distortion.

Phonemes, which are the smallest sound units in words, however, cannot always be clearly pronounced. When said in isolation, phonemes are often distorted. For example, the first two phonemes in the first syllable of the word *blanket,* /b/ and /l/, cannot be pronounced without some distortion. When attempts are made to isolate them, the schwa phoneme is added (*buh* and *ul*).

2. *Every syllable contains one vowel sound.*

The distinguishing characteristic of all syllables is that each contains one vowel sound. For example, in the words *famous, station,* and *complete,* all of the syllables, *fa* and *mous, sta* and *tion,* and *com* and *plete,* contain only one vowel sound. Syllables may contain more than one vowel letter such as *mous, tion,* and *plete,* but they contain only one vowel sound.

3. *Some words are also syllables.*

The words *jump, bone, seat, bird,* and *stretch* are words, but they are also syllables because they contain only one vowel sound.

4. *Phonics works only in syllables.*

Phonics is a study of the letter–sound relationships existing between written and spoken words. However, it is only within the context of the syllable that phonics makes sense. Consider, for example, the following words: <u>rob</u>, <u>robot</u>, <u>met</u>, and <u>meter</u>. Why does the letter *o* represent its short sound in the word *rob,* but represent its long sound in the word *robot?* Why does the letter *e* represent its short sound in the word *met,* but represent its long sound in the word *meter?* The answer lies with the syllable.

The word *rob* is a single-syllable word. In the word *robot,* the syllables are *ro* and *bot.* Even though the reader may focus on the first three letters (*rob*) in the word *robot,* the first syllable in that word is *ro,* not *rob.* The syllables, *rob* and *ro,* are different. The syllable *rob* contains one vowel sound, but that sound is followed by a consonant. However, the syllable *ro,* which also contains only one vowel sound, is not followed by a consonant. Therefore, the syllables are different.

Syllables ending with vowels are different than syllables ending with consonants. These differences affect the sound the vowel letter represents.

The word *met* is a single-syllable word. In the word *meter,* the syllables are *me* and *ter.* Therefore, since the syllables *met* and *me* are different, the sound represented by the letter *e* in each word is also different.

5. *Syllables ending in consonant sounds are called "closed syllables." The vowel sounds in these syllables are usually short.*

All of the following words are examples of closed syllable words: *stretch, end, odd, class, stand, wish, lunch.* Each of these words end in consonant sounds, and in each of them, the vowel letter represents its short sound. The first syllable in the following words are closed: *discharge, athlete, cabin, festival.* These syllables end in consonant sounds, and the vowel in each syllable represents its short sound: *dis, ath, cab,* and *fest.*

6. *Syllables ending in vowel sounds are called "open syllables." The vowel sounds in these syllables are usually long.*

All of the following words are examples of open syllable words: *she, go, we, so.* Each of these words ends in vowel sounds, and in each of them, the vowel represents its long sound. The first syllable in the following words are open: *silence, secret, relax, paper, hero, fable.* These syllables end in vowel sounds, and the vowel in each syllable represents its long sound: *si, se, re, pa, he,* and *fa.*

7. *Syllables ending in one vowel, followed by one consonant, followed by e are called vowel-consonant-e syllables. The vowel sounds in these syllables are usually long.*

Consider the words *complete, translate, polite* and *athlete.* The syllables for these words are *com* and *plete, trans* and *late, po* and *lite,* and *ath* and *lete.* The second syllable in each word is a vowel-consonant-*e* syllable, and the first vowel letter in those syllables represents its long sound.

8. *Syllables containing vowel teams are called vowel team syllables. The vowel sounds in these syllables are determined by the individual vowel team.*

Consider the words *needle, beneath, repeat, rainbow,* and *explain.* The syllables for these words are *nee* and / *dul/, be* and *neath, re* and *peat, rain* and *bow,* and *ex* and *plain.* All of the vowel team syllables, *nee, neath, peat, rain, bow,* and *plain,* contain vowel teams that predict their own phonemes without depending upon whether the syllable ends in a consonant or vowel.

9. *Vowel letters in unstressed or unaccented syllables usually represent the schwa sound.*

Consider the following words: *famous, station, maple, notice, cabin, silence, secret, fable.* In each word the first syllable is stressed, or emphasized, and the second syllable is unstressed. The vowel letter in the unstressed syllables represents the shwa sound, or the short sound of /u/: *fa.mus, sta.shun, ma.pul, no.tus, cab.un, si.luns, se.crut, fa.bul.* (Incidentally, you may notice other phonics patterns in these words. For example, the *ce* ending representing the /s/ sound, and the *tion* ending representing /shun/.)

10. *The le endings at the end of multisyllabic words represents the "ul" sound.*

When words of more than one syllable end in *le,* such as *candle, bundle, able,* and *example,* the *le* represents the sound /ul/. The /ul/ sound is the schwa sound combined with the phoneme /l/.

Syllabication. The key to syllabication is the vowel. As stated, each syllable contains one vowel sound. For example, *me, box, bone, stretch, seed, boat,* and *bird* are all single-syllable words containing one vowel sound. The words *paper, complete, discharge,* and *yesterday* are polysyllabic words containing more than one vowel sound. However, since not all vowels in words represent sounds, the number of vowel letters in a word is not equivalent to the number of vowel sounds in the word. For example, the emphasized letters in each of the sample words listed represent vowel sounds while the others do not. After examining each of the four syllable patterns, one can quickly see that the vowel-consonant-*e* syllable and the vowel team syllable each contain more vowel letters than vowel sounds. In the open and closed syllable patterns, however, there is one vowel letter representing one vowel sound in each syllable.

Since each syllable contains only one vowel sound, if children can identify the number of sounding vowels in a word they automatically identify the number of syllables in the word. Furthermore, they also identify a part of a syllable since each grapheme representing a vowel sound is a part of a syllable. Therefore, a beginning point for the identification of syllable boundaries is to locate the vowels in a word that represent vowel sounds. This process is relatively easy for children if they are familiar with phonics elements and patterns. They will know that vowel teams represent only one vowel sound, that the letters *ge* at the end of words represent a consonant sound (/j/) rather than a vowel sound, and that the *e* at the end of vowel-consonant-*e* syllables is silent. See if you can identify the letters representing vowel sounds in the following words: *complete, merchant, misjudge, cabin, certain, discharge.*

Once children can identify the vowel letters representing sounds in polysyllabic words, they are ready to discover some basic linguistic patterns related to syllabication. Consider the words listed in the following two columns:

Column 1	Column 2
letter	*tiger*
except	*pilot*
complete	*fever*
athlete	*bacon*
enchant	*panic*
discharge	*cabin*
harmful	*robin*

Identify the vowel letters representing vowel sounds in each word, in both columns. How many vowel sounds are in each word? How many syllables are in each word? How are all of the words in both columns alike?

The words in column 1 are different and alike in several ways. Some of them contain consonant blends while others do not, some contain consonant digraphs while others do not, and so on. Some linguists have developed syllabication rules to account for the differences noted in the words. Would you be surprised to know that some linguists have developed a different syllabication rule for each of the seven words listed in column 1?

All of the words in column 1 contain two syllables, but they are also alike in another way. What other common feature do you notice about these words?

The words in column 2 are also both different and alike. The differences among the words in this column, however, are not as great as those found in the first column.

Each of the words in column 2 contains two syllables, but they are also like each other in another respect. Do you notice another feature common to all of the words in column 2?

Consider the number of consonant letters between the sounding vowels in each word in both columns. The difference between the number of consonant letters between sounding vowels in the words is what differentiates the words in column 1 from those listed in column 2.

The words in both columns deliberately contain only two syllables. The linguistic patterns affecting syllabication can be perceived easier in two-syllable words, and once perceived, the knowledge acquired can be applied to all types of multisyllabic words.

All multisyllabic words (words ending with *le* are a special case discussed shortly) have either one consonant unit separating the letters representing vowel sounds (see column 2), or two or more consonant units separating those sounds (see column 1). A *consonant unit* is a grapheme representing one consonant phoneme. A consonant unit can be either a single consonant or a consonant digraph. In the word *fiber,* there is only one consonant unit between the two vowel sounds, a single consonant *b.* In the word *ether,* there is only one consonant unit between the two vowel sounds, a *th* consonant digraph.

When two or more consonant units separate vowel sounds, the first syllable ends with the first consonant unit, and the second syllable begins with whatever consonant units are left. The first syllable is always closed, (i.e., it always ends in a consonant).

let-ter

ex-cept

com-plete

ath-lete

en-chant

dis-charge

harm-ful

In most multisyllabic words there are two or more consonant letters between two sounding vowels, as in the words in column 1. Children eventually learn that the first vowel in these situations represents its short sound. Notice that all of the vowels in the list represent their short sounds except the words *complete* and *harmful.* If the vowel doesn't represent its short sound in closed syllables, it is because the vowel is a vowel team (*ar in harmful*), or the syllable is unaccented (*com in complete*). In unaccented syllables, the vowel letter represents the /u/ sound regardless of the letter(s) representing the sound (*alone, lemon, pencil, open, circus, certain, famous*). This situation occurs in all English words. In two-syllable words, the second syllable is usually the one unaccented, unless the first syllable is a prefix. Prefixes are usually unaccented.

When only one consonant unit separates vowel sounds, the first syllable either ends with the vowel (see column A) or ends with the consonant after the vowel (see column B):

A	B
ti-ger	*pan-ic*
pi-lot	*cab-in*
fe-ver	*rob-in*
ba-con	

An analysis of words with only one consonant unit between sounding vowels suggests that in 55% of the words we find pattern A, and in 45% we find pattern B. If the first syllable ends with a vowel (pattern A) the vowel letter represents its long sound (open syllable pattern). If the first syllable ends with the consonant (pattern

B), the vowel letter represents its short sound (closed syllable pattern). When children encounter unfamiliar polysyllabic words where vowel sounds are separated by one consonant unit, they quickly learn to say the first syllable using the long sound of the vowel first. If that strategy doesn't work, they say the first syllable using the short sound.

A special linguistic pattern involves the use of *le* at the end of multisyllabic words, for example, *maple, candle, babble, bottle, able,* and *bugle.* In these situations, the *le* stands for the /ul/ sound and the first syllable ends before the consonant letter preceding the *le: ma-ple, can-dle, bab-ble, bot-tle, a-ble,* and *bu-gle.* When the first syllable is open, the vowel letter represents its long sound (*ma-ple, a-ble, bu-gle*), and when the first syllable is closed, the vowel letter represents its short sound (*can-dle, bab-ble, bot-tle*).

The Decoding "Path of Least Resistance"

Students should be helped to decode words efficiently. The most efficient of all decoding processes is sight word recognition. Accurate, automatic, fluent sight word recognition is one of the hallmarks of a good reader, and is the objective and focus of this book. Identification strategies (analogy, context, phonics, morphemic analysis, and syllabic analysis/phonics) are only a means to this goal. Identification strategies are important for readers to learn, however, if their word recognition abilities are inadequate for successful independent reading. These strategies help students decode when sight vocabularies are underdeveloped. Furthermore, when children learn those identification strategies that focus their attention on the letter–sound sequences of words, word recognition is enhanced.

When students' word recognition abilities are weak or underdeveloped, they should be provided with many holistic reading experiences where they are assisted to read books they cannot read by themselves (shared book experience, dyad reading, group assisted reading, taped assisted reading, etc.). We discuss these strategies in the next chapter.

When reading independently, some identification strategies are more efficient for students to employ than others. It is hoped that children will learn to choose the most efficient identification strategy available so they spend less time on decoding and more time focusing on the content of the text they are reading. To help students identify words as quickly as possible, encourage them to use the identification strategies as follows:

1. First, try to identify the unknown word by analogy. This is a quick identification process. If the unknown word can't be identified by analogy,
2. try to identify the unknown word using contextual analysis. This is also a fairly quick process. If contextual analysis doesn't work,
3. use phonics to sound out the word if it is a single-syllable word. If the unknown word is a polysyllabic word,
4. look at the word to see if it contains a familiar root word, prefix, suffix, or inflectional ending. The recognition of familiar morphemes may help in the identification of the word. If morphemic analysis doesn't work,
5. locate the word's syllable boundaries and sound out the word.

Application Activities

1. Single vowel letters, regular vowel digraphs, irregular vowel digraphs, vowel diphthongs, murmur diphthongs, single consonant letters, consonant digraphs, and consonant blends comprise the elements of phonics. Analyze a page of text and identify and label each of the phonics elements contained in the words on that page.

2. Consonant sounds are either voiced or voiceless. Sometimes the only difference in the speech mechanisms used to produce two consonant sounds is whether the voice is used. For example, /b/ and /p/ are produced with the tongue, teeth, and lips in the same position, but when producing /b/ the larynx is vibrated, and when producing /p/ air is forced from the mouth. Because the only difference in the production of these two consonant sounds is whether they are voiced or voiceless, we say that /b/ and /p/ are *voiced* and *voiceless complements*. Experiment with the consonant sounds identified in this chapter to see how many voiced and voiceless complements you can find.

3. Analyze the single-syllable words on a page or two of any text and identify those words that are graphophonically regular and those that are graphophonically irregular. Classify the graphophonically regular words by syllable pattern. What percentage of those words represent the closed syllable pattern? What percentage represent the vowel team pattern? What percentage represent the vowel-consonant-*e* pattern? What percentage represent the open syllable pattern?

4. Analyze the polysyllabic words on a page or two of any text and identify those words that are graphophonically regular and those that are graphophonically irregular. Using the syllabication principles taught in this chapter, analyze the graphophonically regular words. How many of them have two or more consonants between sounding vowels? How many of them have only one consonant unit between sounding vowels? In what percentage of the words having only one consonant unit between sounding vowels did you find the first syllable ending with the vowel sound?

5. Visit an elementary school. Listen to several children, at different grade levels, read. Try to identify the decoding strategies they use. Were most of them using word recognition? When children could not recognize words, what strategies did they use? How many of them had developed strategies for identifying unfamiliar words? Were the strategies effective? Were you able to help students by suggesting strategies for them to use?

Chapter 9

Improving Decoding, Fluency, Comprehension, Motivation, and Writing

Improving Decoding, Fluency, and Comprehension

Over the past five decades, educators have experimented with various strategies designed to help beginning and struggling readers cope with comprehension difficulties created by decoding deficiencies. Much of what has been learned about the improvement of decoding, fluency, and comprehension has come from analyses of these experimental efforts.

Poor decoding ability means poor comprehension. The ability to decode written words will not ensure good reading comprehension, but comprehension will certainly not occur without it. One cannot comprehend written text without an understanding of the words used by an author, and written words must be decoded before they can be understood. However, vocabulary knowledge and the ability to decode writing are not sufficient, by themselves, for reading comprehension. Readers must decode text fast enough to hold all of the words of a sentence in short-term memory until they get to the end. If a sentence is read too slowly—say, one word every 5 seconds—its structure collapses and what remains is a string of words producing little meaning. Many teachers have observed "word-by-word readers" who took so much time to decode that they forgot the words at the beginning of a sentence by the time they got to the end.

Fluent reading requires high-speed word recognition, but fluency includes the ability to chunk words into meaningful grammatical units for comprehension as well (Schreiber, 1980, 1987). The ability to fluently group words into grammatical units requires the automatic interpretation of prosodic features of print which enables readers to make appropriate pauses, emphasize appropriate words, and apply proper intonation or expression while reading orally, or using inner speech. Thus, fluency not only provides the reader with more cognitive resources, or attention, for comprehension, but it also requires some comprehension.

The speed at which one hears words or decodes them definitely affects listening (McNeill, 1968) and reading comprehension. Smith (1975) believed that one must read close to 250 words per minute for good comprehension. Yet, a common characteristic of poor readers is that they tend to read word by word, rather than fluently. Slow, halted reading limits the number of words readers can focus on within relevant time periods, which, in turn, affects the meaning they are able to construct from text. This conclusion is supported by research indicating that fluent readers perceive phrases while reading whereas less able, word-by-word readers do not (Kowal, O'Connell, O'Brian, & Brant 1975).

The theory of automatic information processing developed by LaBerge and Samuels (1974) several years ago was based upon the assumption that reading fluency affected reading comprehension. LaBerge and Samuels suggested that readers with good comprehension decoded fluently and automatically, enabling them to focus on the content of written text rather than on its form. They claimed that good readers not only decoded fluently, but they did so without being consciously aware that decoding was even taking place.

Because good readers decode text automatically, they are able to give full attention to comprehension. Beginning and word-by-word readers, however, do not decode automatically, and because most of their attention is on written words, comprehension suffers.

LaBerge and Samuels' theory of automaticity was based on "attention" research suggesting that the brain acts as a single-channel processor, normally processing only one source of information at a time. Yet readers must process two sources of information simultaneously: they must be able to translate the written text into inner speech, and they must be able to construct meaning while reading. According to the theory, the brain is able to process both sources of information simultaneously only when one source (decoding) is brought to the level of automaticity. Driving a "stick-shift" car might be analogous to reading in this sense. Driving a car with a manual transmission, like reading, requires an individual to focus on the task of shifting the car, and also on moving the car safely down the road. Drivers unaccustomed to manual shifting usually have to master this task before driving on public roads, since the safety of the people around them is affected by this ability. In other words, if too much of a driver's attention is on shifting, not enough is left for safe driving.

According to LaBerge and Samuels, beginning and struggling readers have to give competing attention to both decoding and comprehension tasks because decoding is not automatic. Mature readers, however, possess large "word recognition" vocabularies and read fluently. Since their decoding no longer requires conscious attention, they are able to give full attention to the text message. Samuels (1976) stated that "to have both fluent reading and good comprehension, the student must be brought beyond accuracy to automaticity in decoding" (p. 323).

Assisted Reading Strategies

Various assisted reading strategies have been used with struggling readers since the early 1950s to remove the "decoding problems" hindering their reading comprehension. All of these strategies possess common characteristics. All of them also support the notion that an individual's decoding and fluency can be improved by someone "assisting" them to read text material they are unable to read by themselves—either accurately or fluently.

Historical Use of Assisted Reading Strategies

The Neurological Impress Method. Heckelman seems to have been the first to remediate reading handicaps by helping poor readers get involved with reading natural text. Heckelman (1962, 1966, 1968, 1969) developed in the early 1950s the *neurological impress method,* a technique of impressing mature reading behaviors upon students with severe reading disabilities.

The method was a system of unison reading whereby the student and the teacher read aloud, simultaneously, at a rapid rate. The disabled reader was placed slightly to the front of the teacher with the student and the teacher holding the book jointly. As the student and teacher read the material in unison, the voice of the teacher was directed into the ear of the student at close range. The teacher tracked the words on the page with a finger as they were being spoken. At times the instructor read louder and faster than the student and at other times read softer and slower than the student. The goal was to cover as many pages of reading material as possible within the time available.

Heckelman (1969) worked over a 6-week period with 24 remedial secondary students with severe reading handicaps in selected schools in Merced, California. All of them had reading levels at least 3 years below grade level, and all had IQ scores of 90 or above on the WISC. At the end of the treatment period, Heckelman reported a range of achievement gains from 0 grade levels to 5.9 grade levels. Many studies using the neurological impress method produced similar achievement results (Cook, Nolan, & Zanotti, 1965; Cook, Nolan, & Zanotti, 1980; Embrey, 1968; Gardner, 1963; Gardner, 1965; Langford, Slade, & Barnett, 1974; Miller, 1969; Robin, 1977; Stinner, 1979). Three studies failed to find significant achievement differences (Arnold, 1972; Gibbs & Proctor, 1977; Lorenz & Vockell, 1979).

Gardner (1965) believed that some reading disabilities were due to an interruption of synaptic transmissions in the brain brought on by anxiety (Smith & Carrigan, 1959). He believed that anxiety raised the circuit-breaking effect of two body chemicals interacting with each other: cholinestraerase (CHE) and acetylcholise (ACH). He suggested that the neurological impress method (NIM) lowered student anxiety as they read because they were freed from the failure experiences they encountered using traditional methods of reading instruction.

Hoskisson's Assisted Reading. Smith (1971, 1973, 1976) argued that children learned to read by reading, and a teacher's prime task was to do as much reading as was necessary for them until they could go on their own. Influenced by Smith, Hoskisson (1974) proposed a technique for parents to use to help their children learn to read. He called this technique *assisted reading.* Assisted reading was based on the premise that if children saw written words, heard them pronounced, and followed their patterning in sentences, they would learn to read. He stated (1975a) that children could learn to read by reading, much as they learned to talk by talking, claiming (1975b) that children would discover the orthographic patterns in written language if they were provided with enough assisted reading practice. Using Hoskisson's method, a parent moved one finger slowly under the line of print being read to get the child to begin to focus on the words. After repeated visual exposures to words as they were pronounced by the parent, the child was eventually able to read the book.

Hoskisson and others (Hoskisson, Sherman, & Smith, 1974) reported both qualitative and quantitative data suggesting that the strategy was effective with preschoolers and poor readers in the elementary grades. Krohm (Hoskisson & Krohm, 1974) implemented assisted reading strategies in her second-grade classroom as a supplement to her regular reading program. She taped stories, prepared from supplemental reading texts, that were on or just above her students' reading level. Students read the stories while listening to the prepared tapes. They shared the stories they read with their classmates. Krohm reported that the students enjoyed the experience, poor readers became more confident, and overall student achievement was improved.

The Method of Repeated Readings. Dahl and Samuels (1974) developed the *method of repeated readings* to increase the automaticity of poor readers' word recognition skills. Unskilled readers, they claimed, could access meaning by rereading a passage several times. They believed the first few readings would bring the written material to the phonological level as if the students were "listening" to it rather than reading it.

The method involved the use of short selections (50–200 words), taken from interesting stories selected by students, which were marked off for reading practice (Samuels, 1979). Students read a selection to an assistant, or onto a tape, and immediately afterward their reading speed and number of recognition errors were calculated and recorded on a graph. The students then reread the selection, which was again timed, and a new word error count calculated. The procedure was repeated until the student reached an 85-word-per-minute (wpm) criterion rate (the speed at which student comprehension was defined as successful for the study; Dahl (1974) set the original criterion rate at 100 wpm). Then the student went on to the next selection.

Samuels (1979) found that as a student's reading rate increased, word recognition errors decreased, and reading comprehension improved, observing also that reading comprehension improved with each additional rereading. He reasoned that improvement resulted because the decoding barrier to comprehension was gradually overcome. Gonzales and Elijah (1975) studied the effects of repeated readings on informal reading inventory (IRI) performance. They found that when a student read material at a "frustrational reading level" twice, the difficulty of the material on the second reading moved to "instructional level."

The method of repeated readings was implemented with or without audio support. With audio support, the student initially read the passage silently while listening to the recorded narration over earphones. It was believed that the key to the success of the method, with or without taped support, was practice. Samuels (1976) concluded that students would learn to read fluently only if they practiced reading. Subsequent research substantiated the positive benefits of repeated readings on both decoding and reading comprehension (Amlund, Kardash, & Kulhavy, 1986; Dowhower, 1987; Herman, 1985; Taylor, Wade, & Yekovich, 1985).

Dyad Reading. In 1983, a colleague and I (Eldredge & Butterfield, 1984), using some of the basic practices of the neurological impress method, developed an assisted reading strategy to be used with young children in the regular classroom. We named the strategy *dyad reading*. It has also been called *buddy reading*. The strategy differed from Heckelman's Neurological Impress Method in some very significant ways. First, the strategy was used with primary age children rather than teenagers and adults. Second, it was used in the regular classroom setting rather than in a clinical setting. Third, students rather than trained clinicians were used. Fourth, "frustrational" level text material was used rather than "instructional" level material.

In dyad reading, "lead readers" (students in the classroom able to read grade level books and beyond) read books with "assisted readers" (students *unable* to read grade level books without help). (The terms "lead reader" and "assisted reader" *are used only for explanation purposes in this text*). Assisted readers worked with different lead readers each week.

In dyad reading, the difficulty level of the reading material was not as important as the content of the material. As long as a book a) could be read by the lead reader, b) could not be read independently by the assisted reader, and c) was of interest to both the lead reader and the assisted reader, it was appropriate for use in dyad reading.

The first dyad reading study was conducted in 50 Utah second-grade classrooms (Eldredge & Butterfield, 1984, 1986). Struggling readers in experimental classrooms were placed in dyad groups where they read grade-level, or above-grade-level, material with lead readers, while struggling readers in control classrooms were grouped according to their reading levels and read below-grade-level material appropriate for individual reading. The students in the dyads sat side by side, reading aloud from the same book. The lead reader touched each word as it was read, while the assisted reader read along with the lead reader. The lead reader read the book at a normal oral reading speed, avoiding word-by-word reading. Over a period of time, the assisted readers were able to read the regular school material without any assistance. At the end of the school year, children in the experimental classrooms obtained significantly higher scores in both reading achievement and reading attitudes than those in the control classrooms. These findings were supported by a follow-up study conducted in 24 second-grade classrooms in two Utah school districts (Eldredge, 1990b).

Struggling readers in the dyad reading groups in both studies read meaningful but "frustrational level" texts with assistance. By doing so, their decoding accuracy, fluency, and reading achievement significantly improved. The findings of both studies seemed to contradict the generally accepted notion that children need to be taught to read with "instructional level" materials. These studies found that poor readers made better reading achievement gains when *assisted* to read "frustrational level" material than when provided "instructional level" material to read without any assistance. A third study (Eldredge & Quinn, 1988) confirmed those findings. The struggling readers in the dyad groups in this study made greater achievement gains on all reading outcomes than their matched controls. At the end of the year, 27 out of 32 experimental students (84%) scored at or above grade level, while only 6 out of 32 control students (19%) achieved that level. Poor readers in the experimental group outperformed the poor readers in the control situation by an average of 49 percentile points.

A fourth study on dyad reading was conducted in 1997 (Morgan, Wilcox, & Eldredge, 2000). The study sought to determine how far above a poor reader's instructional level dyad reading should be used to promote the greatest growth in reading level, word recognition, comprehension, and fluency. Fifty-one poor readers in the second grade were identified and randomly assigned to one of three experimental groups: a) dyad reading at their instructional level; b) dyad reading two grades above their instructional level; or c) dyad reading four grades above their instructional level. All dyads read for 15 minutes each day during their classroom recreational read time for 95 days. Every group improved with dyad reading regardless of the level of difficulty of materials. However, it was found that children using text materials two grade levels above their "instructional reading" level achieved the most growth.

The results of these dyad reading studies indicate that a) children do not always have to be taught to read with relatively easy "instructional level" text; b) poor readers can significantly improve their word recognition, fluency, and reading comprehension abilities when helped to read material too difficult for them to read by themselves; and c) children who are assisted to read difficult material in dyad groups for a period of time become able to read difficult material independently.

Group Assisted Reading. *Group assisted reading* is a strategy intended to adapt dyad reading to groups of children who are unable to independently read grade-level material. The teacher of the group becomes the lead reader and a small group of students become the assisted readers. Since repeated readings are generally involved in group assisted reading, the strategy has also been called "Guided Repeated Oral Reading" (National Reading Panel, 2000). A study of group-assisted reading with struggling third-grade readers suggests that it is an effective strategy for improving children's decoding, reading fluency, and reading comprehension (Eldredge, 1990a). The teacher in this study read the text material along with the students, modeling correct phrasing, intonation, and pitch. As the students read the material in unison with the teacher, they tracked the words in the text with a finger.

The students receiving the assisted reading treatment read eight paperback books with the teacher over an 8-week period. The books selected were drawn from the literature books supplied in each third-grade classroom as a part of their literature-based reading program. They were selected because the experimental students were interested in the books, but could not read them without help. During the assisted reading period, the students were grouped in dyads, and each dyad had one copy of the day's text. The teacher also had a copy. The teacher and the students in the dyad groups read the story together orally. The teacher set the pace for reading and provided the expressive model, reading the story in phrase units, emphasizing correct stress, pitch, and juncture. The students in the dyads took turns tracking the words on the page with a finger as it was being read; each tracked the words on the page nearest him. Both students kept their eyes on the words while reading. They read the story several times so they could read it expressively without teacher assistance. At the end of the period, the students in the dyads read a part of the story together orally without teacher assistance.

The students receiving the unassisted reading treatment read literature books silently during this same period of time. The same eight books used by the assisted reading group were provided for students to read if they chose. However, they did not select them because they were more difficult than other books available. The children used "trial and error" procedures until they found books they could read. They read books silently during the 15-minute reading period while the teacher made herself available to help them read unfamiliar words.

The students in the unassisted group made no achievement gains over the 8-week period while the average total reading achievement gain for the students in the assisted group was 10 raw score points on the Gates MacGinitie Reading Test. The difference was significant, and the size of the effect large. The struggling readers in the group assisted reading experiment outgained the poor readers in the control situation by an average of 26 percentile points.

These results clearly indicated that a) teachers can assist children, in groups, to read material that is too difficult for them to read by themselves; b) when poor readers are assisted to read difficult material, their decoding, fluency, and reading comprehension abilities improve; and c) poor readers who are assisted to read difficult material achieve better than poor readers who independently read interesting, but simple, material matched to their "instructional reading levels."

Using Group Assisted Reading with First-Grade Students. We have successfully used group assisted reading activities with first-grade children in three elementary classrooms in Utah (Eldredge, 1991). Ten-minute daily phonics lessons (see Chapter 10) accompanied the group assisted reading activities, as did writing and other activities consonant with holistic classroom practices. The effects of group assisted reading, and phonics mini-lessons, on the reading attitudes and achievement of these first-grade children were compared with those obtained in three first-grade basal classrooms.

Students involved in the experimental program made significantly greater vocabulary, comprehension, total reading, and phonics gains than students involved in the basal program. The average total reading achievement on the Gates MacGinitie Reading Test, Level A, Form 1, for the basal group at the end of the year was 59. The average score for the holistic group was 70. An analysis of covariance indicated a significant treatment effect, $F = 40.33$, df = 1, 102, $p < .0001$. In addition, we noted significant reading attitude differences in favor of the holistic group.

Taped Assisted Reading. William Jordan popularized the combined use of audiotapes and written text to help poor readers become more meaningfully involved in reading. Adapting Heckelman's neurological impress method, Jordan (1965, 1966, 1967) in the mid-1960s developed Prime-O-Tec, a combination visual-audio-tactile-kinesthetic-motor input form of reading instruction (Meyer, 1982). Learners used teacher-made prerecorded tapes and headphones. They were instructed to listen to a tape, follow the print with a finger, and finally to read along with the tape. The listening, seeing, saying, and touching was all done in unison.

Railsback (1969) and Hollingsworth (1970, 1978) conducted studies using audiotaped programs similar to Jordan's. Railsback reported that his subjects gained a half year or more in test scores per instructional month involved. Hollingsworth (1970) did not find significant achievement gains in his first study. He repeated his study (1978) several years later, doubling his previous treatment time, and found significant achievement differences. The experimental group gained 1 year's growth while the control group gained only .04 of a year.

Chomsky (1976, 1978) reported a successful experiment using tapes with five slow readers in the third grade. Chomsky recorded two dozen storybooks ranging from second- to fifth-grade reading level, most of which were 20 to 30 pages long. The students selected the books they wanted to read, listened to the tapes, read along with the tapes, and tried to memorize each book before moving on to another.

Chomsky (1976) said, "Mechanical as the idea of memorization may seem in itself, it gives these children practice in reading connected discourse, and it put them in touch with a variety of books. They had a feeling of success right from the start, and a sense of progress as book after book was added to their repertoire" (p. 296). Chomsky reported that the students' passivity about reading declined dramatically over the 15 weeks they were involved in the experiment. Their confidence also increased and they began to pick up new books of their own choosing. Pretest and posttest scores on several reading tests showed encouraging gains. Children averaged 5 months' gain on the Wide Range Achievement Test (WRAT) reading subtest, and several months' to one-year gains in oral speed on the Durrell Analysis of Reading Difficulty.

Carbo (1978) taped stories with correct phrasing for eight average-intelligence learning-disabled students in grades two and six to listen to and mimic. She recorded entire books and parts of books, varying the reading rate and phrase length depending on the reading ability of the student. Students usually listened to their individual tapes three or four times and then read the passage aloud. The students were able to read the stories with fluency and expression. In her uncontrolled study she reported impressive gains for all eight students in word recognition, comprehension, and attitudes toward reading. Carbo's students had memory problems, attention difficulties, and auditory perception difficulties. She believed that the taped assisted reading method worked because it possessed the following characteristics:

- It was multisensory and helped compensate for the students' perception deficits.
- It was interesting and held the students' attention.
- It removed the decoding burden so students were able to attend to comprehension.
- It was highly structured so steady growth and feelings of security were obtained.
- It was fail-safe, so self-concept was not weakened.
- It provided the repetition the students needed to overcome their deficiencies in memory.

A more recent report regarding the use of audiotapes with diverse learners suggests that recorded books work well even with students for whom English is a second language (Koskinen et al., 1999).

Common Characteristics of Assisted Reading Strategies

All of the assisted reading strategies reviewed in this chapter are designed to help readers with decoding problems have better experiences with written text. When the method of repeated readings is accompanied by audiotape support, all strategies share the following characteristics:

1.   All are "psychologically safe" strategies. No student should experience failure, and all students should be able to learn from their reading errors without embarrassment.

2.   All help students read material they cannot read by themselves.

3.   All involve students in reading activities where they "see" written words while simultaneously "hearing" the pronunciations of those words. The strategies provide students with sight word recognition "drill," naturally, subconsciously, and painlessly.

4.   All provide students with multiple exposures to the most frequently used words in the English language (see Chapter 7).

5.   All involve students in holistic, connected reading activities. Phrase and sentence reading make the reading experience more meaningful, and students are able to focus on what is said rather than on the words.

6.   All of the strategies provide students with good oral reading models.

7.   All provide students with more experiences with written language than they would otherwise have if left on their own.

8.   All provide students with experiences known to enhance reading comprehension. Background knowledge, vocabulary knowledge, and syntax knowledge are enhanced because of their increased involvement with books. Likewise, experiences with narrative and expository discourse structures, opportunities for inferencing and imagery, and opportunities to engage in metacognitive processes are increased.

9.   All utilize the principle of scaffolding. Once individual performance levels are established, students move to higher-performance tasks and are provided the necessary assistance needed to perform those higher-level tasks.

10. All involve students in interesting reading material, improving students' attitudes toward reading and motivating them to read more.

Struggling readers are unable to read for meaning because they have to concentrate so heavily on decoding tasks. Therefore, helping students read interesting material in phrases and sentences helps word-by-word readers experience reading differently than they usually experience it. In other words, assisted reading frees readers from their decoding burdens for a while, so they can focus more on reading for meaning. Even so, the method of repeated readings, without taped support, eventually brings the printed material to the phonological level as if the students were "listening" to it rather than reading it, so it also makes reading-for-meaning more apparent and important.

Providing struggling readers with considerable reading practice, by assisting them to read many interesting books, eventually improves their schemata, vocabulary knowledge, syntax knowledge, discourse knowledge, inferencing and imagery, and metacognitive abilities. All of these factors positively influence reading comprehension.

Assisted reading also helps struggling readers decode better, because of their increased exposures to written words while simultaneously hearing the pronunciations they represent. Students' decoding, fluency, and comprehension, then, can be improved using assisted reading strategies that model fluent reading, and increase reading practice.

Modeling and Teaching Fluent Reading

Reading fluency is now recognized as an important component of a comprehensive reading program (Allington, 1983, 1984, 2001; National Reading Panel, 2000; Opitz & Rasinski, 1998; Rasinski, 2000; Rasinski & Padak, 1996). Allington (1983) was probably the first to suggest publicly that fluency goals were neglected by teachers, while in 1995 the National Assessment of Educational Progress (NAEP) confirmed Allington's position by reporting that 44% of the fourth graders in the United States couldn't read fluently (Pinnell et al., 1995). The National Reading Panel (2000) addressed fluency in their report, and they and others (Kuhn & Stahl, 2000) support fluency as a necessary reading instruction component.

Fluency involves rapid, automatic word recognition, but it also involves the ability to rapidly interpret prosodic features of print (commas, question marks, exclamation points, bold print, italics, etc.) in order to read with proper intonation, make appropriate pauses while reading, emphasize appropriate words, and phrase text appropriately. Schreiber (1980, 1991) claims that nonfluent readers lack the ability to read a text in phrases, an ability critical for fluent reading.

Teachers can help students improve their reading fluency by a) modeling expressive oral reading, b) guiding students to discover the essential characteristics of fluent reading, and c) providing classroom time for reading practice. Several scholars have developed strategies for modeling and teaching fluency. Three of my favorites are a) the Oral Recitation Lesson (ORL) developed by Hoffman and Crone (1985; Hoffman, 1987), b) the Support-Reading Strategy (SRS) developed by Morris and Nelson (1992), and c) the Fluency Development Lesson (FDL) developed by Rasinski and his colleagues (Rasinski, Padak, Linek, & Sturtevant, 1994). All three are research-proven strategies.

One Example: The Oral Recitation Lesson. (see Aslett, 1990; Reutzel, Hollingsworth, & Eldredge, 1994).

Three subroutines are used in the ORL:

Routine One: The reading/presentation phase

1. The teacher introduces a literature story with an emphasis on the title and the setting. After the story is introduced, the students make predictions concerning the outcome of the story to be read.
2. The teacher reads the story expressively to the students. The students follow with their own traditionally sized copy of the trade book. The teacher receives student remarks during the reading.
3. The teacher invites the students to respond personally to the story after the reading is completed.

4. The teacher leads a discussion of the story on the elements of the story structure, such as story setting, character exposition and development, goals, problems, plans, and resolution.
5. The teacher makes a story summary statement directed by the information gathered through discussion. After the teacher models story summaries, the students make their own summaries and share them with the students in the classroom.
6. New vocabulary words are discussed.

Routine Two: The rehearsal/practice phase

1. The teacher reviews the story as previously described. The students are encouraged to summarize the story.
2. The teacher reminds the students that this is a practice session to read more fluently and with expression.
3. The students open their books to the first page. The teacher models oral reading and encourages the students to focus on various aspects of expressive oral reading. Aspects such as *sings* (how the language flows), *stresses* (some words are stressed more than others giving meaning to the sentence), and *stops* (pauses) are discussed.
4. The teacher models reading again. The whole class reads the same segment, then one child is asked to read it. If the child needs help, the teacher models reading it again.
5. The teacher calls attention to individual word miscues after each student is finished reading.
6. The teacher sets high standards for expression and fluency in oral reading.
7. The teacher makes performance assignments for the next day.
8. Time is allowed for the students to practice their assignments while the teacher helps individual students.

Routine Three: The performance/recitation phase

1. During this phase the teacher tells the students that they will perform or read orally for others in the class.
2. The teacher begins this session by reading orally. When she reaches a section previously assigned to a student, she invites the student to read his or her assigned part. The teacher comments on each student's performance and invites other students to comment also.
3. This pattern is repeated until all assigned readings had been completed by the students.

Classroom Application of Specific Strategies

Dyad Reading. Dyad reading is an effective strategy to use with students who are unable to read books they want to read, or need to read. It is also effective for improving the reading fluency of students serving as lead readers. When lead readers assist others to read books, they should do so with the intent of practicing their own oral reading skills while doing it. In this way, dyad reading benefits *both* members of the dyad team.

If you decide to use dyad reading groups, spend time teaching all of your students how to be good oral readers. Model good oral reading, help students learn to group words appropriately into meaningful grammatical units while reading orally, and provide opportunities for them to practice oral reading. Also provide training for students willing to serve as lead readers. Teach them how to "track print" as they read expressively. This makes it possible for struggling readers to match spoken words with print while also getting involved with the book's message.

Dyad reading involves the following steps and guidelines:

1. *Identify the students who could benefit from the strategy.* If you use dyad reading in a first-grade classroom, probably all of your students will qualify as candidates for assistance. If you use it at higher grade levels, you can ask students needing help to identify themselves, or you can identify those in need by observing students read.

To identify students needing help, ask all of the children to read some book in quiet but audible voices. Since everyone reads aloud at the same time, students are preoccupied with their own performance rather than the performance of others, and no one is embarrassed by the activity. As you move around the classroom listening to students read, you can easily identify those with reading problems.

2. *Identify lead readers.* Lead readers do not have to be gifted readers. They must, however, be able to read grade-level material, material difficult for struggling readers. If dyad reading is used in first grade, recruit older students in the upper grades as lead readers. Both groups of students will probably benefit from the experience. You may also ask parents or other volunteers to be lead readers instead of classmates or older students.

3. *Match lead readers with assisted readers.* A lead reader and an assisted reader form a dyad group for a specified time, usually no longer than four or five days. New dyads with new lead readers are formed, as old ones are eliminated. This makes it possible for struggling readers to receive continued reading help, but also provides time for lead readers to be engaged in other types of reading activities.

4. *Encourage dyad teams to read both expository and narrative text.* Sometimes the reading material for dyad groups is predetermined: basal readers, science, social studies, and so on. It is also a good practice, however, to give dyad groups the opportunity to select books, from the school or classroom library, they want to read.

5. *Dyad members share one book.* Members of a dyad group sit side by side, sharing one book between them. The lead reader sets the reading pace. The lead reader touches each word as it is read while the assisted reader tries to read aloud with the lead reader. It is important for the struggling reader to look at each word as it is touched and read. It is seeing and hearing words simultaneously that eventually impacts the word recognition abilities of struggling readers.

The lead reader should read in a natural, fluent manner so that both students are able to become meaningfully involved in the book. If this happens, both students will eventually forget about tracking print and words. Above all, there should be no deliberate, word-by-word reading.

6. *Lead readers should be able to read the books selected or assigned.* If a word appears in the book that the lead reader doesn't recognize, or can't identify, she may skip it and simply move on. If she misses too many words, however, the material may be too difficult for her.

7. *It is important for children to read extensively.* An important goal of dyad reading is to increase the amount of reading done by both students in a dyad group. Classrooms equipped with books interesting to children will help teachers achieve this goal. Students are encouraged to read as much as they can during the time available to them.

8. *Scaffolding should be a part of the dyad reading experience.* As the poorer readers gain word recognition skill they need opportunities to read books silently on their own. They also need opportunities to read aloud to a parent volunteer, teacher, or older student, who will silently monitor their word recognition accuracy and fluency. In these situations, the monitor should read aloud any words difficult for the struggling reader, so he can repeat them and move on. It is important that this experience flows naturally so the reader is able to maintain interest in the book.

Group Assisted Reading. Group assisted reading can be used with small or large groups. In first-grade classrooms it is generally used with all of the children in the class. With students in grades two through six, it is generally used with small groups of children—those unable to read certain books independently.

Group assisted reading guidelines

1. *The text material to be read must be visible to all students participating in the activity.* A big book, transparencies, charts, or one book for every two students in the classroom allows all students to see the text being read.

2. *Teachers and students read the story or text together out loud.* The teacher is the lead reader and all students in the classroom, or group, are assisted readers. Each book is read at a normal, or slightly slower than normal, speed, modeling correct phrasing and intonation.

3. *Teachers touch each word in the text as it is read.* Students are encouraged to read with the teacher, and to look at each word as it is touched and read. If basal readers or textbooks are used, the students are organized into dyads and each dyad is given one book. As the teacher and students read the book out loud together, students in each dyad take turns tracking print. Each student tracks the print on the side of the text nearest her/him.

Taped Assisted Reading. Taped assisted reading is an appropriate strategy to use when students can't read a book by themselves. It is like dyad reading, but a tape is used rather than a lead reader. It is important that the taped story or text is read at a proper speed. Teacher-made tapes are generally best; commercial tapes are generally read too fast. Children who listen to tapes should be taught to finger-track print while reading aloud with the tape. Listening to the tape, instead of reading with it, doesn't seem to have the same impact on students' decoding, fluency, and comprehension growth.

Taped assisted reading works particularly well when two students, each wearing earphones connected to a tape recorder or tape junction box, share one book while they read with the tape. As they listen to the tape recording of the story, each student takes turns tracking the print as they read aloud; this helps to keep both students focused on the print while reading.

The Shared Book Experience. Holdaway (1979) was impressed with the impact parents had on their preschool children when they read to them, or shared books with them. Therefore, he developed the *shared book experience* for primary-grade teachers, modeled after the routines parents used when they read to their own children. He used the term "shared book experience" to suggest that the reading experiences he wanted young school children to have went beyond the "reading aloud" activities school children normally experienced. Holdaway wanted school children to see the written text and the book's pictures while hearing a story read, just as children sitting on their parents' laps did. Therefore, he developed "big books" so children and teachers could jointly "share" the pictures and text while reading the book aloud.

In those homes where parents read stories to children regularly, some books are read more often than others. That is, children select "favorites" and ask parents to read them over and over again, often "exhausting" parents with requests to read them. Holdaway believed that children should have these kinds of experiences with books at school. Therefore, he encouraged teachers to create a "homelike" environment in the classroom, with many different kinds of books, and to provide opportunities for children to identify stories that could be read over and over again.

Guidelines for Shared Book Activities. Big books are very popular with young children and their teachers. When using a big book, teachers glide their hands under the words as they are read so students develop a sense of print directionality. This teaches, or reinforces, the concept that the print goes from the left to the right, and from the top to the bottom. As words are tracked, children also begin to develop a concept of written words. They begin to notice that the spaces between letters within words are not as large as the spaces that separate words.

After teachers read a story once with students, children are often invited to read along with the teacher, if they desire, or feel ready to do so. When the stories read contain "predictable" elements, children are encouraged to read those parts without help. For example, the ". . . run, run, as fast as you can. You can't catch me, I'm the Gingerbread man." is a predictable element in the *Gingerbread Man* that can be read by children after repeated readings of the book. As stories are read repeatedly, children begin to memorize them. Children are then able to read all, or parts, of the story without help. It is at this point that some children begin to match the written words with the spoken ones. When this happens, they begin to notice characteristics of written words, and decoding knowledge begins to develop.

Shared Music and Rhythm Experiences. The concept of shared reading can also be applied to music and poetry. During whole-class singing or poetry reading, place a large chart containing the words of the song or poem at the front of the room. Track the words with a pointer, finger, or pencil as you and the children sing or say them. In addition to songs and poetry, raps and other language-play activities can be read using this procedure.

Motivation

Motivation Variables

Motivation occurs within people. It is a feeling inside that influences people to behave in certain ways. Sometimes individuals are concerned about an undesirable consequence that may accompany some behavior. If they have enough concern, they will avoid the behavior. They may want a reward they believe will come to them if they behave in a certain way. If they think they can get the reward, and if they want it badly enough, their behavior will be directed towards receiving the reward. In these circumstances, individuals behave in certain ways because they perceive that something they want will follow the behavior, or something they don't want can be avoided by not behaving in a certain way. At other times, people might be influenced to do things for others because they love them. These and other sources of influence on human behavior are referred to as *motivation variables*.

The major motivation variables are a) concern, b) positive or negative feelings associated with tasks, c) interest, d) feedback, e) success, f) positive or negative consequences associated with behaviors (rewards or punishment), g) love, h) values, and i) perceptions. Teachers can use these sources of influence to encourage students to behave in specific ways. However, they cannot "force" or "control" students. No one really motivates anyone else in the sense that they make them "do things." All that teachers, or anyone else for that matter, can do is *influence*, and hope for the best.

The most important sources of influence for literacy teachers to use are the motivational variables of feelings, success, feedback, interest, and reward. Children who do not read much have negative attitudes toward reading, and have a history of unsuccessful experiences with it (Quandt & Selznick, 1984). Children will probably want to read if a) they have learned to associate positive feelings with reading; b) are successful at reading; c) receive feedback to reinforce those feelings of success; and d) find reading personally interesting and rewarding. All of the assisted reading strategies discussed incorporate these motivational variables. Teachers using these strategies assist children to read until they experience success in independent reading, minimizing negative experiences generally associated with reading failure and enhancing feelings of success. Students are provided with holistic, connected reading experiences with relevant books so reading will most likely be interesting and rewarding to them.

Success Motivates

Informal decoding strategies, such as the assisted reading strategies, work. They work because children develop word recognition through the kinds of practice these strategies provide. When children simultaneously see written words and hear their pronunciations, over time strong connections are made between print and speech. Under these circumstances, the more children read, the more proficient they become at reading. Furthermore, children's fluency and comprehension also appear to be enhanced through assisted reading.

In Chapter 2 qualitative and quantitative dimensions of word recognition practice were discussed. The qualitative dimension of word recognition focuses on the alphabetic principle. When teachers help students understand how the letters in written words are related to the sounds in spoken words, they are focusing on the qualitative dimension of word recognition. The quantitative dimension involves the amount of practice students receive—the number of experiences students have associating written words with spoken words. When teachers keep students continuously involved with reading experiences that reinforce written–spoken word associations, they are focusing on the quantitative dimension of word recognition. Assisted reading strategies emphasize the quantitative dimension. Teachers who wish to improve students' word recognition through assisted reading will find ways to provide them with lots of reading practice. In the process of doing so, fluency and comprehension will also be enhanced.

In Chapter 7 issues of word frequency were discussed. About 66% of the words in most written material will be comprised of about 220 words. Within the 220 most frequently used words we find a much higher percentage of graphophonically irregular words than we would find in the 5,000 most frequently used words. Furthermore, we also find most of the abstract words used in the language (*was, of, the, were, there, their,* etc.) in these 220 words. Children learn to read concrete words (*elephant, door*) quicker than they learn to read semiconcrete words (*surprise, happy*). They generally have the most difficulty learning to read abstract words. When students have the types of practice experiences assisted reading strategies provide, they will encounter the most frequently used words many, many times. Ultimately, that practice will pay off in an increased ability to make print–speech connections without any assistance.

Independent Reading, Motivation, and Achievement

The National Reading Panel (2000) made some interesting comments in their report about independent reading practice. They questioned the conventional wisdom that reading is improved by reading. They reported that most of the evidence linking reading ability to the amount of time children spend reading is correlational. They said:

> Although correlational findings may be useful, they also can be deceptive because correlations tell nothing about the direction or sequence of a relationship. That good readers read more could be because reading practice contributes to reading attainment, but it could also be simply that better readers chose to read more because they are good at it. If this is true, then it is reading achievement that stimulates reading practice, not the reverse. Although there is an extensive amount of correlational data linking amount of reading and reading achievement (Cunningham & Stanovich, 1998; Krashen, 1993), such studies do not permit a clear delineation of what is antecendent and what is consequent.

In 1983 Dennie Butterfield and I conducted a year-long study, using a pretest-posttest experimental-control design, involving 1,149 students, 24 schools, and 50 second-grade classrooms (Eldredge & Butterfield, 1984; Eldredge & Butterfield, 1986). One of the topics under study was the effect of literature books in classrooms. In our study some of the experimental classrooms used literature books to teach reading instead of basal readers. Children in these experimental classrooms were encouraged to read as much as possible each day. They selected the books they wanted to read, and the bulk of the reading time available was spent reading. The experimental classrooms were stocked with paperback literature books, and library books from the school and public libraries. Their parents were involved, and the children's reading experiences were extended into the home. No book reports were required; children simply read books and shared their feelings about favorite books with other students. The amount of time spent on reading was controlled in all of the experimental classrooms; therefore, the children in the literature classrooms spent more time reading than students in the other experimental and control classrooms.

At the end of the study, it was found that children in the classrooms using literature books (after the effects of other variables were controlled) made significantly greater reading gains than children in basal classrooms in a) total reading achievement gains, b) reading vocabulary gains, c) phonics gains, and d) interest in reading gains. One of the conclusions drawn from the study was that the involvement of students "in a lot of reading" contributed significantly to growth in reading (Eldredge & Butterfield, 1984, p. 65). We believe that children's reading abilities are improved by reading. We also believe that teachers who provide opportunities for their students to read extensively, and who motivate them to do so, will have a positive impact on their reading growth.

Motivation and Literature Books

The quality of the reading material provided for students is crucial for motivation. Children will, generally speaking, enjoy reading if the material is relevant, interesting, and meaningful. Therefore, selecting appropriate books to read with students, and making available the very best books for them to choose to read by themselves, is important.

Students need many "easy" books in the classroom, easy enough for them to read independently. However, readability, while important, is not the primary criterion to use for book selection. The most important question to ask is, "Will children enjoy reading this book?" Books are meant to be read, and children find it difficult to stay away from books interesting and appealing to them.

Good classroom libraries include a variety of books; different types of books (mystery, humorous, informational, etc.), with different content (dinosaurs, circus clowns, rocks, etc.), focusing on different aspects of life (conflicts with others, conflicts with nature, etc.). Children have a variety of interests, and what is appealing to one child may not be appealing to another. If teachers stock their classrooms with books, dealing with a wide range of topics, they will more likely meet the diverse needs and interests of their students.

Other aspects of books appeal to children besides type, content, and focus. For example, the physical features of a book—its cover and illustrations—are important to children. The book's characters, its plot, and the author's writing style are important as well. Authors of the best fictional books use plot, characterization, setting, theme, style, and point of view to create stories that children will want to read many times. You will want to consult with librarians, children's literature specialists, and the list of children's book choices published yearly in *The Reading Teacher* to identify some of these special books.

Readability. Readability estimates provide helpful information for teachers about the difficult level of books, but should never be viewed as sacred, infallible, or even as necessarily valid. In fact, educators should constantly remind themselves that all readability estimates from traditional formulas share three characteristics that render their credibility suspect: a) they are based upon early notions about what makes a text difficult to read (word difficulty and sentence difficulty); b) they do not include information about those reader variables (interest, background knowledge, motivation, etc.) that influence a reader's ability to comprehend text material; and c) they are subject to the usual flaws associated with traditional methods of determining difficult words and sentences within the book.

Readability estimates obtained from traditional formulas may be inflated by unusual situations, such as the one found in Wendy Watson's *Lollipop* (Viking), whose readability estimate is 13.3. This is a delightful picture book that young children enjoy and find rather easy to read. A close examination reveals that the entire 25-page book is one sentence long. Each page contains a picture and a line of text. Each line of text contains a clause (sometimes two clauses) that the reader is able to read like a sentence (remember that clauses contain subjects and predicates). Each line of text, other than the first line, begins with the words *and, so,* or *but.* If a period is inserted after each line of text, the readability estimate obtained is 1.29, which more nearly reflects the difficulty of the text. If teachers know that estimates are based on sentence length and word difficulty they can visually scan books with questionable estimates to determine if and why those estimates might be "out of line."

The Ratio of Unique to Total Words. Because of readability limitations, literature books should also be analyzed to determine the ratio of unique words to total words used in the book. It is logical to assume that books containing fewer different words for students to read would be simpler than books containing more different words. Therefore, a book's "ratio of unique to total words" can be used by teachers to differentiate difficulty estimates of literature books with identical or similar readability estimates. For example, *Lollipop* contains 151 words, but there are only 62 unique words used in the entire book: *a, and, asked, asleep, began, bunny, but, cry, dark, did, door, down, fell, finally, for, gave, he, hear, heard, her, him, his, in, it, kept, kissed, let, lollipop, lollipops, mom, no, one, out, penny, piggybank, ran, said, sat, saw, she, so, someone, spanked, still, store, street, the, this, time, to, told, took, up, wanted, wanting, was, were, when, where, woke, worried,* and *you.* Some of these words are repeated multiple times. If the total words used in the book are divided by the number of unique words used, a ratio of unique words to total words is found. That ratio for *Lollipop* is 1:2.4, which means that if each unique word was repeated the same number of times as every other unique word used in the story, each word would be repeated an average of 2.4 times. Difficulty level is not only affected by the percentage of difficult words and average sentence length, but also by the number of unique words, the difficulty of those words, and the number of times they are repeated. For example, in *Lollipop,*

52 of the 62 unique words (84%) are easy words, according to the Spache and Dall Chall readability formulas. (Only the words *asked, kissed, lollipop, lollipops, mom, piggybank, spanked, wanted, wanting,* and *worried* were considered difficult.)

Readability estimates plus unique-to-total-word-ratio data, when combined, give teachers more insight into the difficulty level of books. For example, the books *Daniel's Duck; "Quack," Said the Billy Goat; Q Is For Duck; Wet Cats;* and *This Is Bear* all have readability estimates of 1.0. However, the unique-to-total word ratios for those books are 1:4, 1:1.55, 1:2.65, 1:1.85, and 1:2.18, respectively. The ratio differences are significant, and are probably important readability factors. Word repetitions are particularly important when using assisted reading strategies; the more often readers see words while hearing them pronounced, the more quickly they store their letter sequences in lexical memory.

Book Leveling. Many teachers now rely heavily on a system for leveling books, which provides a finer gradient system than that provided by readability data (Fountas & Pinnell, 1999). In essence, books within a particular readability grade range are arrayed along a continuum based on the book's a) length, b) size and layout of print, c) vocabulary and concepts, d) language structure, e) text structure and genre, f) predictability, g) pattern of language, and H) supportive illustrations. Leveling provides a system for teachers to organize books according to difficulty level so students can learn to read by progressing from simple books to more difficult books. This leveling process also helps teachers find books: a) appropriate for independent reading (easiest books), b) appropriate for guided reading (more difficult books), and c) appropriate for assisted reading (most difficult books).

Some scholars warn against the dangers of using leveled books exclusively for independent reading (Szymusiak & Sibberson, 2001). They claim that a continual diet of reading leveled books leads children to read for teachers, rather than to read for themselves. I certainly agree. Children know what books they can and can't read as soon as they try to read them. By giving children the opportunity to select books to read independently, through a process of trial and error, greater motivation for reading results.

Decoding Is Improved by Reading Good Literature

The amount of time children spend reading may be the most important factor in reading achievement. Children who read extensively become better readers and decoders than children who do not read much. Once basic letter–sound relationships have been taught, students need repeated opportunities to read to increase their familiarity with written words so they can be recognized rapidly and automatically. Students' decoding abilities are improved through reading practice, and the evidence for this proposition is convincing (Barron, 1986; Gough & Hillinger, 1980; Perfetti, 1985; Reitsma, 1983, 1988; Seidenberg, 1985; Snow, Burns, & Griffin, 1998). Therefore, one of the most effective ways to improve students' decoding abilities is to stock the classroom with interesting books, allow students to select books they want to read, provide time for them to read, encourage them to read, and provide opportunities for them to share what they have read with others.

Reading provides enjoyment, adventure, excitement, knowledge, and therapy. It helps children cope with the problems they face in life because they can read about others who have problems similar to their own and vicariously share in the solutions to those problems. Reading helps children learn about the human condition because they are able to objectively examine the consequences of people's moral and amoral actions through books. Literature transmits knowledge in a powerful way. It nurtures and expands children's imaginations, and it stimulates their language, personality, social, and cognitive growth. When teachers make good literature available for children, and help them discover the treasures waiting to be found therein, reading will become a lifetime habit for them.

Integrating Phonics Instruction with Holistic Literature Experiences. Teachers can integrate their phonics instruction with children's holistic reading activities in several ways. Phonics instruction might involve the book's title only, or it might incorporate many of the words found in the book. All phonics lessons should take no more than 10 minutes of classroom time.

The following principles are important to remember:

1. Phonics instruction should be process or strategy oriented instead of skills oriented; it should be taught so students can identify unfamiliar written words.
2. Instruction should help students associate graphemes with the phonemes they represent.
3. Students should learn to isolate sounds represented by graphemes without distorting them.
4. Phonics instruction should help students blend word sounds without distorting them so unfamiliar words can be identified without a "grunting and groaning" sounding-out process.

Using Book Titles for Phonics Activities. The title of a book may be used for phonics teaching either before or after reading the book. The book may be read with teacher assistance or without it.

Model Lesson. Literature book: *The Very Hungry Caterpillar,* by Eric Carle (Puffin Books, 1985). Grouping format: Dyads.
Materials needed:

1. Eleven 1-inch blank paper squares for each dyad. The squares may be prepared in advance or students may be given paper, and shown how to fold and cut it into squares.
2. Eleven lettered squares containing the following letters:

c a t e r p i l l a r

The squares must be large enough for all children in the classroom to see. They may be magnetic letters for a magnet board, tagboard squares with tape on the back to stick on the chalkboard, or squares made from a transparency to place on an overhead projector and projected on a screen.

Approach:

1. Form student dyads.
2. Distribute 11 blank paper squares to each student team or distribute blank sheets and have students make the squares.
3. Write the word *caterpillar* on the chalkboard.
4. Read the word to the children if they cannot read it themselves. Ask them to write each letter in the word on one of their squares.
5. After lettering the squares, ask each student team to put the squares together to spell the word *caterpillar*. Spell the word with your lettered squares so the students can check their work against your model.
6. Ask the student teams to take a letter out of the word that stands for the /a/ sound. After each team responds, display the *a* square to reinforce their correct responses, or help them self-correct.
7. Ask the student teams to take a letter out of the word that stands for the /t/ sound, and to put it with the letter *a* to make the word *at*. After each team responds, place your *t* after the *a* to make the word *at*.
8. Continue this activity, moving and replacing letters, to make the following words:

cat	cell	ape	eat
rat	call	car	treat
rate	tall	cart	
ate	all	part	pal
late	ail	tart	
plate	pail	tar	lip
pat	tail	art	tip
pit	rail	rare	rip
pet	trail	care	trip
let	lap		
lit	tap	pear	
it	rap		
ill	trap	pie	
pill	cap	tie	
till	cape	lie	
tell	tape		

Using Words in Literature Books for Phonics Instruction. Teachers may also integrate phonics lessons with books by organizing the lessons around the words used in the book. Again, phonics lessons should be brief, occupying no more than 10 minutes of classroom time.

There seemingly is no end to the phonics lesson possibilities available from just one literature book, as most if not all of the phonics elements and patterns described in Chapter 8 are found naturally in children's literature. If literature books are used for teaching phonics, some systematic approach should be followed. The following sequence is recommended: short vowel sounds, initial consonant sounds, syllable patterns affecting vowel sounds, vowel team sounds, final consonant sounds, consonant digraph sounds, consonant blends, and y as a vowel (see Chapter 8).

Model Lesson. We use here Harry Allard's *I Will Not Go to Market Today* (Dial, 1992) to demonstrate the phonics lesson possibilities contained in just one children's literature book. The book contains words that include the following sounds:

Short Vowel Sounds
a *am, an, and, as, ask, at, jam, had, last, that, bag, bath*
e *bed, fell, get, leg, next, rest, well, went*
i *him, his, if, it, in, did, six, will, with*
o *fog, hot, not, off, stop*
u *but, just, must, run, up, luck*

Initial Consonant Sounds
b *bag, bath, bed, but, by*
d *day, did, down*
f *fell, fibbed, fog, foot, for, forced, found*
g *get, go, good*
h *had, he, heat, him, his, home, hot, house*
j *jam, jar, just*
l *laid, last, late, leg, like, looked, luck*
m *made, mean, must, my*
n *next, night, nine, no, not*
r *rest, right, road, run*
s *seem, six, so*
t *tea, teeth, toast, too*
w *wave, well, went, will, with*

Syllable Patterns Affecting Vowel Sounds
Closed Syllable
   bag, bath, bed, did, but, fell, will, fog, him, jam, leg, next, run, with, get, his, just, luck, not, six, had, hot, last, must, rest, well

Open Syllable
   go, no, so, he, my, by

Vowel-Consonant-*e*
   made, wave, time, home, nine, late, like, shake, stile

Vowel Team Sounds
oa *coast, road, toast*
ea *heat, mean, tea, screamed*
ea *heavy, weather, weatherman*
ee *seem, teeth, peeked*

or	*for, forced*
ou	*found, house, out*
ow	*down, however*
igh	*night, night's, right*
ar	*jar, yard*
oo	*foot, good, looked, tootsies*
oo	*too*
ay	*day*
ai	*laid*
er	*clerk, perfect*

Final Consonant Sounds

m	*am, him, jam, seem, time*
n	*an, in, mean, mine, nine, run*
t	*at, but, foot, get, it, late*
g	*bag, fog, leg*
d	*bed, did, good, had, laid, made, road, yard*
l	*fell, well, will, stile*
t	*heat, hot, not, out*
f	*if, off*
x	*six*
p	*stop, up*

Consonant Digraph Sounds

tch	*kitchen*
ng	*sang*
th	*with, bath, teeth*
<u>th</u>	*that, this*

Consonant Blends

bl	*blew, blocks, blizzard*
br	*broke, brushed*
cl	*clear, clerk*
dr	*dreaming*
fr	*from, front*
st	*steps, stop, stile*
tr	*traffic*
ck	*luck*
nd	*and*
nt	*front, went*
st	*just, last, must, rest*
xt	*next*

Y as a Vowel

by, my

The following **sample lesson** uses those words containing the short vowel sound /a/.

1. Write the following words on the chalkboard: *am, an, and, as, ask, at, jam, had, last, that, bag, bath.* Say, "These words were used in the story, *I Will Not Go to Market Today.* Notice that all of the words contain the vowel letter *a.*" Touch the letter *a* in each of the words.

2. Focus the children's attention on the first six words (those that begin with the vowel sound): *am, an, and, as, ask, at.* Say, "Let's read the first six words." Touch each word as you read it with the students.

3. Underline the *a* in each of the first six words. Say, "Can you hear the /a/ sound at the beginning of each of these words? Listen for the /a/ sound as I read them again." Read the words again, and as you read each one touch the letter *a* and isolate the vowel sound /a/ before you add the sounds represented by the consonant(s) that follow it. Say, "Did you notice that the sounds in each of these words are represented by letters? In the word *am* the letter *a* stands for the /a/ sound and the letter *m* stands for the /m/ sound. Say the sounds in each of these words with me as I touch the letters that stand for those sounds." Say the sounds in each word with the students as you touch the appropriate letters.

4. Say, "Notice that the letter *a* in each of these words is followed by one or more consonant sounds. When this happens the sound represented by the letter *a* will usually be /a/."

5. Say, "If you don't recognize written words or cannot identify them using context clues, you can use your phonics knowledge to sound them out. When you sound out words, follow these steps:
    a. Look at the vowel in the word, identify its sound, and say it.
    b. Blend the consonant sounds that come before the vowel with the vowel sound.
    c. Isolate the consonant sound(s) that follows the vowel.
    d. Blend all of the sounds together so the word can be identified.
Let's use that process to sound out the other six words used in our story." Focus the students' attention on the last six words: *jam, had, last, that, bag, bath.* Point to the letter *a* in the word *jam.* Say, "What is the sound of this letter?" Wait for a response. Say, "When we blend the letter *j* with the /a/ sound, we get /ja/." Point to the letters *ja* in the word *jam.* "Say /ja/." Wait for a response. Say, "The letter *m* in the word (point to the letter) stands for the /m/ sound. Say /m/." Wait for a response. Say, "Blend /ja/ and /m/ together and identify the word." Wait for a response. Repeat this process with the remaining five words: *had, last, that, bag, bath.*

6. Write the following sentences on the chalkboard: *But Fenimore <u>had</u> not gone two blocks before he found himself caught in a <u>traffic</u> <u>jam</u>. "This isn't the <u>jam</u> I <u>had</u> in <u>mind</u>," he said.* Say, "These sentences are taken from the story we read today. Notice that the underlined words contain the letter *a.* Let's read these sentences together and when we get to the underlined words, let's identify them

by their sounds." Read the sentences with the students and have them sound out the underlined words.

Note: Since the students at this age would probably be unfamiliar with syllabication, sound out the first syllable in the word *traffic,* and say the second one with or for them. It helps students begin to grasp syllabication principles if you rewrite the word *traffic,* placing a hyphen within the word to separate the two syllables: *traf-fic.*

The Language Experience Approach (LEA)

The Language Experience Approach (LEA) to reading has been used effectively in classrooms for years. This strategy can be traced to the old sentence and story methods popular in the middle of the nineteenth century, the experience story material in the progressive education movement of the 1930s, and the work of Roach Van Allen in the late 1950s (Hall, 1981).

The rationale behind the LEA is that what children say can be written down and read. The approach uses children's oral language to help them bridge oral and written language. Since vocabulary, syntax patterns, and schema all originate from the child when using this approach, the written material produced is considered easier for children to read and comprehend than text material produced by someone else. As children see their own spoken words written, their interest is heightened and they tend to focus more carefully on the letter sequences in words, a task necessary for word recognition. As they read their written compositions, and study the words used in those compositions, word recognition abilities are further enhanced.

Follow the listed steps when using the LEA with a group of children:

1. *Provide a common experience for the group.* Examples: read a story to them, take them on a trip to the bakery, or have a cooking experience in the classroom.
2. *Talk, write, and read about the experience with the group.* Example:
   a. Ask questions about the experience. (After reading the story, *The Stonecutter,* you might ask, "Why do you think the stonecutter trembled at the end of the story?")
   b. The students respond to the questions, and the statements made by individual children are written on large paper that can be read by the entire class. Each child's statement is written with different colored chalk or felt-tipped pen so students can remember who said what. Another approach is to begin each statement with the speaker's name: "Michelle said . . . ."
   c. Read each sentence after it is written and ask the child who dictated the sentence to read it.
   d. After writing all student statements, read the story aloud once or twice to the children, emphasizing left-to-right progression using a sweeping hand movement. After reading the story, ask questions to individual children, such as, "Whose sentence is the blue one? Nicole, can you read it?"

Children take turns reading the story, a line at a time, or even the entire story in some cases. Help with the rereading as much as needed.

3. *Study individual words in the story.* Write separately on the chalkboard words used in the dictated story to study so the children can eventually recognize them in isolation; or make devices to frame individual words in the story for study, while blocking out other words that might provide contextual clues.

4. *Make tagboard word cards, phrase cards, and sentence cards for children to study.* Provide individual children, or student teams, with cards containing story words, phrases or sentences to be matched with those found in the story. Copy the individual story sentences on sentence strips for children to reassemble in proper order.

5. *Make copies of the story.* Type the story on a computer using a large font. Make enough copies of the story so each child has a copy from which to work. Ask children to illustrate the story and encourage them to read their illustrated stories to others (students, other teachers, or parents). As children read their copies of the story, ask them to underline the words they are able to recognize by sight. Have each child print each word underlined on a small card, to be filed in an individual word bank for use in building sentences, playing word games, or phonics instruction later on.

Using the LEA with Individual Children

After students have worked in groups for a time, you may wish to give them opportunities to dictate their individual stories or experiences. The motivation for these written records or stories will come from family trips or vacations, a pet, a gift, a holiday, or a reaction to a movie or TV show.

During dictation, ask leading questions, but be careful not to structure the children's written work. After children dictate their stories or experiences, read aloud what you have written. Later the documents will be read, with adult help, by the children who dictated them. Eventually, the children should be able to read their own compositions without assistance.

Because of the time involved in transcribing individual work, you may wish to use aides, parent volunteers, or older children to transcribe children's compositions.

The Writing Process

Writing is considered to be an integral component of a balanced, comprehensive literacy program. Children write daily for intrinsic purposes, on personally relevant topics. Since content is considered more important than form, teachers encourage children to write anything they can say even when they don't know how to spell the words they want to use. If children are unsure about a word's spelling, they try to spell it by its sounds, using invented spelling. When children attempt to spell words as they write, they are constantly reflecting on the relationships between word sounds and letters. These kinds of writing experiences contribute significantly to an understanding of the relationships between spoken and written language, which improves students' decoding abilities. Researchers have found writing to have a positive influence on the word recognition ability of young children, especially when they were encouraged to write using invented spelling (Clarke, 1988; Tierney & Shanahan, 1991).

Some level of phonemic awareness and phonics knowledge is necessary before children can begin to write with invented spellings. Then, as children continue to write words they can't spell, segmenting them into phonemes and assigning letters to those phonemes, their phonemic awareness abilities, phonics knowledge, and word recognition increase through the experience (see Chapter 3).

Will children's normal exposures to the written language in both their home and school environments be sufficient for them to develop the phonemic awareness and phonics knowledge needed to begin writing with invented spellings naturally, or should teachers help students write words by sounds? Although educators are presently divided on this issue, the more popular position seems to be that the ability to use invented spelling develops naturally in most children. Proponents present evidence to support their position from studies of children's early writing, indicating that many children go through predictable writing stages.

Children come to school with varying degrees of knowledge about the written language, knowledge they have acquired through their exposures to print in the home and community. Many of them have already experimented with writing by the time they enter school. These early preschool experiences are immediately followed by writing experiences in school, since writing is a normal part of the daily curriculum in most kindergarten and first-grade classrooms. Researchers studying children's early writing (from pre-kindergarten through grade two) have concluded that most of them go through predictable writing stages reflecting varying levels of understanding of the alphabetic principle. Different scholars have given these stages different names, but the descriptions of those stages are fairly consistent.

The term *invented spelling* describes children's spellings before they learn the orthographic (spelling) system of the language. The first writing stage, the *precommunicative* or *prephonemic* stage, is characterized by the random use of letters. At this stage, children string letters together so their writing looks something like it should, but the letters do not relate in any way to the sounds they represent. Children at this stage are generally always nonreaders, but they know that words are represented by letters.

During the second stage, the *semiphonetic* or *early phonemic* stage, children begin to realize the connection between letters in written words and sounds in spoken ones. However, at this stage they write letters for only one or two sounds in a word, either the beginning, or the beginning and ending. For example, the word *dog* might be spelled *d,* or *dg.*

During the third writing stage, the *phonetic, phonemic,* or *letter–name* stage, vowels begin to appear in children's invented spellings. It is at this stage that children consistently try to break words into their phonemes and represent them with letters. Children often choose letters to represent phonemes on the basis of their letter–name sounds. They try to match each phoneme in a word with one alphabet letter, perceiving a one-to-one match between word sounds and letters.

The letter–name spelling stage is a time when children's concept of a written word is beginning to stabilize:

> Children who produce letter-name spelling have developed a system of spelling that can be read by others who understand the system. Letter–name spelling represents the high-water mark of children's intuitive spelling development, and their spellings during this period are their most original. From this point on, children will become increasingly aware of the details of standard spelling, and their spelling will grow closer to that of adults.
>
> Most children become letter–name spellers by Thanksgiving in first grade. Some begin sooner, and several may wait until late first grade to start using the letter–name strategy. Letter–name spellings will persist into second grade, though most second graders will use transitional strategies, especially in the second half of the year. (Temple, Nathan, Temple, & Burris, 1993, p. 113)

Children begin letter–name spelling before they begin to recode words since they acquire the ability to spell words by sounds before they are able to read words by sounds (Bryant & Bradley, 1980; Huxford, Terrell, & Bradley, 1991). Evidently the ability to segment sounds in words and match them with letters is easier for children than blending sounds in written words. However, phonemic spelling seems to be an indicator that children will profit from recoding instruction.

During the fourth, or *transitional,* writing stage, children abandon the habit of trying to match each phoneme in a word with one letter. They recognize that sometimes word sounds are represented by chunks of letters. They begin to include silent letters and incorporate spelling patterns in their spellings (silent *e* to represent long vowel sounds, etc.), but not consistently. Words with irregular spellings are often misspelled. Children at the transitional stage are readers.

The last stage is called the *correct* or *conventional* stage. Even though children at this stage misspell words, they have learned enough about English orthography to spell a large number of words correctly, even many of the irregularly spelled ones.

Do all children invent spelling? Probably not. "If every child spontaneously wrote out invented spelling at the kitchen table, the phenomenon would be as widely known a writing behavior as baby talk is a speech behavior. But they don't and it's not. Many children do not explore writing before they enter school, and there they usually practice writing only words they have memorized" (Temple, Nation, Temple, & Burris, 1993, p. 79).

Although we know much about children's writing stages, there is still much to learn. Many questions are unanswered about the factors influencing children's writing development. What causes children to move from one developmental stage to another? Can teachers help children move through developmental stages by using intervention strategies? If so, what kinds of intervention strategies are most effective?

Application Activities

1. Find a reader who does not decode well. Identify a book this reader wants to read, but cannot read independently. Using the dyad reading strategy described in this chapter, read the book with the student for 20 minutes a day, over a 5- to

6-day period. Discuss and evaluate the experience with the student when the activity is completed.

2. Suppose four literature books had unique-to-total word ratios of 1:4, 1:8, 1:2.5, and 1:1, respectively. In which book would the words used be repeated most frequently? Which book would be best suited for group assisted reading? Why?

3. How many words can you make from the letters used in the title, *Make Way for Ducklings?*

4. Analyze a preschool or kindergarten child's written composition. Which writing stage is the child in?

   (a) precommunicative or prephonemic

   (b) semiphonetic or early phonemic

   (c) phonetic, phonemic, or letter–name

   (d) transitional

   (e) correct or conventional

Justify your conclusion.

Chapter 10

Teaching Phonics in 10 Minutes a Day

In the previous chapter, we discussed strategies for teaching phonics in the context of children's meaningful reading experiences. In this chapter, we present strategies for teaching phonics as a brief, but separate and isolated, activity. Although the present sentiment among some educators is against teaching phonics "out of context," there are legitimate reasons for ignoring that censure. Critics of isolated phonics instruction argue that it is ineffective and meaningless to children, and that children dislike it, but offer little evidence against "out of context" phonics instruction other than personal reasoning generated from a whole language philosophical perspective. However, some research findings (Eldredge & Butterfield, 1986; Eldredge, 1988–1989; Eldredge, 1991) reveal that brief, isolated phonics instruction in an otherwise predominantly holistic environment improves children's reading achievement, helps them understand how print and speech are related, and is associated with positive attitudes toward reading rather than negative ones. In fact, "out of context" phonics instruction may actually make it possible for children to have better experiences with literature, since their experience is not encumbered with a phonics component. However, making the decision to teach phonics in or out of context is a choice that, as a teacher, you must make for yourself. I describe both approaches in this book. The features of effective phonics instruction noted in Chapter 4 are more important to successful instruction than whether you teach phonics in or out of "context."

Effective phonics instruction does not need to absorb much classroom time. You can teach each of the lesson models presented in this chapter to large or small groups of children in no more than 10 minutes. Many teachers presently using them teach one lesson per day (short vowel lessons excepted) to all of the children at one time, and complete their instruction in about 7 minutes.

Young children need two types of experiences with written language to become fully literate individuals. They need personally relevant reasons to use it, and they need to be involved in metalinguistic awareness activities to help them understand how it works. Children need to be involved in holistic reading and writing experiences, and they need to understand the spelling–sound system that underlies these experiences. Effective phonics instruction provides the metalinguistic experiences children need to become literate individuals.

The 10-minute phonics lessons described in this chapter support the efforts of teachers by helping them teach children how the alphabetic system works. Using these lessons, teachers may allocate more classroom time for children to enjoy other reading and writing activities:

1. engage in shared book experiences, taped assisted reading, dyad reading, and group assisted reading;
2. write on topics relevant to them;
3. read extensively (magazines, books, and other text material);
4. explore topics of interest; and
5. engage in other practices consistent with a balanced, comprehensive literacy program (see Chapter 1).

Phonics Lessons

The phonics elements and patterns described in Chapter 8 are taught in the lessons presented in this chapter. The following lessons have been designed based on this text's intent to teach phonics as a strategy to use rather than skills to learn. However, as important as word identification strategies are to nonfluent readers, the major benefits young readers will reap from these lessons will be increased understanding of how the spoken language maps onto the written language, and the increased ability to access written words into lexical memory (see Chapter 4).

When teaching the phonics lessons, the principles of social mediation and scaffolding discussed in Chapter 7 will be used. You will be interacting with students, acting as mediators for them, when needed, as they interact with written text. In the initial lessons, you will do the majority of the tasks *with* students, while they do only a small number of tasks independently. In the later lessons they will need less assistance.

All of the lessons are "strategy oriented." Phonics elements and patterns are introduced systematically, in the following order:

1. Short vowel sounds
2. Initial consonant sounds
3. Final consonant sounds
4. Vowel principles (determining vowel sounds by syllable pattern)
5. Vowel teams (determining vowel sounds by letter clusters)
6. Consonant digraph sounds
7. Consonant blends (two alternate approaches)
8. The letter *y* as a vowel

The lessons progress in the following steps. While every lesson does not contain all steps, the steps for each lesson follow the same order:

1. Association
2. Synthesizing

3. Application (sentences)
4. Word formation
5. Word discrimination
6. Dictation
7. Advanced synthesizing

Note: In each step of a lesson, except dictation, you are asked to write something on the chalkboard. I have organized the lessons to help you better visualize how what you say in each lesson step relates to what you write on the chalkboard. When teaching the lessons to children you should write everything needed for all of the lesson steps on the chalkboard before you begin.

Word lists for all of the phonics lessons are found in Appendix D.

Short Vowel Sounds

The 6 steps in each short vowel lesson are designed to help students a) learn to associate the appropriate sounds with a specific vowel letter, and b) learn to identify written words by sounds.

Sample Vowel Lesson—Vowel A

Association. Write the words *am, at, an,* and *add* on the chalkboard. Underline the letter *a* in each of the words, and say, "Notice that each word I have written on the chalkboard begins with the same letter. Each word also begins with the same sound. Listen carefully to the words as I read them to see if you can hear the /a/ sound at the beginning of each one." As you read each word point to the letter *a* and emphasize the /a/ sound.

Point to the word *am.* Say, "Listen as I say the two sounds in the word *am.*" Point to the appropriate letters as you say the two sounds, and then glide your finger under both letters as you say the word: "/a/. . /m/. . . /am/." Say, "The letter *a* (point to the letter) in the word *am* stands for the /a/ sound." Keep pointing to the letter *a* in the word *am.* "Say /a/." Wait for a response. Point to the appropriate letters as you continue. "Say /a/. . /m/. . . /am/." Wait for a response. Repeat this process with the words *at, an,* and *add.*

Synthesizing. Write the words *ask, and,* and *ant* on the chalkboard. Point to the letter *a* in each of the words. Say, "You know the sound of this letter. We are going to identify each of the words on the chalkboard by their sounds. You say the sound of the letter *a* in each of the words, and I will say the sounds after the letter *a.* After you hear all of the sounds in a word, blend them together quickly in your mind, and tell me what the word is."

Point to the letter *a* in the word *ask.* Say, "Say the sound of this letter." Wait for a response. Say, "The last two letters in the word (point to the letters *sk*) stand for the /sk/ sound. What is the word?" Wait for a response. Repeat this process with the words *and* and *ant.*

Application (Sentences). Write the following sentence on the chalkboard: *That man can dance fast.* Say, "I taught you to isolate the /a/ sound at the beginning of words because it's easier to hear it there. However, most of the time the /a/ sound will be found in the middle of words." Point to the letter *a* in each of the words in the sentence on the chalkboard. Say, "If you don't recognize written words, and if you can't identify them using context clues, then you can sound them out by doing the following:

1. Say the vowel sound of the word.
2. Blend the sound of the letter or letters before the vowel *with* the vowel sound.
3. Say the sound of the letter or letters after the vowel.
4. Put all of the sounds together to identify the word."

Say, "Let's see if we can sound out the words in this sentence." Point to the letter *a* in the word *That.* "What is the sound of this letter?" Wait for the students to respond with the appropriate sound. Point to the letters *Tha* in the word *That.* Say, "In this word the letters *T h a* say /tha/." Point to the letter *t* at the end of the word. Say, "In this word the letter *t* comes after the vowel and the sound of *t* is /t/." Say, "When you blend the sounds /tha/ and /t/ together, what word do you get?" Wait for a response. Continue this process with all of the words in the sentence, and then ask the students to read the entire sequence as quickly as they can.

Word Formation. Write the following on the chalkboard: _n. Run your finger under the _ and then the *n* while you say, "This word is /a/. . /n/. What sound is missing?" Wait for a response. "What letter is missing?" Wait for a response. Repeat this process with _m, _dd, _ct.

Word Discrimination. Write the following on the chalkboard:

at

it

Point to the letter *t* in both *at* and *it* as you say, "What letter is the same in these two words?" Wait for a response. Point to the letters *i* and *a* in *it* and *at.* Say, "What letters are different?" Wait for a response. Say, "What sounds are different?" Point to the letter *a* in the word *at.* Wait for the students to say /a/. Point to the letter *i* in the word *it.* "The sound of this letter is /i/." Point to each of the letters in the word *at* as you say, "/a/. . /t/ is . . . ?" Wait for the students to say "at." Point to each of the letters in the word *it* as you say, "/i/. . /t/ is . . . ?" Wait for the students to say "it." Repeat this process with other word pairs: *an, on; add, odd,* and so on.

Dictation. Provide the students with "magic" slate boards, small chalkboards, or scrap paper on which to write. Say, "Write the letter that stands for the /a/ sound you hear at the beginning of the word /a/. . /sk/. At the count of three hold up what you have written. One . . . two . . . three." Scan the room to assess the accuracy of individual responses. Write the letter *a* on the chalkboard. Say, "Most of you have written the letter *a* on your paper. The letter *a* stands for the /a/ sound we hear at the beginning of the word *ask*. Write the letters *sk* after the *a* as you say the word *ask*. Repeat this process with the words *at, add,* and *am*.

Note: Word lists for the other vowel lessons are found in Appendix D.

Beginning Consonant Sounds

The seven steps in the beginning consonant lessons are designed to help students a) learn to associate the appropriate sounds with specific consonant letters; b) learn to blend beginning consonant sounds in words with the vowel sounds that follow them; and c) learn to identify words by sounds.

Sample Beginning Consonant Lesson—Consonant W

Association. Write the words *wax, with, west,* and *wish* on the chalkboard. Underline the letter *w* in each of the words, and say, "Notice that each word I have written begins with the same letter. Each word also begins with the same sound. Listen carefully to the words as I read them to see if you can hear how they sound alike at the beginning." As you read each word, point to the letter *w*.

Point to the letter *a* in the word *wax*. Say, "You know the /a/ sound in the word *wax*. When you blend the first sound of the word with the /a/ sound you get /wa/. Listen as I say the word *wax* in two parts . . . ." Point to the appropriate letters as you say, "/wa/. . /ks/. . . /waks/." Ask the students to say the word *wax* in two parts as you point to the appropriate letters. Repeat this process with the words *with, west,* and *wish*.

Synthesizing. Write the words *wag, win, web,* and *wind* on the chalkboard. Say, "We are going to identify these words by sounds." Point to the vowel letters in each word and say, "You know the vowel sounds in each of these words. Say the vowel sound in each word first. Then blend the sound of *w* with the vowel sound, and then I will say the sound or sounds after the vowel. After you hear all of the sounds in the word, blend them together quickly in your mind, and tell me what the word is."

Point to the letter *a* in the word *wag*. "Say the sound of this letter." Wait for a response. Point to the letters *wa* in the word *wag*. "Say the sound of the first two letters." Wait for a response. Point to the letter *g*. "The last letter in the word says /g/. What is the word?" Wait for a response. Repeat the process above with the words *win, web,* and *wind*.

Application (Sentences). Write the following sentence on the chalkboard: _The witch of the west wept_. Say, "We will read the underlined words in this sentence and sound out the words that are not underlined." Point to the first word and read it with the students. Point to the letter *i* in the word *witch*. Say, "Say the sound of this letter."

Wait for a response. Point to the letters *wi* in the word *witch*. "Say the sound of the first two letters." Wait for a response. Point to the letters *tch*. Say, "The last three letters in the word say /ch/. What is the word?" Wait for a response. Continue this process with all of the words in the sentence, and then ask the students to read the entire sentence as quickly as they can.

Word Formation. Write the following on the chalkboard: _ _*pt*. Run your finger under the _ _ and the *pt* while you say, "This word is /we/. . /pt/. What sound is missing?" Wait for a response. "What letters are missing?" Wait for a response. Repeat this process using the words *wish*, *west*, *web*, and *witch*.

Word Discrimination. Write the following on the chalkboard:

west

test

Point to each of the letters *est* in both *west* and *test*, and say, "What letters are alike in these two words?" Point to the letters *w* and *t* in *west* and *test*. Wait for a response. Say, "What letters are different?" Wait for a response. Say, "What sounds are different?" Point to the letters *we* in the word *west*. Prompt the students to say /we/. Point to the letters *te* in the word *test*. "The sounds of these letters are /te/." Point to the appropriate letters in the word *west* as you say, "/we/. . /st/ is . . . ?" Wait for the students to say "*west*." Point to the appropriate letters in the word *test* as you say, "/te/. . /st/ is . . . ?" Wait for the students to say "*test*." Repeat this process with word pairs: *will, hill; wept, kept; wed, bed.*

Dictation. Provide the students with "magic" slate boards, small chalkboards, or scrap paper on which to write. Say, "Write the two letters that stand for the /wi/ sound you hear at the beginning of the word /wi/. . /th/. At the count of three hold up what you have written. One . . . two . . . three." Scan the room to assess the accuracy of individual responses. Write the letters *wi* on the chalkboard. Say, "Most of you have written the letters *w* and *i* on your paper. The letters *w* and *i* stand for the /wi/ sound we hear at the beginning of the word *with*." Write the letters *th* after the *wi* as you say the word *with*. Repeat this process with the words *wept* and *wish*.

Advanced Synthesizing. Write the word *wade* on the chalkboard. Point to the letter *a* in the word *wade*. Say, "In this word this letter says /ā/." Glide your finger under the letters *wa* in the word *wade*. Say, "What is the sound of the first two letters?" Wait for a response. Point to the letters *de* in the word *wade*. Say, "The last two letters say /d/. What is the word?" Wait for a response. Continue this process with the words *waist, wait, wake, wave, way, we, weak, week, weed, weep, wide, wife, wipe, wood, wool.*

Note: It is recommended that the consonant lessons be taught in the following order: *m, p, s, b, t, d, f, l, r, n, w, h, c/k/, k, j, g, g/j/, c/s/, y, v, z, qu.* Word lists for the other beginning consonant lessons are found in Appendix D.

Final Consonant Sounds

The seven steps in a final consonant lesson are designed to help students a) identify short vowel sounds in words; b) blend the beginning consonant sounds in words with the vowel sounds that follow them; c) identify consonant sounds in the final position of words; and d) synthesize all of the sounds in the words so the words can be identified.

Sample Final Consonant Lesson—Consonants P and B

Association. Write the words *map, hop, nap,* and *lip* on the chalkboard. Underline the letter *p* in each of the words, and say, "Notice that each word I have written on the chalkboard ends with the same letter. Each word also ends with the same sound. Listen carefully to the words as I read them to see if you can hear how they sound alike at the end." As you say the /p/ sound in each word, point to the letter *p*.

Point to the word *map*. Say, "Listen as I say the word *map* in two parts," Point to the appropriate letters as you say the sounds, and then glide your finger under the appropriate letters as you say, "/ma/../p/.../map/." Ask the students to say the word in two parts as you glide your finger under the appropriate letters. Say, "The letter *p* (point to the letter) in the word *map* stands for the /p/ sound." Keep pointing to the letter *p*. "Say /p/." Repeat this process with the words *hop, nap,* and *lip*.

Write the words *cab, web, bib,* and *cub* on the chalkboard. Repeat the association step using each of the words.

Synthesizing. Write the words *cap, hub, tip, rub, pup,* and *rip* on the chalkboard. Say, "We are going to identify these words by their sounds. First, say the vowel sound in each word; second, blend the beginning consonant sound with the vowel sound; third, say the consonant sound after the vowel; and after you have heard all of the sounds in the word, blend them together quickly in your mind to identify the word."

Point to the letter *a* in the word *cap* and say, "Say the sound of this letter." Wait for a response. Point to the letters *ca* in the word *cap*. "Say the sounds of the first two letters." Wait for a response. Point to the letter *p* in the word *cap*. "Say the sound of the last letter in the word." Wait for a response. "Say the word." Wait for a response. Repeat the process above with the words *hub, tip, rub, pup,* and *rip*.

Application (Sentences). Write the following sentence on the chalkboard: <u>A</u> *pup* <u>with</u> <u>much</u> *pep* <u>can</u> <u>eat</u> *ripe grapes*. Say, "We will read the underlined words in this sentence and sound out the words that are not underlined." Point to the first word and read it with the students. Point to the letter *u* in the word *pup* and say, "Say the sound of this letter." Wait for a response. Point to the letters *pu* in the word *pup*. "Say the sound of the first two letters." Wait for a response. Point to the letter *p* at the end of the word *pup*. "Say the sound of the last letter in the word." Wait for a response. Ask, "What is the word?" Wait for a response. Continue this process with all of the words in the sentence, and then ask the students to read the entire sentence as quickly as they can.

Write the following sentence on the chalkboard: *Rob* <u>got</u> *a job* <u>driving</u> <u>a</u> *cab*. Have the students read this sentence the same way they did the first sentence.

Word Formation. Write the following on the chalkboard: *ca_*. Run your finger under the *ca* and the _ while you say, "This word is /ka/. . /p/. What sound is missing?" Wait for a response. Ask, "What letter is missing?" Wait for a response, and write the correct letter. Repeat this process using the words *lap, dip, web, mop, nap, ripe, hope,* and *tribe*.

Word Discrimination. Write the following on the chalkboard:

> *cup*
> *cub*

Point to the letters *cu* in both *cup* and *cub* and ask, "What letters are alike in these two words?" Wait for a response. Point to the letters *p* and *b* in *cup* and *cub*. "What letters are different?" Wait for a response. "What sounds are different?" Wait for a response. "What are the words?" Wait for a response. Repeat this process with word pairs: *cab, cap; rope, robe; mop, mob; gap, gab*.

Dictation. Provide the students with "magic" slate boards, small chalkboards, or paper on which to write. Say, "Write the letter that stands for the /p/ sound that you hear at the end of the word /ho/. . /p/. At the count of three hold up what you have written. One . . . two . . . three." Scan the room to assess the accuracy of individual responses. Write the letter *p* on the chalkboard. "Most of you have written the letter *p* on your paper. The letter *p* stands for the /p/ sound we hear at the end of the word *hop*." Write the letters *ho* before the letter *p* as you say the word *hop*. Repeat this process with the words *leap, tub, rob,* and *hip*.

Advanced Synthesizing. Write the word *tape* on the chalkboard. Point to the letter *a* in the word *tape*. Say, "In this word the letter *a* says /ā/." Glide your finger under the letters *ta* and say, "What is the sound of the first two letters?" Wait for a response. Point to the letters *pe* and say, "What is the ending sound of the word?" Wait for a response. Continue this process with the words *robe, pipe, tribe, hope, soap, rope,* and *deep*.

Note: Word lists for the other ending consonant lessons are found in Appendix D.

Vowel Principles

Write the words *jump* and *robin* on the chalkboard. Point to the *u* in the word *jump*. Say, "Words that have one vowel sound are one-syllable words." Point to the letters *o* and *i* in the word *robin*. Say, "Words that have two vowel sounds are two-syllable words." Rewrite the word *robin*, adding a space between the syllables: *rob in*. Point to the *rob*, and then point to the *in*. Say, "A syllable is the part of the word that contains one vowel sound. The word *robin* is a two-syllable word." Point to *rob*. "This syllable says /rob/." Point to *in*. "This syllable says /un/."

Write the word *men* on the chalkboard. Point to the letter *e* in the word *men*. "The vowel sound in the word *men* is /e/. When a single vowel word or syllable ends with consonant letters, the vowel says its short sound. Another way of saying this principle is, if a vowel letter is followed by one or more consonants that vowel is 'protected' and says its calm short sound—the sound you have already learned."

Write the word *me* on the chalkboard right under the word *men*. Point to the letter *e* in the word *me*. Say, "When a single vowel word or syllable does not end with consonant letters, the vowel says its long sound. Another way of saying this principle is, if a vowel letter is not followed by consonant letters that vowel is 'unprotected' and says its long sound. The vowel's long sound is its own name. For example, the long sound of *a* is /ā/. Unprotected vowels yell out in frustration and say their own names because they are not protected by consonants." Point to the letter *e* in the word *me*. Say, "In this word the vowel sound is /ē/ and the word is *me*."

Continue this discussion of open (unprotected) vowels and closed (protected) vowels and syllables using the following words:

on	*it*	*at*	*up*
so	*pi-lot*	*ba-con*	*fu-ture*

Write the word *cap* on the chalkboard. Point to the letter *a* in the word *cap*. Say, "What is the vowel sound in this word?" Wait for a response. "The vowel letter *a* says /a/ because it is a protected vowel."

Write the word *cape* on the chalkboard underneath the word *cap*. Point to the letter *a* in the word *cape*. Say, "The vowel letter *a* in the word *cape* has a consonant (point to the *p*) after it to protect it, but the vowel letter *e* (point to the letter) has no protector. Guess what happens in these types of words? The letter *a* cries out and says his own name /ā/ because he is worried about his vowel friend *e*. His friend *e* doesn't say anything. We call this syllable a lonely *e* syllable. Whenever you see a vowel in a lonely *e* word or syllable, give the vowel its long sound."

Continue this discussion of closed syllables and vowel-consonant-*e* syllables using the following words:

us	*it*	*end*	*odd*
use	*ice*	*eve*	*ode*

Write the words *not, no,* and *note* on the chalkboard. Say, "Let's summarize what we have learned today. There are three types of word or syllable patterns." Point to the word *not*. "There is the protected vowel syllable." Point to the word *no*. "There is the unprotected vowel syllable." Point to the word *note*. "There is the lonely *e* syllable." Point to the vowel in the word *not*. "Protected vowels say their short sounds." Point to the vowel in the word *no*. "Unprotected vowels and (point to the vowel in the word *note*) vowels in lonely *e* syllables say their long sounds."

Synthesizing. Ask students to say the vowel sounds in the following words. Ask them to tell you why they chose the sounds they chose, and ask them to identify the words by sounds. When blending sounds in polysyllabic words, ask students to sound out the first syllable only. You sound out the second syllable for them.

ate, ba-by, bake, back, ba-sic, ape, came, fame, age, ba-con, cap, cape, fan, da-ta, cat, cage, fa-vor, fat, fate, la-ter, face, fast, la-dy, safe, sat, la-bor, eve, be-came, he, hen, be-gan, wed, we, fete, ce-dar, tweed, fled, flee, get, ce-ment, beg, bee, e-ven, trend, tree, fe-ver, bed, be, hem, he, yet, ye, fret, free, she, shed, gee, spree, three, thresh, when, whee, ice, ci-der, bite, bit, wife, di-ver, bike, line, fi-ber, lid, time, i-cy, wide, size, li-lac, sit, side, bone, bo-ny, owe, cone, co-bra, rock, rope, do-nate, sob, so, fo-cus, poke, ho-ly, pond, pop, lo-cal, doze, dog, lo-cate, go, got, log, lo, fro, frost, pro, prod, tho, use, hu-mor, cut, cute, mu-sic, mule, mud, pu-pil, fuse, fuss, u-nit, ute, fume, fun

Note: Six phonograms violate the closed (protected) vowel principle: *ost, old, oll, olt, ind,* and *ild.* We call these phonograms "foolers."

ost	old	oll	olt	ind	ild
post	*bold*	*toll*	*bolt*	*bind*	*wild*
most	*cold*	*roll*	*colt*	*wind*	*mild*
ghost	*told*	*poll*	*jolt*	*mind*	*child*
host	*sold*	*stroll*		*rind*	
	mold	*troll*		*hind*	
	gold			*kind*	
	hold			*find*	
	fold			*grind*	

Vowel Teams

The six steps outlined below are to be followed when teaching any of the vowel teams. However, you will need to modify your word formation and dictation steps when teaching vowels represented by more than one vowel team. For example, the vowel team *oi* represents the same sound as the vowel team *oy*. If you ask students to write the letters that stand for the /oi/ sound in a particular word they could logically give either spelling. Therefore, if you ask the students to write the letters that stand for the /oi/ sound in the word *boy* and they write *oi*, ask them to write the other two letters that also represent the /oi/ sound, and explain to them that the /oi/ sound in the word *boy* is spelled *oy*.

Sample Vowel Team Lesson—Murmur Diphthong AR

Association. Write the words *arm, art, arch,* and *ark* on the chalkboard. Underline the letters *ar* in each of the words and say, "Notice that each word I have written on the chalkboard begins with the same two letters. Each word also begins with the same sound. Listen carefully to the words as I read them to see if you can hear how they sound alike at the beginning." As you read each word point to the letters *ar* and emphasize the /ar/ sound.

Point to the letters *ar* in the word *arm*. Say, "This word says *arm*. Listen to the /ar/ and the /m/ sounds in the word /ar . . m/." Repeat the word, isolating the /ar/ and the /m/ sounds so the students can hear them. "Say the sounds of each part of the word as I underline the parts: /ar/. . /m/." Wait for a response. Point to the letters *ar*. Say, "The letters *ar* in the word *arm* stand for the /ar/ sound. Say /ar/. . /m/. . . /arm/." Wait for a response. Repeat this process with the words *art, arch,* and *ark*.

Synthesizing. Write the words *barn, start, shark,* and *march* on the chalkboard. Say, "We are going to identify these words by their sounds." Point to the letters *ar* in the word *barn*. "Say the sound of these letters." Wait for a response. Draw a line under the letters *bar* in the word *barn*. Say, "Say the sounds represented by the first three letters." Wait for a response. Draw a line under the letter *n* in the word *barn*. Say, "Say the sound of the last letter." Wait for a response. Ask, "What is the word?" Wait for a response. Repeat this process with the words *start, shark,* and *march.*

Application (Sentences). Write the following sentence on the chalkboard: *March the large cow out of the yard and put her in the barn.* Say, "We will read the underlined words in this sentence and sound out the words that are not underlined." Underline the letters *ar* in the word *March.* Say, "Say the sound of these letters." Wait for a response. Draw a line under the letters *Mar* in the word *March.* Say, "Say the sounds represented by the first three letters." Wait for a response. Draw a line under the letters *ch* in the word *March.* Say, "The sound of the last two letters of the word is /ch/." Ask, "What is the word?" Wait for a response. (*Note:* The ending grapheme *ch* in the word *march* had not been taught up to this point. Therefore, the students were told the sound.)

Underline the letters *ar* in the word *large.* Say, "Say the sound of these letters." Wait for a response. Draw a line under the letters *lar* in the word *large.* Say, "Say the sounds represented by the first three letters." Wait for a response. Draw a line under the letters *ge* in the word *large.* "Say the sound of the last two letters of the word." Wait for a response. Ask, "What is the word?" Wait for a response. (*Note:* The students should remember that *ge* represents the /j/ sound at the end of words.)

Continue this process with all of the words in the sentence, and then ask the students to read the sentence as quickly as they can.

Word Formation. Write the following on the chalkboard: *sh_ _ k.* Run your finger under *sh_ _* and the letter *k* while you say, "This word is /shar/. . /k/. What sound is missing?" Wait for a response. Ask, "What letters are missing?" Wait for a response, and write the letters. Repeat this process using the words *starch, smart, spark,* and *charge.*

Word Discrimination. Write the following on the chalkboard:

> *hard*
> *hid*

Point to the letters *h* and *d* in both *hard* and *hid.* Ask, "What letters are alike in these two words?" Wait for a response. Point to the letters *ar* and *i* in *hard* and *hid.* Ask, "What letters are different?" Wait for a response. Point to the vowel letters in both words again. Ask, "What sounds are different?" Wait for a response. "What are the words?" Wait for a response. Repeat this process with the word pairs: *card, cod; harm, him; part, pot.*

Dictation. Provide the students with "magic" slate boards, small chalkboards, or scrap paper to write on. Say, "Write the letters that stand for the /ar/ sound that you hear in the word /spar/. . /k/. At the count of three hold up what you have written. One . . . two . . . three." Scan the room to assess the accuracy of individual responses. Write the letters *ar* on the chalkboard. Say, "Most of you have written the letters *a* and *r* on your paper. These letters stand for the /ar/ sound we hear in the word *spark.*" Write the letters *sp* before the letters *ar,* and the letter *k* after those letters as you say the word *spark.* Repeat this process with the words *arm, shark,* and *march.*

Note: It is recommended that the vowel team lessons be taught in the following order: *ai, ay, ee, oa, ir, er, ur, ar, or, ea, oy, oi, ou, ow, oo, au, aw, ew, ue, igh.* Word lists for the other vowel team lessons are found in Appendix D.

Beginning Consonant Digraph Sounds

The six steps in a beginning consonant digraph lesson are designed to help students a) learn to associate specific sounds with specific consonant digraphs; b) learn to blend consonant digraph sounds in words with the vowel sounds that follow them; c) identify the consonant sounds in the final position of words; and D) synthesize all of the sounds in the words so they can be identified.

Sample Beginning Consonant Digraph Lesson—Digraph CH

Association. Write the words *chin, chop, chess, chat,* and *chum* on the chalkboard. Underline the letters *ch* in each of the words and say, "Notice that each word I have written on the chalkboard begins with the same letters. Each word also begins with the same sound. Listen carefully to the words as I read them to see if you can hear the /ch/ sound at the beginning." As you read each word point to the letters *ch* and emphasize the /ch/ sound.

Point to the word *chin.* Say, "Listen as I say the word *chin* in two parts, . . . " Point to the appropriate letters as you say, "/chi/. . /n/. . . /chin/." Ask the students to say the word in two parts as you glide your finger under the appropriate letters. Say, "The letters *chi* (point to the letters) in the word *chin* stand for the /chi/ sound." Repeat this process with the words *chop, chess, chat,* and *chum.*

Synthesizing. Write the words *check, chest, chain,* and *cheat* on the chalkboard. Say, "We are going to identify these words by sounds. First, say the vowel sound in each word; second, blend the /ch/ sound with the vowel sound; and then say the sound or sounds after the vowel. After you have heard all of the sounds in the word, blend them together quickly in your mind, and identify the word."

Point to the letter *e* in the word *check* and say, "Say the sound of this letter." Wait for a response. Point to the letters *che* and say, "Say the sounds of the first three letters." Wait for a response. "Say the sound of the last two letters in the word." Wait for a response. Repeat the process above with the words *chest, chain,* and *cheat.*

Application (Sentences). Write the following sentence on the chalkboard: <u>Do</u> <u>you</u>, <u>by</u> chance, <u>have</u> <u>a</u> chess <u>game</u> <u>in</u> <u>that</u> chest? Say, "We will read the underlined words in this sentence and sound out the words that are not underlined." Point to the first three words and read them with the students. Point to the letter *a* in the word *chance* and say, "Say the sound of this letter." Wait for a response. Point to the letters *cha* and say, "Say the sounds of the first three letters." Wait for a response. Point to the letters *nce* and ask, "What is the ending sound of the word?" Wait for a response. Ask, "What is the word?" Wait for a response. Continue this process with all of the words in the sentence, and then ask the students to read the entire sentence as quickly as they can.

Word Formation. Write the following on the chalkboard: _ _ _p. Run your finger under the _ _ _ and the p while you say, "This word is /cho/. . . /p/. What sound is missing?" Wait for a response. Ask, "What letters are missing?" Wait for a response. Repeat this process using the words *check, chin, chess, champ,* and *chum.*

Word Discrimination. Write the following on the chalkboard:

> *chart*
> *smart*

Point to the letters *art* in both *chart* and *smart.* Say, "What letters are alike in these two words?" Wait for a response. Point to the letters *ch* and *sm* in *chart* and *smart* and ask, "What letters are different?" Wait for a response. "What sounds are different?" Point to the letters *char* in the word *chart.* Wait for the students to say /char/. Point to the letters *smar* in the word *smart.* Say, "The sounds of these letters are /smar/." Point to the first word and say, "/char/. . /t/ is. . .?" Wait for a response. Point to the second word and say, "/smar/. . /t/is. . .?" Wait for a response. Repeat this process with word pairs: *chin, spin; chop, drop; cheat, treat; chain, drain.*

Dictation. Provide the students with "magic" slate boards, small chalkboards, or paper on which to write. Say, "Write the three letters that stand for the /chi/ sound that you hear at the beginning of the word /chi/. . /p/. At the count of three hold up what you have written. One . . . two . . . three." Scan the room to assess the accuracy of individual responses. Write the letters *chi* on the chalkboard and say, "Most of you have written the letters *chi* on your paper. These letters stand for the /chi/ sound we hear at the beginning of the word *chip.*" Write the letter *p* after the letters *chi* as you say the word *chip.* Repeat this process with the words *chirp, chop,* and *choke.*

Note: It is recommended that the beginning consonant digraph lessons be taught in the following order: *th, ch, sh, wh.* Word lists for the other beginning consonant digraph lessons are found in Appendix D.

Ending Consonant Digraph Sounds

The six steps in a final consonant digraph lesson are designed to help the students independently decode unfamiliar words that end with consonant digraphs.

Sample Ending Consonant Digraph Lesson—Digraph CH, Trigraph TCH

Association. Write the words *beach, coach,* and *teach* on the chalkboard. Underline the letters *ch* in each of the words and say, "Notice that each word I have written on the chalkboard ends with the same letters. Each word also ends with the same sound. Listen carefully to the words as I read them to see if you can hear the /ch/ sound at the end of each one." As you say the /ch/ sound in each word, point to the letters *ch.*

Point to the word *beach*. Say, "Listen as I say the word *beach* in two parts." Glide your finger under the appropriate letters as you say, "/bē/. . /ch/. . . /bē ch/. "Ask the students to say the word in two parts, and say, "The letters *ch* (point to the letters) at the end of the word *beach* represent the /ch/ sound." Repeat this process with the words *coach* and *teach*.

Write the words *catch, witch, fetch,* and *notch* on the chalkboard. Repeat the association step with each of the words.

Synthesizing. Write the words *peach, rich, hatch, ditch,* and *couch* on the chalkboard. Say, "We are going to identify these words by their sounds. First, say the vowel sound in each word; second, blend the beginning consonant sound with the vowel sound; third, say the consonant sound after the vowel; and after you have heard all of the sounds in the word, blend them together quickly in your mind to identify the word."

Point to the letters *ea* in the word *peach*. "Say the sound of these letters." Wait for a response. Point to the letters *pea* and say, "Say the sounds of the first three letters." Wait for a response. Point to the letters *ch*. "Say the sound of the last two letters in the word." Wait for a response. "Say the word." Wait for a response. Repeat the process above with the words *rich, hatch, ditch,* and *couch*.

Application (Sentences). Write the following sentence on the chalkboard: <u>Can</u> <u>you</u> catch <u>the</u> witch <u>with</u> <u>the</u> patch <u>on</u> <u>her</u> <u>cape</u>? Say, "We will read the underlined words in this sentence and sound out the words that are not underlined." Point to the first two words and read them with the students. Point to the letter *a* in the word *catch* and say, "Say the sound of this letter." Wait for a response. Point to the letters *ca* in the word *catch*. "Say the sounds of the first two letters." Wait for a response. Point to the letters *tch* at the end of the word and say, "Say the sounds of the last three letters in the word." Wait for a response. Ask, "What is the word?" Wait for a response. Continue this process with all of the words in the sentence, and then ask the students to read the entire sentence as quickly as they can.

Word Formation. Write the following on the chalkboard: *tea* _ _. Run your finger under the _ _ and the *tea* while you say, "This word is /tē/ /ch/. What sound is missing?" Wait for a response. "What letters are missing?" Wait for a response and write the missing letters. Repeat this process using the words *switch, peach, scratch, poach,* and *twitch*.

Note: The sound /ch/ is represented by both the consonant digraph *ch* and the consonant trigraph *tch*. The *ch* spelling follows long vowel sounds, such as in the word *peach,* and the *tch* spelling follows short vowel sounds, such as in the word *patch*. (There are five exceptions to this generalization: *such, much, rich, which,* and *touch*.) Ask your students to listen to the vowel sound before the /ch/ sound to help them know when to write the letters *tch* or *ch*.

Word Discrimination. Write the following on the chalkboard:

catch

cash

Point to the letters *ca* in both *catch* and *cash*. Ask, "What letters are alike in these two words?" Wait for a response. Point to the letters *tch* and *sh* in *catch* and *cash* and ask, "What letters are different?" Wait for a response. "What sounds are different?" Wait for a response. "What are the words?" Wait for a response. Repeat this process with word pairs: *witch, win; ditch, dig; match, mad.*

Dictation. Provide the students with "magic" slate boards, small chalkboards, or paper on which to write. Say, "Write the letters that stand for the /ch/ sound that you hear at the end of the word /kō/ /ch/. At the count of three hold up what you have written. One . . . two . . . three." Scan the room to assess the accuracy of individual responses. Write the letters *ch* on the chalkboard and say, "Most of you have written the letters *ch* on your paper. These letters stand for the /ch/ sound we hear at the end of the word *coach*." Write the letters *coa* before the letters *ch* as you say the word *coach*. Repeat this process with the words *couch, sketch, ditch,* and *batch.*

Note: Word lists for the other ending consonant digraph lessons are found in Appendix D.

Consonant Blends

Students who have learned their individual consonant sounds well usually have little difficulty in learning to blend two or more of them together when they occur in words like *black, stop, blond, street,* and *last.* This lesson is designed to help students learn to blend consonant sounds together so they can identify words containing consonant clusters that are unfamiliar to them in print.

There are two types of consonant blends. The most common type is when two or more consonant letters are clustered together in words, and each consonant letter represents its individual sound. The words *stand, strip,* and *list* contain examples of this type of blend. The second type of blend is where three consonant letters are clustered together in words, and at least two of those letters represent a consonant digraph sound. For example, the letters *ch* in the consonant cluster *nch* (found in such words as *lunch* and *bench*) are a consonant digraph, so the three letters in the *nch* cluster represent only two sounds rather than three, such as we find in the word *street.*

If students have learned to identify and recall the appropriate sounds of the consonant digraphs presented in previous lessons they should have few problems with consonant clusters, regardless of the type they encounter.

There are two major strategies used to teach students to synthesize consonant blends. The first, presented here, is to blend each consonant one at a time to the vowel in the word. The second strategy (see approach 2, following) is to present words containing one specific blend over and over again. With this approach, students learn to recognize the blend as a unit just as they learned to recognize individual consonant letters and the sounds represented by those letters. Approach 1 is best suited for students who have strong consonant letter/sound knowledge, as well as strong blending abilities.

Sample Consonant Blends Lesson (Approach 1)

Synthesizing. Write the word *slip* on the chalkboard. Draw a line under the letter *i* in the word *slip*. Say, "What is the sound of this letter?" Wait for a response. Draw a line under the letters *li* and ask, "What is the sound of these two letters?" Wait for a response. Draw a line under the letters *sli* and ask, "What is the sound of the first three letters?" Wait for a response. Draw a line under the letter *p* and ask, "What is the ending sound?" Wait for a response. "What is the word?" Wait for a response.

Write the word *must* on the chalkboard. Draw a line under the letter *u* and ask, "What is the sound of this letter?" Wait for a response. Draw a line under the letters *mu* and ask, "What is the sound of the first two letters?" Wait for a response. Draw a line under the letter *s* and ask, "What is the sound of this letter?" Wait for a response. "What is the sound of the first three letters?" Wait for a response. Draw a line under the letter *t* and ask, "What is the ending sound?" Wait for a response. "What is the word?" Wait for a response.

Continue this synthesizing activity using selected words from the following list, representing all beginning and ending blends.

stiff, sketch, stamp, skimp, step, skin, sled, block, slump, blond, slept, bless, brick, plan, brisk, pledge, bridge, plush, clip, crack, clutch, crash, clash, crutch, glad, grab, gland, grudge, glimpse, gruff, press, trap, print, trick, prank, trust, frog, drop, fresh, dress, frost, drill, flag, smog, flat, smell, flesh, smack, snack, swim, snob, swept, sniff, swift, spend, scab, spill, scat, spin, scuff, stretch, scrub, strip, scrap, strict, scram, spring, thrill, sprint, thrust, sprung, thrift, split, shrub, splash, shrimp, splint, shred, twin, crop, twist, plug, twelve, dust, risk, pest, mask, cost, brisk, camp, sense, sent, clamp, spent, limp, mint, pond, honk, band, sink, mend, mink, pinch, felt, bench, tilt, punch, melt, rinse, lift, tract, theft, fact, wept, soft, kept, pact, script, gasp, judge, lisp, dodge, grasp, ledge, hinge, dance, plunge, since, cringe, fence, tense

Word Formation. *Beginning Blends.* Write the following on the chalkboard: _ _ _*p*. Run your finger under the _ _ and the *p* while you say, "The last part of this word is /te/. ./p/. What sound is missing?" Wait for a response. "What letters are missing?" Wait for a response and write the missing letters: _ *tep*. Run your finger under the _ *te* and the *p* while you say, "This word is /s/. ./te/. ./p/. What sound is missing?" Wait for a response. "What letter is missing?" Wait for a response and write the missing letter, *step*. "What is the word?" Wait for a response. Repeat this process using the words *splash, shred, strict, fresh,* and *mask*.

Ending Blends. Write the following on the chalkboard: *pi*_. Run your finger under the *pi* and the _ while you say, "This word is /pi/. ./n/. What sound is missing?" Wait for a response. "What letters are missing?" Wait for a response and write the missing letter. Write the following on the chalkboard: *pin*_ _. Run your finger under the *pin* and the _ _ while you say, "This word is /pin/. ./ch/. What sound is missing?" Wait for a response. "What letters are missing?" Wait for a response and write the missing letters. "What is the word?" Wait for a response. Repeat this process using the words *spent, theft, clamp, script,* and *cringe*.

Word Discrimination. *Beginning Blends.* Write the following on the chalkboard:

stamp
tramp

Point to the letters *amp* in both *stamp* and *tramp.* Say, "What letters are alike in these two words?" Wait for a response. Point to the letters *st* and *tr* in *stamp* and *tramp* and ask, "What letters are different?" Wait for a response. Ask the students to sound out each word to hear the different beginning sounds. First, ask them to say the vowel sound in the first word (/a/). Next, ask them to blend the first consonant with that vowel sound (/ta/). Next, ask them to blend the second consonant with /ta/ (/sta/). Next, ask them to add the first consonant after /sta/ (/stam/). Next, ask them to add the last consonant to /stam/ (/stamp/). Finally, ask them to identify the word. Repeat that process with the second word.

Repeat the entire step with word pairs: *skin, spin; brick, trick; strip, clip.*

Ending Blends. Write the following on the chalkboard:

limp
list

Point to the letters *li* in both *limp* and *list.* Say, "What letters are alike in these two words?" Wait for a response. Point to the letters *mp* and *st* in *limp* and *list* and ask, "What letters are different?" Wait for a response. Ask the students to sound out each word to hear the different ending sounds. First, ask them to say the vowel sound in the first word (/i/). Next, ask them to blend the beginning consonant with that vowel sound (/li/). Next, ask them to add the consonant after the vowel to /li/ (/lim/). Next, ask them to add the last consonant to /lim/ (/limp/). Finally, ask them to identify the word. Repeat that process with the second word.

Repeat the entire step using word pairs: *dust, dump; rinse, risk; wept, west.*

Dictation. Provide the students with "magic" slate boards, small chalkboards, or paper on which to write. Say, "Write the four letters that stand for the /spla/ sound you hear at the beginning of the word /spla/. . ./sh/. At the count of three hold up what you have written. One . . . two . . . three." Scan the room to assess the accuracy of individual responses. Write the letters *spla* on the chalkboard and say, "Most of you have written the letters *spla* on your paper. These letters stand for the /spla/ sound we hear at the beginning of the word *splash.*" Write the letters *sh* after the letters *spla* as you say the word *splash.*

Say, "Write the two letters that stand for the /sk/ sound in the word /ma/. . ./sk/. At the count of three hold up what you have written. One . . . two . . . three." Scan the room to assess the accuracy of individual responses. Write the letters *sk* on the chalkboard and say, "Most of you have written the letters *sk* on your paper. These letters stand for the /sk/ sound we hear at the end of the word *mask.*" Write the letters *ma* before the letters *sk* as you say the word *mask.* Continue the dictation activities using any of the words listed in this lesson.

Sample Consonant Blends Lesson (Approach 2—Initial Position, ST)

These lessons are designed for students who have difficulty blending two or more consonant sounds as presented in Approach 1.

Association. Write the words *stick, stem, stop,* and *step* on the chalkboard. Underline the letters *st* in each of the words, and say, "Notice that each word I have written on the chalkboard begins with the same letters. Each word also begins with the same sound. Listen carefully to the words as I read them to see if you can hear how they sound alike at the beginning." As you read each word point to the letters *st*.

Point to the letter *i* in the word *stick*. Say, "You know the /i/ sound in the word *stick*. When you blend the /s/ and /t/ sounds with the /i/ sound you get /sti/. Listen as I say the word *stick* in two parts . . . ." Point to the appropriate letters as you say the sounds, and glide your finger under the appropriate letters as you say, "/sti/. . /k/. . . /stik/." Ask the students to say the word *stick* in two parts, and point to the appropriate letters while you do so. Wait for a response. Repeat this process with the words *stem, stop,* and *step*.

Synthesizing. Write the words *stamp, stack, stiff,* and *stuff* on the chalkboard. Say, "We are going to identify these words by their sounds." Point to the vowel letters in each word and say, "You know the vowel sounds in each of these words. First, say the vowel sound in each word; second, blend the /s/ and /t/ sounds with the vowel sound; I will say the sound or sounds after the vowel if you need help. After you hear all of the sounds in the word, blend them together quickly in your mind, and identify the word."

Point to the letter *a* in the word *stamp*. "Say the sound of this letter." Wait for a response. Point to the letters *sta* and say, "Say the sound of the first three letters." Wait for a response. Point to the letters *mp* and say, "The last two letters in the word say /m/. . /p/. What is the word?" Wait for a response. Repeat the process with the words *stack, stiff,* and *stuff*.

Application (Sentences). Write the following sentence on the chalkboard: *Stop, don't step on that stamp.* Say, "We will read the underlined words in this sentence and sound out the words that are not underlined." Point to the letter *o* in the word *Stop* and say, "Say the sound of this letter." Wait for a response. Point to the letters *Sto*. "Say the sounds of the first three letters." Wait for a response. Point to the letter *p* and ask, "What is the sound of the last letter in this word?" Wait for a response. "What is the word?" Wait for a response. Continue this process with all of the words in the sentence, and then ask the students to read the entire sentence as quickly as they can.

Word Formation. Write the following on the chalkboard: _ _ _ *p*. Run your finger under the _ _ _ and the *p* while you say, "This word is /sto/. . /p/. What sound is missing?" Wait for a response. "What letters are missing?" Wait for a response. Repeat this process using the words *stem, stitch,* and *storm*.

Word Discrimination. Write the following on the chalkboard:

stop
mop

Point to the letters *op* in both *stop* and *mop*. Ask, "What letters are alike in these two words?" Wait for a response. Point to the letters *st* and *m* in *stop* and *mop* and ask, "What letters are different?" Wait for a response. "What sounds are different?" Encourage the students to say /sto/ and /mo/. Say, "The ending sound in these words is /p/. What is the first word?" Wait for a response. "What is the second word?" Wait for a response. Repeat this process with word pairs: *stock, flock; stitch, hitch; stem, them.*

Dictation. Provide the students with "magic" slate boards, small chalkboards, or paper on which to write. Say, "Write the three letters that stand for the /sti/ sound that you hear at the beginning of the word /sti/../f/. At the count of three hold up what you have written. One . . . two . . . three." Scan the room to assess the accuracy of individual responses. Write the letters *sti* on the chalkboard and say, "Most of you have written the letters *sti* on your paper. These letters stand for the /sti/ sound we hear at the beginning of the word *stiff.*" Write the letters *ff* after the *sti* as you say the word *stiff.* Repeat this process with the words *stuff* and *stamp.*

Advanced Synthesizing. Write the word *start* on the chalkboard. Point to the letters *ar* and say, "What is the sound of these letters?" Wait for a response. Glide your finger under the letters *star* and ask, "What are the sounds of the first four letters?" Wait for a response. "What is the sound of the last letter?" Wait for a response. "What is the word?" Wait for a response. Continue this process with the words *starch, starve, stay, steal, stern, stew, stir, stone, storm,* and other similar words.

Note: It is recommended that the beginning consonant blends lessons be taught in the following order: *st, pr, tr, gr, pl, cl, cr, str, br, dr, sp, fl, fr, bl, sl, sw, sm, sc, thr, sk, gl, tw, scr, spr, sn, spl, shr.* Word lists for the other beginning consonant blends lessons are found in Appendix D.

Sample Consonant Blends Lesson (Approach 2—Final Position, ST)

Association. Write the words *cost, nest, fast,* and *dust* on the chalkboard. Underline the letters *st* in each of the words, and say, "Notice that each word I have written on the chalkboard ends with the same letters. Each word also ends with the same sound. Listen carefully to the words as I read them to see if you can hear how they sound alike at the end." As you say the /st/ sound in each word point to the letters *st.*

Point to the word *cost.* Say, "Listen as I say the word *cost* in two parts." Glide your finger under the appropriate letters as you say, "/ko/. . /st/. . . . /kost/." Ask the students to say the word *cost* in two parts, and point to the appropriate letters as they say "/ko/. . /st/. . . . /kost/." Say, "The letters *s* and *t* (point to the letters) in the word *cost* stand for the /st/ sound." Keep pointing to the letters *st*. "Say /st/." Repeat this process with the words *nest, fast,* and *dust.*

Write the words *risk, mask, desk,* and *ask* on the chalkboard. Repeat the association step with each of the words.

Synthesizing. Write the words *test, dusk, lost, task, bust,* and *whisk* on the chalkboard. Say, "We are going to identify these words by their sounds. First, say the vowel sound in each word; second, blend the beginning consonant sound with the vowel sound; third, say the consonant sound after the vowel; and after you have heard all of the sounds in the word, blend them together quickly in your mind to identify the word."

Point to the letter *e* in the word *test.* Say, "Say the sound of this letter." Wait for a response. Point to the letters *te* and say, "Say the sounds of the first two letters." Wait for a response. Point to the letters *st* and say, "Say the sound of the last two letters in the word." Wait for a response. "Say the word." Wait for a response. Repeat the process with the words *dusk, lost, task, bust,* and *whisk.*

Application (Sentences). Write the following sentence on the chalkboard: <u>At</u> *dusk* <u>you</u> *must rest* <u>in</u> <u>my</u> *best* <u>chair</u>. Say, "We will read the underlined words in this sentence and sound out the words that are not underlined." Point to the first word and read it with the students. Point to the letter *u* in the word *dusk* and say, "Say the sound of this letter." Wait for a response. Point to the letters *du.* "Say the sound of the first two letters." Wait for a response. Point to the letters *sk.* "Say the sound of the last two letters in the word." Wait for a response. Ask, "What is the word?" Wait for a response. Continue this process with all of the words in the sentence, and then ask the students to read the entire sentence as quickly as they can.

Word Formation. Write the following on the chalkboard: *fro_ _.* Run your finger under the *fro* and the _ _ while you say, "This word is /fro/. . /st/. What sound is missing?" Wait for a response. "What letters are missing?" Wait for a response. Repeat this process using the words *risk, crust, mask, blast, desk,* and *twist.*

Word Discrimination. Write the following on the chalkboard:

rust

rush

Point to the letters *ru* in both *rust* and *rush.* Ask, "What letters are alike in these two words?" Wait for a response. Point to the letters *st* and *sh* in *rust* and *rush* and ask, "What letters are different?" Wait for a response. "What sounds are different?" Wait for a response. "What are the words?" Wait for a response. Repeat this process with word pairs: *disk, dish; mast, mask; ask, ash; cast, cash.*

Dictation. Provide the students with "magic" slate boards, small chalkboards, or paper on which to write. Say, "Write the letters that stand for the /st/ sound that you hear at the end of the word /lo/. . /st/. At the count of three hold up what you have written. One . . . two . . . three." Scan the room to assess the accuracy of individual responses. Write the letters *st* on the chalkboard and say, "Most of you have written the letters *st* on your paper. These letters stand for the /st/ sound we hear at the end of the word *lost*." Write the letters *lo* before the letters *st* as you say the word *lost*. Repeat this process with the words *pest, desk, bust,* and *dusk*.

Note: Word lists for the other beginning consonant blends lessons are found in Appendix D.

Y as a Vowel

The letter *y* is a consonant when it begins a word or a syllable, as in *yellow* and *canyon*. The letter *y* is a vowel when it occurs in a vowel position in a closed syllable *(myth);* in an open syllable *(my);* or in a vowel-consonant-*e* syllable *(rhyme)*.

The letter *y* represents the /i/ sound in a closed syllable *(myth)*. It represents the /ī/ sound in an open syllable in single-syllable words or in an accented open syllable in polysyllabic words *(cry, de-ny)*. It represents the /ē/ sound in an unaccented syllable in polysyllabic words *(hap-py, ba-by)*. Note that in some dialect areas of the country the *y* represents the /i/ sound in unaccented syllables rather than the /ē/ sound.

When teaching *y* as a vowel to students, help them learn that *y* represents the /i/ sound in protected syllables, the /ī/ sound in unprotected single-syllable words, and either /ī/ or /ē/ when it occurs in the last syllable of polysyllabic words.

Association. Write the words *gym, hymn,* and *myth* on the chalkboard. Underline the letter *y* in each of the words and say, "Notice that the vowel letter in each word I have written on the chalkboard is *y*. The letter *y* in each of these words represents the /i/ sound. It is the same sound the letter *i* represents in protected syllables. Listen carefully to the words as I read them to see if you can hear the /i/ sound in each one." As you read each word point to the letter *y* and emphasize the /i/ sound.

Write the words *my, fly,* and *by* on the chalkboard. Underline the letter *y* in each of the words and say, "Notice that the vowel letter in each word I have written on the chalkboard is *y*. The letter *y* in each of these words represents the /ī/ sound. It is the same sound the letter *i* represents in unprotected syllables. Listen carefully to the words as I read them to see if you can hear the /ī/ sound in each one." As you read each word point to the letter *y* and emphasize the /ī/ sound.

Write the words *deny, July,* and *defy* on the chalkboard. Underline the letter *y* in each of the words and say, "Notice that the ending vowel letter in each word I have written on the chalkboard is *y*. The letter *y* in each of these words represents the /ī/ sound. Listen carefully to the words as I read them to see if you can hear the /ī/ sound in each one." As you read each word point to the letter *y* and emphasize the /ī/ sound.

Write the words *jolly, happy,* and *baby* on the chalkboard. Underline the letter *y* in each of the words and say, "Notice that the ending vowel letter in each of these words is *y*. This time the *y* represents the /ē/ sound. Listen carefully to the words as I read them to see if you can hear the /ē/ sound in each one." As you read each word point to the letter *y* and emphasize the /ē/ sound.

Say, "When the letter *y* is at the end of words of more than one syllable, *y* can represent either the /ī/ sound or the /ē/ sound."

Synthesizing. Ask the students to say the vowel sounds in the following words; ask them to tell you why they chose the sounds they chose; and ask them to identify the words by sounds. When blending the sounds in polysyllabic words, ask the students to try both sounds until they get a word that makes sense:

fly, by, cy-cle, my, myth, why, gyp-sy, thy, gym, cry, dry, hymn, fry, pry, sly, spy, sty, try, spry, de-ny, hap-py, diz-zy

Application (Sentences). Write the following sentence on the chalkboard: <u>A</u> *dirt-y fly* <u>flew</u> *by* <u>the</u> *hap-py ba-by.* Say, "We will read the underlined words in this sentence and sound out the words that are not underlined." Point to the first word and read it with the students. Point to the letters *ir* in the word *dirt-y* and say, "Say the sound represented by these letters." Wait for a response. Point to the letters *dir.* "Say the sounds represented by the first three letters." Wait for a response. Point to the letter *t.* "Say the sound represented by this letter." Wait for a response. Ask, "What is the first syllable in the word?" Wait for a response. Point to the letter *y* in the word and ask, "What is the sound of *y* in this word?" Wait for a response. "What is the word?" Wait for a response. Continue this process with all of the words in the sentence, and then ask the students to read the entire sentence as quickly as they can.

Write the following sentence on the chalkboard: <u>That</u> *cand-y* <u>is</u> *chunk-y,* <u>not</u> *cream-y.* Have the students read this sentence the same way they read the first one.

Word Discrimination. Write the following words on the chalkboard:

gem
gym

Point to the letters *g* and *m* in both *gem* and *gym.* Ask, "What letters are alike in these two words?" Wait for a response. Point to the letters *e* and *y* in *gem* and *gym* and ask, "What letters are different?" Wait for a response. Point to the vowel letters in both words again. Ask, "What sounds are different?" Wait for a response. Repeat this process with word pairs: *me, my; sly, slay; free, fry; myth, math; spry, spree; tree, try; be, by; flea, fly.*

Dictation. Provide the students with "magic" slate boards, small chalkboards, or paper on which to write. Say, "Write the two letters that stand for the /mi/ sound you hear at the beginning of the word /mi/ /th/. At the count of three hold up what you have written. One . . . two . . . three." Scan the room to assess the accuracy of individual responses. Write the letters *my* on the chalkboard and say, "Most of you have written the letters *my* on your paper. These letters stand for the /mi/ sound we hear at the beginning of the word *myth.*" Write the letters *th* after the letters *my* as you say the word *myth.* Repeat this process using any of the words listed in the synthesizing step.

Application Activities

1. Obtain a copy of any basal first-grade teacher's manual. Find a lesson on beginning consonant sounds. Read the teaching instructions for that lesson. Compare it with the 10-minute phonics lessons described in this chapter. Answer the following questions regarding both approaches: Is phonemic awareness taught? Is segmentation taught? Are children helped to associate sounds with letters? Are children taught how to blend word sounds? How much time will be needed to teach the lesson? Will the children be able to apply what is taught to help them be better readers?

2. Find a child needing help with phonics. Teach an appropriate phonics lesson to this child following the steps outlined in the chapter. Write all of the information you need to teach the lesson on the chalkboard before you begin to teach. Time yourself. Did you teach the lesson in 10 minutes or less?

3. Volunteer to teach a class of first graders one of the 10-minute phonics lessons. After teaching the lesson, ask the children to evaluate their experience. Ask them if they enjoyed the lesson. Ask them if they think it was helpful.

Chapter 11

Assessment

Concepts About Print

For years children's concepts about print were either ignored or misunderstood. It was assumed that children understood what books were for and how they were used. However, many of the early literacy problems young children experience are directly linked to a lack of understanding regarding the conventions of print most adults assume are understood by children. Before expecting children to read books, teachers need to determine what they know about letters, words, print directionality, book pictures, parts of books, and prosodic features of print. Marie Clay (1985) designed the *Concepts About Print (CAP)* test for this purpose. She assesses about 24 basic print awareness elements using one of two books specifically constructed for the assessment. Her test is widely used by teachers of emergent readers.

Parents or teachers can get some idea of children's concepts about print by giving them a book and asking them to show you what they know about it. Concepts about print assessments are conducted with one child at a time. An informal assessment of selected print concepts follows:

1. Show me the front of the book.
2. Show me where to start reading the story.
3. Which way do I go when I start reading the story?
4. Where do I go when I get to the end of the line?
5. After I read this page, where do I go?
6. Point to the words while I read them.
7. Show me the last part of this story.
8. Show me the top (or bottom) of this picture.
9. Show me a letter in this word.
10. (Point to a period at the end of a sentence) Ask, "What is this mark for?"
11. (Point to a question mark) Ask, "What is this mark for?"
12. (Point to a comma) Ask, "What is this mark for?"
13. (Point to an exclamation mark) Ask, "What is this mark for?"

14. (Point to quotation marks) Ask, "What are these marks for?"
15. Ask the child to show you specific capital or "uppercase" letters by name.
16. (Point to an uppercase letter in a word that begins a sentence) Ask, "Why does this word begin with a capital letter?"
17. Ask the child to show you specific "lowercase" letters by name.
18. Show me the first letter in this word.
19. Show me the last letter in this word.

Assessing Phonemic Awareness

The assessment of phonemic awareness was discussed in Chapter 3. Two phonemic awareness assessment instruments were presented in Figure 3.1 of that chapter. The beginning assessment contains 32 two- and three-phoneme words. Those words are listed at the top of Figure 3.1. The first 16 words in this group are sufficient to identify phonemic awareness deficits. The last 16 words in the group are to be used for assessment purposes after providing phonemic awareness training for the student.

The eight tasks listed in Figure 3.1 are to be assessed using each of the 16 words in the beginning assessment. That is, each of the 16 words are used to assess the student's ability to do phoneme blending, phoneme association with beginning phonemes, phoneme segmentation with beginning phonemes, and so on. The assessment questions used to assess each of the eight assessment tasks are found in Chapter 3 under the heading, *What Are Some Phonemic Awareness Tasks?*

The advanced phonemic awareness assessment contains 3 three- and four-phoneme words. Those words are listed at the bottom of Figure 3.1. Again, only the first 17 words in the group are needed for the phonemic awareness assessment of the more difficult words. The last 17 words in the group are to be used for posttesting purposes.

In sum, the results of the initial phonemic awareness testing, either initial or advanced, should be used to identify those areas where instruction is needed. After phonemic awareness training has been provided, assessments should be made to evaluate the effectiveness of the instruction.

Informal Reading Inventories

An informal reading inventory (IRI) is an assessment instrument designed to provide an approximation of children's ability to read graded reading materials. The inventory generally consists of graded word lists, graded reading selections, and comprehension questions. The graded reading selections generally begin at a preprimer level and continue on up through the eighth or ninth grade. The selections have been graded by either a readability formula or some "book leveling" procedure.

The informal reading inventory is an individually administered assessment, and provides information regarding students' "independent reading level," "instructional reading level," and "frustration level." The independent level is the point where a student can read the graded material without any assistance. The instructional level identifies the graded material appropriate for teaching purposes, and the frustration level identifies the graded material considered to be too difficult for the student.

There are many commercially produced IRIs available for teachers. However, teachers may also construct their own. Teacher-made IRIs are made by taking 100- to 200-word passages from basal stories. These passages are taken from each grade level, from the preprimer level up through the level that ends the basal series. Once the selections have been identified, five or six comprehension questions are developed for each selection. Some of the questions are literal questions ("What do the words say?"), and some of them are inferential questions ("What do the words imply?").

As the students read the selections, the teacher marks the word errors made. Errors are counted when students a) leave out a word, b) insert a word, c) read a word incorrectly, or d) indicate they don't know a word. After the selection has been read, the teacher asks the comprehension questions. For each selection a word accuracy and a comprehension score are determined.

The graded material is considered to be at a student's independent level when comprehension is 90% or higher and word recognition accuracy is 99% or higher. Instructional level material is the graded material where comprehension is at least 75%, and word accuracy is from 95% to 98%. Frustration level is reached when either word recognition is 94% or lower or comprehension is less than 75%.

If a student reaches frustration with word recognition before comprehension, the teacher continues the assessment. However, the teacher reads the next selection to the student. After the material is read, the comprehension questions are asked. If the student gets a comprehension score higher than 75%, the teacher reads the next selection. This process continues until the student reaches frustration with comprehension. For example, the student might reach frustration on word recognition at the third-grade-level material, but not reach frustration on comprehension until the sixth-grade-level material. If so, the teacher could conclude that the student could read and understand sixth-grade-level material if the student had better decoding abilities.

If a student reaches frustration with comprehension before word recognition, the teacher asks the student to read the next selection, but does not ask any of the questions. The student continues decoding until frustration is reached. For example, the student might reach frustration on comprehension at the third-grade-level material, but not reach frustration on word recognition until the fifth-grade material. This does not happen very often, but occasionally does. If so, the teacher could conclude that the student's language and/or thinking development is lagging behind his decoding development.

Informal reading inventories not only provide estimates of students' reading levels, but also provide information regarding the instructional areas needing the greatest attention. Refer to Figure 1.1 in Chapter 1. The word recognition scores on an informal reading inventory are improved by addressing one or more of the areas listed under the "Decoding/Encoding" box. The comprehension scores on an informal reading inventory are improved by addressing one or more of the areas listed under the "Language" and/or the "Thinking" box.

Running Records

Running records evolved from Marie Clay's (1967) study of the oral reading errors of emergent readers. Running records (Clay, 1985) can be used for determining students' a) word identification strategies, b) word recognition development, and c) oral reading fluency. They are also used for determining the suitability of reading material for "guided," or independent reading. If teachers ask students questions about the content of the selection used for the running record, or if they have students retell the story used for the running record, reading comprehension can also be assessed.

Running records, like IRIs, are administered individually. A running record is essentially a record of everything a student says and does while reading the selection. The materials used for running records are either short books or book selections of about 100 to 200 words in length. For beginning readers, the text may be less than 100 words. The text selections used for running records are often "leveled" material, leveled according to the procedures described under "Book Leveling" in Chapter 9.

Running record data are usually recorded on a separate sheet of paper. All of the words students read correctly and all of the errors students make while reading are coded on a sheet of paper in a special code. Word recognition errors are basically the same as those considered for IRIs (word omissions, word insertions, word recognition errors, and words not recognized). Since teachers are trying to record everything students say or do while reading the selections, the coding system used for this purpose is shown in Figure 11.1. You may notice that there is a mark for each word in the text. When a new line of text begins, the teacher starts recording on a new line so the running record has the same number of lines as the selection being read. When a word is read correctly, a check mark is made. When a word is omitted, the omitted word is written, a line is written above it, and a dash mark is made above the line. When a word is inserted, the inserted word is written above the dash and line. When a word is read incorrectly, it is written above the correct word. When a child cannot read a word, and the teacher tells her the word, a *T* is written to represent "told." When children read a word incorrectly, but then immediately self-correct the error, the word read incorrectly is written but an *sc* for self-correction follows it. The self-corrections are *not* counted as errors.

The running records are scored by determining the percentage of words read correctly in the selection. This is calculated by a) subtracting the number of errors from the number of words in the selection, resulting in the number of words read correctly, and then by b) dividing the number of words read correctly by the number of words in the selection. For example, if there were 120 words in the selection, and the student made 5 errors, subtract 5 from 120. The answer (115) represents the number of words read correctly. By dividing the number of words read correctly (115) by the number of words in the selection (120), the result (96%) represents the percentage of words read correctly.

Reading levels are determined as follows:

Independent	95%–100%
Instructional	90%–94%
Difficult	50%–89%

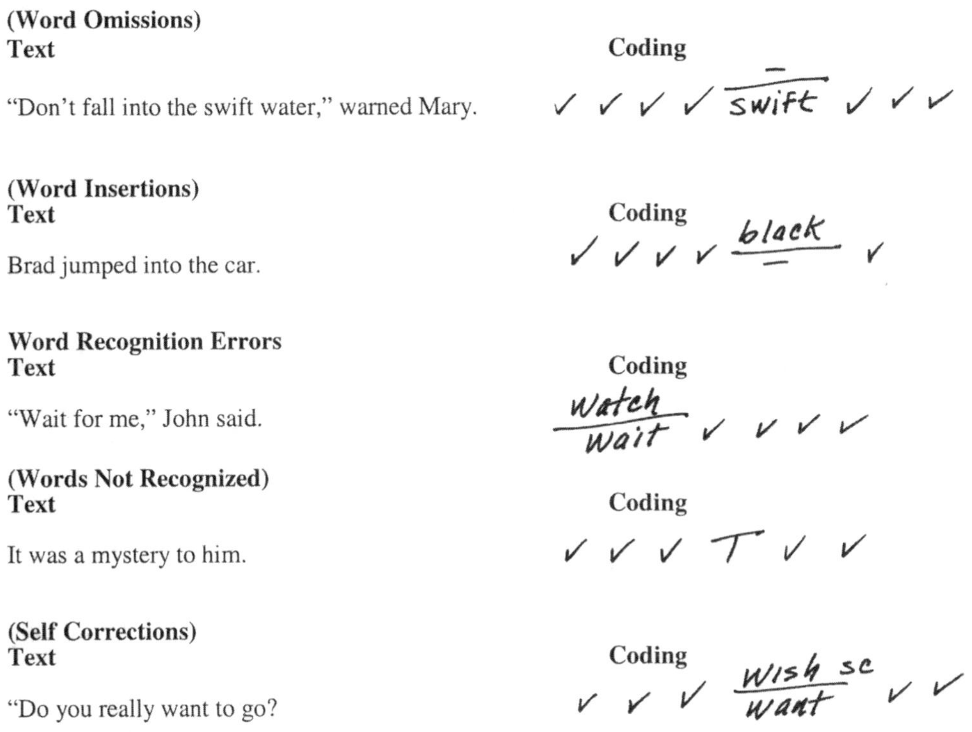

(Word Omissions)
Text   Coding

"Don't fall into the swift water," warned Mary.   ✓ ✓ ✓ ✓ sw̄ift ✓ ✓ ✓

(Word Insertions)
Text   Coding

Brad jumped into the car.   ✓ ✓ ✓ ✓ black̄ ✓

Word Recognition Errors
Text   Coding

"Wait for me," John said.   watch / wait ✓ ✓ ✓ ✓

(Words Not Recognized)
Text   Coding

It was a mystery to him.   ✓ ✓ ✓ T ✓ ✓

(Self Corrections)
Text   Coding

"Do you really want to go?   ✓ ✓ ✓ wish sc / want ✓ ✓

FIGURE 11.1   Coding Running Records

The errors students make during a running record can be analyzed to help teachers understand the strategies students are using when they encounter unfamiliar words. Review the information about the three cueing systems in written language found in the section *Teaching Children to Use Contextual Information* in Chapter 7 to help you understand the analysis of reading errors.

If a student was using the semantic cue to identify an unknown word, the error made would make sense in the sentence even though it doesn't even look like the correct word. For example, the text might be, "Nicole loved to ride her horse in the late afternoon." The student might read the text, "Nicole loved to ride her pony in the late afternoon." In this instance, the letter *M* for *meaning* is marked by the error, indicating that the error made sense, and the student was reading for meaning.

If a student was using the syntax cue, then the error will be the right kind of word (noun, verb, adjective, etc.) even if it doesn't make a lot of sense. For example, the text might be, "The fish pulled the fishing pole into the water." The student might read the text, "The fish bounced the fishing pole into the water." The student read *bounced* instead of *pulled*. The error doesn't make a lot of sense, but both words are verbs so the error is syntactically correct. The error would be marked with the letter *S* to indicate that the student was probably using the *syntax cue* (or sentence *structure* cue) to identify the unknown word.

If a student was using both the graphophonics and the syntax cue she might read the sentence, "The fish poured the fishing pole into the water." The words *poured* and *pulled* begin with the same letter (and phoneme), and both words are verbs so the error is graphophonically correct and syntactically correct, but not semantically appropriate. The letter *V* is marked by the error to indicate that the student was probably using more *visual* information (graphophonics) than anything else to identify the word. The teacher might also use the *V/S* symbol to indicate the error was also syntactically appropriate. If the student read, "The fish pilled the fishing pole into the water," it would be obvious that she was using the graphophonics cue almost exclusively.

An analysis of reading errors helps teachers know which of the written language cueing systems students are using when reading. This information helps them plan an appropriate instructional program for students.

Decoding Strategies—IRIs and Running Records

Students need to learn how to use the three cueing systems of written language. However, children also need to learn how speech maps onto print so word recognition growth occurs. As children become fluent in word recognition, their reliance on semantics and syntactic cues diminish. They no longer have the need to guess words through context because words are immediately recognized by sight.

Word recognition grows when students develop phonemic awareness and phonics knowledge. As phonemic awareness and phonics knowledge grows, students begin to look at all of the letter sequences within words, enabling them to store the visual images of words in lexical memory. Therefore, teach children about all of the decoding processes, and teach them to use whatever strategy they are able to use that will least interfere with reading comprehension. Decoding by word recognition is the best of all of the decoding strategies, not only because it is the strategy the very best readers use, but also because it enhances the likelihood of comprehension rather than interferes with it. Therefore, teach students to decode by analogy, context, phonics, morphemic analysis, and syllabic analysis/phonics, *in that order,* when word recognition doesn't happen. Teach children about recognizing words. Teach them about the various word identification strategies. If they don't recognize a word, encourage them to use analogy. If they can't use analogy, encourage them to use the three cueing systems (context). If context doesn't work, encourage them to use phonics (if the word has one vowel sound), or morphemic analysis (if the word has more than one vowel sound). If morphemic analysis doesn't work, encourage them to "chunk" the multisyllabic word into syllables and use phonics to sound it out.

During mini-lessons and/or guided reading, help students learn how to use all of the strategies in the order outlined. While observing children read during the administration of IRIs and running records, watch how they apply what you have taught. Keep individual records regarding the strategies they use, and guide them in the development of fluent word recognition abilities.

Assessing Decoding Accuracy and Fluency Through IRIs and Running Records

Throughout this book, I have emphasized that decoding accuracy and fluency have important positive effects on reading comprehension. Fluent readers recognize words accurately, rapidly, and automatically. Fluent readers comprehend better than children who have poor decoding abilities simply because they have less difficulty translating print into language. During the administration of IRIs and running records, teachers are able to assess students' word recognition and fluency as they listen to them read.

The information which follows will help you use a running record to assess reading fluency as well as word recognition accuracy. It is recommended that the following materials be used: a) a specific literature book, or literacy book selection of at least 100 words for the student to read; b) a sheet of paper to do a running record; and c) a stopwatch to record the time taken to read the selection. It is also recommended the number of words in the reading selection be determined before the selection is read.

Testing Procedures

1. Write the student's name and the test date on the paper used for the running record.
2. Give the student an unmarked copy of the literature book or reading selection. Say, "I would like you to read this book for me. Read it with expression if you can. If you come to a word you cannot read, tell me and I will read it for you. Do you understand what I want you to do?" Wait for a response. Say, "Begin reading."
3. Push the button on the stopwatch as soon as the child begins to read. Use the running record coding system to complete the running record. Also note whether or not the student uses prosodic features of print, and reads in phrases to make the oral reading more fluent and expressive.
4. As soon as the child finishes reading the selection, push the button on the stopwatch and record the time taken (in seconds) by the child's name. Also make comments about reading fluency.

Fluency Measures

After the test is completed, count the errors, calculate the number of words read correctly, and determine the percentage of words read correctly. Also calculate the number of words the student read correctly per minute (Stanovich, Cunningham, & Freeman, 1984b). This score will give you some information about the student's word recognition fluency.

To determine the number of *words read correctly per minute (wcpm)* divide the total number of words read correctly by the number of seconds taken to read them. This will identify the number of words read correctly per second. Then multiply the number of words read correctly per second by 60 and the result will be the number of words read correctly per minute. For example, let's say a second-grade student read a 200-word selection in 2 minutes and 50 seconds, and made six errors. The number of words read correctly would be 194, and the percentage of words read correctly would be 97%. The 2 minutes and 50 seconds it took to read the selection would be 170 seconds. The 194 words read correctly divided by the 170 seconds it took to read them would result in 1.14 words read correctly per second. The 1.14 words read correctly per second multiplied by 60 would result in 68.4 words read correctly per minute. The student's wcpm could then be compared to other students of his age to see if he is above or below the average for students of his age and time of year.

Tim Rasinski and Nancy Padak (2004), using the work of Hasbrouck and Tindal (1992) and Howe and Shinn (2001), developed the following oral reading norms for grade level and time of year (p. 111):

Grade	Fall	Winter	Spring
1			60 wcpm
2	53	78	94
3	79	93	114
4	99	112	118
5	105	118	128
6	115	132	145
7	147	158	167
8	156	167	171

Assessing Reading Comprehension with Running Records

After students complete a running record of a story, ask them to retell the story as though they were telling it to someone who had never read it before. Tape record their retellings for later analysis. Children's story retellings have proven to be an extremely good indicator of reading comprehension. Since stories have a predictable structure (characters, a setting, a problem, a sequence of events leading to solving the problem, and a solution to the problem), record the number of these elements students include in their retellings as evidence of comprehension.

Also develop a story grammar test to get another comprehension measure. A sample test is included in Appendix E.

Assessing Phonics Knowledge

According to Ehri and Wilce (1983, 1985), the difference between skilled and unskilled readers is that skilled readers possess the phonics knowledge needed to form complete connections between word spellings and word pronunciations in memory, while unskilled readers do not. Skilled readers have stored many written words in lexical memory that they can easily retrieve when seen in print. Unskilled readers, however, form partial or incomplete word spelling–pronunciation connections because of insufficient phonics knowledge. Their word recognition vocabularies are small and their decoding is slow and inaccurate. Phonics knowledge is necessary for children to form the visual–phonological connections in memory necessary for word storage and retrieval. This knowledge is used by children to learn both regular and irregular words.

Research suggests that students' phonics knowledge can be assessed by giving them pseudo-words to read. The speed and accuracy of reading pseudo-words is not only a measure of phonics knowledge, but also clearly differentiates students with good reading comprehension from those who do not comprehend well.

Appendix G contains an individual phonics test. This test was developed and validated in a Masters study at the Brigham Young University (Hutchings, 1995), and a 1994 decoding research project. There are three separate tests in the phonics test battery. All of the phonics elements and patterns described in Chapter 8 are assessed by the complete test. Phonics test one contains 22 pseudo-words. All of the words contain a single vowel, and most of them contain a single consonant at the end and beginning (*bab, wep, yat,* etc.). Test two contains 33 pseudo-words with a single vowel, and either a consonant digraph or consonant blend at the end or beginning (*swush, strisp, spitch,* etc.). Test three contains 28 pseudo-words containing either a vowel digraph, vowel diphthong, murmur diphthong, or a single vowel in a vowel-consonant-*e* pattern (*toak, coise, birt, lope,* etc.).

All of the pseudo-words used in the tests were created according to the graphophonic structure of real words. The spelling–sound relationship of each pseudo-word on the test was checked against the common spelling–sound relationships found in the written language. This was done by first comparing the spelling of the pseudo-word up to and including the vowel with spelling relationships found in commonly used words. For example, in the pseudo-word *bab,* the *ba* spelling for the /ba/ sound is consistent with the *ba* spelling in words like *bat, back, bag, band,* and so on. Second, the spelling of the pseudo-word from the vowel to the end of the word was checked. In the pseudo-word *bab* the *ab* spelling for the /ab/ sound is consistent with the *ab* spelling in words like *lab, tab, stab, crab,* and so on. A pseudo-word like *mik* would not be used since there are no single-syllable words where the /ik/ sound is spelled *ik.* In real words the /ik/ sound is spelled *ick* such as in *pick, stick, quick, trick,* and so on.

The individual phonics tests were administered twice to 233 children: first in February and then in November. The test was highly reliable using auto-correlations as test-retest reliability indexes. The auto-correlation for the individual phonics test was .81. The test results revealed that students, generally speaking, were able to read a higher percentage of pseudo-words correctly in test three than in test two. Phonics test two may be slightly more difficult for students than phonics test three. Perhaps students find it more difficult to read pseudo-words with consonant blends and digraphs in both the initial and final position of the words, than pseudo-words containing vowel teams (vowel digraphs, vowel diphthongs, murmur diphthongs).

The test results also revealed a consistent pattern of scores in each test among the different age groups. This supports the validity and reliability data obtained for the test in the Hutchings study (1995). The results are reported in Table 11.1. The mean scores can be used as norms for score comparisons of other primary grade students.

Appendix H presents a group phonics test. The production tasks on the individual phonics test is more difficult for students than the recognition tasks on the group test. Therefore, students are generally able to recognize a phonics element before they are able to produce the sound represented by the element. However, the correlations between the test results obtained from children taking both tests are high ($r = .81$, $p < .01$), indicating that tests are related and that the group test can be used as a valid indicator

TABLE 11.1 Phonics Mean Scores

Groups	Test One	Test Two	Test Three	Total Phonics Score
	22 items	33 items	28 items	83 items
Group 1 (N=92)				
Grade 1/Feb.	14 (63%)	12.7 (39%)	10.7 (38%)	37.1 (45%)
Grade 2/Nov.	16.8 (76%)	17.6 (53%)	15.4 (55%)	49.5 (60%)
Group 2 (N=92)				
Grade 2/Feb.	18.4 (84%)	22.1 (67%)	18.5 (66%)	58.7 (71%)
Grade 3/Nov.	19.2 (87%)	24.0 (73%)	21.6 (77%)	64.8 (78%)
Group 3 (N=49)				
Grade 3/Feb.	19.6 (89%)	23.8 (72%)	21.4 (76%)	64.7 (78%)
Grade 4/Nov.	19.7 (90%)	24.7 (75%)	22.4 (80%)	66.7 (80%)

Note: The two test results listed under each group are test-retest results for the same children. The numbers in parentheses refer to the percentages of pseudo-words read correctly in the test.

for the individual test (Hutchings, 1995, p. 12). It is interesting to note that the correlation between the individual phonics test and the group phonics test was identical to the test-retest correlation of the individual phonics test noted earlier.

A careful observation of both the individual and group phonics tests reveals that the same pseudo-words are used in both tests. In the individual test, the student is asked to read the pseudo-word (*bab*) on the first test item. In the group test, the student is presented with four pseudo-words (*bab, dab, beb, bap*) on the first test item, and asked to circle the word *bab*. The three distractor pseudo-words are identical to the target word in all areas, but one. The word *dab* has a different beginning, the word *beb* has a different vowel, and the word *bap* has a different ending. Therefore, the distractor circled by the student provides an indicator of where the phonics problem resides.

Both tests measure the same phonics elements and both tests predict each other. The group phonics test is more efficient than the individual test. It can be administered to all of the students in a classroom at one time, while the individual test must be administered to one student at a time. Therefore, teachers who want to assess the phonics knowledge of many students at one time will want to use the group test.

Both phonics tests are significantly related to word recognition and reading comprehension. The correlations of both tests to word recognition and reading comprehension are as follows:

Group phonics test and word recognition r = .83, p < .01

Individual phonics and word recognition r = .88, p < .01

Group phonics test and comprehension r = .41, p < .01

Individual phonics and comprehension r = .52, p < .01

Using the Phonics Tests as Diagnostic Tools

The phonics tests provide a measure of phonics knowledge that can be used to identify students' phonics growth over time. Phonics scores can also be used to compare the phonics knowledge of different groups of students. However, the greatest value of the phonics tests is their diagnostic potential. Both phonics measures can be used to identify specific phonics elements students need to be taught. For example, if a student read the pseudo-word *bab* as *dab*, on the individual test, the phonics element the student was unable to use was the consonant *b* at the beginning of the word. Therefore, the teacher would go to Appendix D and find the word lists for the beginning consonant *b*, and teach a beginning consonant lesson as outlined in Chapter 10, focused on that phonics element.

If a student read the pseudo-word *bab* as *beb*, the phonics element missed would be the short vowel *a*. Therefore, the teacher would go to Appendix D, find the word lists for the short vowel *a*, and teach a short vowel lesson as outlined in Chapter 10.

If a student read the pseudo-word *bab* as *bap*, the phonics element missed would be the ending consonant *b*. Therefore, the teacher would go to Appendix D, find the word lists for the ending consonant *b*, and follow the lesson outline in Chapter 10 for ending consonants lessons. All of a student's test errors can be used for diagnostic purposes, on both the individual and the group phonics tests. When using the group test, the item circled would reveal the phonics elements missed. For example, if a child circled the pseudo-word *dab* when asked to circle *bab*, the phonics element missed would be the beginning consonant *b*.

The phonics tests have been carefully developed so that all of the phonics elements and patterns are assessed. An error on each test item provides important diagnostic data that can be used to identify a specific phonics element or pattern students need to be taught.

Assessing Word Recognition

Running Records

A measure of word recognition is found when doing running records. The number of words read correctly is calculated from this assessment instrument, and if students make little or no errors, word recognition is considered to be satisfactory—at least with the particular graded materials used.

High-Frequency Word Lists

Sight word recognition can also be assessed by using high-frequency word lists. In Chapter 7 the list of the 300 most frequently used words in children's literature books and first grade basal readers is found. In Appendix A the 919 most frequently used words derived from 235 children's literature books are listed in the order of their frequency of use. In Appendix B the 275 most frequently used graphophonic irregular words are listed in the order of their frequency of use. Graphophonic irregular words are particularly important because children do not learn them (store them in lexical memory) as quickly as they learn graphophonic regular words.

Teachers can use high-frequency word lists as assessment instruments for word recognition. By asking students to read groups of words on the list, you can identify which words they recognize and which ones they don't recognize. This information can be used for instruction.

If a child can read the first 30 words on a high-frequency word list in about 18 seconds without any errors, those words are probably in that child's word recognition vocabulary. If they pause on any word for a second or more, the student is trying to use some identification strategy to identify it.

Sight Word Tests

One of the best ways to estimate the size of a student's word recognition vocabulary is by using the Individual Sight Word Test in Appendix F. The sight word test has four parts, or subtests. All of the words on the tests were taken from the Carroll, Davies, and Richman (1971) word frequency book. Each test contains 30 words. The first test is comprised of high-frequency, regular graphophonic words (*see, back, man,* etc.). The second test is comprised of high-frequency, irregular graphophonic words (*to, one, most,* etc.). The third test is comprised of low-frequency, regular graphophonic words (*trapeze, spade, unselfish,* etc.). The fourth test is comprised of low-frequency, irregular graphophonic words (*fluent, stingy, beverage,* etc.).

The sight word tests were administered twice to 233 children: first in February and then in November. The test was very reliable using the auto-correlations as test-retest reliability indexes. The auto-correlation for the sight words test was .87. The word recognition test results revealed that students, generally speaking, demonstrated consistent growth in word recognition development over the nine-month period. The test results also revealed a consistent pattern of scores in each test among the different age groups. Furthermore, the results indicated that test one is the easiest test, test two next, test three next, and that test four is the most difficult test.

The test results also raised some interesting questions regarding "decodable text." They suggested that word frequency was a more important word recognition variable than graphophonic regularity. Students were able to read high-frequency irregular words (test 2) better than low-frequency regular graphophonic words (test 3). The results are reported in Table 11.2. The mean scores can be used as norms for score comparisons of other primary grade students.

The sight word tests appear to be a valuable tool for estimating the size of students' word recognition vocabularies. While the results of all four sight word tests provide important information, the best predictor of vocabulary size appears to be the score obtained on test four. *Knowing the size of a student's sight vocabulary is extremely important since the use of analogy, context, and morphemic analysis as decoding strate-*

TABLE 11.2 Word Recognition Mean Scores

Group	Test One	Test Two	Test Three	Test Four	Total Score
Group 1 (N=92)					
Grade 1/Feb.	23.9 (80%)	20.9 (70%)	10.1 (34%)	4.4 (15%)	59.3 (49%)
Grade 2/Nov.	28.9 (96%)	26.8 (89%)	18.5 (62%)	10.2 (34%)	84.3 (70%)
Group 2 (N=92)					
Grade 2/Feb.	29.4 (98%)	27.9 (93%)	21.9 (73%)	14.1 (47%)	93.3 (78%)
Grade 3/Nov.	29.6 (98.7%)	29.0 (97%)	25.2 (84%)	17.0 (59%)	101.1 (84%)
Group 3 (N=49)					
Grade 3/Feb.	29.7 (99%)	28.8 (96%)	25.6 (85%)	17.9 (60%)	102.0 (85%)
Grade 4/Nov.	29.7 (99%)	29.0 (97%)	26.9 (90%)	21.1 (70%)	106.8 (89%)

Note: The two test results listed under each group are test-retest results for the same children. Each test contained 30 words. The numbers in parentheses refer to the percentages of words read correctly.

gies are dependent upon a large sight vocabulary. Unless students have enough words stored in lexical memory they will be unable to effectively use these strategies as tools for decoding.

Assessing Word Recognition Fluency

Sight word fluency can also be assessed by using the 120 sight word test found in Appendix F. If a stopwatch is used to record the time taken to read the words in each of the four sight word tests, word recognition fluency scores can also be calculated. Simply determine the number of words read correctly per minute as is done when using running records.

The sight word tests administered to the 233 children were timed both in February and again in November. The timed test was very reliable using the auto-correlations as test-retest reliability indexes. The auto-correlation for the fluency test was .86. The test results revealed that students demonstrated consistent growth in word recognition fluency over the nine-month period. The test results also revealed a consistent pattern of scores in each test among the different age groups. Again, the results suggested that test one was the easiest while each subsequent test became more difficult. The results are reported in Table 11.3. The mean scores can be used as norms for score comparisons of other primary grade students.

Assessing Students' Ability to Use Analogy as a Decoding Strategy

It was mentioned in Chapter 2 that the main advantage of using analogy as a word identification strategy is the speed at which the strategy produces results. However, students cannot use analogy as a decoding strategy unless there are already enough words in their lexical memories to compare with unknown words.

TABLE 11.3 Word Recognition Fluency Scores

Group	Test One	Test Two	Test Three	Test Four	Total Score
Group 1 (N=92)					
Grade 1/Feb.	38.4 wcpm	30.0 wcpm	6 wcpm	2.4 wcpm	12.0 wcpm
Grade 2/Nov.	78.6 wcpm	61.8 wcpm	18 wcpm	7.8 wcpm	25.2 wcpm
Group 2 (N=92)					
Grade 2/Feb.	94.8 wcpm	79.8 wcpm	28.2 wcpm	14.4 wcpm	36 wcpm
Grade 3/Nov.	101.4 wcpm	94.2 wcpm	41.4 wcpm	21.6 wcpm	48.6 wcpm
Group 3 (N=49)					
Grade 3/Feb.	97.8 wcpm	87.6 wcpm	39 wcpm	21 wcpm	45.6 wcpm
Grade 4/Nov.	112.2 wcpm	102.6 wcpm	49.8 wcpm	29.4 wcpm	57.0 wcpm

Note: The two test results listed under each group are test-retest results for the same children. wcpm = words read correctly per minute.

I have developed a names test where each name on the test contains either a common rime (first 23 items), or a familiar word part (last 13 items). If students can read the names on this test in about 28 seconds, it is assumed that they are able to use analogy as a decoding strategy for the identification of many different words. If they can read the rimes in less than a second, it is assumed that they can use analogy for at least some words.

Analogy Test

1. Jack
2. Glade
3. Gail
4. Jake
5. Stan
6. Mark
7. Dave
8. Jean
9. Jed
10. Jen
11. Brent
12. Jess
13. Chet
14. Dick
15. Sid
16. Mike
17. Bill
18. Tim
19. Skip
20. Kit
21. Bob
22. Dot
23. Ross
24. Davy
25. Jason
26. Mabel
27. Tony
28. Sunny
29. Margo
30. Carter
31. Bobby
32. Molly
33. Nelly
34. Jenny
35. Billy
36. Kimberly

Assessing Students' Ability to Use Context as a Decoding Strategy

Running Records

When students use context as a decoding strategy, they use the three written language cueing systems (semantics, syntax, and graphophonics) to identify unfamiliar words. One way to determine students' ability to use context for word identification is through a running record. Observe the way students attempt to identify unfamiliar words, and analyze their reading errors after the record is completed.

Modified Cloze Tests

Another way to assess students' abilities to use context for decoding is the modified cloze test constructed with reading material on their *instructional reading level*. Modified cloze tests provide the beginning letter/s for missing words. This enables students to use the graphophonic text cue as well as the semantics and syntax cues. The students are given a copy of the modified cloze test and they are asked to complete the words in the blank spaces. A sample modified cloze test follows:

The Stumpy-Tailed Bear

All of the animals lived in the dark woods. It was winter and the sn_____ was very deep. There was not much food. The animals were all friends. That is, all of th_____ except Fox. Fox was too sly. He liked to play tr_____ on the other animals.

One day Bear saw Fox sneaking through the woods. Fox had stolen a string of fish. He was going to eat them.

"Where did you get such big f_____?" Bear growled.

"Well, my good friend," lied Fox. "I have been out fishing and c_____ them."

Fox knew Bear loved fish. He knew it was Bear's favorite f_____. Fox decided to play a trick on Bear.

"Bear," said Fox. "Would you like some big fish like mine? I can tell you how to c_____ some."

"Oh yes," Bear cried. "Please tell me how."

"It's easy," fibbed Fox. "First, go to the frozen l_____. Then cut a hole in the ice and stick your long t_____ down into the water. It will get very cold. But you must hold your tail in the water a long, long time. You must sit very still."

"Okay, okay, I will. Thank y_____ very much, Fox."

Bear hurried down the path.

"Bear, oh, Bear," Fox called. "I almost forgot to t_____you. If you move, you will sc_____ the fish away. And don't worry when your tail begins to hurt. That only means the fish are b_____ it. But when it really hurts, yank it out of the w_____ and you will have lots of fish."

Bear's eyes got big. Lots of fish! He could have fat, tasty fish for d_____. He ran as fast as he could down the path. Fox watched Bear go. Then he dashed through the woods. He r_____ until he reached the lake. Then he hid behind a tree and waited.

Bear came to the frozen lake. He did as Fox said. He c_____ a hole in the ice and stuck his long tail down into the water. It was so cold. But he held it there a long, long time. He sat very still. He did not want to scare the fish away.

Soon his tail really h_____.

"The fish are biting hard. I must have lots of fish for dinner by now," Bear thought. "It is time to yank on my tail." Bear tried to yank his tail out of the water. But his tail was fr_____. It snapped right off!

Fox laughed and laughed at Bear. But the other animals did not laugh when they saw Bear's sh_____ tail. Poor Bear! Fox had played a very mean trick. And that is why the bear has a stumpy-tail to this day.

Assessing Students' Ability to Use Morphemic Analysis as a Decoding Strategy

It was mentioned in Chapter 2 that morphemic analysis can be a fairly rapid word identification process for students who have large sight vocabularies. Children can use their knowledge of morphemic units (root words, suffixes, prefixes, and inflectional endings) to identify unfamiliar word variants and word derivatives *if* they have stored enough words containing these units in lexical memory. However, students cannot use morphemic analysis as a decoding strategy unless their sight vocabularies include enough word variants and derivatives to make such comparisons.

I have developed two morphemic analysis tests: a simple one and a more difficult one. Each test consists of 17 items. Some of the items are compound words, some of them are word variants, and some are word derivatives.

Instructions for test administration: Give a student a copy of either one of the tests. Ordinarily, younger students are given the simple test, and older students the more difficult test. Ask the student to underline the root word in each word. If the word is a compound word, two words will be underlined. After the root word is underlined, ask the student to read the word.

Morphemic Analysis Tests

Simple	Difficult
1. bedroom	1. lawnmower
2. armchair	2. heavyweight
3. bathtub	3. windowpane
4. butterfly	4. spendthrift
5. buses	5. marches
6. harder	6. sooner
7. smallest	7. strongest
8. asking	8. burning
9. added	9. mended
10. darkness	10. dampness
11. hateful	11. mouthful
12. agreement	12. employment
13. dislike	13. displease
14. unsafe	14. unlucky
15. joyous	15. poisonous
16. selection	16. correction
17. agreeable	17. fashionable

Assessing Syllabication and Phonics Knowledge

Phonics can be used to decode words of more than one syllable if their syllable boundaries can be identified. Therefore, ways to assess whether or not students can syllabicate multisyllabic words and use phonics to identify them are the subject of discussion here.

Students need to understand certain concepts before they are able to decode words of more than one syllable. These concepts were discussed in Chapter 8. Among some of the most important concepts students should understand are: every syllable contains one vowel sound; phonics works only in syllables; closed syllables end in consonants, and the vowel in closed syllables are usually short; open syllables end in vowels, and the vowels in open syllables are usually long; the vowels in vowel-consonant-*e* syllables are usually long; vowel letters in unstressed syllables usually represent the schwa sound; and the *le* endings at the end of multisyllabic words represent the /ul/ sound.

Syllable boundaries are generally identified by determining how many consonant units are found between vowels: a) If there are two or more consonant units between vowels *(holster)*, the first syllable ends after the first consonant unit *(hol-ster)*; b) If there is only one consonant unit between vowels *(Friday, blemish)*, sometimes the first syllable ends before the consonant *(Fri-day)*, and sometimes the first syllable ends after the consonant *(blem-ish)*. Students are instructed to use the "trial and error" method with these words, but to begin by trying the first syllable ending with a vowel.

If a multisyllabic word ends in *le (dwindle, bible)*, the last syllable begins with the consonant before the *le (dwin-dle, bi-ble)*. The main purpose of finding syllable boundaries is to determine whether the vowels in multisyllabic words are in closed or open syllables so proper vowel sounds can be predicted.

I have developed a syllabication/phonics assessment test. It contains 40 words. Some of the words have two or more consonants between vowels, some of them have only one consonant between vowels, and some of them end in *le*.

Instructions for test administration: Give a student a copy of the test. Ask the student to draw a line separating the two syllables in each word. After the syllable boundaries are identified, ask the student to read the word. Remind her that the vowel sound in the second syllable of some of these words will be the schwa sound (/u/).

Syllabic Analysis/Phonics Test

1. bony	21. rifle
2. waken	22. label
3. silent	23. cactus
4. ambush	24. cancel
5. ignite	25. pencil
6. bandit	26. lemon
7. edit	27. cabin
8. wagon	28. camel
9. satin	29. music
10. fatal	30. bugle
11. fiber	31. yodel
12. donate	32. erase
13. justice	33. china
14. napkin	34. matter
15. lantern	35. witness
16. finish	36. mildew
17. robin	37. comic
18. vanish	38. level
19. marble	39. metal
20. diver	40. beetle

Application Activities

1. Assess a selected elementary school child's decoding accuracy and fluency with a literature book, following the steps outlined in the chapter. Assess the child's comprehension of the book using the retelling strategy outlined in the chapter.
2. Assess a child's sight word accuracy and fluency using the sight word test in Appendix F. Share your findings with the child, and if appropriate, with the child's parents and/or teacher.
3. Assess a child's phonics knowledge using the individual phonics test in Appendix H. Share your findings with the child, and if appropriate, with the child's parents and/or teacher.

Appendix A

919 High-Frequency Words Obtained From 235 Children's Literature Books

(Listed According to Frequency of Use)

the	then	too	look	that's	along
and	what	asked	cried	head	another
a	me	if	long	am	ate
to	as	came	or	great	bed
said	him	don't	I'm	door	dark
I	have	did	boy	has	three
he	there	over	us	never	let's
you	be	good	well	thought	tree
of	were	house	off	called	than
was	when	away	ran	new	even
it	big	looked	going	yes	sat
in	do	know	saw	eat	give
on	went	by	way	help	heard
she	can	how	think	something	nothing
that	this	bear	two	next	blue
is	down	day	more	only	toad
his	no	Mr.	because	run	wizard
they	will	right	after	can't	its
for	like	it's	again	play	soon
all	your	would	cat	night	been
but	into	who	baby	frog	last
her	man	time	home	first	much
with	now	put	want	dog	witch
we	mother	around	make	still	found
little	from	about	other	water	walked
my	very	come	why	through	red
up	back	oh	take	morning	always
out	could	some	didn't	our	let
at	just	got	made	once	while
had	them	an	I'll	tell	you're
so	old	here	find	king	began
one	see	their	father	must	fast
not	go	where	say	told	bad
are	get	took	Mrs.	rabbit	before

under	I've	side	anything	grandfather	porridge
gave	ice	hat	opened	hole	mean
eyes	lady	four	stood	kitchen	large
room	these	shall	pocket	whole	cry
shouted	fox	suddenly	teeny	straight	bone
dinosaurs	garden	cake	bones	sun	we're
everyone	teeth	goose	own	table	sky
things	really	tail	picked	playing	honey
inside	hill	grasshopper	truck	ball	feel
children	smiled	round	elephant	lost	milk
looking	end	six	himself	bit	stand
stopped	catch	which	grow	book	slowly
small	maybe	work	fine	beautiful	sitting
any	skeleton	name	cow	kind	wish
behind	he's	dinosaur	we'll	police	ready
until	birthday	farmer	course	yellow	mind
girl	street	trees	most	crocodile	kept
fish	met	tried	pretty	such	waited
store	feet	should	voice	quiet	nobody
woman	please	cats	whispered	thank	sorry
couldn't	box	wasn't	brought	far	legs
happy	sleep	enough	jump	girls	arms
young	full	without	try	black	they're
road	across	laughed	faster	story	isn't
together	tiny	need	rain	white	you'll
thing	gingerbread	clothes	read	teacher	sad
left	pumpkin	hard	funny	hungry	wall
better	gone	same	family	balloon	watch
started	top	getting	eggs	doesn't	flying
front	bird	chair	days	world	fat
people	school	mom	skinny	love	town
sure	won't	cream	doing	grass	care
every	umbrella	someone	brown	walrus	car
ever	hear	mouse	almost	horse	asleep
high	may	nose	bunny	friend	five
nice	jumped	window	giant	everybody	lot
each	yelled	open	watched	show	ten
wanted	coming	many	turn	dear	sit
best	those	boys	food	held	past
stop	goat	ground	cave	caught	sea
seen	air	friends	foot	outside	later
knew	walk	wind	today	stay	birds
green	does	lucky	hiccup	happened	says
fell	turned	else	pulled	moon	set
place	lived	hand	flew	bat	felt
keep	poor	tired	parson	climbed	word
sister	fly	everything	running	fun	live
snow	soup	wait	basket	rest	eating

goodnight	mouth	pig	thin	tall	telephone
near	answered	ahead	thinking	dry	smaller
there's	hello	animals	though	bread	meat
cook	city	cheep	quack	zoo	hope
orange	spot	bee	lake	tomorrow	visit
tea	dropped	indeed	goes	listen	Nazis
stone	loved	cannot	perhaps	onto	grandmother
shoes	mama	rolled	color	she's	seven
sometimes	gold	chickens	followed	broomstick	real
floor	yet	sound	deep	light	pockets
liked	yard	silly	different	easier	bet
hurry	wouldn't	chocolate	dad	walking	matter
kittens	fire	sick	call	warm	blanket
duck	Halloween	pat	crying	quick	swim
talk	I'd	lowly	cloud	pick	moved
brother	quickly	step	wrong	daddy	broke
idea	follow	making	wonderful	row	flat
few	shook	buy	showed	makes	stars
close	pond	what's	robin	marigold	heavy
trumpet	page	breakfast	game	mice	spring
rose	done	being	holding	instead	mallard
chicken	comes	sang	lamb	field	likes
carry	also	change	land	sing	doctor
egg	face	wet	coat	pink	except
button	toward	taking	helped	already	blew
picture	winter	afraid	move	year	song
noise	bag	pie	myself	supper	soldier
grew	vine	stairs	upon	sighed	shopping
star	farm	train	pushed	rabbi	roll
guess	reached	seemed	frightened	mountain	start
ask	ride	money	finally	lunch	line
apple	mad	hot	against	leaves	laughing
might	soft	journey	worry	everywhere	hardly
river	glad	bigger	wearing	strong	okay
sign	son	flowers	loud	shut	finger
miss	boat	closed	berries	biggest	hen
remember	violet	threw	special	gate	here's
alone	surprise	fall	clean	grabbed	above
worm	bring	forget	hide	empty	toys
piece	woods	hold	hurried	become	gets
sorceress	both	pot	hall	Nazi	cross
paint	stupid	prince	wood	grandma	club
others	hands	late	climb	lovely	clock
paper	cookies	sheep	surprised	hid	grade
park	corner	men	forgot	waiting	breath
answer	leave	swam	letter	used	bottom
anyone	mother's	trying	life	terrible	steps
party	covered	bottle	short	wants	afternoon

passed	uncle	crowd	owl	free	monkey
bath	filled	became	moth	doll	moving
carried	cars	stepped	mitt	ago	plant
castle	class	higher	leaving	true	private
busy	roof	hung	led	landed	rice
bear's	dinner	louder	rooster	believe	rushed
arm	falling	babies	valley	broom	sandwich
throw	dumb	turkey	knows	hop	send
till	brush	snake	half	closer	sent
smell	bye	bright	onions	coach	ship
pair	bark	case	cents	cut	somebody
palace	wise	fair	fallen	haven't	speak
market	signor	fur	music	hopped	stuck
marsh	second	canoe	trouble	department	talking
jar	part	dug	cupboard	earth	turtle
houses	nest	beside	eater	eight	use
hair	nine	smile	dancing	either	wagon
policeman	kitten	sharp	cold	eye	watching
hey	animal	safe	plants	finished	week
suit	bears	ring	Jewish	glasses	
ladder	cards	stick	join	herself	
butterfly	ears	sugar	dogs	lots	
played	apples	pin	heart	meadow	
easy	lie	pail	dressed	middle	

Appendix B

275 High-Frequency Irregular Words Obtained From 235 Children's Literature Books

(Arranged According to Frequency of Use)

the	where	everyone	clothes	mind	done
a	cried	small	chair	sorry	comes
to	I'm	any	someone	they're	also
said	two	behind	many	you'll	toward
you	more	store	friends	wall	son
of	again	woman	tired	watch	violet
was	want	couldn't	anything	care	both
they	other	young	elephant	says	cookies
all	I'll	together	course	word	mother's
one	find	front	most	live	covered
are	father	people	pretty	near	rolled
what	Mrs.	sure	brought	there's	buy
have	great	wanted	doing	shoes	what's
there	door	knew	almost	sometimes	change
were	thought	I've	giant	floor	pie
do	something	full	watched	talk	stairs
your	only	gone	today	brother	money
into	water	school	pulled	idea	journey
mother	through	won't	whole	carry	fall
very	our	hear	straight	picture	hold
could	once	coming	ball	guess	though
old	told	air	beautiful	sign	goes
don't	another	walk	kind	worm	color
know	give	does	police	piece	call
bear	heard	poor	doesn't	others	wrong
Mr.	nothing	soup	world	answer	wonderful
would	wizard	four	love	anyone	holding
who	been	work	walrus	answered	lamb
put	walked	dinosaur	friend	loved	move
come	always	tried	dear	mama	pushed
oh	you're	should	caught	gold	against
some	before	wasn't	climbed	wouldn't	worry
here	eyes	enough	we're	fire	wearing
their	dinosaurs	laughed	honey	I'd	berries

special	field	Nazis	pair	babies	believe
hurried	already	grandmother	hair	turkey	haven't
hall	year	moved	policeman	fair	earth
climb	everywhere	soldier	hey	canoe	eight
tall	become	roll	suit	sugar	either
tomorrow	Nazi	laughing	falling	knows	eye
listen	grandma	here's	dumb	half	monkey
onto	lovely	above	bye	onions	moving
easier	terrible	carried	signor	trouble	somebody
walking	wants	castle	bears	cupboard	talking
warm	telephone	busy	ears	cold	watching
marigold	smaller	bear's	lie	heart	

Appendix C

Sample Words Containing Low-Frequency Letter–Sound Relationships

Graphemes representing the /f/ sound: _phone, laugh, calf_

Graphemes representing the /g/ sound: _ghost, guest_

Graphemes representing the /k/ sound: _ache, mechanic, bisque, walk_

Graphemes representing the /m/ sound: _climb, hymn_

Graphemes representing the /n/ sound: _know, gnat, pneumonia_

Graphemes representing the /r/ sound: _write, rhyme_

Graphemes representing the /s/ sound: _scene, psalm, listen_

Graphemes representing the /sh/ sound: _partial, sugar, precious, machine, session_

Graphemes representing the /ch/ sound: _question, future_

Graphemes representing the /zh/ sound: _measure, azure, division, garage_

Graphemes representing the /a/ sound: _plaid, laugh_

Graphemes representing the /ē/ sound: _seize money, field, police_

Graphemes representing the /e/ sound: _said, heifer, friend, says, many_

Graphemes representing the /ī/ sound: _aisle, sign, height, pie, aye_

Graphemes representing the /i/ sound: _sieve, build_

Graphemes representing the /ō/ sound: _soul, toe, though_

Graphemes representing the /o/ sound: _cough_

Graphemes representing the /ō/ sound: _through, fruit_

Graphemes representing the /u/ sound: _double, come_

Grapheme representing the /oo/ sound: _could_

Grapheme representing the /ou/ sound: _bough_

Appendix D

Word Lists for Chapter 10 Phonics Lessons

Short Vowels:

a

at, an, add, as, am, ash, act, ask, asp, apt, and, ant

hat, pan, fan, lamp, lap, hand, sack, cat, ham, an, bat, wax, back, bad, bag, band, mad, map, rat, sad, sand, sat, rag, ran, had, nap, land, gas, tack, tap, pat, cap, catch

ac-tion, ac-tor, ad-dress, ad-just, ad-mit, af-ter, ap-ple, am-bush, ap-ply

e

Ed, edge, etch, end, else, ebb

web, wet, well, bed, beg, bell, bend, best, set, send, fed, felt, fell, fence, desk, deck, den, men, mend, mess, met, jet, red, hen, neck, nest, next, vest, led, less, let, yes, yell, yet, ten, test, tense, peck, pen, pest, pet, zest, gem

ed-it, ef-fort, en-force, en-try, ex-pel

i

it, in, if, itch, inch, is

wig, win, wish, with, witch, will, wind, bib, big, bid, bit, sit, sick, sin, fix, fin, fish, fist, fit, did, dig, dip, ditch, dish, mix, mill, mint, miss, mist, mitt, jig, rid, rich, risk, rip, hid, hill, hip, hit, lick, lid, lift, lint, lip, list, lit, kick, kill, tin, tip, pill, pin

ig-loo, im-age, ig-nite, im-press, in-crease, it-self, in-deed

o

on, odd, ox, oz, off, oft

box, boss, bond, sob, sock, sod, fox, fog, fond, dog, dock, dodge, dot, mob, mock, mop, job, jot, rob, rock, rod, rot, hog, hop, hot, nod, not, lock, log, loss, lost, lot, got, toss, top, tot, pop, pot, cot, cob, cost

ob-tain, Oc-to-ber, of-fer

u

up, us

bus, bump, bud, budge, bunch, but, sub, suck, sum, fun, fudge, fuss, dust, duck, dug, much, mud, mug, mush, must, just, jump, rub, runt, rush, rut, rust, hum, hug, hush, hut, hunch, hunt, nut, nudge, luck, lug, lump, lunch, luck, gum, gush, tub, puff, pump, punch, pup, punt, cut, cup, cuff, cuss

ug-ly, un-der, un-til, ut-ter, un-bend, up-per, un-mask, up-set

Beginning Consonants:

m

mad, melt, much, mob, mix, man, men, milk, mock, mud, map, mend, mill, mop, mug, mash, mesh, mink, mum, mass, mess, mint, mumps, met, miss, munch, match, mist, mush, math, mitt, muss, must, mat, midst

maid, mail, maim, make, male, mane, mar, march, mark, maul, may, maze, me, meal, mean, meant, meat, meek, meet, merge, mice, mile, mine, mode, moist, mole, mood, moon, moose, morn, mount, mound, mouse, mouth, mule, my, myth

mag-ic, mag-net, ma-jor, mam-mal, man-age, man-sion, ma-ple

p

pack, peck, pick, pod, puff, pact, peg, pig, pong, pulp, pad, pelt, pill, pop, pulse, pan, pen, pin, pot, pump, pant, pest, pinch, pun, pants, pet, pink, punch, pat, pit, punk, patch, pitch, punt, path, pup, pull

pace, page, paid, pail, pain, paint, pale, pane, park, part, pave, paw, pawn, pay, pea, peace, peak, peek, peel, peep, perch, perk, pew, pile, pine, pipe, poach, point, poise, poke, pole, pool, porch, pork, pouch, pound, pout, purse

pack-et, pad-dle, pam-per, pan-el, pan-ic, pa-per, part-ner, pat-tern, par-ty, pay-ment, pen-cil, pun-ish

s

sit, sack, self, sob, sub, sick, sin, sad, sell, sift, sock, such, sag, send, silk, sixth, sod, suck, sand, sense, sill, solve, suds, sang, sent, silt, sum, sank, set, sun, sap, since, sung, sunk, sat, sing, singe, sink

safe, sail, saint, sake, sale, same, sauce, saw, say, sea, seam, seat, serve, so, soak, soap, soil, soon, soothe, sort, sound, south, sown

sa-cred, sad-dle, sat-in, sam-ple, sil-ver, sel-fish, sev-en, sig-nal, sim-ple, si-lent, sis-ter, sud-den

b

back, box, bus, bib, bed, bad, botch, bump, big, beg, badge, boss, bat, buck, bud, bid, bond, budge, bell, bag, bench, ban, bug, bend, band, batch, bath, bum, bun, bunch, bunk, bunt, but, buzz, bit, best, bet, bent

beach, bead, bean, beast, beet, boil, book, boot, born, bound, burst

ban-dit, ban-jo, bash-ful, bas-ket, bo-ny, bot-tle, bu-gle, buc-kle, bun-dle, buz-zer

t

ten, tack, tell, toss, tub, test, tab, Ted, tick, top, till, tuck, tact, tempt, tilt, tot, tug, tag, tin, tan, tend, tinge, tang, tense, tint, tank, tent, tip, tap, tenth, text

toy, type, tail, take, tale, tame, tape, tar, tart, taunt, taut, tea, teach, team, tease, tee, teem, teeth, term, terse, tight, tile, time, toad, toast, toe, toil, tone, took, tool, toot, tooth, torch, torn, tow, town

ta-ble, tab-let, tac-kle, tai-lor, tar-dy, tar-get, tar-nish, tat-tle, tem-per, tem-ple, ten-der, ten-sion, ti-dy, tick-et, tim-ber

d

did, dust, dog, desk, dash, dab, debt, dock, dub, dad, deck, dig, dodge, duck, Dutch, daft, dense, dill, damp, dent, dip, doll, dud, Dan, depth, ditch, Don, dug, dance, dish, dot, duff, dash, dull, dam, den, dumb, dump, dunce, dawn, day, daze, dead

deaf, dealt, deal, death, deed, deep, dew, dice, dime, dine, dive, dome

dab-ble, dai-ly, dain-ty, daz-zle, dea-con, de-fy, dim-ple, du-ty, do-nate, diz-zy, di-ver, dip-per, de-ny

f

fox, fib, fan, fed, fun, fact, felt, fix, fog, fudge, fad, fell, fifth, fond, fence, fig, font, fund, fang, fetch, fill, fuss, fast, fat, film, fin, finch, fish, fist, fit

face, fade, fail, faint, faith, fake, fame, farm, fate, fault, fawn, feast, feat, fee, feed, feel, feet, fete, few, file, fine, firm, first, five, foam, foil, food, fool, foot, for, force, form, fort, forth, foul, found, fowl, fume, fur, fuse

fa-ble, fa-tal, fau-cet, fa-vor, fee-ble, fi-ber, fe-ver, fid-dle, fin-ish, fiz-zle

l

lap, led, lick, lock, luck, lack, lass, lug, lad, latch, ledge, lid, lodge, lull, lag, lax, left, lift, log, lump, lamp, lamb, leg, limb, loss, lunch, lend, limp, lost, lung, lance, lens, lint, lot, lunge, land, less, lip, luck, lap, lest, lisp, lapse, let, list, lash, lit, lace, laid, lake, lame, lane, large, lark, late, launch, law, lawn, lay, least, leave, leech, life, light, like, line, lo, loaf, loan, loaves, lone, look, loom, loop, loose, loot, loud, lounge, louse, low, lurk

la-bel, la-bor, lad-der, la-dy, lan-tern, laun-dry, law-yer, lead-er, leath-er, lem-on, les-son, lev-el

r

rat, red, rob, rug, rid, rack, rich, risk, rub, rag, rent, rock, ram, rest, ridge, rod, rum, ramp, rift, romp, run, ran, rig, rot, rung, ranch, rim, runt, rang, ring, rush, rank, rink, rust, rap, rinse, rut, rash, rip

race, rage, raid, rail, rain, raise, rake, rate, rave, raw, ray, reach, read, realm, ream, reap, reed, reef, reel, rice, ride, right, ripe, rise, road, roam, roast, robe, rode, role, roof, room, roost, root, rope, rose, round, rout, rove, rude, rule, row rab-bit, rac-coon, ra-cer, ram-ble, rid-dle, ri-der, ri-fle, rob-in, ro-bot

n

neck, nod, nag, nick, nudge, nap, nest, nip, not, numb, nab, net, nil, notch, nut, next

nail, name, nay, neat, need, nerve, new, news, nice, night, nine, no, noise, noon, noose, nook, nor, north, nose, note, noun, now, nurse

nap-kin, nas-ty, na-tion, na-vy, nee-dle, neg-lect, nev-er, nib-ble, nim-ble, no-ble, nor-mal, noz-zle, num-ber, ny-lon

w

web, wig, went, win, wet, wish, wept, wag, wit, wax, with, witch, wedge, width, wed, will, wilt, weld, well, wind, west, wing, wink, welt, wisp

wade, wage, waist, wait, waive, wake, wave, way, we, weak, wealth, wean, weave, wee, week, weed, weep, wide, wife, wipe, wood, wool, worn, wove, wine

wag-on, wa-ken, wig-gle, win-dow, win-ter, wit-ness, wob-ble, wish-ful

h

hum, had, hid, hog, hedge, hack, hag, heft, help, hill, hilt, hub, huff, hug, hull, husk, hush, hut, ham, hem, him, honk, hump, hand, hen, hinge, hop, hot, hunch, hung, hunk, hunt, hint, hip, his, hiss, hit, hitch, hence, hang, hat, hatch, have, has

hard, harm, harp, harsh, hate, haul, haunt, hawk, hay, haze, head, heal, health, heap, heat, heave, heed, heel, her, herb, herd, hew, hide, hike, hive, hoe, hoist, hole, home, hood, hoof, hook, hoop, hoot, hope, horn, horse, hose, hound, house, how, howl, hue, hurl, hurt

hab-it, ham-mer, ham-ster, han-dle, hap-pen, har-den, hatch-et, ho-tel

c/k/

can, cot, cub, cob, cast, cap, cad, calf, cut, catch, cup, cat, cuff, cog, cash, cuss, cod, camp, cab, cost

carp, carve, cause, coach, coal, coast, coat, coax, code, coil, cook, cool, cork, corn, couch, count, cow, coy, cube, curb, curl, curse, curve, cute

cab-in, ca-ble, cac-tus, cam-el, can-cel, can-dle, can-yon, car-go, cat-tle, com-ic, com-ma, cop-y

k

kick, keg, kiss, kit, kin, kill, kid, kelp, king, kink

kite, keep

ket-tle, ketch-up, ken-nel, ker-nel, kid-nap, kin-dle, kitch-en

j

just, job, jig, judge, jam, jack, jet, jug, jag, jilt, jest, Jill, jinx, John, jump, jot, junk, jut, jamb, jazz

jail, jar, jaunt, jaw, jeans, jeep, jerk, join, joint, joke, joy

jac-ket, jeal-ous, jel-ly, jew-el, jif-fy, jig-gle, jol-ly, jug-gle, jum-ble, junc-tion, jus-tice

g/g/

gum, get, got, gag, gift, gab, gild, gob, gulf, gill, God, gull, gang, golf, gulp, gas, gash, gasp, gap, gush, gust, gut

gage, gain, game, gape, gate, gauze, gave, gaze, geese, goal, goat, good, goose, gorge, gouge, gown

gal-lant, gam-ble, gar-den, gar-gle, gar-lic, gob-ble, gob-lin, go-pher, gos-sip, gut-ter

g/j/—(before *e, i, y*)

gem, gin, gist, gym (but gift, get, gild, gill)

gene, germ, gent (but geese)

gen-tle, gin-ger, gen-er-al, gen-er-ous, ge-ni-us, gen-tle-man, gent-ly, gi-ant, gyp-sy (but gig-gle, giz-zard)

c/s/

cent, cinch, cell, cit-y, cen-ter, cig-ar, cin-der, cel-lar, cen-sus, civ-ic, cyn-ic

cite

ce-dar, ce-ment, cir-cle, cir-cus, cy-press, civ-il

y

yes, yam, yet, yank, yap, yelp, yank, yell, yak

yard, yarn, yawn, yeast, yoke, yowl, yule

yel-low, yes-ter-day, yo-del, yon-der

v

vest, van, vat, vent, valve, vend, vast, vex

verb, verse, vice, vile, vise, voice, void, vote, vouch, vow va-cant, va-ca-tion, vac-cin-a-tion, van-ish, va-por, vi-o-lin, vis-it, vow-el, vic-tim, viv-id, vol-ume

z

zap, zest, zip, zonked, zinc, zom-bie, zing

zone, zoo, zoom

ze-bra, ze-ro

qu

quack, quit, quest, quiz, quick, quench, quill, quell, quilt, quip

quail, quaint, quake, queen, quite, quote

ques-tion, qui-et, quit-ter, quiv-er, quo-ta

Final Consonants:

m

sum, yam, gem, him, mum, ram, hem, mom, hum, ham, vim, bum, gum, jam, rim, yum, Sam, dim, rum

shame, blame, came, fame, flame, frame, game, lame, name, same, slime, crime, dime, grime, home, dame, tame, lime, time, dome, Rome, fume, theme, chime, prime, slime, scheme

beam, room, seam, seem, team, zoom, ream, roam, maim, boom, deem, doom, down, foam

dim-ple, fum-ble, gam-ble, hum-ble, jum-ble, mum-ble, nim-ble, sam-ple, sim-ple, cam-er-a, com-ic, dam-age, im-age, lem-on, lim-it, mem-o, mim-ic, com-ma, com-pound, dum-my, em-ploy, ham-per, mum-my, mem-ber, num-ber, tim-ber

p

cap, pep, tip, top, cup, tap, hep, zip, sop, sup, zap, sip, pop, pup, sap, rip, mop, rap, quip, hop, nap, pip, map, dip, lap, lip, gap, hip, up, nip, lop

ape, cape, drape, grape, scrape, shape, pipe, dope, hope, rope, slope, gape, nape, tape, wipe, cope, lope, mope, snipe, tripe, grope, scope, slope, stripe, swipe

seep, soap, weep, peep, reap, leap, loop, coop, deep, heap, hoop, jeep, keep

s

mess, mass, yes, miss, boss, bus, hiss, toss, cuss, lass, less, kiss, moss, pus, sass, Bess, loss, muss, fuss, pass, Russ, us

base, case, chase, dose, vase, curse, verse, terse, horse, purse, loose, house, louse, moose, mouse, noose, geese, goose, lease, blouse, crease, grease, grouse, spouse, sparse

(*s* after voiceless consonants) pups, ducks, hats, locks, maps, cuffs, socks, sacks

bas-ket, blos-som, blis-ter, clas-sic, clus-ter, cus-tom, dis-cuss, dis-tant, des-troy, dras-tic, dis-turb, dis-tort, dis-like, dis-count, sis-ter, ves-sel, whis-per, wit-ness, plas-tic, roos-ter, res-cue, es-cape, es-say, es-cort, es-tate, es-teem, flus-ter, fos-sil, fos-ter, frus-trate, gos-sip, gos-pel, hos-tage, les-son, las-so, lus-ter, les-sen, mis-hap, mus-ket, mus-tang, mas-ter, mes-sage, mis-take, nas-ty, nos-tril, con-sists, car-cass, sys-tem, e-rase, de-crease, en-dorse

n

ban, ten, bin, Don, ran, bun, can, yen, tin, sun, tan, pen, sin, run, van, den, pin, pun, pan, man, fin, nun, man, dun, fan, gun, Dan, fun, gin, in, win

lane, plane, shine, dine, line, bone, cone, lone, cane, mane, pane, sane, vane, wane, gene, mine, nine, pine, vine, wine, tone, zone, crane, scene, whine, brine, spine, swine, thine, twine, drone, prone, shone, shrine, throne, stone, phone

bean, been, seen, wean, noon, noun, pain, pawn, rain, roan, lain, lawn, lean, loan, loin, loon, main, mean, moan, moon, boon, coin, dawn, dean, down, fain, fawn, gain, gown, jean, join, keen

b

hub, gob, dub, jab, rub, job, sub, mob, dab, rob, tub, nab, fib, sob, tab, rib, cob, cub, cab, web, bib, bob, bub

globe, robe, gibe, lobe, tribe, probe, scribe

t

bat, bet, bit, tot, but, cat, yet, sit, rot, cut, vat, pet, wet, quit, pot, rut, sat, set, pit, not, putt, rat, mitt, dot, nut, pat, net, hit, lot, mutt, nat, met, fit, got, gut, mat, let, wit, hot, hut, hat, fat, get, jot

kite, ate, date, fate, slate, gate, hate, late, mate, plate, rate, vote, note, cute, fete, mete, bite, mite, site, dote, mote, rote, mute, crate, grate, skate, slate, state, white, smite, spite, trite, smote, sprite, quote, write, wrote bait, beat, beet, boat, root, seat, soot, toot, wait, loot, lout, mail, maim, maul, meal, meat, meet, moat, neat, boot, bout, coat, feat, feet, foot, goat, heat, hoot

bot-tle, bat-tle, cat-tle, ket-tle, lit-tle, rat-tle, set-tle, at-om, met-al, bet-ter, bot-tom, bat-ter, but-ter, but-ton, bit-ter, gut-ter, pat-tern, mot-to, wit-ness, kit-ten, let-ter, mit-ten, mat-ter

d
bad, pad, bed, bid, cod, bud, cad, wed, rid, sod, mud, sad, red, did, rod, dad, led, hid, pod, mad, fed, nod, lad, had, fad, kid, lid, cud, God

blade, fade, grade, made, side, slide, bride, hide, ride, jade, wade, cede, bide, tide, wide, ode, bode, code, lode, mode, rode, glade, shade, spade, trade, Swede, chide, glide, stride, strode, guide, bead, seed, toad, void, weed, wood, paid, raid, read, reed, road, laid, laud, lead, load, loud, tweed, maid, mood, need, dead, deed, feed, feud, food, good, heed, hood

cud-dle, fid-dle, grid-dle, hud-dle, mud-dle, med-dle, mid-dle, pad-dle, rid-dle, sad-dle, bod-y, cred-it, mod-ern, mod-el, med-al, mod-est, prod-uct, stud-y, ad-mit, ad-vice, ad-vance, dad-dy, sud-den, glad-den, hid-den, kid-nap, kid-ney, lad-der, mud-dy, mid-night

l
mill, bell, dull, doll, cell, till, moll, lull, tell, will, gull, yell, sill, well, pill, sell, dill, quell, gill, dell, jell, hill, fill, fell, bill, loll, kill, cull

smile, tile, male, file, mile, pile, stole, hole, mole, pole, mule, bale, gale, hale, pale, sale, tale, vale, bile, vile, wile, dole, role, sole, yule, scale, shale, stale, whale, while, stile, whole, bail, seal, soil, tail, toil, tool, veal, wool, pail, pool, rail, mail, maul, meal, nail, boil, bowl, coal, coil, cool, fail, feel, foal, foul, foil, fool, foul, fowl, hail, haul, heal, heel

col-umn, frol-ic, jol-ly, mel-on, sol-id, bel-low, bal-lot, bol-ster, cel-lar, cul-prit, fil-ter, hel-lo, hol-low, hel-met, hol-ly, yel-low, mil-dew, pil-low, sil-ver, sil-ly, sel-dom, vel-vet, wel-come

g
fog, bag, big, bog, bug, tag, peg, zig, dog, rug, zag, meg, wig, log, dug, wag, leg, rig, hog, mug, sag, pig, jog, lug, rag, dig, hug, nag, fig, lag, gag, jig, hag, jag

wag-on, big-ger, beg-ger, dag-ger, sig-nal, drag-gle, gig-gle, hag-gle, jug-gle, jig-gle, snug-gle, drag-on, fig-ure, bug-gy, drug-gist, drag-net, dag-ger, fog-gy, mag-net

f
puff, off, if, muff, doff, huff, buff

safe, life, fife, wife, knife, strife, beef, roof, reef

ck
buck, back, peck, wick, sock, suck, tack, neck, sick, rock, puck, sack, deck, quick, dock, duck, rack, heck, pick, mock, muck, quack, Dick, lock, luck, pack, lick, hock, tuck, hack, nick, jack, tick, lack

x
tax, six, fox, tux, wax, Rex, box, sax, hex, fix, pox, Max, vex, ox, lax, ax, mix, sex

z
quiz, razz, fuzz, jazz, fizz, daze, gaze, glaze, graze, haze, doze, maze, raze, size, craze, prize, froze, blaze

haz-ard, liz-ard, wiz-ard, daz-zle, driz-zle, fiz-zle, muz-zle, puz-zle, bliz-zard, buz-zard, buz-zer, diz-zy, giz-zard

k
shake, wake, bake, brake, cake, fake, flake, make, rake, snake, dike, hike, like, choke, poke, lake, sake, take, bike, coke, joke, woke, drake, slake, spake, spike, broke, choke, smoke, spoke, strike, stroke, beak, seek, soak, week, weak, took, nook, peak, peek, reek, leak, look, meek, book, cook, hawk, hook

ge
stage, cage, gage, page, rage, huge, age, sage, wage, verge, forge, gorge, large, merge, purge, surge

dge
judge, fudge, bridge, badge, budge, dodge, edge, ridge, madge, grudge, lodge, hedge, fridge, ledge, nudge, pledge, smudge, wedge, sludge, sledge, drudge, fledge

s/z/
has, as, is, his

fuse, hose, chose, rise, close, rose, ruse, muse, wise, nose, pose, use, phase, prose, these, those, whose, phrase

choose, clause, noise, pause, poise, raise, tease, please, praise (*s* after voiced consonants) jobs, pigs, hams, bells, dogs, beds, guns, hills

pris-on, vis-it, hus-band, com-pose, sup-pose, sur-prise, be-cause, dis-please, ex-er-cise, en-close, ad-ver-tise, like-wise

ce

ace, ice, lace, lice, dice, face, race, rice, mice, nice, pace, vice, brace, grace, place, price, slice, space, spice, trace, truce, twice, splice, spruce, thrice

farce, force, peace, sauce, voice, choice, fleece, Greece

ap-ple-sauce, clock-face, en-force, re-trace, dis-place, re-place, de-face, dis-grace

ve

eve, five, gave, hive, cave, cove, dive, dove, pave, rave, save, wave, wove, brave, crave, drive, drove, grave, grove, clove, knave, strove, shave, slave, stove, strive, thrive

carve, curve, delve, valve, heave, leave, waive, weave, cleave, groove, sleeve, eaves, elves, sheaves

cav-ern, bev-el, clev-er, civ-ic, crev-ice, driv-en, grav-el, gav-el, hav-oc, liv-er, lev-el, riv-er, sev-en, trav-el, nov-ice, bee-hive, de-prive

Vowel Teams:

ai

drain, frail, gain, hail, jail, maid, mail, main, paid, pail, pain, paint, quail, rail, rain, raise, sail, saint, snail, sprain, stain, straight, strain, tail, train, trait, waist, wait, aim, bait, braid, brain, chain, claim, drain, fail, faint, faith, nail, wail, grain, lain, plain, aid, laid, maim, taint, praise

ay

stay, day, gay, hay, jay, lay, may, nay, pay, ray, say, way, bray, clay, flay, gray, play, tray, spray, slay, pray, bay, stray

ee

freeze, bee, free, knee, see, three, tree, bleed, deed, feed, need, seed, speed, tweed, weed, cheek, creek, meek, peek, seek, week, eel, feel, heel, kneel, peel, reel, steel, wheel, seem, green, keen, queen, screen, seen, creep, deep, keep, peep, sheep, sleep, sweep, weep, steep, beet, feet, meet, sheet, sleet, breeze,

sneeze, squeeze, wheeze, fee, flee, glee, greed, greet, jeep, screech, sleek, sleeve, speech, street, sweet, tweet, beef

oa

coach, poach, roach, load, road, toad, loaf, oaf, cloak, oak, soak, coal, foal, shoal, loan, moan, roan, soap, boast, coast, roast, toast, boat, coat, float, gloat, goat, oats, throat, coax, croak, foam, groan, oath, goal, hoax

ir

firm, dirt, girl, first, bird, third, twirl, swirl, whirl, flirt, shirt, skirt, squirt, fir, sir, gird, chirp, shirk, smirk, stir, thirst, birch, birth

er

fern, verb, germ, stern, herd, her, per, herb, term, serf, perk, pert, clerk

ur

urn, nurse, burn, curb, turn, blur, cur, spur, fur, purr, churn, spurn, purse, curse, hurl, hurt, spurt, curd, curl, curt, turf, surt, lurk, murk, blurt, purge

ar

arm, art, arch, ark, march, bar, car, far, jar, mar, scar, star, tar, mark, starch, card, hard, lar, yar, charge, large, bark, dark, lark, park, shark, spark, charm, farm, harm, barn, darn, yarn, harp, sharp, cart, chart, part, smart, start, tart, barb, snarl

or

or, cord, cork, fork, pork, stork, form, storm, born, corn, horn, morn, scorn, thorn, short, sort, fort, port, sport, torn, for

core, bore, fore, score, shore, swore, tore, wore, snore, store, sore

ea

heat, flea, plea, sea, tea, beach, bleach, each, peach, preach, reach, teach, bead, lead, plead, deal, heal, meal, seal, squeal, steal, veal, beam, dream, gleam, scream, steam, stream, team, clean, lean, mean, wean, cheap, heap, leap, reap, please, tease, east, feast, least, yeast, beat, cheat, eat, meat, neat, peat, seat, treat, wheat, feat, freak, grease, heave, leaf, leak, lean, league, lease, leave, peace, peach, peal, please, plead, pleat, ream, seam, sneak, speak, squeak, streak, tease, weak, weave, teak, beast, bleach, cease, cream, dean, ease bread, breadth, meant, breath, cleanse, dead, deaf, dealt, death, dread, head, health, spread, sweat, thread, threat, tread, wealth, realm, stead, read

oy

toy, boy, coy, joy, en-joy, des-troy, an-noy, em-ploy, de-coy, loy-al, voy-age

oi

coin, choice, voice, boil, broil, coil, foil, oil, soil, spoil, toil, join, noise, poise, joint, point, void, foist, groin, hoist, loin, moist

ou

trout, couch, crouch, ouch, pouch, slouch, cloud, loud, proud, shroud, bound, found, ground, hound, mound, pound, round, sound, count, mount, flour, our, scour, sour, clouse, house, louse, mouse, out, pout, scout, snout, spout, stout, noun, south, foul

ow

brown, cow, bow, how, plow, row, vow, fowl, growl, howl, owl, prowl, scowl, brown, clown, crown, down, drown, frown, gown, town

snow, bow, mow, row, sow, blow, crow, flow, glow, grow, know, low, show, slow, stow, throw, bowl, blown, flown, grown, known, own, strown, sown

oo

fool, roof, proof, cool, drool, pool, school, spool, loose, tool, bloom, boom, broom, gloom, loom, room, goose, coon, croon, moon, noon, spoon, soon, coop, moose, droop, hoop, loop, scoop, stoop, swoop, troop, noose, boot, hoot, loot, shoot, toot

good, hood, stood, wood, hoof, book, brook, crook, hook, look, shook, took

au

pause, fraud, sauce, caught, clause, launch, vault, cause, taunt, jaunt, fault, taught

aw

lawn, caw, claw, draw, flaw, gnaw, jaw, law, paw, raw, slaw, squaw, straw, thaw, squawk, brawl, crawl, shawl, scrawl, dawn, drawn, yawn, bawl, hawk

ew

chew, flew, grew, knew, stew, brew, new, crew, drew, slew, threw, shrew, blew, screw, dew, news, shrewd, strewn

few, hew, mew, pew

ue

glue, clue, true, blue, sue, due, rue

cue, hue

igh

light, blight, bright, right, sight, tight, fight, might, night, flight, fright, knight, plight, slight, high, sigh, nigh

are

fare, flare, glare, hare, mare, pare, rare, scare, share, snare, spare, square, care

air

chair, fair, flair, hair, lair, pair, air

eer

cheer, deer, jeer, peer, sheer, sneer, steer

ear

clear, dear, ear, fear, gear, hear, rear, shear, smear, spear, year

ire

fire, hire, mire, wire, sire

Consonant Digraphs:
ch—beginning

chop, chat, chap, chaff, check, chess, chick, chill, chin, chip, chub, chuck, chug, chum, champ, chance, chant, chest-chain, charge, charm, chart, chase, cheap, cheat, cheep, cheese, chime, chirp, choice, choke, choose, chow, church, churn

chan-nel, chap-ter, char-coal, chat-ter, chick-en, chim-ney, chi-na, cho-sen, chow-der, chuc-kle, chal-lenge, chap-el, charm-ing, char-ter, chas-tise, cheap-en, check-ers, chil-ly, chim-pan-zee, chis-el, chub-by, en-chant-ing, en-chant-ment, mer-chant, mer-chan-dise, pur-chase, un-chain, wood-chuck

ch and *tch*—endings

beach, leech, peach, beech, poach, pouch, coach, couch, reach, teach, vouch, bleach, breach, broach, crouch, grouch, preach, slouch, speech

rich, which, such, much

ditch, catch, batch, witch, blotch, clutch, etch, pitch, patch, notch, snatch, fetch, stitch, hatch, hitch, batch, thatch, sketch, snitch, latch, itch, crotch, crutch, stretch, match, switch, splotch, Dutch, wretch, scratch, twitch, Scotch, hutch arch-er, at-tach, bleach-ers, sand-wich, coach-man, cock-roach, grouch-y, rich-es, hatch-et, treach-er-ous, treach-er-y, dis-patch, im-peach

sh—beginning
shut, shop, sham, shack, shag, shall, shed, shell, ship, shod, shock, shot, shun, shuck, shaft, shalt, shank, shelf, shift, shade, shake, shale, shame, shape, shark, sharp, shave, shawl, she, sheaf, sheen, sheep, sheet, shine, shirk, shirt, shone, shoo, shook, shoot, short, shout, show, shown

shab-by, shad-ow, sha-dy, shag-gy, sha-ky, shal-low, sham-bles, sharp-en, shiv-er, show-er, shac-kle, sha-ding, sha-ken, sham-poo, shat-ter, shel-ter, sher-bet, shi-ny, ship-ment, shiv-er, short-en, shop-ping, shoot-ing, short-cake, ship-yard, shop-keep-er, shift-less

sh—ending
rush, cash, rash, blush, wish, flesh, gosh, brush, dish, fresh, bosh, sash, fish, thresh, clash, slush, swish, mesh, slash, crush, crash, flush, splash, gush, dash, hush, flash, mush, smash, plush, thrash, gash, trash, hash, lash, bash, mash, ash

leash, harsh

sel-fish, cash-ew, fin-ish, Dan-ish, ab-o-lish, ad-mon-ish, ban-ish, bash-ful, blem-ish, boy-ish, dem-ol-ish, fool-ish, dim-in-ish, fash-ion, fash-ion-a-ble, fresh-ness, fur-nish, gar-nish, harsh-ness, pol-ish, pun-ish, rad-ish, round-ish, snob-bish, tar-nish, tick-lish, rel-ish, pun-ish-ment

wh—beginning
whiz, whip, whack, when, whiff, whet, whim, whit, which, whisk, whale, wheat, wheel, while, whine, whirl, white, why

wheez-y, wheth-er, which-ev-er, whim-per, whim-sic-al, whirl-pool, whirl-wind, whis-ker, whis-per, whit-tle

ng—ending
long, sing, bang, bring, flung, rang, bong, rung, string, clang, song, cling, hung, slang, slung, fang, strong, ding, dong, lung, tang, sling, sprung, swing, gang, gong, fling, stung, sang, spring, strung, thing, hang, prong, king, sung, sprang, pong, swung, wing, pang, throng, ring, clung, sting, bung, ting, zing, wring, wrong

king-dom, cong-ress, gang-ster, ang-ry, hung-ry, ang-le, ang-er, fing-er, fung-us, hung-er, jing-le, jung-le, ling-er, mang-le, ming-le, sing-le, tang-le

Note: When the first syllable of a two-syllable word ends in *ng* and the second syllable begins with a vowel sound, the /g/ sound begins the second syllable.

th—beginning
voiceless: thin, thick, thong, thud, thence, thug, thank, thing, think, thump, thumb, thaw, theme, third, thirst, thorn

thir-ty, thir-teen, thun-der, thank-ful, ther-mom-et-er, ther-mos-tat, thick-en, thick-et, thick-ness, thim-ble, think-er, thirst-y, thorn-y, thous-and, thun-der-cloud, thun-der-storm, Thurs-day, thy-roid, e-ther, leng-then, leng-thy, streng-then, syn-thet-ic

voiced: that, than, them, then, this, thus, these, thine, those

fur-ther, far-ther, them-selves, hea-then

th—ending
voiceless: bath, broth, with, Beth, path, cloth, lath, moth, pith, hath, smith, math, froth, myth, wroth, wrath, mouth, booth, death, faith, south, teeth, tooth, growth, sleuth, wreath, wealth, twelfth

meth-ods, ath-lete, ath-let-ic, auth-or, auth-en-tic, auth-or-ize, death-ly, sab-bath, eth-ic-al, eth-ics, math-em-at-ics, meth-od-ic-al, mouth-ful, orth-od-ox, sev-enth, sym-path-et-ic, sym-path-ize

voiced: loath, smooth, soothe

gath-er, wheth-er, hith-er

Consonant Blends:
st—beginning
stop, stick, stab, stack, staff, stag, stem, step, stiff, still, stock, stub, stuck, stuff, stun, stamp, stance, stand, stench, stilt, sting, stint, stomp, stink, stitch, stump, stung, stunk, stunt

star, starch, start, starve, state, stay, steal, steam, steel, steep, stern, stew, stir, stone, stood, stool, storm, stove

sta-ble, stam-mer, stam-pede, sta-ple, sta-tion, stee-ple

pr—beginning
prop, press, prim, prick, prod, prom, prance, prank, prince, print, prong, prompt

praise, pray, preach, price, pride, prime, prize, pro, probe, prone, proof, proud, prowl, prine, pry prin-cess, prob-lem, prof-it, pro-gram, pro-noun, pro-nounce, prop-er

tr—beginning

trot, tram, trap, trek, trick, trill, trim, trip, truss, truck, track, tract, tramp, trance, trash, trench, trend, trump, trund, trust

trace, trade, trail, train, trait, tray, tread, treat, tree, tribe, trite, troop, trounce, trout, truce, true, try

trac-tor, tra-der, traf-fic, tram-ple, trans-fer, trans-late, trap-eze, trav-el, trem-ble, tric-kle

gr—beginning

grip, grab, gram, grass, grill, grid, grim, grin, grit, grub, gruff, graft, grand, grant, graph, grasp, grudge, grunt, grump

grace, grade, grain, grape, grave, graze, grease, greed, green, greet, grew, grime, groan, groom, groove, grope, grouch, ground, grove, grow, growl, grown, growth

gram-mar, grav-el, gra-vy, grid-dle, griz-zly, gro-cer

pl—beginning

plot, pled, plod, pluck, plug, plum, plus, plank, plant, pledge, plump, plunge, plush, plan

place, plain, plane, plate, play, plea, plead, please, pleat, plight, plow, plume, ply

plan-et, plas-tic, plas-ter, plen-ty, plat-ter, Plu-to

cl—beginning

clip, clack, clam, clan, clap, class, clef, click, cliff, clock, clod, clog, clot, cluck, club, clamp, clang, clasp, clash, clench, cleft, clinch, cling, clink, clump, clutch, clung

claim, clause, claw, clay, clean, cloud, clown, clue, cleanse

clas-sic, clat-ter, clev-er, cli-mate, clip-per, clos-et, clo-ver, clum-sy, clus-ter

cr—beginning

crop, crack, crag, crab, cram, crib, crock, cross, craft, cramp, crank, crash, crept, crest, cringe, crisp, crotch, crumb, crunch, crush, crutch

crate, crave, crawl, craze, cream, crease, creek, creel, creep, crew, crime, cry, croak, crook, croon, crouch, crow, crowd, crown, crude

cra-dle, crank-y, cra-ter, cra-yon, cra-zy, cred-it, crick-et, crip-ple, crum-ble, cru-sade, crys-tal

str—beginning

stretch, strap, stress, strip, struck, strut, strand, strict, string, strong, strung

strain, strait, straw, stray, streak, stream, street, strewn, stride, strife, strike, stripe, stroke

strad-dle, stretch-er, stri-king, strug-gle

br—beginning

bronze, brat, brag, bran, brass, bred, brick, brig, brim, brand, branch, bridge, bring, brink, brisk, broth, brunt, brush

brace, braid, brake, brave, brawl, brawn, breach, bread, breath, breeze, brew, bribe, bride, bright, broil, broke, bronze, brood, brook, broom, brow, brown, browse, brute

brace-let, breez-y, bri-dle, bright-en, brit-tle, bro-ken, bron-co, bru-net, bru-tal

dr—beginning

drip, drop, drab, dram, drag, dreg, dress, drill, dross, drug, drub, drum, draft, drank, dredge, drench, drift, drink, drunk, drudge

drain, drape, draw, drawl, drawn, dread, dream, drew, drive, drone, droop, drove, dry

drag-on, dras-tic, draw-er, dream-er, driv-en, dri-ver, driz-zle, drow-sy, drum-mer

sp—beginning

spend, spot, span, spat, speck, sped, spell, spill, spin, spit, spun, spank, spent, spilt, spunk

space, Spain, spake, spark, sparse, spawn, speak, speech, speed, spice, spike, spine, spite, spoil, spoke, spook, spool, spoon, sport, spout, spy

spa-cious, spar-kle, spi-cy, spi-der, spin-dle, spin-ster, spin-et, spon-sor

fl—beginning

flat, flag, flap, flax, fled, fleck, flex, flick, flit, flip, flock, flog, floss, flop, fluff, flank, flash, flask, flesh, flinch, fling, flint, flung, flunk, flush

flake, flame, flaunt, flaw, flea, flee, fleece, fleet, flew, fly, flight, flirt, float, flood, flout, flow, flown, flu, flute

flan-nel, flat-ter, fla-vor, flim-sy, flow-er, flut-ter

fr—beginning

frog, fret, frill, frizz, frock, from, frank, French, fresh, fringe, frisk, frost

frail, frame, fraud, freak, free, freeze, fright, fro, frown, froze, fry

frac-tion, fra-grance, fran-tic, frec-kle, free-dom, fren-zy, fric-tion

bl—beginning

bless, blush, black, bled, blip, bliss, blob, block, blot, bluff, bland, blank, blast, blend, blimp, blink, blond, blotch, blunt

bleak, bleed, blight, bloat, blood, bloom, blouse, blow, blown, blue, blur, blurt

bleach-ers, blem-ish, bless-ing, blis-ter, bliz-zard, blos-som, blow-er, blub-ber, blun-der

sl—beginning

slap, slim, sled, slid, slot, slum, slam, slob, slack, slip, slug, slag, slick, slit, slop, slog, slang, slant, slash, sledge, slept, sling, slink, sludge, slump, slush, slat

slate, slave, slay, sleek, sleep, sleet, sleeve, slew, slice, slide, slight, slime, slope, slouch, slow, sly, slur

slan-der, slen-der, slug-gish, slum-ber

sw—beginning

swift, swim, swam, swell, switch, swum, swish, swank, swept, swung, swing, swift, Swiss

sway, sweat, sweep, sweet, swerve, swirl, swoon, sworn

swiv-el

sm—beginning

smog, smug, smut, smock, smack, smell, smash, smudge, smelt

smart, smile, smirk, smite, smoke, smooth, smote

smel-ter, smo-ky, smug-gle

sc—beginning

scat, scuff, scab, scoff, scan, scum, Scott, Scotch, scamp, scud

scale, scar, scarf, scoop, scoot, scope, scorch, scorn, scout, scowl

scaf-fold, scam-per, scan-dal, scant-y, scar-let, scat-ter, scoot-er, scoun-drel

thr—beginning

thrill, throb, thrash, thresh, thrift, thrust, throng, thrush

thread, threat, three, threw, thrice, thrive, throat, throne, throw

threat-en, thrift-y, throt-tle

sk—beginning

skin, sketch, skip, skunk, skill, skull, skim, skid, skiff, skit, skimp

skirt, sky, state

skel-et-on, skin-ny, skill-ful, skip-per, sky-line

gl—beginning

glum, glad, glen, glib, gloss, glass, glance, gland, glimpse, glint

glaze, gleam, glee, glide, glean, gloat, globe, gloom, glow, glue

gli-der, glim-mer, glit-ter, glut-ton

tw—beginning

twin, twig, twill, twang, twelve, twinge, twist, twitch

tweed, twice, twine, twirl

scr—beginning

scrub, scrap, scrag, scram, scrim, scruff, scratch, scrimp, script, scrunch, scrod

scrape, scrawl, scream, screech, screen, scribe, screw

scrab-ble, scram-ble, scrib-ble, scru-ples

spr—beginning

spring, sprig, sprag, sprung, sprint, sprang

sprain, sprawl, spray, spread, spree, sprite, sprout, spruce, spry

sn—beginning

snack, sniff, snob, snub, snatch, snap, snip, snug, snag, snuff

snail, snake, snarl, sneak, sneeze, snipe, snoop, snooze, snort, snout, snow

snap-py, snap-shot, snif-fle, snob-bish, snor-kel, snug-gle, snoop-ing

spl—beginning

splash, split, splotch, spling, splat

spleen, splice

splat-ter, splen-did, splin-ter

shr—beginning
shrub, shrill, shred, shrug, shrank, shrunk, shrink, shrimp

shrew, shrine, shrewd

shriv-el

st—ending
zest, dust, just, nest, past, cost, rest, blast, frost, fist, bust, best, fast, lost, twist, crust, vast, list, rust, chest, last, mist, thrust, west, cast, gist, gust, crest, mast, trust, jest, must, vest, pest, test

sk—ending
risk, mask, ask, brisk, desk, dusk, flask, disk, husk, frisk, musk, task, bask, whisk, cask

mp—ending
damp, camp, bump, skimp, stomp, pump, stamp, dump, imp, hemp, rump, clamp, hump, limp, slump, romp, cramp, jump, shrimp, stump, clomp, lamp, lump, crimp, thump, chomp, ramp, plump, pomp, trump

nt—ending
sent, bent, ant, tent, blunt, tint, font, chant, went, bunt, hint, vent, grant, dent, grunt, lint, pent, plant, rent, hunt, mint, slant, punt, print, pant, spent, runt, splint, stint, can't, lent, flint, glint, cent, stunt, sprint, rant, scent, squint

nd—ending
tend, sand, and, bend, blond, fund, band, blend, bond, strand, bland, end, fond, brand, lend, pond, gland, mend, grand, send, hand, spend, land, stand, trend

nk—ending
honk, bank, blink, bunk, blank, rink, flank, brink, chunk, crank, zonk, sunk, drink, drunk, drank, sink, trunk, ink, hunk, frank, stink, flunk, kink, plank, junk, think, stunk, link, punk, rank, wink, tank, pink, shrunk, sank, clink, thank, shrink, spunk, spank, mink, clank

lt—ending
felt, belt, jilt, quilt, knelt, stilt, melt, tilt, pelt, wilt, smelt, hilt, welt, lilt, milt, silt

ft—ending
lift, craft, drift, left, soft, tuft, draft, gift, theft, loft, raft, deft, oft, sift, shaft, shift, heft, daft, graft, swift, thrift, rift

ct—ending
tract, fact, act, pact, tact, duct, strict

pt—ending
slept, kept, script, wept, crept, swept

sp—ending
lisp, wisp, clasp, gasp, grasp, hasp, rasp, crisp

nge—ending
hinge, lunge, binge, plunge, singe, tinge, fringe, twinge, cringe

nce—ending
dance, fence, mince, glance, dunce, lance, hence, since, whence, wince, stance, prince, trance, pence, chance, thence, prance

nse—ending
rinse, sense, dense, tense

nch—ending
pinch, bench, clench, branch, munch, scrunch, trench, ranch, punch, clinch, winch, French, wench, crunch, finch, cinch, quench, hunch, flinch, drench, bunch, lunch, inch, brunch, wrench, lynch

Y as a Vowel:
fly, by, my, why, thy, cry, dry, fry, pry, sly, spy, sty, try, spry

myth, hymn, gym

de-ny, de-fy, re-ly, Ju-ly, im-ply, cyn-ic, cy-cle, gyp-sy, wood-y, room-y, starch-y, speed-y, chunk-y, mud-dy, fun-ny, snap-py, slop-py, hap-py, pen-ny, sun-ny, jol-ly, sil-ly, ba-by, po-ny, la-dy, ti-ny, gra-vy, na-vy, ho-ly, mush-y, fish-y, storm-y, rain-y, bod-y, bo-ny, cand-y, cook-y, dirt-y, diz-zy, dress-y, dum-my, dust-y, du-ty, emp-ty, weed-y, frost-y, leaf-y, brain-y, spook-y, cloud-y, gloom-y, bump-y, crisp-y, cream-y, rat-if-y, oc-cu-py, mag-nif-y, i-den-tif-y, syl-la-ble, sys-tem, sym-bol, cyl-in-der, cym-bal, syc-a-more, syn-thet-ic, sym-path-et-ic, sym-path-ize, typ-ic-al, sym-path-y, sym-pho-ny, symp-tom, syn-dic-ate, hyp-no-sis, hyp-no-tize, hyp-oc-ris-y, phys-ics, phys-ic-al, pyg-my, mys-ter-y, mys-tic, mys-tic-al, myth-ic-al

Appendix E

Sample Story

Grammar Test for Peter's Chair, *by Ezra Jack Keats (Harper & Row, 1967)*

1. Where did this story take place?
   a. Mostly inside Peter's house—one point
   b. Some of the story took place outside Peter's house—another point
2. Who was this story mostly about?
   a. Peter—one point
   b. Peter's dog—another point
   c. Peter's family: Mom, Dad, and Susie, his sister—give another point for identifying his family, or one or more family member(s)
3. What was bothering Peter in this story?
   a. His father was painting Peter's things pink so they could be given to his new baby sister, Susie—one point
   b. If the student mentions that the father was painting Peter's *cradle, high chair,* or *crib* pink—give another point
   c. If the student mentions that Peter did not want his father to paint his *old blue chair* pink—give another point

4. What did Peter decide to do because he was unhappy?
   a. He decided to run away—one point
   b. If the student says he decided to run away with his *dog,* or his *blue chair,* or with some of his things—give another point
5. How did Peter solve his problem?
   a. When he tried to sit in his old blue chair he couldn't because he was too big—one point
   b. He decided to ask his dad to paint his old blue chair pink for his sister—another point
   c. He played a trick on his mother by putting his shoes under the curtain to make her think he was hiding behind the curtain—another point

Total points _____ (13 possible)

Appendix F

Individual Sight Word Test, Parts 1, 2, 3, and 4

Teacher Directions

Materials Needed:

1. Two copies of the test (one for the teacher to use for marking, and one for the student to read)
2. Stopwatch

Administration of the Test:

1. Write the student's name on one test. Keep this copy.
2. Give the student the other copy of the test.
3. Say, "Look at the words on Part 1 of this test." Allow the student a few seconds to look at the words. "Touch each word as you read it, and read the words on this test as quickly as you can. If you feel you can't read a word on the test, just say 'skip' and go to the next word."
4. Say, "Put your finger on the first word and begin reading."
5. Push the button on the stopwatch as soon as the student begins to read. On your test copy: write a *C* next to each word read correctly; write an *I* next to each word read incorrectly; and write an *S* next to each word skipped.
6. As soon as the student finishes with word number 30 on Part 1 of the test, push the button on the stopwatch and record the time taken (in seconds) by the student's name.
7. Repeat steps 1 through 6 with Parts 2, 3, and 4 of the test. Note that each part has 30 items.

Sight Word Test, Part 1

1.	that	16.	than
2.	with	17.	first
3.	this	18.	made
4.	when	19.	down
5.	can	20.	way
6.	will	21.	just
7.	each	22.	get
8.	how	23.	back
9.	out	24.	man
10.	them	25.	day
11.	like	26.	same
12.	him	27.	right
13.	see	28.	came
14.	time	29.	part
15.	make	30.	place

Sight Word Test, Part 2

1.	to	16.	other
2.	you	17.	two
3.	they	18.	could
4.	from	19.	who
5.	have	20.	people
6.	one	21.	only
7.	what	22.	find
8.	were	23.	use
9.	there	24.	water
10.	your	25.	very
11.	their	26.	words
12.	said	27.	where
13.	many	28.	most
14.	some	29.	through
15.	would	30.	our

Sight Word Test, Part 3

1. gunshot
2. outlast
3. cookout
4. pocketful
5. handcart
6. trucking
7. spade
8. waistline
9. refill
10. salesgirl
11. mousetrap
12. freezer
13. toothbrush
14. minnow
15. mixer
16. bathrobe
17. noose
18. hiked
19. cobweb
20. spaceman
21. rainstorm
22. trapeze
23. insults
24. hinted
25. snowflake
26. houseboat
27. hanger
28. unpaid
29. unselfish
30. bleach

Sight Word Test, Part 4

1. inconvenient
2. custodian
3. seagull
4. stoneworker
5. persecute
6. invention
7. innocent
8. fluent
9. elevate
10. inquire
11. unforgettable
12. withhold
13. conflicting
14. creamy
15. alerted
16. tinted
17. licorice
18. inflation
19. deodorant
20. duet
21. stingy
22. defy
23. shoeshine
24. bachelor
25. badger
26. resented
27. workroom
28. beverage
29. salads
30. watercolor

Appendix G

Individual Phonics Test, Parts 1, 2, and 3

Teacher Directions

Materials Needed:

1. Two copies of the test (one for the teacher to use for marking, and one for the student to read)
2. Stopwatch

Administration of the Test:

1. Write the student's name on one test. Keep this copy.
2. Give the student the other copy of the test.
3. Say, "Look at the words on this test." Allow the student a few seconds to look at the words. "They are not real words, but they were made just like real words are made. Try to read the words on this test just like you would read real words. Touch each word as you read it, and read the words as quickly as you can. If you feel you can't read a word on the test, just say 'skip' and go to the next word."
4. Say, "Put your finger on the first word and begin reading."
5. Push the button on the stopwatch as soon as the student begins to read. On your test copy: write a *C* next to each word read correctly; write an *I* next to each word read incorrectly; and write an *S* next to each word skipped.
6. As soon as the student finishes with word number 22 on part 1 of the test, push the button on the stopwatch and record the time taken (in seconds) by the student's name.
7. Repeat steps 1 through 6 with parts 2 and 3 of the test. Note that there are 33 items on part 2 of the test, and 28 items on part 3.

Individual Phonics Test, Part 1

1.	bab	12.	pux
2.	cem	13.	nell
3.	cuzz	14.	dag
4.	tive	15.	mot
5.	ved	16.	lin
6.	yat	17.	gam
7.	zin	18.	heb
8.	wep	19.	juck
9.	soss	20.	kix
10.	ruff	21.	fot
11.	quix	22.	geb

Individual Phonics Test, Part 2

1.	glact	18.	blence
2.	scash	19.	plense
3.	squist	20.	springe
4.	crith	21.	swush
5.	smilt	22.	clomp
6.	splesk	23.	skint
7.	scradge	24.	gratch
8.	strisp	25.	tredge
9.	frept	26.	flost
10.	slift	27.	shunk
11.	twing	28.	choft
12.	drent	29.	whinse
13.	brunk	30.	thesk
14.	stend	31.	thung
15.	snamp	32.	thrug
16.	spitch	33.	shreb
17.	prench		

Individual Phonics Test, Part 3

1.	lope	15.	birt
2.	ye	16.	herk
3.	knod	17.	har
4.	phope	18.	saud
5.	wrem	19.	sawn
6.	gnad	20.	coise
7.	cly	21.	boun
8.	shay	22.	plowl
9.	paim	23.	groot
10.	feep	24.	dewn
11.	heach	25.	strow
12.	toak	26.	tood
13.	curge	27.	voy
14.	reath	28.	hight

Appendix H

Group Phonics Test,

Parts 1, 2, and 3

Teacher Directions, Group Phonics Test, Part 1

Distribute place markers and a test to each student. Tell students, "Look at the words on your test. Most of the words are nonsense words. However, they can be read as if they were real words. I am going to read one of the words on each row. Please circle each word that I read."

Print the words *tep, mep, tup,* and *teb* on the chalkboard. Say, "Place your markers under the sample row on your test. It looks like this row." Point to the chalkboard row of words. Check to be sure that each student has the marker under the sample row. Say, "Circle the word *tep.*" Wait for the students to respond. Circle the word *tep* in the chalkboard sample. Ask, "Did you circle this word?" Point to the word *tep.* Say, "If you did, you circled the correct word. Now, place your markers under Row 1 and circle the word *bab.*" Repeat the word: *"bab."* Continue dictating words for the students to circle:

2. cem (pronounced /sem/)
3. cuzz (rhymes with *fuzz*)
4. tive (rhymes with *give*)
5. ved (rhymes with *bed*)
6. yat (rhymes with *fat*)
7. zin (rhymes with *tin*)
8. wep (rhymes with *pep*)
9. soss (rhymes with *boss*)
10. ruff (rhymes with *cuff*)
11. quix (pronounced /kwiks/)
12. pux (rhymes with *tux*)
13. nell (rhymes with *tell*)
14. dag (rhymes with *bag*)
15. mot (rhymes with *hot*)
16. lin (rhymes with *sin*)
17. gam (rhymes with *ham*)
18. heb (rhymes with *web*)
19. juck (rhymes with *duck*)
20. kix (rhymes with *fix*)
21. fot (rhymes with *hot*)
22. geb (pronounced /jeb/)

Group Phonics Test, Part 1

Sample:	tep	mep	tup	teb
1.	bab	dab	beb	bap
2.	kem	cen	cem	cam
3.	cizz	cuzz	cux	guzz
4.	tive	bive	tave	tiff
5.	veb	vid	med	ved
6.	yut	zat	yat	yad
7.	yin	zin	zan	ziff
8.	wep	vep	wip	weg
9.	noss	sess	sozz	soss
10.	roff	rux	ruff	luff
11.	quax	quiss	quix	pix
12.	pum	pux	gux	pex
13.	nell	zell	noll	nep
14.	dap	pag	deg	dag
15.	mit	mox	mot	fot
16.	vin	len	lig	lin
17.	cam	gom	gam	gat
18.	heb	beb	hib	hed
19.	jeck	jut	juck	yuck
20.	kizz	kix	pix	kex
21.	fet	yot	foss	fot
22.	geb	gib	gep	keb

Teacher Directions, Group Phonics Test, Part 2

Distribute place markers and a test to each student. Tell students, "Look at the words on your test. Most of the words are nonsense words. However, they can be read as if they were real words. I am going to read one of the words on each row. Please circle each word that I read."

Print the words *plint, phint, plent,* and *plift* on the chalkboard. Say, "Place your markers under the sample row on your test. It looks like this row." Point to the chalkboard row of words. Check to be sure that each student has the marker under the sample row. Say, "Circle the word *plint.*" Wait for the students to respond. Circle the word *plint* in the chalkboard sample. Ask, "Did you circle this word?" Point to the word *plint.* Say, "If you did, you circled the correct word. Now, place your markers under Row 1 and circle the word *glact.*" Repeat the word: *"glact."* Continue dictating words for the students to circle:

2. scash (rhymes with *cash*)
3. squist (rhymes with *fist*)
4. crith (rhymes with *with*)
5. smilt (rhymes with *built*)
6. splesk (rhymes with *desk*)
7. scradge (rhymes with *badge*)
8. strisp (rhymes with *crisp*)
9. frept (rhymes with *kept*)
10. slift (rhymes with *lift*)
11. twing (rhymes with *sing*)
12. drent (rhymes with *bent*)
13. brunk (rhymes with *sunk*)
14. stend (rhymes with *bend*)
15. snamp (rhymes with *damp*)
16. spitch (rhymes with *pitch*)
17. prench (rhymes with *bench*)
18. blence (rhymes with *fence*)
19. plense (rhymes with *sense*)
20. springe (rhymes with *singe*)
21. swush (rhymes with *mush*)
22. clomp (rhymes with *stomp*)
23. skint (rhymes with *flint*)
24. gratch (rhymes with *patch*)
25. tredge (rhymes with *wedge*)
26. flost (rhymes with *frost*)
27. shunk (rhymes with *trunk*)
28. choft (rhymes with *soft*)
29. whinse (rhymes with *rinse*)
30. thesk (pronounced /thesk/)

31. thung (pronounced /thung/)
32. thrug (rhymes with *rug*)
33. shreb (rhymes with *web*)

Group Phonics Test, Part 2

Sample: plint   phint   plent   plift

1.	glact	gract	gluct	glaft
2.	swash	scosh	scask	scash
3.	squest	squift	swist	squist
4.	crint	crith	clith	crath
5.	shilt	smilt	smalt	smint
6.	splisk	splesh	spresk	splesk
7.	scradge	stradge	scridge	scrand
8.	strist	strasp	stisp	strisp
9.	fropt	flept	frept	frest
10.	skift	slift	slaft	slith
11.	tring	twing	twang	twint
12.	drent	trent	drunt	drend
13.	brund	brank	brunk	blunk
14.	stund	stend	stemp	strend
15.	snand	slamp	snamp	snump
16.	pritch	spetch	spitch	spith
17.	spench	princh	prench	pretch
18.	blance	flence	blent	blence
19.	plinse	plench	plense	prense
20.	squinge	springe	sprenge	sprinse
21.	swesh	swust	swush	spush
22.	glomp	climp	clomp	clonk
23.	skift	skint	slint	skent
24.	gritch	glatch	gratch	grath
25.	twedge	tredge	tresk	tridge
26.	flost	flopt	flist	slost
27.	slunk	shink	shunk	shund
28.	cheft	choth	choft	cloft
29.	shinse	whinse	whint	whense
30.	thesk	twesk	thisk	thept
31.	thang	thunk	thung	tung
32.	trug	thrug	thrag	thrup
33.	sheb	shreb	shrab	shrep

Teacher Directions, Group Phonics Test, Part 3

Distribute place markers and a test to each student. Tell students, "Look at the words on your test. Most of the words are nonsense words. However, they can be read as if they were real words. I am going to read one of the words on each row. Please circle each word that I read."

Print the words *scrade, scade, scride,* and *scrafe* on the chalkboard. Say, "Place your markers under the sample row on your test. It looks like this row." Point to the chalkboard row of words. Check to be sure that each student has the marker under the sample row. Say, "Circle the word *scrade.*" Wait for the students to respond. Circle the word *scrade* in the chalkboard sample. Ask, "Did you circle this word?" Point to the word *scrade.* Say, "If you did, you circled the correct word. Now, place your markers under Row 1 and circle the word *lope.*" Repeat the word: "*lope.*" Continue dictating words for the students to circle:

2. ye (rhymes with *we*)
3. knod (pronounced /nod/)
4. phope (pronounced /fop/)
5. wrem (pronounced /rem/)
6. gnad (pronounced /nad/)
7. cly (rhymes with *my*)
8. shay (rhymes with *may*)
9. paim (rhymes with *game*)
10. feep (rhymes with *keep*)
11. heach (rhymes with *teach*)
12. toak (rhymes with *cloak*)
13. curge (rhymes with *merge*)
14. reath (rhymes with *death*)
15. birt (rhymes with *dirt*)
16. herk (rhymes with *jerk*)
17. har (rhymes with *tar*)
18. saud (rhymes with *fraud*)
19. sawn (rhymes with *lawn*)
20. coise (rhymes with *noise*)
21. boun (rhymes with *town*)
22. plowl (rhymes with *howl*)
23. groot (rhymes with *boot*)
24. dewn (rhymes with *noon*)
25. strow (rhymes with *grow*)
26. tood (rhymes with *good*)
27. voy (rhymes with *boy*)
28. hight (rhymes with *night*)

Group Phonics Test, Part 3

Sample:	scrade	scade	scride	scrafe
1.	lop	lope	loip	lupe
2.	ye	yue	yo	yew
3.	noad	nood	knod	knode
4.	phope	fop	foop	foip
5.	ruem	wrem	reem	reme
6.	gnad	nade	gnod	naid
7.	clee	clo	cly	clu
8.	shaw	shi	shar	shay
9.	gaim	pam	peam	paim
10.	flep	feep	fep	fuep
11.	huech	heach	heak	hoach
12.	toak	tok	tock	toap
13.	corge	curge	curn	carge
14.	rith	reath	roath	reat
15.	bort	girt	bart	birt
16.	herk	herm	hork	hark
17.	hir	har	hor	hur
18.	sud	saud	soad	saun
19.	soan	sain	sawn	rawn
20.	coase	coise	coese	cose
21.	boun	boin	boan	buen
22.	plaul	plown	plool	plowl
23.	groot	groat	gloot	grot
24.	deen	dewn	dewd	doan
25.	strue	strow	strew	stroy
26.	tode	tod	tood	tord
27.	voy	vay	vo	vow
28.	hoat	hight	huet	haught

References

Adams, M. J. (1990). *Beginning to read, thinking and learning about print.* Cambridge, MA: MIT Press.

Adams, M. J. (1991). A talk with Marilyn Adams. *Language Arts, 68,* 206–212.

Adams, M. J. (2001). Alphabetic anxiety and explicit, systematic phonics instruction: A cognitive science perspective. In S. B. Neuman & D. K. Dickinson (Eds.), *Handbook of early literacy research.* New York: Guildford Press.

Allington, R. L. (1977). If they don't read much, how they ever gonna get good? *Journal of Reading, 21,* 57–61.

Allington, R. L. (1980). Poor readers don't get to read much in reading groups. *Language Arts, 57,* 872–876.

Allington, R. L. (1983). Fluency: The neglected reading goal. *The Reading Teacher, 36,* 556–561.

Allington, R. L. (1984a). Content coverage and contextual reading in reading groups. *Journal of Reading Behavior, 16,* 85–96.

Allington, R. L. (1984b). Oral reading. In R. Barr, M. L. Kamil, & P. Mosenthal (Eds.), *Handbook of Reading Research.* New York: Longman.

Allington, R. L. (2001). *What really matters for struggling readers: Designing research-based programs.* New York: Addison Wesley Longman.

Allington, R. L., & Cunningham, P. M. (1996). *Schools that work: Where all children read and write.* New York: Harper Collins.

Altwerger, B., Edelsky, C., & Flores, B. (1987). Whole language: What's new? *The Reading Teacher, 41,* 144–155.

Amlund, J. T., Kardash, C. A. M., & Kulhavy, R. W. (1986). Repetitive reading and recall of expository text. *Reading Research Quarterly, 21,* 49–58.

Anderson, R. C., Hiebert, E. H., Scott, J. A., & Wilkinson, I. A. G. (1985). *Becoming a nation of readers.* Washington, DC: National Institute of Education.

Armbruster, B., & Anderson, T. (1981). *Content area textbooks* (Reading Education Report No. 23). Urbana-Champaign, IL: University of Illinois at Urbana-Champaign, Center for the Study of Reading.

Armbruster, B. B., Lehr, F., & Osborn, J. (2001). *Put reading first: The research building blocks for teaching children to read kindergarten through grade 3.* Washington, DC: National Institute for Literacy.

Arnold, R. D. (1972). *A comparison of the neurological impress method, the language experience approach, and classroom teaching for children with reading disabilities* (Final Report). Purdue Research Foundation, Lafayette, IN.

Asher, S. R. (1980). Topic interest and children's reading comprehension. In R. J. Spiro, B. C. Bruce, & W. F. Brewer (Eds.), *Theoretical issues in reading comprehension* (pp. 525–534). Hillsdale, NJ: Erlbaum.

Aslett, R. (1990). *Effects of the oral recitation lesson on reading comprehension of fourth grade developmental readers.* Unpublished doctoral dissertation, Brigham Young University, Provo, UT.

Backman, J., Bruck, M., Herbert, M., & Seidenberg, M. S. (1984). Acquisition and use of spelling–sound correspondences in reading. *Journal of Experimental Child Psychology, 38,* 114–133.

Ball, E. W., & Blachman, B. A. (1991). Does phoneme segmentation training in kindergarten make a difference in early word recognition and developmental spelling? *Reading Research Quarterly, 26,* 49–66.

Balmuth, M. (1992). *The roots of phonics: A historical introduction.* Timonium, MD: York Press.

Balota, D., Pollatsek, A., & Rayner K. (1985). The interaction of contextual constraints and parafoveal visual information in reading. *Cognitive Psychology, 17,* 364–390.

Barr, R. C. (1972). The influence of instructional conditions on word recognition errors. *Reading Research Quarterly, 7,* 509–529.

Barrett, F. L. (1982). *A teacher's guide to shared reading.* Richmond Hill, Ontario, Canada: Scholastic-TAB.

Barron, R. W. (1981). Reading skill and spelling strategies. In A. Lesgold & C. A. Perfetti (Eds.), *Interactive processes in reading* (pp. 299–327). Hillsdale, NJ: Erlbaum.

Barron, R. W. (1986). Word recognition in early reading: A review of the direct and indirect access hypotheses. *Cognition, 24,* 93–119.

Bauman, J. F., Hoffman, J. V., Moon, J., & Duffy-Hester, A. M. (1998). What are the teachers' voices in the phonics/whole language debate? Results from a survey of U.S. elementary classroom teachers. *The Reading Teacher, 51,* 636–650.

Beck, I. L., Perfetti, C. A., & Mckeown, M. G. (1982). Effects of long-term vocabulary instruction on lexical access and reading comprehension. *Journal of Educational Psychology, 74,* 506–521.

Beers, J., & Henderson, E. (1977). A study of developing orthographic concepts among first graders. *Research in Teaching English, 11,* 133–148.

Bennett, W. J. (2001, April 24). A cure for the illiteracy epidemic. *Wall Street Journal,* p. A24.

Bergeron, B. (1990). What does the term whole language mean? Constructing a definition from the literature. *Journal of Reading Behavior, 22,* 301–329.

Biemiller, A. (1970). The development of the use of graphic and contextual information as children learn to read. *Reading Research Quarterly, 6,* 75–96.

Biemiller, A. (1979). Changes in the use of graphic and contextual information as functions of passage difficulty and reading achievement level. *Journal of Reading Behavior, 11,* 307–319.

Bissex, G. (1980). *Gyns at wrk: A child learns to write and read.* Cambridge, MA: Harvard University Press.

Blachman, B. (1983). Are we assessing the linguistic factors critical in early reading? *Annals of Dyslexia, 33,* 91–109.

Blachman, B. (1984). Language analysis skills and early reading acquisition. In G. Wallach & K. Butler (Eds.), *Language learning disabilities in school-age children* (pp. 271–287). Baltimore, MD: Williams & Wilkins.

Blachman, B. (1989). Phonological awareness and word recognition: Assessment and intervention. In A. G. Kamhi & H. W. Catts (Eds.), *Reading disabilities: A developmental language perspective* (pp. 133–158). Boston: College-Hill.

Blachman, B. (1991). Phonological awareness: Implications for prereading and early reading instruction. In S. A. Brady & D. P. Shankweiler (Eds.), *Phonological processes in literacy: A tribute to Isabelle Y. Liberman* (pp. 29–36). Hillsdale, NJ: Erlbaum.

Blachman, B., & James, S. (1985). Metalinguistic abilities and reading achievement in first-grade children. In J. Niles & R. Lalik (Eds.), *Issues in literacy: A research perspective. Thirty-fourth yearbook of the National Reading Conference* (pp. 280–286). Washington, DC: National Reading Conference.

Blevins, W. (1998). *Phonics from A to Z.* New York: Scholastic.

Bond, G. L., & Dykstra, R. (1967). The cooperative research program in first-grade reading instruction. *Reading Research Quarterly, 6,* 75–96.

Bradley, L., & Bryant, P. E. (1983). Categorizing sounds and learning to read: A causal connection. *Nature, 30,* 419–421.

Bradley, L., & Bryant, P. E. (1985). *Rhyme and reason in reading and spelling.* Ann Arbor, MI: University of Michigan Press.

Breznitz, Z. (1997a). Effects of accelerated reading rate on memory for text among dyslexic readers. *Journal of Educational Psychology, 89,* 289–297.

Breznitz, Z. (1997b). Enhancing the reading of dyslexic children by reading acceleration and auditory masking. *Journal of Educational Psychology, 89,* 103–113.

Bridge, C., & Burton, B. (1982). Teaching sight vocabulary through patterned language materials. In J. A. Niles & L. A. Harris (Eds.), *New inquiries in reading research and instruction: Thirty-first yearbook of the National Reading Conference* (pp. 119–123). Washington, DC: National Reading Conference.

Bridge, C., Winograd, P., & Haley, D. (1983). Using predictable materials vs. preprimers to teach beginning sight words. *The Reading Teacher, 36,* 884–891.

Bruner, J. S. (1978). The role of dialogue in language acquisition. In A. Sinclair, R. J. Jarvella, & W. M. Levelt (Eds.), *The child's conception of language* (pp. 241–256). New York: Springer-Verlag.

Bryant, P., & Bradley, L. (1980). Why children sometimes write words which they do not read. In U. Frith (Ed.), *Cognitive processes in spelling* (pp. 355–370). New York: Academic Press.

Burns, J., & Richgels, D. (1989). An investigation of task requirements associated with invented spellings of 4-year-olds with above average intelligence. *Journal of Reading Behavior, 21,* 1–14.

Burns, M. S., Griffin, P., & Snow, C. E. (1999). *Starting out right: A guide to promoting children's reading success.* Washington, DC: National Academy Press.

Byrne, B. (1992). Studies in the acquisition procedure for reading. Rationale, hypotheses, and data. In P. B. Gough, L. C. Ehri, & R. Treiman (Eds.), *Reading acquisition* (pp. 1–35). Hillsdale, NJ: Erlbaum.

Calfee, R. C., & Drum, P. (1986). Research on teaching reading. In M. C. Wittrock (Ed.), *Handbook of research on teaching* (pp. 804–849). New York: Macmillan.

Calfee, R. C., Lindamood, P., & Lindamood, C. (1973). Acoustic-phonetic skill and reading—Kindergarten through twelfth grade. *Journal of Educational Psychology, 64,* 293–298.

Calkins, L. M. (1982). Writing taps a new energy source: The child. In R. D. Walsh (Ed.), *Donald Graves in Australia.* Portsmouth, NH: Heinemann Educational Books.

Campbell, R. (1992). *Reading real books.* Philadelphia: Open University Press.

Carbo, M. (1978). Teaching reading with talking books. *The Reading Teacher, 32,* 267–273.

Cardoso-Martins, C., Michalick, M. F., & Pollo, T. C. (2002). Is sensitivity to rhyme a developmental precursor to sensitivity to phoneme?: Evidence from individuals with Down syndrome. *Reading and Writing: An Interdisciplinary Journal, 15,* 439–454.

Carnine, L., Carnine, D., & Gersten, R. (1984). Analysis of oral reading errors made by economically disadvantaged students taught with a synthetic-phonics approach. *Reading Research Quarterly, 19,* 343–356.

Carroll, J. B., Davies, P., & Richman, B. (1971). *The American heritage word frequency book.* Boston: Houghton Mifflin.

Cattell, J. M. (1886). The time it takes to see and name objects. *Mind, 11,* 63–65.

Chall, J. (1967). *Learning to read: The great debate.* New York: McGraw-Hill.

Chall, J. (1983). *Learning to read: The great debate* (2nd ed.). New York: McGraw-Hill.

Chall, J. (1996). *Learning to read: The great debate* (3rd ed.). New York: McGraw-Hill.

Chomsky, C. (1971). Write first, read later. *Childhood Education, 47,* 296–299.

Chomsky, C. (1976). After decoding: What? *Language Arts, 53,* 288–296.

Chomsky, C. (1978). When you still can't read in third grade: After decoding, what? In S. J. Samuels (Ed.), *What research has to say about reading instruction* (pp. 13–30). Newark, DE: International Reading Association.

Clarke, L. K. (1988). Invented versus traditional spelling in first graders' writings: Effects on learning to spell and read. *Research in the Teaching of English, 22,* 281–309.

Clay, M. (1983). Getting a theory of writing. In B. M. Kroll & G. Wells (Eds.), *Explorations in the development of writing, theory, research, and practice* (pp. 23–32). New York: Wiley.

Clay, M. M. (1967). The reading behaviour of five year old children: A research report. *New Zealand Journal of Educational Studies, 2,* 11–31.

Clay, M. M. (1985). *The early detection of reading difficulties: A diagnostic survey with recovery procedures.* Portsmouth, NH: Heinemann.

Cohen, A. S. (1974–1975). Oral reading errors of first-grade children taught by a code-emphasis approach. *Reading Research Quarterly, 10,* 616–650.

Cohen, D. (1968). The effect of literature on vocabulary and reading achievement. *Elementary English, 45,* 209–213, 217.

Content, A., Kolinsky, R., Morais, J., & Bertelson, P. (1986). Phonetic segmentation in prereaders: Effect of corrective information. *Journal of Experimental Child Psychology, 42,* 49–72.

Cook, J. E., Nolan, G., & Zanotti. R. J. (1965). *The effect of neurological impress on reading disabled children with auditory perception impairments.* Arlington, VA. (ERIC Document Reproduction Service No. ED128781)

Cook, J. E., Nolan, G., & Zanotti, R. J. (1980). Treating auditory perception problems: The NIM helps. *Academic Therapy, 15,* 473–481.

Corno, L., & Randi, J. (1997). Motivation, volition, and collaborative innovation in classroom literacy. In J. T. Guthrie & A. Wigfield (Eds.), *Reading engagement: Motivating readers through integrated instruction.* Newark, DE: International Reading Association.

Cullinan, B., Jaggar, A., & Strickland, D. (1974). Language expansion for black children in the primary grades: A research report. *Young Children, 29,* 98–112.

Cunningham, P. M., & Cunningham, J. W. (1978). Investigating the "print to meaning" hypothesis. In P. D. Pearson & J. Hansen (Eds.), *Reading: Disciplined inquiry in process and practice. Twenty-seventh Yearbook of the National Reading Conference* (pp. 116–120). Clemson, SC: National Reading Conference.

Cunningham, J. W., Cunningham, P. M., Hoffman, J. V., & Yopp, H. K. (1998). *Phonemic awareness and the teaching of reading: A position statement from the board of directors of the International Reading Association.* Newark, DE: International Reading Association.

Cunningham, A. E., & Stanovich, K. E. (1998). What reading does for the mind. *American Educator, 22,* 8–15.

Dahl, P. (1974). *An experimental program for teaching high-speed word recognition and comprehension skills* (Final Report Project #3-1154). Washington, DC: National Institute of Education. (ERIC Document Reproduction Service No. ED099812)

Dahl, P., & Samuels, J. (1974). *A mastery-based experimental program for teaching poor readers high-speed word recognition skills.* Unpublished manuscript.

Dale, E., & Chall, J. S. (1948). A formula for predicting readability. *Educational Research Bulletin, 27,* 11–20; 28, 37–54.

Dale, E., & O'Rourke, J. (1976). *The living word vocabulary.* Elgin, IL: Dorne.

Dank, M. E. (1976). *A study of the relationship of miscues to the mode of formal reading instruction received by selected second graders.* Unpublished doctoral dissertation, University of Massachusetts. (ERIC Document Reproduction Service No. ED126431)

DeLawter, J. A. (1975). Three miscue patterns: The relationship of beginning reading instruction and miscue patterns. In W. D. Page (Ed.), *Help for the reading teacher: New directions in research.* Urbana, IL: National Conference on Research in English, ERIC Clearinghouse on Reading and Communication Skills, National Institute of Education.

Devries, T. (1970). Reading, writing frequency and expository writing. *Reading Improvement, 7,* 14–15.

Dickinson, D. K., & Tabors, P. O. (2001). *Beginning literacy with language.* Baltimore, MD: Paul H. Brookes.

Dionisio, M. (1983). Write? Isn't this reading class? *The Reading Teacher, 36,* 746–750.

Doake, D. L. (1987). Learning to read: It starts in the home. In D. R. Tovey & J. E. Kerber (Eds.), *Roles in literacy learning* (pp. 2–9). Newark, DE: International Reading Association.

Doctorow, M., Wittrock, M. C., & Marks, C. (1978). Generative processes in reading comprehension. *Journal of Educational Psychology, 70,* 109–118.

Doehring, D. G., Trites, R. L., Patel, P. G., & Fiedorowicz, C. A. M. (1981). *Reading disabilities: The interaction of reading, language, and neuropsychological deficits.* New York: Academic Press.

Dolch, E. W. (1936). A basic sight vocabulary. *Elementary School Journal, 36,* 456–460.

Dolch, E. W. (1948). *Problems in reading.* Champaign, IL: Garrard.

Dole, J. A., Brown, K. J., & Trathen, W. (1996). The effects of strategy instruction on the comprehension performance of at-risk students. *Reading Research Quarterly, 31,* 62–88.

Dowhower, S. L. (1987). Effects of repeated reading on second-grade transitional readers' fluency and comprehension. *Reading Research Quarterly, 22,* 389–406.

Duke, N. K. (2000a). For the rich it's richer; Print experiences and environments offered to children in very low- and very high-socioeconomic status first-grade classrooms. *American Educational Research Journal, 37,* 441–478.

Duke, N. K. (2000b). 3.6 minutes per day: The scarcity of informational texts in first grade. *Reading Research Quarterly, 35,* 202–224.

Durkin, D. (1978). What classroom observations reveal about reading comprehension instruction. *Reading Research Quarterly, 14,* 482–533.

Durkin, D. (1989). *Teaching them to read* (5th ed.). New York: Allyn & Bacon.

Ehri, L. C. (1991). Development of the ability to read words. In R. Barr, M. L. Kamil, P. Mosenthat, & P. D. Pearson (Eds.), *Handbook of reading research* (Vol. II, pp. 383–417). New York: Longman.

Ehri, L. C. (1992). Reconceptualizing the development of sight word reading and its relationship to recoding. In P. B. Gough, L. C. Ehri, L. C. & R. Treiman (Eds.), *Reading acquisition* (pp. 107–143). Hillsdale, NJ: Erlbaum.

Ehri, L. C. (1994). Development of the ability to read words: Update. In R. Ruddell, M. Ruddell, & R. Treiman (Eds.), *Reading acquisition* (pp. 107–143). Hillsdale, NJ: Erlbaum.

Ehri, L. C. (1998). Research on learning to read and spell: A personal-historical perspective. *Scientific Studies of Reading, 2,* 97–114.

Ehri, L. C., & McCormick, S. (1998). Phases of word learning: Implications for instruction with delayed and disabled readers. *Reading and Writing Quarterly: Overcoming Learning Disabilities, 14,* 135-1.

Ehri, L. C., Nunes, S. R., Willows, D. M., Schuster, B. V., Yaghoub-Zadeh, Z., & Shanahan, T. (2001). Phonemic awareness instruction helps children learn to read: Evidence from the National Reading Panel's meta-analysis. *Reading Research Quarterly, 36,* 250–287.

Ehri, L. C., & Robbins C. (1992). Beginners need some decoding skill to read words by analogy. *Reading Research Quarterly, 27,* 13–26.

Ehri, L. C., & Wilce, L. (1983). Development of word identification speed in skilled and less skilled beginning readers. *Journal of Educational Psychology, 75,* 3–18.

Ehri, L. C., & Wilce, L. (1985). Movement into reading: Is the first stage of printed word learning visual or phonetic? *Reading Research Quarterly, 20,* 163–179.

Ehri, L. C., & Wilce, L. (1987). Does learning to spell help beginners learn to read words? *Reading Research Quarterly, 12,* 47–65.

Eldredge, J. L. (1988–1989). A fifty-two-year-old dyslexic learns to read. *Journal of Reading, Writing & Learning Disabilities International, 4,* 101–106.

Eldredge, J. L. (1990a). Increasing the performance of poor readers in the third grade with a group-assisted strategy. *Journal of Educational Research, 84,* 69–77.

Eldredge, J. L. (1990b). "You'll never get me in the corner again!": Effective practices in literature-based instruction. *The California Reader, 23,* 2–21.

Eldredge, J. L. (1991). An experiment with a modified whole language approach in first grade classrooms. *Reading Research and Instruction, 30,* 21–38.

Eldredge, J. L. (2004). *Phonics for teachers: Self-instruction, methods, and activities* (2nd ed.). Upper Saddle River, NJ: Pearson\Merrill\Prentice Hall.

Eldredge, J. L., & Baird, J. E. (1996). Phonemic awareness training works better than whole language instruction for teaching first graders how to write. *Reading Research and Instruction, 35,* 193–208.

Eldredge, J. L., & Butterfield, D. D. (1984). *Sacred cows make good hamburger: A report on a reading research project titled "Testing the sacred cows in reading."* (ERIC Document Reproduction Service ED255861)

Eldredge, J. L., & Butterfield, D. D. (1986). Alternatives to traditional reading instruction. *The Reading Teacher, 40,* 32–37.

Eldredge, J. L., & Quinn, D. W. (1988). Increasing reading performance of low-achieving second graders by using dyad reading groups. *Journal of Educational Research, 82,* 40–46.

Eldredge, J. L., Quinn, D. W., & Butterfield, D. D. (1990). Causal relationships between phonics, reading comprehension, and vocabulary achievement in the second grade. *Journal of Educational Research, 83,* 201–214.

Eldredge, J. L., Reutzel, D. R., & Hollingsworth, P. M. (1996). Comparing the effectiveness of two oral reading practices: Round-robin reading and the shared book experience. *Journal of Literacy Research, 28,* 201–225.

Elkonin, D. B. (1963). The psychology of mastering the elements of reading. In B. Simon & J. Simon (Eds.), *Educational psychology in the U.S.S.R.* (pp. 165–179.). London: Routledge & Kegan Paul.

Elkonin, D. B. (1973). U.S.S.R. In J. Downing (Ed.), *Comparative reading* (pp. 551–580). New York: Macmillan.

Embrey, A. (1968). *A study of the effectiveness of neurological impress as a remedial reading technique.* Unpublished master's thesis, Central Washington State College, Ellenburg, WA.

Evanechko, P., Ollila, L., & Armstrong, R. (1974). An investigation of the relationships between children's performance in written language and their reading ability. *Research in the Teaching of English, 8,* 315–326.

Evans, M. A., & Carr, T. H. (1985). Cognitive abilities, conditions of learning, and the early development of reading skill. *Reading Research Quarterly, 20,* 327–347.

Farris, P. J., & Kaczmarski, D. (1988). Whole language: A closer look. *Contemporary Education, 59,* 77–81.

Ferguson, C. A. (1986). Discovering sound units and constructing sound systems: It's child's play. In J. S. Perkell & D. H. Klatt (Eds.), *Invariance and variability in speech processes* (pp. 36–51). Hillsdale, NJ: Erlbaum.

Ferroli, L., & Shanahan, T. (1987). Kindergarten spelling, Explaining its relationship to first-grade reading. In J. E. Readence & R. S. Baldwin (Eds.), *Research in literacy: Merging perspectives. Thirty-sixth yearbook of the National Reading Conference* (pp. 93–99). Rochester, NY: National Reading Conference.

Fielding, L. G., Wilson, P. T., & Anderson, R. C. (1986). A new focus on free reading: The role of trade books in reading instruction. In T. E. Raphael (Ed.), *The contexts of school-based literacy* (pp. 149–160). New York: Random House.

Fielding-Barnsley, R. (1997). Explicit instruction of decoding benefits children high in phonemic awareness and alphabet knowledge. *Scientific Studies of Reading, 1*(1), 85–98.

Fitzgerald, J. (1984). The relationship between reading ability and expectations for story structure. *Discourse Processes, 7,* 211–241.

Fitzgerald, J. (1999). What is this thing called "balance"? *The Reading Teacher, 53,* 100–115.

Fitzgerald, J., & Spiegel, D. L. (1983). Enhancing children's reading comprehension through instruction in narrative structure. *Journal of Reading Behavior, 15,* 1–17.

Fitzgerald, J., & Teasley, A. B. (1986). Effects of instruction in narrative structure on children's writing. *Journal of Education Psychology, 78,* 424–432.

Foorman, B. R., Fletcher, J. M., Francis, D. J., Schatschneider, C., & Mehta, P. (1998). The role of instruction in learning to read: Preventing reading failure in at-risk children. *Journal of Educational Psychology, 90,* 37–55.

Foorman, B. R., Jenkins, L., & Francis, D. J. (1993). Links among segmenting, spelling, and reading words in first and second grades. *Reading and Writing: An Interdisciplinary Journal, 5,* 1–15.

Fountas, I. C., & Hannigan, I. L. (1989). Making sense of whole language: The pursuit of informed teaching. *Childhood Education, 65,* 133–137.

Fountas, I. C., & Pinnell, G. S. (1996). *Guided reading instruction: Good first teaching for all children.* Portsmouth, NH: Heinemann Educational Books.

Fountas, I. C., & Pinnell, G. S. (1999). *Matching books to readers: Using leveled books in reading, K-3.* Portsmouth, NH: Heinemann.

Fountas. I. C., & Pinnell, G. S. (2001). *Guiding readers and writers: Grades 3–6. Teaching comprehension genre, and content literacy.* Portsmouth, NH: Heinemann.

Fowler, A. E. (1991). How early phonological development might set the stage for phoneme awareness. In S. A. Brady & D. P. Shankweiler (Eds.), *Phonological processes in literacy: A tribute to Isabelle Y. Liberman* (pp. 97–117). Hillsdale, NJ: Erlbaum.

Fox, B., & Routh, D. K. (1975). Analyzing spoken language into words, syllables and phonemes: A developmental study. *Journal of Psycholinguistic Research, 4,* 331–342.

Fox, B., & Routh, D. K. (1976). Phonemic analysis and synthesis as word-attack skills. *Journal of Educational Psychology, 68,* 70–74.

Fox, B., & Routh, D. K. (1980). Phonemic analysis and severe reading disability in children. *Journal of Psycholinguistic Research, 9,* 115–119.

Fox, B., & Routh, D. K. (1984). Phonemic analysis and synthesis as word-attack skills: Revisited. *Journal of Educational Psychology, 76,* 1,059–1,061.

Freedman, S. W., & Calfee, R. C. (1984). Understanding and comprehending. *Written Communication, 1,* 459–490.

Frith, U. (1980). Unexpected spelling problems. In U. Frith (Ed.), *Cognitive processes in spelling* (pp. 495–516). New York: Academic Press.

Frith, U. (1985). Beneath the surface of developmental dyslexia. In K. Patterson, J. Marshall, & M. Coltheart (Eds.), *Surface dyslexia* (pp. 301–330). London: Erlbaum.

Fry, E. (1980). The new instant word list. *The Reading Teacher, 34,* 284–289.

Funke, A. (1997). *The effect of phonemic awareness training as an integrated component of a balanced literacy program on at-risk first-grade students' reading skills.* Unpublished masters thesis, Brigham Young University, Provo, UT.

Gardner, C. E. (1963). *Sonoma county schools office research project.* Unpublished.

Gardner, C. E. (1965). *The experimental use of the impress method of reading habilitation* (U.S. Office of Education Co-op Reading Project No. S167). (ERIC Document Reproduction Service No. ED003838)

Gibbs, V., & Proctor, S. (1977). Reading together: An experiment with the neurological-impress method. *Contemporary Education, 48,* 156–157.

Goldenberg, C. (1991). Learning to read in New Zealand: The balance of skills and meaning. *Language Arts, 68,* 555–562.

Golinkoff, R. M. (1978). Phonemic awareness skills and reading achievement. In F. B. Murray & J. H. Pikulski (Eds.), *The acquisition of reading: Cognitive, linguistic, and perceptual prerequisites* (pp. 23–41). Baltimore, MD: University Park.

Gonzales, P. G., & Elijah, D. V. (1975). Rereading: Effect on error patterns and performance levels on the IRI. *The Reading Teacher, 28,* 647–652.

Goodman, K. S. (1967). Reading: A psycholinguistic guessing game. *Journal of Reading Specialist, 6,* 126–135.

Goodman, K. S. (1986). *What's whole in whole language.* Portsmouth, NH: Heinemann.

Goodman, K. S. (1989). Whole language is whole: A response to Heymsfeld. *Educational Leadership,* (March), 69–70.

Goodman, K. S. (1992a). I didn't found whole language. *The Reading Teacher, 46,* 188–199.

Goodman, K. S. (1992b). Why whole language is today's agenda in education. *Language Arts, 69,* 354–363.

Goodman, K. S. (1993). *Phonics phacts.* Portsmouth, NH: Heinemann.

Gordon, C. J. (1985). Modeling inference awareness across the curriculum. *Journal of Reading, 28,* 444–447.

Goswami, U. (1986). Children's use of analogy in learning to read: A developmental study. *Journal of Experimental Child Psychology, 42,* 73–83.

Goswami, U. (1988). Orthographic analogies and reading development. *Quarterly Journal of Experimental Psychology, 40,* 239–268.

Goswami, U. (2001). Early phonological development and the acquisition of literacy. In S. B. Neuman & D. K. Dickinson (Eds.), *Handbook of early literacy research* (pp. 111–125). New York: Guilford Press.

Gough, P. B., Ehri, L. C., & Treiman, R. (Eds.). (1992). *Reading acquisition.* Hillsdale, NJ: Erlbaum.

Gough, P. B., & Hillinger, M. L. (1980). Learning to read: An unnatural act. *Bulletin of the Orton Society, 30,* 179–196.

Gough, P. B., Juel, C., & Griffith, P. L. (1992). Reading, spelling, and the orthographic cipher. In P. B. Gough, L. C. Ehri, & R. Treiman (Eds.), *Reading acquisition* (pp. 35–48). Hillsdale, NJ: Erlbaum.

Gough, P. B., & Tummer, W. E. (1986). Decoding, reading, and reading disability. *Remedial and Special Education, 7,* 6–10.

Gough, P. B., & Walsh, M. A. (1991). Chinese, Phoenicians, and the orthographic cipher of English. In S. A. Brady & D. P. Shankweiler (Eds.), *Phonological processes in literacy: A tribute to Isabelle Y. Liberman* (pp. 199–209). Hillsdale, NJ: Erlbaum.

Graves, D. H. (1983). *Writing: teacher and children at work.* Portsmouth, NH: Heinemann Educational Books.

Griffith, P. L. (1991). Phonemic awareness helps first graders invent spellings and third graders remember correct spellings. *Journal of Reading Behavior, 23,* 215–233.

Griffith, P. L., & Olson, M. W. (1992). Phonemic awareness helps beginning readers to break the code. *The Reading Teacher, 45,* 517–522.

Guthrie, J. T., & McCann, A. D. (1997). Characteristics of classrooms that promote motivations and strategies for learning. In J. T. Guthrie & A. Wigfield (Eds.), *Reading engagement: Motivating readers through integrated instruction.* Newark, DE: International Reading Association.

Hall, M. (1981). *Teaching reading as a language experience.* Columbus, OH: Merrill.

Halliday, M. A. K. (1973). *Explorations in the functions of language.* London: Edward Arnold.

Harris, A. J., & Sipay, E. R. (1980). *How to increase reading ability.* White Plains, NY: Longman.

Harris, A. J., & Sipay, E. R. (1990). *How to increase reading ability* (9th ed.). New York: Longman.

Hasbrouck, J. E., & Tindal, G. (1992). Curriculum-based oral reading fluency forms for students in grades 2 through 5. *Teaching Exceptional Children, 24,* 41–44.

Hatcher, P. J., Hulme, C., & Ellis, A. W. (1994). Ameliorating early reading failure by integrating the teaching of reading and phonological awareness skills: The phonological linkage hypothesis. *Child Development, 65,* 41–57.

Heckelman, R. G. (1962). *A neurological impress method of reading instruction.* Merced, CA: Merced County Schools Office.

Heckelman, R. G. (1966). The phonics-bound child. *Academic Therapy Quarterly, 1,* 12–13.

Heckelman, R. G. (1968). Is reading an instantaneous memory process? *Academic Therapy Quarterly, 3,* 231–232.

Heckelman, R. G. (1969). A neurological-impress method of remedial-reading instruction. *Academic Therapy, 4,* 277–282.

Helfgott, J. (1976). Phoneme segmentation and blending skills of kindergarten children: Implications for beginning reading acquisition. *Contemporary Educational Psychology, 1,* 157–169.

Henk, W. A., & Holmes, B. C. (1988). Effects of content-related attitude on the comprehension and retention of expository text. *Reading Psychology, 9,* 203–225.

Herman, P. A. (1985). The effect of repeated readings on reading rate, speech pauses, and word recognition accuracy. *Reading Research Quarterly, 20,* 553–565.

Hoffman, J. V. (1987). Rethinking the role of oral reading in basal instruction. *Elementary School Journal, 87,* 367–373.

Hoffman, J. V., & Crone, S. (1985). The oral recitation lesson: A research-derived strategy for reading basal texts. In J. A. Niles & R. A. Lalik (Eds.), *Issues in literacy: A research perspective. Thirty-fourth yearbook of the National Reading Conference* (pp. 76–83). Rochester, NY: National Reading Conference.

Hohn, W., & Ehri, L. (1983). Do alphabet letters help prereaders acquire phonemic segmentation skills? *Journal of Educational Psychology, 75,* 752–762.

Holbrook, H. T. (1987). Writing to learn in the social studies. *The Reading Teacher, 41,* 216–219.

Holdaway, D. (1979). *The foundations of literacy.* Sydney, Australia: Ashton Scholastic.

Hollingsworth, P. M. (1970). An experiment with the impress method of teaching reading, *The Reading Teacher, 24,* 112–114, 187.

Hollingsworth, P. M. (1978). An experimental approach to the impress method of teaching reading. *The Reading Teacher, 31,* 624–626.

Hollingsworth, P. M., & Reutzel, D. R. (1988). Get a grip on comprehension. *Reading Horizons, 29,* 71–78.

Hoover, W., & Gough, P. B. (1990). The simple view of reading. *Reading and Writing: An Interdisciplinary Journal, 2,* 127–160.

Hopkins, C. J. (1979). The spontaneous oral vocabulary of children in grade 1. *The Elementary School Journal, 79,* 240–249.

Horn, E. (1926). *A basic writing vocabulary—10,000 words most commonly used in writing.* Iowa City, IA: State University of Iowa.

Hoskisson, K. (1974). Should parents teach their children to read? *Elementary English, 51,* 295–299.

Hoskisson, K. (1975a). The many facets of assisted reading. *Elementary English, 52,* 312–315.

Hoskisson, K. (1975b). Successive approximation and beginning reading. *The Elementary School Journal, 75,* 443–445.

Hoskisson, K., & Krohm, B. (1974). Reading by immersion: Assisted reading. *Elementary English, 51,* 832–836.

Hoskisson, K., Sherman, T. M., & Smith, L. L. (1974). Assisted reading and parent involvement. *The Reading Teacher, 27,* 710–714.

Howe, K. B., & Shinn, M. M. (2001). *Standard reading assessment passages (RAPS) for use in general outcome measurements: A manual describing development and technical features.* Eden Prairie, MN: Edformations.

Huey, E. B. (1908). *The psychology and pedagogy of reading.* New York: Macmillan.

Hutchings, K. A. (1995). *Validating a group phonics test,* Unpublished Masters study, Brigham Young University, Provo, Utah.

Huxford L., Terrell, C., & Bradley, L. (1991). The relationship between the phonological strategies employed in reading and spelling. *Journal of Research in Reading, 14,* 99–105.

Iversen, S., & Tunmer, W. E. (1993). Phonological processing skills and the Reading Recovery Program. *Journal of Educational Psychology, 85,* 112–126.

Jeffrey, W. E., & Samuels, S. J. (1967). The effect of method of reading training on initial learning and transfer. *Journal of Verbal Learning and Verbal Behavior, 6,* 354–358.

Jenkins, J. R., Bausell, R. B., & Jenkins, L. M. (1972). Comparison of letter name and letter sound training as transfer variables. *American Educational Research Journal, 9,* 75–86.

Johnson, D. D. (2001). *Vocabulary in the elementary and middle school.* Needham Heights, MA: Allyn & Bacon.

Johnson, D. D., & Baumann, J. F. (1984). Word identification. In P. D. Pearson (Ed.), *Handbook of reading research.* White Plains, NY: Longman.

Johnston, F. P. (2001). The utility of phonic generalizations: Let's take another look at Clymer's conclusions. *The Reading Teacher, 55,* 132–143.

Jordan, W. C. (1965). Prime-O-Tec: A new approach to reading. *Instructor, 7,* 108–111.

Jordan, W. C. (1966). Six-year-olds reading faster, better with electronic aids. *Audio-Visual Instructor, 11,* 542–543.

Jordan, W. C. (1967). Prime-O-Tec: The new reading method. *Academic Therapy Quarterly, 2,* 248–250.

Jorm, A. F., & Share, D. L. (1983). Phonological recoding and reading acquisition. *Applied Psycholinguistics, 4,* 103–147.

Jorm, A. F., Share, D. L., Maclean, R., & Matthews, R. (1984). Phonological recoding skills and learning to read: A longitudinal study. *Applied Psycholinguistics, 5,* 201–207.

Juel, C., & Minden-Cupp, C. (2000). Learning to read words: Linguistic units and instructional strategies. *Reading Research Quarterly, 35,* 458–492.

Juel, C. (1988). Learning to read and write: A longitudinal study of 54 children from first through fourth grades. *Journal of Educational Psychology, 80,* 437–447.

Juel, C., Griffith, P., & Gough, P. B. (1986). Acquisition of literacy: A longitudinal study of children in first and second grade. *Journal of Educational Psychology, 78,* 243–255.

Jusczyk, P. (1986). Toward a model of the development of speech perception. In J. Perkell & D. Klatt (Eds.), *Invariance and variability in speech perception* (pp. 1–33). Hillsdale, NJ: Erlbaum.

Just, M. A., & Carpenter, P. A. (1980). A theory of reading: From eye fixations to comprehension. *Psychological Review, 4,* 329–354.

Just, M. A., & Carpenter, P. A. (1987). *The psychology of reading and language comprehension.* Boston, MA: Allyn & Bacon.

Kroese, J. M., Hynd, G. W., Knight, D. F., Hall, J., & Hiemenz, J. R. (2000). Clinical appraisal of spelling ability and its relationship to phonemic awareness (blending, segmenting, elision, and reversal), phonological memory, and reading in reading disabled, ADHD, and normal children. *Reading and Writing: An Interdisciplinary Journal, 13,* 105–131.

Kahneman, D. (1973). *Attention and effort.* Englewood Cliffs, NJ: Prentice Hall.

Koskinen, P. S., Blum, I. H., Bisson, S. A., Phillips, S. M., Creamer, T. S., & Baker, T. K. (1999). Shared reading, books, and audiotapes: Supporting diverse students in school and at home. *The Reading Teacher, 52,* 430–444.

Kowal, S., O'Connell, D., O'Brian, E., & Bryant, E. (1975). Temporal aspects of reading aloud and speaking: Three experiments. *American Journal of Psychology, 88,* 549–569.

Krashen, S. (1993). *The power of reading: Insights from the research.* Englewood, CO: Libraries Unlimited.

Kucera, H., & Francis, W. N. (1967). *Computational analysis of present-day American English.* Providence, RI: Brown University Press.

Kuhn, M., & Stahl, S. (2000). *Fluency: A review of developmental and remedial reading practices.* CIERA Report #2–008. Ann Arbor, MI: University of Michigan, Center for the Improvement of Early Reading Achievement.

Labbo, L. D. (2001). Supporting children's comprehension of informational text through interactive read alouds. *Literacy and Nonfiction Series, 1,* 1–4.

LaBerge, D., & Samuels, S. J. (1974). Toward a theory of automatic information processing in reading. *Cognitive Psychology, 6,* 293–323.

Langford, K., Slade, K., & Barnett, A. (1974). An examination of impress techniques in remedial reading. *Academic Therapy, 9,* 309–319.

Lass, B., & Davis, B. (1985). *The remedial reading handbook.* Upper Saddle River, NJ: Prentice Hall.

Leong, C. K., & Haines, C. F. (1978). Beginning readers' awareness of words and sentences. *Journal of Reading Behavior, 10,* 393–407.

Lesgold, A. M., & Curtis, M. E. (1981). Learning to read words efficiently. In A. M. Lesgold & C. A. Perfetti (Eds.), *Interactive processes in reading.* Hillsdale, NJ: Erlbaum.

Lesgold, A. M., Resnick, L. B., & Hammond, K. (1985). Learning to read: A longitudinal study of word skill development in two curricula. In G. E. Mackinnon & T. G. Waller (Eds.), *Reading research: Advances in theory and practice* (Vol. 4, pp. 107–138). San Diego, CA: Academic Press.

Liberman, A. M. (1989). Reading is hard just because listening is easy. In C. von Euler (Ed.), *Wenner-Gren International Symposium series: Brain and reading.* Basingstoke, England: Macmillan.

Liberman, A. M., Cooper, F. S., Shankweiler, D., & Studdert-Kennedy, M. (1967). Perception of the speech code. *Psychological Review, 74,* 731–761.

Liberman, I. Y. (1971). Basic research in speech and lateralization of language: Some implications for reading disability. *Bulletin of the Orton Society, 21,* 72–87.

Liberman, I. Y. (1973). Segmentation of the spoken word and reading acquisition. *Bulletin of the Orton Society, 23,* 65–67.

Liberman, I. Y. (1983). A language-oriented view of reading and its disabilities. In H. R. Mykebust (Ed.), *Progress in learning disabilities* (Vol. 5, pp. 81–101). New York: Grune & Stratton.

Liberman, I. Y., & Liberman, A. M. (1992). Whole language versus code emphasis: Underlying assumptions and their implications for reading instruction. In P. B. Gough, L. C. Ehri, & R. Treiman (Eds.), *Reading acquisition* (pp. 343–366). Hillsdale, NJ: Erlbaum.

Liberman, I. Y., Shankweiler, S., Fischer, F. W., & Carter, B. (1974). Explicit syllable and phoneme segmentation in the young child. *Journal of Experimental Child Psychology, 18,* 201–212.

Liberman, I. Y., Shankweiler, D., & Liberman, A. M. (1989). The alphabetic principle and learning to read. In D. Shankweiler & I. Y. Liberman (Eds.), *Phonology and reading disability: Solving the reading puzzle* (pp. 1–33). Ann Arbor, MI: University of Michigan Press.

Lomax, R. G., & McGee, L. M. (1987). Young children's concepts about print and reading: Toward a model of word reading acquisition. *Reading Research Quarterly, 22,* 237–256.

Lorenz, L., & Vockell, E. (1979). Using the neurological impress method with learning disabled readers. *Journal of Learning Disabilities, 12,* 420–422.

Lovett, M. W. (1987). A developmental approach to reading disability: Accuracy and speed criteria of normal and deficient reading skill. *Child Development, 58,* 234–260.

Lundberg, I., Frost, J., & Petersen, O. (1988). Effects of an extensive program for stimulating phonological awareness of preschool children. *Reading Research Quarterly, 23,* 263–284.

Lundberg, I., Olofsson, A., & Wall, S. (1980). Reading and spelling skill in the first school years predicted from phonemic awareness skills in kindergarten. *Scandinavian Journal of Psychology, 21,* 159–173.

Lyon, G. R. (1997). Statement of G. Reid Lyon to The Committee on Education and the Workforce, U.S. House of Representatives (July 19, 1997). Washington, DC.

Maclean, M., Bryant, P., & Bradley, L. (1987). Rhymes, nursery rhymes, and reading in early childhood. *Merrill-Palmer Quarterly, 33,* 266–281.

Mandler, J. M., & Johnson, N. S. (1977). Remembrance of things parsed: Story structure and recall. *Cognitive Science, 9,* 111–151.

Manis, F. R., & Morrison, F. J. (1985). Reading disability: A deficit in rule learning? In L. S. Siegel & F. J. Morrison (Eds.), *Cognitive development in atypical children* (pp. 1–26). New York: Springer-Verlag.

Manis, F. R., Szeszulski, P. A., Howell, M. J., & Horn, C. C. (1986). A comparison of analogy- and rule-based decoding strategies in normal and dyslexic children. *Journal of Reading Behavior, 18,* 203–218.

Mann, V. A. (1984). Longitudinal prediction and prevention of early reading difficulty. *Annals of Dyslexia, 34,* 117–136.

Mann, V. A., & Liberman, I. Y. (1984). Phonological awareness and verbal short-term memory: Can they presage early reading problems? *Journal of Learning Disabilities, 17,* 592–599.

Mann, V. A., Tobin, P., & Wilson, R. (1987). Measuring phonological awareness through the invented

spellings of kindergarten children. *Merrill-Palmer Quarterly, 33,* 365–391.

Marsh, G., Friedman, M., Desberg, P., & Saterdahl, K. (1981). Comparison of reading and spelling strategies in normal and reading disabled children. In M. P. Friedman, J. P. Das, & N. O'Connor (Eds.), *Intelligence and learning* (pp. 363–367). New York: Plenum.

Marsh, G., Friedman, M., Welch, V., & Desberg, P. (1981). A cognitive developmental theory of reading acquisition. In G. E. Mackinnon & T. G. Waller (Eds.), *Reading research: Advances in theory and practice* (Vol. 3, pp. 199–221). New York: Academic Press.

May, F. B. (1994). *Reading as communication.* New York: Macmillan.

McCarrier, A., Pinnell, G. S., & Fountas, I. C. (1999). *Interactive writing: How language & literacy come together, K–2.* Portsmouth, NH: Heinemann.

McCutcheon, D., Bell, L. C., France, I. M., & Perfetti, C. A. (1991). Phoneme-specific interference in reading: The tongue-twister effect revisited. *Reading Research Quarterly, 26,* 87–103.

McKenna, M., Stahl, S., & Reinking, D. (1994). A critical commentary on research, politics, and whole language. *Journal of Reading Behavior, 26,* 211–233.

McKeown, M. G., Beck, I. L., Omanson, R. C., & Perfetti, C. A. (1983). The effects of long-term vocabulary instruction on reading comprehension: A replication. *Journal of Reading Behavior, 15,* 3–18.

McKeown, M. G., Beck, I. L., Omanson, R. C., & Pople, M. T. (1985). Some effects of the nature and frequency of vocabulary instruction on the knowledge and use of words. *Reading Research Quarterly, 20,* 522–535.

McNeill, D. (1968). Production and perception: The view from language. *Ontario Journal of Educational Research, 10,* 181–185.

Menyuk, P., & Menn, L. (1979). Early strategies for the perception and production of words and sounds. In P. Fletcher & M. Garman (Eds.), *Language acquistion* (pp. 49–70). Cambridge, England: Cambridge University Press.

Metsala, J., & Ehri, L. (Eds.). (1998). *Word recognition in beginning reading.* Mahwah, NJ: Erlbaum.

Meyer, V. (1982). Prime-O-Tec: A successful strategy for adult disabled readers. *Journal of Reading, 25,* 512–515.

Meyer, B., Brandt, D., & Bluth, G. (1980). Use of top-level structure in text for reading comprehension of ninth-grade students. *Reading Research Quarterly, 16,* 72–103.

Meyer, B. J. (1979). Organizational patterns in prose and their use in reading. In M. L. Kamil & A. J. Moe (Eds.), *Reading research: Studies and applications* (pp. 109–117). Twenty-eighth Yearbook of the National Reading Conference.

Miller, M. Z. (1969). Remediation by neurological impress, *Academic Therapy Quarterly, 4,* 313–314.

Mills, E. (1974). Children's literature and teaching written composition. *Elementary English, 51,* 971–973.

Moe, A. J., Hopkins, C. J., & Rush, R. T. (1982). *The vocabulary of first-grade children.* Springfield, IL: Charles C. Thomas.

Mooney, M. E. (1990). *Reading to, with, and by children.* Katonah, NY: Owen.

Morais, J. (1991). Constraints on the development of phonemic awareness. In S. A. Brady & D. P. Shankweiler (Eds.), *Phonological processes in literacy* (pp. 5–27). Hillsdale, NJ: Erlbaum.

Morais, J., Cary, L., Alegria, J., & Bertelson, P. (1979). Does awareness of speech as a sequence of phonemes arise spontaneously? *Cognition, 7,* 323–331.

Morgan, A., Wilcox, B. R., & Eldredge, J. L. (2000). Effect of difficulty levels on second-grade delayed readers using dyad reading. *The Journal of Educational Research, 94,* 113–119.

Morris, D. (1983). Concept of word and phoneme awareness in the beginning reader. *Research in the Teaching of Reading, 17,* 359–373.

Muller, D. (1973). Phonic blending and transfer of letter training to word reading in children. *Journal of Reading Behavior, 5,* 13–15.

NAEP 1992 reading report card for the nation and the states (Report No. 23–ST06). Washington, DC: National Center for Education Statistics, USDOE.

Nagy, W. E., Herman, P. A., & Anderson, R. C. (1985). Learning words from context. *Reading Research Quarterly, 20,* 233–253.

Nathan, R. G., & Stanovich, K. E. (1991). The causes of consequences of differences in reading fluency. *Theory Into Practice, 30,* 176–184.

National Reading Panel. (2000). *Teaching children to read: An evidence-based assessment of the scientific research literature on reading and its implications for reading instruction.* Washington, DC: National Institute of Child Health and Human Development.

National Research Council. (1998). *Preventing reading difficulties in young children.* Washington, DC: U.S. Department of Education.

Neuman, S. B. (1999). Books make a difference: A study of access to literacy. *Reading Research Quarterly, 34,* 2–31.

Newman, J. (1985). *Whole language: Theory in use.* Portsmouth, NH: Heinemann.

Newman, J. M., & Church, S. M. (1990). Myths of whole language. *The Reading Teacher, 44,* 20–26.

Nicholson, T., Lillas, C., & Rzoska, M. (1988). Have we been misled by miscues? *The Reading Teacher, 42,* 6–10.

Norton, D. E. (1976). A comparison of the oral reading errors of high and low ability first and third graders taught by two approaches—Synthetic phonic and analytic-eclectic. (Doctoral dissertation, University of Wisconsin-Madison). *Dissertation Abstracts International, 37,* 3399A.

Norton, D. E., & Hubert, P. (1977). *A comparison of the oral reading strategies and comprehension patterns developed by high, average, and low first grade students taught by two approaches—Phonic emphasis and eclectic basal.* College State: Texas A & M University. (ERIC Document Reproduction Service No. ED145393)

Norris, A. N., & Hoffman, P. R. (2002). Phoneme awareness: A complex developmental process. *Topics in Language Disorders, 22,* 1–34.

Olofsson, A., & Lundberg, I. (1985). Evaluation of long term effects of phonemic awareness training in kindergarten: Illustrations of some methodological problems in evaluation research. *Scandinavian Journal of Psychology, 26,* 21–34.

Opitz, M. (1998). Children's books develop phonemic awareness—For you and parents, too! *The Reading Teacher, 51,* 526–528.

Opitz, M. F., & Ford, M. P. (2001). *Reaching readers: Flexible and innovative strategies for guided reading.* Portsmouth, NH: Heinemann.

Optiz, M. F., & Rasinski, T. V. (1998). *Good-bye round robin: 25 effective oral reading strategies.* Portsmouth, NH: Heinemann.

O'Shea, L. J., Sindelar, P. T., & O'Shea, D. J. (1985). The effects of repeated readings and attentional cues on reading fluency and comprehension. *Journal of Reading Behavior, 17,* 129–142.

Paul, R. (1976). Invented spelling in kindergarten. *Young Children, 21,* 195–200.

Pearson, P. D. (2000a). Reading in the 20th century. In T. Good (Ed.), *American education: Yesterday, today, and tomorrow. Yearbook of the National Society for the Study of Education* (pp. 152–208). Chicago: University of Chicago Press.

Pearson, P. D. (2000b). *What sorts of programs and practices are supported by research? A reading from the radical middle.* Ann Arbor, MI: Center for the Improvement of Early Reading Instruction.

Pearson, P. D., & Duke, N. (2002). Comprehension instruction in the primary grades. In C. Collins-Block & M. Pressley (Eds.), *Comprehension instruction: Research-based best practices* (pp. 247–258). New York: Guilford.

Pearson, P. D., & Fielding, L. (1991). Comprehension instruction. In R. Barr, M. Kamil, P. Mosenthal, & P. Pearson (Eds.), *Handbook of reading research* (Vol. 2, pp. 815–860). White Plains, NY: Longman.

Pearson, P. D., & Gallagher, M. (1983). The instruction of reading comprehension. *Contemporary Educational Psychology, 8,* 317–344.

Perfetti, C. A. (1985). *Reading ability.* New York: Oxford University Press.

Perfetti, C. A. (1986). Cognitive and linguistic components of reading ability. In B. R. Foorman & A. W. Siegel (Eds.), *Acquisition of reading skills: Cultural constraints and cognitive universals* (pp. 1–40). Hillsdale, NJ: Erlbaum.

Perfetti, C. A. (1992). The representation problem in reading acquisition. In P. B. Gough, L. C. Ehri, & R. Treiman (Eds.), *Reading acquisition* (pp. 145–174). Hillsdale, NJ: Erlbaum.

Perfetti, C. A., Goldman, S., & Hogaboam, T. (1979). Reading skill and the identification of words in discourse context. *Memory and Cognition, 7,* 273–282.

Perfetti, C. A., & Hogaboam, T. W. (1975). The relationship between single word decoding and reading comprehension skill. *Journal of Educational Psychology, 67,* 461–469.

Peterson, M. E., & Haines, L. P. (1992). Orthographic analogy training with kindergarten children: Effects on analogy use, phonemic segmentation, and letter–sound knowledge. *Journal of Reading Behavior, 24,* 109–124.

Pflaum, S. W., Walberg, H. J., Karegianes, M. L., & Rasher, S. P. (1980). Reading instruction: A quantitative analysis. *Educational Researcher, 9,* 12–18.

Pikulski, J. J., & Templeton, S. (1997). The role of phonemic awareness in learning to read. *Invitations to Literacy.* Boston: Houghton Mifflin.

Pinnell, G. S., Pikulski, J. J., Wixson, K. K., Campbell, J. R., Gough, P. B., & Beatty, A. S. (1995). *Listening to children read aloud.* Washington, DC: U.S. Department of Education, Office of Educational Research and Improvement.

Pollatsek, A., Rayner, K., & Balota, D. A. (1986). Inferences about eye movement control from the perceptual span in reading. *Perception and Psychophysics, 40,* 123–130.

Pressley, M. (2000). What should comprehension instruction be the instruction of? In M. L. Kamil, P. B. Mosenthal, P. D. Pearson, & R. Barr (Eds.), *Handbook of Reading Research,* Vol. 3. Mahwah, NJ: Erlbaum.

Pressley, M. (2004). Comprehension strategies instruction: A turn-of-the-century status report. In R. D. Robinson, M. C. McKenna, & J. M. Wedman (Eds.), *Issues and trends in literacy education,* 3rd ed. Boston: Pearson.

Pullen, P. C. (2000). *The effects of alphabetic word work with manipulative letters on the reading acquisition of struggling first-grade students.* Unpublished doctoral dissertation, University of Florida, Gainesville, FL.

Quandt, I., & Selznick, R. (1984). *Self-concept and reading.* Newark, DE: International Reading Association.

Rack, J., Snowling, M., & Olson, R. (1992). The nonword reading deficit in developmental dyslexia: A review. *Reading Research Quarterly, 27,* 29–53.

Railsback, L. (1969). Use of automated aural-oral techniques to teach functional illiterates who are upper age level adolescents. *The psychology of reading behavior: Eighteenth yearbook of the National Reading Conference,* 207–211.

Rasinski, T. (2000). Speed does matter. *The Reading Teacher, 54,* 146–151.

Rasinski, T. V., & Padak, N. (1996). Five lessons to increase reading fluency. In L. R. Putnam (Ed.), *How to become a better reading teacher: Strategies for assessment and intervention.* Columbus, OH: Merrill/Prentice Hall.

Rasinski, T., & Padak, N. D. (2004). *Effective reading strategies; Teaching children who find reading difficult.* Upper Saddle River, NJ: Pearson/Merrill/Prentice Hall.

Rasinski, T. V., Padak, N. D., Linek, W. L., & Sturtevant, E. (1994). Effects of fluency development on urban second-grade readers. *Journal of Educational Research, 87,* 158–165.

Rayner, K., & Bertera, J. H. (1979). Reading without a fovea. *Science, 206,* 468–469.

Rayner, K., Foorman, B. R., Perfetti, C. A., Pesetsky, D., & Seidenberg, M S. (2001). How Psychological science informs the teaching of reading. *Psychological science in the Public Interest, 2,* 31–74.

Rayner, K., Foorman, B. R., Perfetti, C. A., Pesetsky, D., & Seidenberg, M. S. (2002, March). How should reading be taught? *Scientific American, 286,* 85–91.

Rayner, K., & Pollatsek, A. (1989). *The psychology of reading.* Englewood Cliffs, NJ: Prentice Hall.

Read, C. (1971). Pre-school children's knowledge of English phonology. *Harvard Educational Review, 41,* 1–34.

Read, C. (1986). *Children's creative spellings.* London: Routledge & Kegan Paul.

Read, C., Zhang, Y., Nie, H., & Ding, B. (1986). The ability to manipulate speech sounds depends on knowing alphabetic writing. *Cognition, 24,* 31–44.

Reitsma, P. (1983). Printed word learning in beginning readers. *Journal of Experimental Child Psychology, 36,* 321–339.

Reitsma, P. (1988). Reading practice for beginners: Effects of guided reading, reading-while-listening, and independent reading with computer-based speech feedback. *Reading Research Quarterly, 23,* 219–235.

Reutzel, D. R., & Hollingsworth, P. M. (1991a). Investigating the development of topic-related attitude: Effect on children's reading and remembering text. *Journal of Educational Research, 84,* 334–344.

Reutzel, D. R., & Hollingsworth, P. M. (1991b). Reading time in school: Effect on fourth graders' performance on a criterion-referenced comprehension test. *Journal of Educational Research, 84,* 170–176.

Reutzel, D. R., & Hollingsworth, P. M. (1993). Effects of fluency training on second grader's reading comprehension. *Journal of Educational Research, 86,* 325–331.

Reutzel, D. R., Hollingsworth, P. M., & Eldredge, J. L. (1994). Oral reading instruction: The impact on student reading development. *Reading Research Quarterly, 23,* 40–62.

Rich, S. J. (1985). Restoring power to teachers: The impact of "whole language." *Language Arts, 62,* 717–724.

Rinsland, H. D. (1945). *A basic vocabulary of elementary school children.* New York: Macmillan.

Robin, K. (1977). *A study of the effectiveness of two impress methods of instruction with elementary school children.* Unpublished manuscript. Highland Park, IL.

Robinson, S. S. (1991, April). *Reading achievement: Contributions of invented spelling and alphabetic knowledge.* Paper presented at the annual meeting of the American Educational Research Association, Chicago, IL.

Rohl, M., & Tummer, W. E. (1988). Phonemic segmentation skill and spelling acquisition. *Applied Psycholinguistics, 9,* 335–350.

Rosenhouse, J., Feitelson, D., & Kita, B. (1997). Interactive reading aloud to Israeli first graders: Its contribution to literacy development. *Reading Research Quarterly, 32,* 168–183.

Rosenshine, B., & Meister, C. (1992). The use of scaffolds for teaching higher-level cognitive strategies. *Educational Leadership, 49,* 26–33.

Rosner, J., & Simon, D. (1971). The auditory analysis test: An initial report. *Journal of Learning Disabilities, 4,* 384–392.

Rozin, P., & Gleitman, L. (1977). The structure and acquisition of reading II: The reading process and the acquisition of the alphabetic principle. In A. Reber & D. Scarborough (Eds.), *Toward a psychology of reading* (pp. 55–141). Hillsdale, NJ: Erlbaum.

Samuels, S. J. (1976). Automatic decoding and reading comprehension. *Language Arts, 53,* 323–325.

Samuels, S. J. (1979). The method of repeated readings. *The Reading Teacher, 32,* 403–408.

Samuels, S. J., Schermer, N., & Reinking, D. (1992). Reading fluency: Techniques for making decoding automatic. In S. J. Samuels & A. E. Farstrup (Eds.), *What research says about reading instruction* (2nd ed., pp. 124–144). Newark, DE: International Reading Association.

Scardamalia, M. (1981). How children cope with the cognitive demands of writing. In C. H. Frederickson & J. F. Dominic (Eds.), *Writing: The nature, development and teaching of written communication.* Vol. 2: *Writing: Process, development, and communication* (pp. 81–104). Hillsdale, NJ: Erlbaum.

Schreiber, P. A. (1980). On the acquisition of reading fluency. *Journal of Reading Behavior, 12,* 177–186.

Schreiber, P. A. (1987). Prosody and structure in children's syntactic processing. In R. Horowitz & S. J. Samuels (Eds.), *Comprehending oral and written language.* New York: Academic Press.

Schreiber, P. A. (1991). Understanding prosody's role in reading acquisition. *Theory into Practice, 30,* 158–164.

Seidenberg, M. S. (1985). The time course of phonological code activation in two writing systems. *Cognition, 19,* 1–30.

Shanahan, T. (1988). The reading-writing relationship: Seven instructional principles. *The Reading Teacher, 41,* 636–647.

Shankweiler, D. (1991). The contributions of Isabelle Y. Liberman. In S. A. Brady & D. P. Shankweiler (Eds.), *Phonological processes in literacy: A tribute to Isabelle Y. Liberman* (pp. 29–36). Hillsdale, NJ: Erlbaum.

Share, D. (1995). Phonological recoding and self-teaching: Sine qua non of reading acquisition. *Cognition, 55,* 151–218.

Share, D. J., Jorm, A. F., Maclean, R., & Mathews, R. (1984). Sources of individual differences in reading achievement. *Journal of Educational Psychology, 76,* 466–477.

Simmons, D. C., & Kameenui, E. J. (1998). *What reading research tells us about children with diverse learning needs: Bases and basics.* Mahwah, NJ: Erlbaum.

Simpson, G. B., & Foster, M. R. (1986). Lexical ambiguity and children's word recognition. *Developmental Psychology, 22,* 147–154.

Slaughter, H. (1988). Indirect and direct teaching in a whole language program. *The Reading Teacher, 42,* 30–34.

Smith, D. E. P., & Carrigan, P. (1959). *The nature of reading disability.* New York: Harcourt, Brace & Co.

Smith, F. (1971). *Understanding reading.* New York: Holt, Rinehart & Winston.

Smith, F. (1973). *Psycholinguistics and reading.* New York: Holt, Rinehart & Winston.

Smith, F. (1975). *Comprehension and learning.* New York: Holt, Rinehart & Winston.

Smith, F. (1976). Learning to read by reading. *Language Arts, 53,* 297–299, 322.

Snow, C. E., Burns, M. S., & Griffin, P. (Eds.). (1998). *Preventing reading difficulties in young children.* Washington, DC: National Academy Press.

Snowling, M. (1980). The development of grapheme-phoneme correspondences in normal and dyslexic readers. *Journal of Experimental Child Psychology, 29,* 294–305.

Snowling, M. (1981). Phonemic deficits in developmental dyslexia. *Psychological Research, 43,* 219–234.

Snowling, M. (1985). The assessment of reading and spelling skills. In M. Snowling (Ed.), *Children's written language difficulties* (pp. 80–95). Windsor, England: NFER-Nelson.

Spangler, K. L. (1983). Reading interests vs. reading preferences: Using the research. *The Reading Teacher, 36,* 876–878.

Spiegel, D. L. (1992). Blending whole language and systematic direct instruction. *The Reading Teacher, 46,* 38–44.

Spiegel, D. L. (1999). The perspective of the balanced approach. In S. M. Blair-Larsen & K. A. Williams (Eds.), *The balanced reading program: Helping all students achieve success* (pp. 8–23). Newark, DE: International Reading Association.

Stahl, S. A. (1986). Three principles of effective vocabulary instruction. *Journal of Reading, 29,* 662–668.

Stahl, S. A. (1998). *Vocabulary development.* Cambridge, MA: Brookline Press.

Stahl, S. A. (1999). Why innovations come and go: The case of whole language. *Educational Researcher.*

Stahl, S. A., & Fairbanks, M. M. (1986). The effects of vocabulary instruction: A model-based meta-analysis. *Review of Educational Research, 56,* 72–110.

Stahl, S. A., & Jacobson, M. G. (1986). Vocabulary difficulty, prior knowledge, and text comprehension. *Journal of Reading Behavior, 18,* 309–319.

Stahl, S., Duffy-Hester, A., & Stahl, K. (1998). Everything you wanted to know about phonics (but were afraid to ask). *Reading Research Quarterly, 33,* 338–355.

Stanovich, K. E. (1980). Toward an interactive-compensatory model of individual differences in the development of reading fluency. *Reading Research Quarterly, 16,* 32–71.

Stanovich, K. E. (1984). The interactive-compensatory model of reading: A confluence of developmental, experimental and educational psychology. *Remedial and Special Education, 5,* 11–19.

Stanovich, K. E. (1985). Explaining the variance in reading ability in terms of psychological processes: What have we learned? *Annals of Dyslexia, 35,* 67–96.

Stanovich, K. E. (1986). Matthew effects in reading: Some consequences of individual differences in the acquisition of literacy. *Reading Research Quarterly, 21,* 360–406.

Stanovich, K. E. (1991). Word recognition: Changing perspectives. In R. Barr, M. L. Kamil, P. B. Mosenthal, & P. D. Pearson (Eds.), *Handbook of reading research* (Vol. 2, pp. 418–452). White Plains, NY: Longman.

Stanovich, K. E. (1992). Speculations on the causes and consequences of individual differences in early reading acquisition. In P. B. Gough, L. C. Ehri, & R. Treiman (Eds.), *Reading acquisition* (pp. 307–342). Hillsdale, NJ: Erlbaum.

Stanovich, K. E. (1994). Romance and reality. *The Reading Teacher, 47,* 280–291.

Stanovich, K. E., Cunningham, A. E., & Cramer, B. B. (1984). Assessing phonological awareness in kindergarten children: Issues of task comparability. *Journal of Experimental Child Psychology, 38,* 175–190.

Stanovich, K. E., Cunningham, A. E., & Freeman, D. J. (1984a). Intelligence, cognitive skills and early reading progress. *Reading Research Quarterly, 19,* 278–303.

Stanovich, K. E., Cunningham, A. E., & Freeman, D. J. (1984b). Relation between early reading acquisiting and word decoding with and without context: A longitudinal study of first-grade children. *Journal of Educational Psychology, 76,* 668–677.

Stanovich, K. E., & West, R. F. (1989). Exposure to print and orthographic processing. *Reading Research Quarterly, 24,* 402–433.

Stanovich, K. E., West, R. F., & Freeman, D. J. (1981). A longitudinal study of sentence context effects in second-grade children: Tests of an interactive-compensatory model. *Journal of Experimental Child Psychology, 32,* 185–199.

Stinner, M. C. (1979). *The use of neurological impress method in accelerating reading levels in selected disabled children.* Unpublished master's project. University of Florida.

Stotsky, S. (1983). Research on reading/writing relationships: A synthesis and suggested directions. *Language Arts, 60,* 627–642.

Stuart, M. (1999). Getting ready for reading: Early phoneme awareness and phonics teaching improves reading and spelling in inner-city second language learners. *British Journal of Educational Psychology, 69,* 587–605.

Studdert-Kennedy, M. (1986). Sources of variability in early speech development. In J. S. Perkell & D. H. Klatt (Eds.), *Invariance and variability of speech processes.* Hillsdale, NJ: Erlbaum.

Studdert-Kennedy, M. (1987). The phoneme as a perceptumotor structure. In A. Allport, D. Mackay, W. Prinz, & E. Scheerer (Eds.), *Language perception and production* (pp. 67–84). London: Academic Press.

Sulzby, E., & Teale, W. (1991). Emergent literacy. In R. Barr, M. L. Kamil, P. B. Mosenthal, & P. D. Pearson (Eds.), *Handbook of reading research, vol. II.* White Plains, NY: Longman.

Sweet, A. (1997). Teacher perceptions of student motivation and their relation to literacy learning. In J. T. Guthrie & A. Wigfield (Eds.), *Reading engagement: Motivating readers through integrated instruction.* Newark, DE: International Reading Association.

Szymusiak, K., & Sibberson, F. (2001). *Beyond leveled books: Supporting transitional readers in grades 2–5.* York, ME: Stenhouse.

Tan, A., & Nicholson, T. (1997). Flashcards revisited: Training poor readers to read words faster improves their comprehension of text. *Journal of Educational Psychology, 89,* 276–288.

Tangel, D. M., & Blachman, B. A. (1992). Effect of phoneme awareness instruction on kindergarten children's invented spelling. *Journal of Reading Behavior, 24,* 233–261.

Tannenhaus, M. K., Flanigan, H., & Seidenberg, M. S. (1980). Orthographic and phonological code activation in auditory and visual word recognition. *Memory and Cognition, 8,* 513–520.

Taylor, B., & Berkowitz, S. (1980). Facilitating children's comprehension of content material. In M. Kamil & A. Moe (Eds.), *Perspectives on reading research and instruction: Twenty-ninth yearbook of the National Reading Conference* (pp. 64–68). Washington, DC: National Reading Conference.

Taylor, I., & Taylor, M. M. (1983). *The psychology of reading.* New York: Academic Press.

Taylor, N. E., Wade, M. R., & Yekovich, F. R. (1985). The effects of text manipulation and multiple reading strategies on the reading performance of good and poor readers. *Reading Research Quarterly, 20,* 566–574.

Temple, C., Nathan, R., Temple, F., & Burris, N. A. (1993). *The beginnings of writing.* Boston: Allyn & Bacon.

Thompson, G. B. (1986). When nonsense is better than sense: Non-lexical errors to word reading tests. *British Journal of Educational Psychology, 56,* 216–219.

Thompson, R. (1997). The philosophy of balanced reading instruction. *The Journal of Balanced Reading Instruction, 4* (D1), 28–29.

Thorndike, E. L., & Lorge, I. (1944). *The teacher's word book of 30,000 words.* New York: Teacher's College Press, Columbia University.

Tierney, R. J., & Cunningham, J. W. (1984). Research on teaching reading comprehension. In P. D. Pearson, R. Barr, M. L. Kamil, & P. Mosenthal (Eds.), *Handbook of reading research* (pp. 609–655). White Plains, NY: Longman.

Tierney, R. J., & Shanahan, T. (1991). Research on the reading–writing relationship: Interactions, transactions, and outcomes. In R. Barr, M. L. Kamil, P. B. Mosenthal, & P. D. Pearson (Eds.), *Handbook of reading research* (Vol. 2, pp. 246–280). White Plains, NY: Longman.

Torgesen, J. K., Wagner, R. K., & Rashotte, C. A. (1997). Prevention and remediation of severe reading disabilities: Keeping the end in mind. *Scientific Studies of Reading, 1,* 217–234.

Torneus, M. (1984). Phonological awareness and reading: A chicken and egg problem? *Journal of Educational Psychology, 76,* 1,346–1,358.

Treiman, R., & Baron, J. (1983). Individual differences in spelling: The Phoenician-Chinese distinction. *Topics in Learning and Learning Disabilities, 3,* 33–40.

Treiman, R., & Breaux, A. (1982). Common phoneme and overall stimulating relations among spoken syllables: Their use by children and adults. *Journal of Psycholinguistic Research, 11,* 569–597.

Tulving, E., & Gold, C. (1963). Stimulus information and contextual information as determinants of tachistoscopic recognition of words. *Journal of Experimental Psychology, 66,* 319–327.

Tummer, W. E. (1989). The role of language-related factors in reading disability. In D. Shankweiler & I. Y. Liberman (Eds.), *Phonology and reading disability: Solving the reading puzzle* (pp. 91–131). Ann Arbor: University of Michigan Press.

Tummer, W. E., Herriman, M. L., & Nesdale, A. R. (1988). Metalinguistic abilities and beginning reading. *Reading Research Quarterly, 23,* 134–158.

Tummer, W. E., & Nesdale, A. R. (1985). Phonemic segmentation skill and beginning reading. *Journal of Educational Psychology, 77,* 417–427.

Vallecorsa, A. L., & deBettencourt, L. U. (1997). Using a mapping procedure to teach reading and writing skills to middle grade students with learning disabilities. *Education and the Treatment of Children, 20,* 173–188.

Vellutino, F. R., & Scanlon, D. M. (1984). Converging perspectives in the study of the reading process: Reactions to the papers presented by Morrison, Siegel and Ryan, and Stanovich. *Remedial and Special Education, 5,* 39–44.

Vellutino, F. R., & Scanlon, D. M. (1987). Phonological coding, phonological awareness, and reading ability: Evidence from a longitudinal and experimental study. *Merrill-Palmer Quarterly, 33,* 321–363.

Venezky, R. L. (1976). *Theoretical and experimental base for teaching reading.* The Hague: Mouton.

Vygotsky, L. S. (1978). *Mind in society.* Cambridge, MA: Harvard University Press.

Vygotsky, L. S. (1986). *Thought and language.* Cambridge, MA: MIT Press.

Wagner, R. (1986). Phonological processing abilities and reading: Implications for disabled readers. *Journal of Learning Disabilities, 19,* 623–630.

Wagner, R., & Torgesen, J. (1987). The nature of phonological processing and its causal role in the acquisition of reading skills. *Psychological Bulletin, 101,* 192–212.

Walker, C. M. (1979). High frequency word list for grades 3 through 9. *The Reading Teacher, 32,* 803–812.

Watson, D. J. (1989). Defining and describing whole language. *Elementary School Journal, 90,* 129–142.

Weber, R. M. (1970). A linguistic analysis of first-grade errors. *Reading Research Quarterly, 5,* 427–451.

Wepman, J. M., & Hass, W. (1969). *A spoken word count (children—ages 5, 6 and 7).* Chicago, IL: Language Research Associates.

Wesseling, R., & Reitsma, P. (2000). The transient role of explicit phonological recoding for reading acquisition. *Reading and Writing: An Interdisciplinary Journal, 13,* 313–336.

West, R. F., & Stanovich, K. E. (1978). Automatic contextual facilitation in readers of three ages. *Child Development, 49,* 717–727.

Williams, J. P. (1986). The role of phonemic analysis in reading. In J. Torgesen & B. Wong (Eds.), *Psychological and educational perspectives on learning disabilities* (pp. 399–416). Orlando, FL: Academic Press.

Yopp, H. K. (1992). Developing phonemic awareness in young children. *The Reading Teacher, 45,* 696–703.

Yopp, H., & Yopp, R. (2000). Supporting phonemic awareness in the classroom. *Reading Teacher, 54,* 130–143.

Zhurova, L. E. (1963). The development of analysis of words into their sounds by preschool children. *Soviet Psychology and Psychiatry, 72,* 17–27.

Zifcak, M. (1981). Phonological awareness and reading acquisition. *Contemporary Educational Psychology, 6,* 117–126.

Zinna, D. R., Liberman, I. Y., & Shankweiler, D. (1986). Children's sensitivity to factors influencing vowel reading. *Reading Research Quarterly, 21,* 465–480.

Index